Sustainable Development

Promoting Progress or Perpetuating Poverty?

Edited by
Julian Morris

P

PROFILE BOOKS

First published in Great Britain in 2002 by
Profile Books Ltd
58A Hatton Garden
London ECIN 8LX
www.profilebooks.co.uk

Designed and typeset in Sabon by MacGuru
info@macguru.org.uk

Printed and bound in Great Britain by
Clays, Bungay, Suffolk

A CIP catalogue record for this book is available from the British
Library.

ISBN I 86197 458 2

Contents

The authors

Jonathan H. Adler is an assistant professor at the Case Western Reserve University School of Law. He holds a doctorate in law and is an expert in environmental and regulatory policy. Dr Adler is the author or editor of several books and numerous scholarly articles on environmental and regulatory policy.

George B. N. Ayittey is a distinguished economist at the American University and president of the Free Africa Foundation (both in Washington DC). A PhD economist, he has been a consultant to the World Bank and US AID. Dr Ayittey has published four books and numerous articles on Africa and the third world.

Robert C. Balling Jr is director of the Office of Climatology and associate professor of geology at Arizona State University. He has been involved in the greenhouse debate throughout his career, has published over a hundred articles in the professional scientific literature, and is the author of several books on the subject.

Roger Bate is co-director of International Policy Network and a research fellow at the Institute of Economic Affairs in London. His PhD thesis focused on water allocation in South Africa. Dr Bate is the author or editor of numerous books and scholarly articles on environmental policy.

Robert L. Bradley Jr is president of the Institute for Energy Research and a senior research fellow in energy history and policy at the University of Houston. He has a PhD in political economy, and is the author of three books and numerous essays on energy policy and related sustainability issues.

Michael De Alessi is director of natural resource policy for the Reason

Public Policy Institute in Los Angeles. An economist and marine policy expert, he is the author of numerous papers and monographs.

Pierre Desrochers is director of research at the Montreal Economic Institute. A PhD economist, he carried out post-doctoral work on industrial ecology issues. The author of numerous scholarly articles, his main research interests are economic development, environmental and urban policy and public finance.

Indur Goklany is an engineer who has worked within and outside the US government on natural resource and environmental issues for about thirty years. He is the author of numerous books and papers on climate change, biodiversity, and the relationship between economic growth and the environment.

Martín Krause is professor of economics at the Law School, University of Buenos Aires, and dean of ESEADE Graduate School. A PhD economist, he is the author of many academic papers and several books. Dr Krause has lectured widely and been awarded numerous prizes and fellowships.

Julian Morris is co-director of International Policy Network and a visiting professor at the University of Buckingham. An economist and lawyer, he is an expert in the role of institutions in economic growth and environmental protection. Professor Morris has written or edited numerous books and articles.

Michael Mortimore is a partner at Drylands Research and a senior research associate at the Department of Geography, Cambridge University. He has worked as a geographer at universities in Nigeria, carried out numerous projects on African dryland environments, and is the author of many books and scholarly articles.

Alan Oxley is director of International Trade Strategies and chairman of the Australian APEC Centre, both in Melbourne. An expert in international trade and environmental issues, he was formerly Australia's ambassador to the GATT (1985–9) and was chairman of the GATT Council.

Fabiano Pegurier is professor of economics at Faculdades IBMEC in Rio de Janeiro, Brazil. He has had extensive experience both in government planning and in business management. Professor Pegurier is the author of numerous studies of economic growth in Latin America.

Gilberto Salgado is a consultant economist based in Rio de Janeiro. He has a PhD in economics and is an expert in competition theory and public economics. Dr Salgado has recently co-authored *Liberdade e Prosperidade*, which focused on how markets achieve coordination.

Douglas Southgate is a professor at Ohio State University and an expert in natural resource economics. A PhD economist, he has studied tropical deforestation and other environmental problems throughout the developing world and is the author of three books and more than fifty journal articles and scholarly papers.

Charles N. Steele is a consultant and economist. He has a PhD in economics and is an expert on the relationship between property rights and economic growth. Dr Steele has taught economics to graduates and undergraduates at universities in the United States, China, Russia and Ukraine.

Mary Tiffen is a partner at Drylands Research. She has a PhD in economics and has worked on agricultural development issues in Africa and the Middle East since the 1960s, including a period at the Overseas Development Institute in London. Dr Tiffen is the author of numerous scholarly articles and books.

Figures and tables

Introduction

Julian Morris

W hat is sustainable development? Is it desirable and if so how can it be encouraged? Why are some countries rich and others poor? What is the relationship between economic growth, human health and welfare, and conservation of the environment? Can economic development continue indefinitely? What can we learn from countries where economic growth has stalled? Are we consuming too many of the earth's resources and thereby undermining humanity's ability to continue its progress? Will global environmental agreements protect the environment and aid human progress? Do we need stronger environmental constraints on free trade? These are some of the questions that authors in this book seek to answer.

Sustainable Development: Promoting Progress or Perpetuating Poverty? is the first project of the Sustainable Development Network, an alliance of individuals and groups from around the world seeking to promote *real* sustainable development – see www.sdnetwork.net. The book and the network originated from a concern that both public debate and political rhetoric relating to 'sustainable development' was being dominated by a narrow and unhelpful interpretation of the meaning of the term. Specifically, the debate has been focused primarily on the relationship between economic growth and the environment. More generally, there has been a tendency to hypothesise about possible long-term constraints to economic growth caused by human activity. While these are undoubtedly important questions, and are addressed in some detail in this book, they are only one aspect of sustainable development. In 1987, the World Commission on Environment and Development released a report entitled *Our Common Future*, in which it stated:

> Sustainable development is development that meets the needs of

the present without compromising the ability of future generations
to meet their own needs.

Most discussions of sustainable development have failed to give
due attention to 'meeting the needs of the present' and many such discussions have focused not on promoting development but on restricting it – typically in the name of protecting the environment.

Since this book project began, the needs of the present have been
brought sharply back into focus. The tragic events of September 11th
in particular have reminded us of the risks of terrorism and the importance of being vigilant against those who seek to destroy civilisation. The worsening AIDS crisis in Sub-Saharan Africa has reminded
us of the importance of investing in the health and education of people who are alive *today*. Economic chaos in Argentina and Zimbabwe
illustrates how quickly inappropriate government policies can destroy
wealth and cause or perpetuate poverty. Meanwhile, famine in Sub-
Saharan Africa reminds us of the importance of promoting policies
that will enable the billion or more malnourished people in the world
to escape from the mire of poverty.

Structure of the book

The book is split into five parts. Part One (chapters 1 to 3) is concerned with the broad picture, examining the meaning of 'sustainable development', the state of humanity, and the motives of
economic actors to use resources sustainably. In chapter 1, I analyse
the meaning of the term 'sustainable development'. After critiquing
the conventional interpretation of the term, which focuses on identifying goals and then implementing policies to meet those goals, I
offer an alternative interpretation that is focused on ensuring that
the underlying social and economic institutions are structured in a
way that enables development to take place in a more sustainable
way. In chapter 2, Indur Goklany evaluates the progress of humanity over the past two centuries. Using several indicators, including
available food supplies per capita, life expectancy, infant mortality,
economic development, education, and political rights and freedoms,
he provides a broad assessment of the state of humanity and how it
has changed. In chapter 3, Pierre Desrochers considers whether the
market system provides economic incentives for companies to reduce
the environmental impact of their products and production
processes. He illustrates his thesis by describing technological devel-

opments that have been driven by a desire to improve the efficiency of use of inputs.

Part Two (chapters 4 to 6) contains three case studies of how regions have *not* developed sustainably, including Africa, Latin America and the Soviet Union. In chapter 4, George Ayittey offers an explanation as to why Africa, a continent with enormous natural resource wealth, remains mired in poverty. To explain this paradox, he contrasts the views of the 'externalists', who blame outsiders for Africa's woes with those of the 'internalists', who argue that Africans have inflicted most of their misery on themselves. He also assesses the impact that foreign aid has had on Africa. In chapter 5, Fabiano Pegurier and Gilberto Salgado consider the impact of 'import substitution industrialisation' and other instances of economic mismanagement that have been imposed on the people of Latin America. By distinguishing both similarities and differences in the policies employed by Latin American governments, they identify many of the causes of the economic problems in the region. In chapter 6, Charles Steele explains how the economy of the USSR worked (or, more accurately, did not work). Steele highlights some of the consequences of central planning for the people of the Soviet Union and also for the environment.

Part Three (chapters 7 and 8) assesses the prospects for specific global policies aimed at promoting sustainable development: a proposal to create systems of national accounts that incorporate environmental quality, and the proposition that trade sanctions should be used to enforce environmental policy. In chapter 7, Martín Krause assesses the case for including environmental factors into the system of national accounts, contrasting the functioning of a conventional system of national accounts with various proposed alternatives. In chapter 8, Alan Oxley considers the impact of the agreement signed in Doha, Qatar, in November 2001, which launched a new round of multilateral trade negotiations in the forum of the World Trade Organization (WTO). He focuses in particular on the possible impact of formally expanding the role of trade sanctions for environmental protection, and he discusses the possible implications of a recent decision concerning the legitimisation of trade sanctions to enforce environmental regulations under existing WTO rules.

In Part Four (chapters 9 and 10), attention turns to the problem of climate change and energy policy. In chapter 9, Robert Balling assesses the current state of understanding of the global climate and the impact which humans may have on it. By discussing the various possible causes of climate change, from solar radiation to El Niño, he provides a balanced perspective of the extent to which humans are influencing the earth's climate and also the possible effects of this influence. In Chapter 10, Robert Bradley Jr discusses the role of energy in achieving sustainable development. Drawing on a wealth of data concerning the availability of resources and the impact of energy use on the environment, he evaluates the arguments for and against diverting resources into non-hydrocarbon forms of energy, especially in the context of providing energy to the poor.

The final part of the book (chapters 11 to 15) addresses resource issues, including the problems of biological diversity loss and species extinction, and how best to manage the world's forests, fish, land and water. In chapter 11, Jonathan Adler considers the threat posed by species extinction and biodiversity loss, as well as measures ostensibly put in place to control these problems. In particular, Adler considers the Convention on International Trade in Endangered Species, the Convention on Biological Diversity and the Biosafety Protocol. In chapter 12, Douglas Southgate considers the problem of managing forests, especially those in tropical and sub-tropical countries, which contain important, biologically diverse habitat. In particular he looks at systems of common property management and the impact that state interventions have had on these systems. In chapter 13, Michael De Alessi discusses the state of the world's fisheries and examines efforts to conserve them. He contrasts political management, perhaps best exemplified by the European Common Fisheries Policy, with experiments in decentralised ownership and control that have taken place over the past twenty years in places such as Iceland and New Zealand. In chapter 14, Mary Tiffen and Michael Mortimore investigate the problem of land degradation. They discuss various international actions that have been launched, ostensibly to tackle it. Using case studies from Africa, they show how people in various arid regions have managed their land. In chapter 15, Roger Bate assesses the problem of conflict over water resources. Employing numerous examples from around the world, he identifies systems of ownership and control that are consistent with efficient, peaceful provision of water. He contrasts these systems with their alternatives, which often result in inefficiency and conflict.

Part One

The Nature of Sustainable Development

1 Reconceptualising 'sustainable development'

Julian Morris

In early February 2002 two colleagues and I were driven from Delhi to Agra to see the Taj Mahal. As we crossed the border of Uttar Pradesh we saw long lines of trucks simply waiting, doing nothing. Their drivers were hanging around smoking bidis. We were shocked. Then it struck me; sustainable transport. The truck drivers must have been given an edict that they should drive less, perhaps to conserve fuel or to reduce nasty emissions to the environment. I asked the driver. 'No sir, not sustainable,' he said, laughing at the ridiculous Englishman. 'The truck drivers must wait to pay a toll to cross the border.' 'But we're still in India,' I protested, 'you mean they have *internal* tariffs here?' 'Yes, sir.'

The term 'sustainable development' has been around for about 30 years but has only recently been popularised. It derives originally from the biological concept of 'sustainable yield' – that is to say, the rate at which species such as cod and elephants may be harvested without depleting the population. Starting in the late 1980s, environmentalists and government officials began applying the terms 'sustainability' and 'sustainable development' when discussing environmental policy. Thus, numerous measures aimed at conservation and pollution prevention have been justified on the grounds that they are necessary to promote sustainable development. More recently, and in light of the AIDS crisis in Africa, the interpretation of sustainable development has been broadened to include issues such as health care and education, the lack of which are seen as constraints on economic development.

The most common definition of the term derives from a report prepared for the World Commission on Environment and Development, which stated in 1987:

> Sustainable development is development that meets the needs of
> the present without compromising the ability of future generations
> to meet their own needs.[1]

So defined, sustainable development is, like motherhood and apple
pie, not a concept to which many would object. It would take a perverse outlook indeed to support the idea that people's needs should
not be met both now and in the future. But, unobjectionable as it is in
principle, the concept is sufficiently broad to allow various different
interpretations. Indeed, a voluminous literature has sprung up debat-
ing its interpretation in periodicals such as the *Journal of Sustainable
Development*, the *International Journal of Sustainable Development*,
the *International Journal of Sustainable Development and World
Ecology* and *Sustainable Development International*.

Most of this literature has focused on identifying specific outcomes, such as controlling the climate or saving periwinkles, and then
setting about developing policies intended to achieve those outcomes.
Usually these policies require stronger systems of global governance
(periwinkles are important).

An alternative interpretation focuses less on specific outcomes and
more on increasing the chances of superior outcomes. It is the purpose
of this chapter, first, to critique the conventional outcome-oriented vision of sustainable development and, second, to offer an alternative
vision.

Unintended consequences of outcome-oriented sustainable development policies

Some environmental groups have claimed that rich countries are
burning too many hydrocarbons (coal, oil, gas) and that this harms
poor countries. In order to redress the balance, these groups demand
a reduction in the consumption of hydrocarbons by rich countries.
While such a policy would almost certainly reduce the differential in
income and wealth between people in rich and people in poor countries, it would do so in the main by destroying wealth and reducing
income in rich countries. The reason for this is twofold. First, energy
is a basic factor of production, so increasing the cost of energy by
mandating a shift to lower-carbon forms will reduce output. Second,
hydrocarbons are used by consumers in all manner of applications,
both directly, for example in cars and gas stoves, and indirectly,
when they turn on their lights, fans, electric ovens, TVs and air con-

ditioners. So, reducing the availability of hydrocarbons will create energy poverty.

Although some middle-income countries might benefit from a shift in the location of industrial production, for the most part people in poor countries would suffer – those in the poorest countries, especially, because they have little industrial capacity. The reason is that reducing income in rich countries will reduce demand for all goods, including agriculture, textiles and apparel, which are the main prod-ucts currently exported from poor to rich countries.

The likely adverse effect on the world's poorest people of con-straining consumption of hydrocarbons by the rich is one instance of a more general phenomenon: the unintended effects of outcome-oriented policies that are justified on the grounds that they promote 'sustainable development'.

Consider the effect of the Basel Convention, an international agreement intended to prevent the illegal dumping of hazardous waste in poor countries. As Alan Oxley points out in chapter 8:

> ... restrictions on the export of used lead to India have
> undermined the formal lead recycling industry in that country
> with perverse environmental consequences. The formal recycling
> industry, which operates under strict environmental and health
> and safety regulations, requires high throughput of lead. Because
> of the relatively low levels of lead use locally, the industry requires
> imported lead in order to operate at a profit. The restriction on
> exports of used lead to India has led to the closure of a number of
> formal-sector lead recycling facilities, which became unprofitable.
> As a result, more of the locally produced waste lead is now
> recycled by the informal sector. These are unregulated backyard
> operations, which typically cause contamination of water and air,
> with adverse health consequences.[2]

Likewise, the ban on trade in elephant ivory, enacted under the Con-vention on International Trade in Endangered Species (CITES), proba-bly does more harm than good by undermining incentives to conserve elephants locally. In Southern Africa governments have, to a greater or lesser extent, decentralised management of wildlife. In many places in Botswana, Namibia, South Africa, Tanzania and Zimbabwe, local peo-ple receive a proportion of the income from hunting, eco-tourism and other economic activities associated with the wildlife with which they share their land. As a result, local people have become stakeholders in the wildlife management system and instead of seeing elephants and other wildlife as a threat they realise that by conserving them they are able to benefit. The ban on international trade in elephant ivory reduced the value of elephants to these people and thereby reduced their incentives to conserve them.

The UN Commission on Sustainable Development is outcome-oriented. One need only search its website for a few minutes to find a hundred outcomes it seems to favour. How would these outcomes be achieved? Through systems of global governance; rules and regulations agreed by every nation. And who would apply this global governance? Why, the UN of course.[3] In 2000, the UN issued *The Millennium Declaration*, which included a commitment to halve the proportion of the world's population whose income is less than $1 a day (bringing the level down to 400 million people) by the year 2015.[4] Now, of course, such an outcome may seem laudable; reducing poverty and its accompanying misery *is* a good thing. But several objections to this proposition could be raised. First, one could object that the outcome is far too modest. How can we accept that in 2015 there will still be 400 million people living on only $1 a day? Second, one could object that simply reducing the number of poor people is not enough. What *happens* to the people who were poor is what is important. Merely ensuring that they have $1.10 per day for a few years by sending them food packages or other forms of emergency aid is hardly much use in the long-run. Increases in wealth must be sustained if they are to be considered sustainable. This points to a general problem of starting with a desired outcome and then attempting to formulate an appropriate policy to achieve that outcome: all sorts of mischief becomes acceptable because the ends justify the means.

Good intentions are not enough

Good intentions are laudable but if good intentions were enough to alleviate poverty, malnutrition and disease, these dreadful problems would no longer plague us. Indeed, the fact that more than 10 million people each year die of preventable or curable diseases and that 800 million people survive on less than $1 per day are testament to the failure of good intentions – and the many billions of dollars spent in their pursuit.[5]

For over fifty years, governments in rich countries have been taking money from their taxpayers and transferring it to governments in poor countries. Hundreds of billions of dollars have been spent on such 'aid', yet a balanced assessment indicates that, although there may have been a few benefits, on average this 'aid' has caused harm. Graham Hancock, former East Africa correspondent for *The Economist*, noted over a decade ago:

> Garnered and justified in the name of the destitute and the vulnerable, aid's main function in the past half century has been to create and then entrench a powerful new class of rich and privileged people. In that notorious club of parasites and hangers-on made up of the United Nations, the World Bank, and the bilateral agencies, it is aid – and nothing else – that has permitted hundreds of thousands of 'jobs for the boys' and that has permitted record-breaking standards to be set in self-serving behaviour, arrogance, paternalism, moral cowardice, and mendacity. At the same time, in the developing countries, aid has perpetuated the rule of the incompetent and venal men whose leadership would otherwise be utterly non-viable; it has allowed governments characterised by historic ignorance, avarice, and irresponsibility to thrive; last but not least, it has condoned – and in some cases facilitated – the most consistent and grievous abuses of human rights that have occurred anywhere in the world since the dark ages.
>
>   In these closing years of the twentieth century the time has come for the lords of poverty to depart.[6]

Since then, there have been few signs that 'aid' is being put to better use.

Institutions for sustainable development

The reason transfers of financial resources from the governments of rich countries to the governments of poor countries have been largely unsuccessful in stimulating economic development is that lack of resources is not the primary problem in poor countries. Take the case of Nigeria, which happens to contain one of the largest oil deposits on the planet. The oil wealth in Nigeria has been controlled by government officials – until recently it was in the hands of the murderous kleptocrat General Sanai Abache – who used it to line their pockets and keep the politically important elite happy, rather than to promote development.

There is little point in pouring money into a country whose government has no intention to encourage economic development. Indeed, as Mengistu showed in Ethiopia, Mobutu in Zaire, Pol Pot in Cambodia, and Amin in Uganda, dictators will happily accept 'aid' if it helps to prop up their regime. In such cases, government-to-government transfers are not merely counterproductive, they are murderous.

The more fundamental problem is that 'aid' is based on a largely false premise, namely that poverty itself is a barrier to development. In most cases this is not true. Economic development in Western Europe did not require massive redistribution from the rich to the poor. Rather, it required a change in the structure of Europe's institutions; a move away from the Feudal system of the early middle ages to a trading economy.[7] Whilst Sub-Saharan Africa now faces a genuine crisis, in the form of disease that is destroying the economically productive sector of society, it is probably unique in the world (if not world history) in requiring external assistance to escape from such a quagmire. And even then, such assistance is unlikely to lead to significant growth; rather, it might prevent total economic collapse. If countries are to develop sustainably, then institutional reform, not aid, is the solution.

But what do we mean by 'institutional' reform? Institutions are the framework within which people act and interact – they are the rules, customs, norms and laws that bind us to one another and act as boundaries to our behaviour. Institutions reduce the number of decisions that we need to take; they remove the responsibility to calculate the effect of each of our actions on the rest of humanity and replace it with a responsibility to abide by simple rules. In a system in which rules emerge spontaneously and are changed by evolutionary processes, good rules will tend to crowd out bad rules. That is to say, over time, rules that result in better outcomes will survive and rules that result in worse outcomes will become extinct.

Some rules are, of course, essentially arbitrary – which side of the road to drive on, for example. Clearly a rule is required here, or the consequences would be fatal. But whether one follows the English rule, which is based on the fact that (right-handed) jousters would pass on the left, or the French rule, which is based on the fact that it is not English, is of no great consequence.

Other rules are not so arbitrary. For example, the rule that contracts should, generally, be upheld in a court of law has a very distinct consequence. It grants people greater certainty in their transactions with one another and thereby encourages such transactions to take place. If the rule were that contracts were not legally binding, the effect on commerce would be devastating. That is why in evolutionary systems of law, such as the English common law, contracts tend to be upheld. The better rule won the evolutionary battle for survival.

In *The Other Path*, Hernando de Soto documented the plight of his fellow countrymen in Peru, most of whom were denied the formality of such law.[8] They were instead forced to rely upon informal mechanisms to enforce contracts, property rights and other relationships. Whilst such informal mechanisms – customs and norms, for example – work well for groups that are relatively homogenous and where there is little trade with outsiders, they impose significant constraints on the ability for groups to improve their lot. Societies that have adopted formal institutions – such as property rights, markets, contract law, tort law, trademarks, patents, copyright, and so on – have tended to do much better economically and socially than societies that have relied primarily on informal institutions.

Property rights[9]

It is the institution of private property that, more than any other, has enabled people to escape from the mire of poverty. Property rights are capital; they give people incentives to invest in their land and they give people an asset against which to borrow, so that they might become entrepreneurs.

As in Peru, the 500 million rural poor in India are not oppressed by multinational companies. Most of them have never even heard of multinational companies and those that have probably dream of working for them. No, India's rural poor are oppressed by tenure rules which make it difficult for them to rent, buy or sell property formally. Land transactions typically involve paying large bribes to local officials, who have a vested interest in maintaining the status quo.

Property rights are created in order to resolve competing claims over resources. Thus, if 10 men all graze their cattle on the same piece of land and there are no rules governing how much each man can graze, then each man has a strong incentive to graze as much of the available land as possible. Under such a system – known as 'open access' – the cattle will quickly denude the land and, in the absence of free land on which to move, they will die.

Historically, open access has been a rarity, occurring only when land is so plentiful that ownership is not necessary, or when people are prevented from owning property. In most cases, before the tragedy occurs, the users of the land will see the advantage of either dividing it up into individual plots or creating rules for using it that reduce the likelihood of denudation. In either case, the land has been privatised – made the exclusive property of one or more people. If the land is split into plots it becomes 'several' or 'individual' property; if the owners agree to common rules, but do not divide the land into several plots, it is called 'common' property.[10]

Privatisation is expected to occur when the costs of exclusion (that is, the costs of limiting access to a piece of previously open land, for example by fencing and policing) are equal to or less than the external costs (which, in this case, means the costs associated with the denudation of the land).[11] But the costs of exclusion will depend upon the exclusion technologies available. Wherever there are externalities present (such as the threat of encroachment by cattle belonging to other ranchers), users would have an incentive to produce new and cheaper exclusion technologies. So, over time, we would expect more and more land to become privately owned and the sum of external costs to decline precipitously.

Land that is owned privately (whether individually or in common) will in general be managed better than land that is unowned or owned by the state. This is because the owner(s) know that they will reap the benefits from any investments made in the land, so they have stronger incentives to make those investments. Going back to our cattle-rancher example: those who graze more cattle than their land can support will soon cease to be cattle ranchers. That creates a strong incentive to discover the 'carrying capacity' of the land – and to increase it through new technologies. Entrepreneurial, land-owning peasants constantly introduce new crops and production methods, creating an environment of diverse agriculture.[12]

Technological innovation not only enables peasants to improve their lot, it also benefits those with whom they trade, by lowering the cost of purchasing food and other goods and reducing the risk of famine. But such innovation will be stifled if those who might develop new technologies are not allowed to benefit from the investments they make through the ownership of property. The individual's *incentive* to *invest* in his land and *innovate* new methods of production will be greater when he can *own* and *exchange property*. Thus, Michael Stahl concludes:

> At the farm level, the presence or absence of clearly defined property rights makes the difference between active interest in

investing in soil conservation measures or apparent indifference to environmental degradation.[13]

Individual property rights also encourage pollution prevention. In the English common law for example, if the owner of property A emits a substance that causes damage to property B, then the owner of A must compensate the owner of B for the harm caused.[14] Thus, even at the height of the industrial revolution a smelting works in an industrial area was enjoined for causing damage to shrubs and trees on a nearby property.[15] There remains an ancient maxim, *sic utere tuo ut in alienum non laedas*, roughly translated as 'so use your own as not to harm another'. Widely applied in the courts of law this rule would protect not only the property of the owner but also neighbouring properties and even the environment – and society – as a whole. However, the maxim has not received sufficiently general application, mostly because states have stepped in and asserted that the polluting activities should continue – on the grounds that they are in the general interests of humankind. As in other cases, policies aimed at improving outcomes probably had the opposite effect because they undermined successful evolved rules.

Property also begets wealth. Once a person owns property, he or she can use it as collateral against a loan. Because such collateral gives lenders security, they will be willing to offer loans at lower rates. So property reduces the cost of becoming an entrepreneur. Of course, some of these entrepreneurs will fail and they may have their property repossessed by the lender. But at least they will have had the opportunity to try to escape from poverty and, of course, most will be no worse than if they never had the property in the first place. In any case, many will succeed in their endeavours. Some may become wealthy; most will simply be less poor.

Intellectual property rights[16]
Another institution that encourages innovation is intellectual property (IP). In 1474, the Venetian Republic enacted a law that entitled inventors to a temporary exclusive right to profit from their inventions. Later such laws were adopted widely throughout Europe and North America. In some cases the laws have been abused, but for the most part they have been very beneficial to humanity.

Strong, readily enforceable intellectual property is particularly important for those products and processes that require large investments in research, development and marketing but for which the costs of copying are relatively low. Chemicals, pharmaceuticals and biotechnology each rely heavily on patents. The music, film, book, art and software industries each rely heavily on copyright. Meanwhile, all manufacturers and sellers of brand goods (which is most manufacturers and most sellers) rely on trademarks and servicemarks to guarantee the identity (and hence brand-associated characteristics) of products.

There are of course drawbacks to IP, including temporarily higher prices of the protected goods, a reduction in the number of goods directly derived from those that are patented,[17] the legal and administrative costs involved in enforcement and so on.[18] These drawbacks have led several commentators to conclude that patents and other forms of intellectual property are not desirable. However, the problem with focusing on these drawbacks is that in doing so one often forgets that the inventions and creative works might never have come about but for the existence of IP.

It is all very well to criticise the excessively broad application of patent to the internal combustion engine or aeroplane wing control (which was patented by Orville Wright) but if there was no patent protection how much longer would we have had to wait for the car and the aeroplane? Perhaps more importantly, without the stimulus of patent protection, would we have had all the wonderful synthetic chemicals and pharmaceuticals that make our lives and the lives of our loved ones so much better? Without copyright protection, would we have enjoyed the explosion of music, art, literature and film that we have experienced over the course of the past century? Without trademarks and servicemarks, how much more complicated would our lives be, constantly battered with confusingly similar marks?

In sum, were we to abandon or significantly diminish our system of intellectual property rights, we might gain in the very short term through lower-cost products, but the cost in the medium to long term would be felt in terms of fewer products, as well as higher expenditures on trade secrecy and other means of protecting knowledge, which might well increase the cost of products.

Freedom of contract

Another fundamental institution for sustainable development is freedom of contract. This includes both the freedom *to* contract – the freedom to make whatever agreements one desires, subject to fair and simple procedural rules – and the freedom *from* contract – the freedom not to be bound by the decisions of others. Freedom of contract is a fundamental part of the freedom to associate with others. It includes the freedom to transact – to buy and sell property – and as such it is an essential adjunct to the right to clearly defined and readily enforceable property rights.

The freedom to contract enables people to bind themselves to agreements and thereby creates greater legal certainty. This in turn encourages people to engage in trade and investment. Armed with enforceable property rights and contracts, the peasant becomes a merchant.

The freedom from contract prevents others from attempting to interfere with one's right to engage in exchange. Sadly, governments rarely respect the rights of parties to freedom from contract. Restrictions on trade abound in every country in the world. As I pointed out, in India they even have tariffs on internal borders, where trucks can wait for days while their drivers pay a small fee (Uttar Pradesh charges 160 rupees – about three dollars). The delay comes from the drivers having to go backwards and forwards filling out ridiculous forms. And as they wait, their loads rot or are stolen. Such interventions are truly unsustainable: they waste capital (the trucks and goods lie idle), and they waste good food, which in turn reduces the value of perishable agricultural goods, and keeps farmers poor.

The rule of law

Property rights and contracts are nothing if they are not enforceable. And enforcement is only possible if there are courts wherein disputes over the rights and duties of parties may be resolved and a legal system that will enforce those judgements. There are two key issues of concern here: the first is the willingness of the state to permit competition in the provision of legal services; the second is the enforcement of whatever decision is made.

When the state exerts a monopoly on the provision of law, the costs of resolving disputes through the formal judicial system are typically large both in monetary terms and, more importantly, in terms of delays. The costs of such dispute resolution can, however, be dramatically reduced if people are able to resolve their disputes privately. Arbitration, for example, is usually far quicker and cheaper than going to court. However, for such arbitration to be enforceable, the courts must accept the rights of parties to settle disputes in this way. This is essentially a matter of freedom of contract: if parties contract to have their dispute settled by arbitration then the courts should only get involved if that contract is breached. Sadly, in most countries the courts have resisted this – presumably because they see it as a threat to their power.

The second issue, enforcement of decisions, requires the existence of a credible system of sanctions. One of the reasons rich countries have been able to become rich is that the police and the administrators of criminal justice are generally trusted and are trustworthy. That is not to say that they are free from corruption, rather that the level of corruption is small in comparison to the levels of corruption in many poor countries. In Indonesia, for example, it is common for wealthy criminals to use a combination of threats and bribes to ensure that they stay out of jail. Similar problems exist in many other countries. In Nigeria and South Africa, people have so little trust in the police that they employ private security agencies. In South Africa these seem on the whole to be rather reliable. In Nigeria they are no doubt better than the police – if you can afford them – but they also run scams, stealing from the very houses they are supposed to protect.

Decentralised decision-making and sound science

If government is to intervene in the actions of its citizens, there must be both a strong justification – the benefits must outweigh the costs – and there must be in place mechanisms to ensure that poor decisions can be changed. Space does not permit a discussion of how in practice costs and benefits would be estimated. Needless to say, however, decisions must at the very least be informed by sound science – that is science which has undergone a rigorous process of peer review.[19]

To prevent mistakes from being perpetuated, decisions must be reviewable. Given the difficulties associated with reviewing legislation, that probably means building in redundancy: legislation should perhaps have a sell-by date of two or three years, after which it must be subject to the same process of assessment to determine whether it is still justified.

In addition, decisions to limit human activities should be taken at the most local level possible but must be bound by the other principles that prevent abuses of local power. Those principles are mostly contained within the other principles already outlined, such as respect for property and freedom from contract.

Generally speaking, state bureaucracy should be avoided because bureaucracies have a tendency to expand and to create justifications for expansion – such as the promotion of unnecessary and often counter-productive legislation. One way to deal with this would be to contract out all government services.[20]

Towards good governance for sustainable development

This combination of property rights, freedom of contract, the rule of law, decentralised decision-making and sound science provides the basis upon which sustainable development can take place. In short, it represents good governance. Sadly, as subsequent chapters in this book attest, few countries have come close to instituting such systems of good governance. The challenge for those eager to see the world become a more sustainable place is clear: stop squealing about the importance of global governance and instead promote good governance.

2 Economic growth and human well-being

Indur Goklany

'If present trends continue, the world in 2000 will be more crowded, more polluted, less stable ecologically, and more vulnerable to disruption than the world we live in now. Serious stresses involving population, resources, and environment are clearly visible ahead. Despite greater material output, the world's people will be poorer in many ways than they are today.'

Global 2000 Report to the President

With this Neo-Malthusian vision of the future, the *Global 2000 Report to the President*[1] began a chilling description of the problems that lay ahead for the world unless radical changes were made. Fifteen years later, Julian Simon[2] quoted these words in his introduction to the monumental collection of essays, *The State of Humanity*. The point of that book, which Simon also edited, was to determine whether trends in human well-being and environmental quality were in accord with a Neo-Malthusian world view.

In 58 chapters by more than fifty scholars, *The State of Humanity* documented the tremendous strides in human well-being over the centuries, as well as trends in natural resource use and environmental quality. Based on these discussions, Simon wrote, 'Our species is better off in just about every measurable material way.'[3]

Yet today anxiety about the future continues. Calls to restructure our economy to avoid the pending insurmountable problems are typical. 'The challenge facing the entire world is to design an economy that can satisfy the basic needs of people everywhere without self-destructing,' said Lester Brown, president of World Watch Institute, in 1998.[4]

This chapter is a conscious effort to emulate, build upon and update the work of Julian Simon, and to provide empirical data to help evaluate the heated rhetoric of Lester Brown and other Neo-Malthusian alarmists. While no-one can confidently predict the future, it is possible to scrutinise the past and present to determine the current state of humanity and identify which factors have helped, and which hindered, progress.

Thus, the goal of this much smaller chapter is to collect in a convenient and portable volume the historical trends for indicators that are widely used to illustrate human welfare. These trends are presented not only across time but, where data are available, across countries with different levels of economic development. In some cases, the data go back to when modern economic growth began – around 1800.[5]

This chapter will address whether and to what extent modern economic growth has improved humanity's lot, using the following indicators.

- *Available food supplies per capita.* Having sufficient food is the first step to a healthy society. It enables the average person to live a productive life, while hunger and undernourishment retard education and the development of human capital, slowing down technological change and economic growth.
- *Life expectancy.* To most people, this is the single most valuable indicator of human well-being. Longer life expectancy is also generally accompanied by an increase in disability-free years.
- *Infant mortality.* Throughout history, high levels of death in early childhood have produced enormous sorrow, reduced population growth and lengthened the time spent by women in childbearing.
- *Economic development.* Gross domestic product (GDP) per capita is a measure of people's income. Thus, it measures the wealth or level of economic development of a country. While wealth is not an end in itself, it indicates how well a nation can achieve the ends its people desire, from greater availability of food, safe water and sanitation to higher levels of education and healthcare.
- *Education.* While education is an end in itself, it also adds to human capital and can accelerate the creation and diffusion of technology. Education (particularly of women) helps to spread knowledge about nutrition and public health practices.

- *Political rights and economic freedom.* The ability to conduct one's life creatively and productively usually depends on having political rights and economic freedom. They are critical to maintaining liberty and the pursuit of happiness, which are among the inalienable rights of human beings.
- *A composite human development index.* Using an approach similar to that employed in the United Nations Development Programme (UNDP), this index combines indicators for life expectancy, education and per capita income.[6]

After examining trends in the above indicators, this chapter will address whether differences in human well-being have widened between developed and developing countries and whether urban residents fare worse than rural residents. Finally, it will discuss the factors that appear to be responsible for the remarkable cycle of progress that has accompanied modern economic growth.

Hunger and undernourishment

Concerns about the world's ability to feed its burgeoning population have been around at least since Thomas Malthus's 'Essay on the Principle of Population' two hundred years ago. Several Neo-Malthusians of the twentieth century confidently predicted apocalyptic famines in the latter part of the century in the developing countries.[7] But even though the world's population is the largest it has ever been, the average person has never been better fed.

Since 1950, the global population has increased by 90%, increasing the demand for food, but at the same time the real price of food commodities has declined 75%.[8] Greater agricultural productivity and international trade have made this possible.[9] As a result, average daily food supplies per person increased 24% globally from 1961–98, as indicated by Table 1. The increase for developing countries was even larger, at 38%.

The Food and Agriculture Organization (FAO) estimates the minimum daily energy requirement for maintaining health and body weight and engaging in light physical activity to be between 1,720 and 1,960 calories (properly, kilocalories) per person per day.[10] Adding to this threshold an allowance for moderate activity results in an estimate of the national average requirement of between 2,000 and 2,310 calories per person per day. (This assumes equal food provisions are likely to be equally available to the population.)

Table 1   **Daily food supplies, c. 1790–1998**
(kcalories per capita, per day)

Area	Pre- or early industrial phase	1961	1975	1985	1998
France	1,753 (1790)	3,193	3,246	3,498	3,541
Developed countries		2.948	3,144	3,284	3,246
India	1,635 (1950–51)	2,073	1,942	2,143	2,466
China	2,115 (1947–48)	1,636	2,084	2.616	2,972
Developing countries		1,930	2,146	2,421	2,663
Sub-Saharan Africa		2,056	2,090	2,043	2,221
World		2,255	2,423	2,637	2,792

Notes: Pre- or early industrial phase data are for the year(s) shown in parenthesis.
Data for China are based on 22 provinces. Many developing countries, such as
India and China, barely embarked on industrialisation until after the Second
World War.
Sources: Burnette and Mokyr (1995); FAO (2000); Fogel (1995); Goklany (1999a).

The improvements in food supply in India and China since the
middle of the twentieth century are especially remarkable. By 1998,
China's food supplies had gone up 82% from a barely subsistence
level of 1,636 calories per person per day in 1961. India's food supplies went up 51% from 1,635 calories per person per day in
1950–51. Between 1969–71 and 1995–7 such increases in food supplies reduced the number of chronically undernourished people in developing countries from 920 million to less than 800 million (or from
35% to 19% of their population), despite a 70% growth in population.[11]

Figure 1, based on cross-country data for 1961 and 1994 from the
World Resources Institute, shows that available food supplies per
capita per day increase with GDP per capita as well as with time.[12] To
better illustrate the change in food supplies for low-income people,
the scale on the graph ends at a GDP per capita of $10,000 (in 1995
dollars).[13] The upward slope for each year probably reflects the fact
that the wealthier the country, the greater its ability to afford more

Figure 1   **Food supply and income, 1961–94**

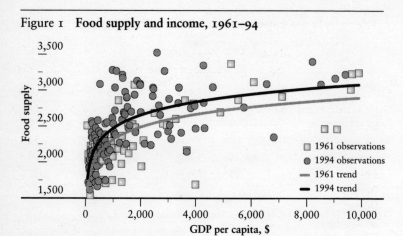

Note: Food supply data in kcalories per day, per capita; income is expressed as GDP per capita in 1995 dollars.
Source: World Resources Institute (1998)

productive technologies to increase crop yields or purchase food in the global market. The upward shift of the available food supply curve through time is consistent with the fact that increases in food production outpaced population growth, largely due to technological change.[14] As a result, the real global price of food commodities declined 75% since 1950, making more food available for people in the lower rungs of the economic ladder. [15]

Life expectancy

Life expectancy at birth is probably the single most important indicator of human well-being. For much of human history, life expectancy was between 20 to 30 years.[16] By 1998 it had increased to 66.9 years worldwide, as Table 2 indicates.[17] For the wealthiest group of nations, the Organization for Economic Co-operation and Development (OECD), life expectancy at birth was 76.4 years in 1998. Life expectancy in the countries that are developed today fluctuated in the early nineteenth century, followed by small declines in the middle two quarters of the nineteenth century. Then, with a few notable exceptions and some minor fluctuations, it began a sustained improvement that continues to this day.

Table 2 **Life expectancy at birth, in years**

Area	Middle ages	Pre- or early industrial phase	1950–55	1975–80	1998
France		30 (1800)	66.5	73.7	78.2
United Kingdom	20–30	35.9 (1799–1803)	69.2	72.8	77.3
Developed countries	20–30		66.5	72.2	74.5
India		24–25 (1901–11)	38.7	52.9	62.9
China		25–35 (1929–31)	40.8	65.3	70.1
Africa			37.8	47.9	53.8
Developing countries			40.9	56.7	63.6
World	20–30		46.5	59.7	66.9

Notes: Pre- or early industrial phase data are for the year(s) shown in parenthesis. UK data, 1799–1803, are for England and Wales only.
Sources: Lee and Feng (1999); Wrigley and Schofield (1981; 529); World Resources Institute (1998); UNDP (2000).

In England and Wales, life expectancy was 35.9 years in 1801. After some ups and downs, it increased to 40.8 years in 1831 but then declined to 39.5 in 1851. After further fluctuations in the range of 40.2 to 41.2 years, it has been climbing since 1871.[18] The same broad pattern seems to fit the United States from the 1850s to the present, with steady improvements from 1880 onwards.[19] The nineteenth-century fluctuations were probably due to a combination of factors. Urbanisation, ignorance of germs and poor sanitation helped spread infectious and parasitic diseases such as cholera, smallpox, malaria, tuberculosis and typhoid.

Once solutions to these diseases were identified – in some cases before their causes were understood – nations cleaned up their water supplies and instituted basic public health measures, such as sanitation, pasteurisation and vaccination. Mortality rates dropped rapidly in the late nineteenth and early twentieth centuries. Then, in the first half of the twentieth century, antibiotics, pesticides such as DDT, and an array of vaccines were added to the arsenal of weapons against disease. Once the traditional infectious and parasitic diseases were essentially conquered, the developed countries turned to dealing with

Figure 2   **Access to safe water and income, 1961–94**

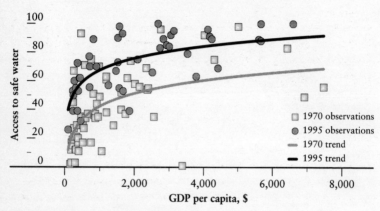

Note: Data represent the per cent of population with access to safe water; income is expressed as GDP per capita in 1995 dollars.
Source: World Bank (1999)

so-called diseases of affluence: cancer, heart diseases and strokes (plus HIV/AIDS, a non-traditional infectious disease).

During the second half of the twentieth century, the diffusion of technology from the developed to developing countries, as well as the greater wealth in the developing countries, increased access to safe water and sanitation services in developing countries. This is shown, for example, in Figure 2.[20] Such access, coupled with increases in per capita food supplies,[21] basic public health services and the newer weapons such as antibiotics, reduced mortality rates.[22] As a result, life expectancies lengthened worldwide, not just in the richest nations.

Figure 3 shows that life expectancy increases as GDP per capita increases, using data for 1962, 1980 and 1997. Average global life expectancy increased from 55.0 to 66.7 years between 1962 and 1997, as technology, including knowledge, was diffused around the world.[23] A country with a GDP per capita of $300 per year would have increased its citizens' average life expectancy from 44.7 years in 1962 to 55.0 in 1997.[24] Figure 3 also suggests that developing countries may have higher life expectancies than did the developed countries at equivalent levels of income. This, indeed, is the case for China and India, countries once synonymous with poverty and wretchedness. In 1913, when the United States had a GDP per capita of $5,305 (in

Figure 3   Income and life expectancy at birth, 1962–97

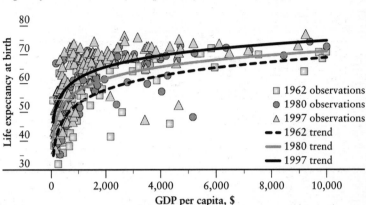

Note: Data represent the life expectancy at birth in years; income is expressed as GDP per capita in 1995 dollars.
Source: World Bank (1999)

1990 dollars),[25] life expectancy at birth was 52.5 years.[26] In 1995, when China and India had GDP per capita of a mere \$2,653 and \$1,568 respectively (also in 1990 dollars), they had life expectancies of approximately 69 and 62 years.[27]

Not only are we living longer; we are also healthier.[28] The World Health Organization reports on disability-adjusted life expectancy, which is calculated by subtracting the years of ill health (weighted according to severity) from the expected overall life expectancy to give the equivalent years of healthy life. According to the 2000 *World Health Report*, disability-adjusted life expectancies for 1997–9 for the United States, China and India were 70.0, 62.3 and 53.2 years respectively.[29] This is substantially more than these countries' corresponding *total* life expectancies before industrialisation (Table 2). Moreover, disability in the older populations of such developed nations as the United States, Canada and France has been declining.[30] In the United States, for instance, the disability rate dropped 1.3% per year between 1982 and 1994 for persons aged 65 and over.

To illustrate the changes in the populous and less affluent countries, Figure 4 shows trends in life expectancies from the years 1950–55 to 1997 for ten countries that together contained 54% of the world's population in 1997.[31] Life expectancy has been increasing for

Figure 4   **Life expectancy at birth, 1950/5–97**

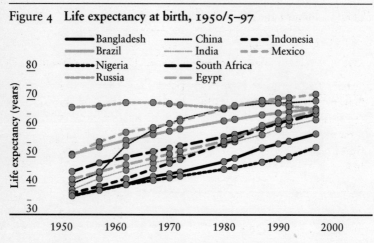

Sources: World Bank (1999); World Resources Institute (1998).

each of the ten except Russia, where it has declined since the late 1980s.[32] Russia's decline reflects economic deterioration. Between 1989 and 1997, Russia's GDP per capita (in real dollars) declined 41%. Yields of cereal, which represent 50% of all crops, fell and food supplies per capita, nutritional levels and public health services all declined.[33] Alcoholism increased, as did accidental deaths, homicides, hypertension and suicides.[34] Life expectancies have similarly declined in other Eastern European countries and those of the former Soviet Union. Life expectancies are also declining in a number of Sub-Saharan countries, seemingly due to a vicious cycle involving HIV/AIDS and a drop in economic output.[35]

Infant mortality

Before industrialisation, one out of every five children died before reaching his or her first birthday. As indicated in Table 3, infant mortality, measured as the number of children dying before reaching one year, typically exceeded 200 per 1,000 live births.[36] The rate fell to 58 per 1,000 worldwide in 1998. This is the same level that more developed countries had reached in the 1950–55 period.[37] In the United States, as late as 1900 infant mortality was about 160 per 1000; but in 1997 it was about 7.[38] In the developing countries, the declines

Table 3 **Infant mortality**

Area	Middle ages	Pre- or early industrial phase	1950–55	1975–80	1998
Sweden		240 (1800)	22	8	4
France		182 (1830)	45	11	5
Developed countries	>200		58	18	9
China			195	52	38
India			190	129	69
Developing countries			179	98	64
Africa			185	120	91
World	>200		156	87	58

Notes: Data represent the number of deaths before age one, per 1,000 live births. Pre- or early industrial phase data are for the year shown in parenthesis.
Sources: Hill (1995); Mitchell (1992, 116–23); World Resources Institute (1998).

started later but may be occurring more rapidly in some areas. For instance, between 1950–55 and 1998, India's infant mortality fell from 190 to 69 and China's from 195 to 38.[39]

It is well known that infant mortality declines as a nation's income increases.[40] Figure 5 illustrates this relationship (using data for 1962, 1980 and 1997). It also shows the general worldwide decline in infant mortality over time. It dropped from a global average of 114 in 1962 to 56 in 1997.[41, 42]

The declines in infant mortality were accompanied by even more spectacular declines in maternal mortality. In the United States, for instance, while infant mortality rates declined from around 100 per 1,000 live births in 1915 to 7.2 per 1,000 in 1996, maternal mortality rates declined from 220 per 100,000 live births to 7.6 per 100,000.[43]

Economic development

Long-term trends in economic growth, based on data from Maddison, are shown in Table 4 for the United States, India, China, Africa, Europe and the world.[44] While these estimates are less than precise, they do indicate that for most of this millennium, GDP per capita

Figure 5   **Infant mortality and income, 1962–97**

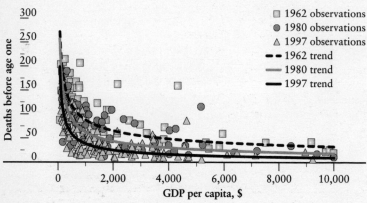

Note: Infant mortality is the number of deaths before age one, per 1,000 live births; income is expressed as GDP per capita in 1995 dollars.
Source: World Bank (1999)

worldwide was below $600, measured in 1990 international dollars.[45] Today, as Figure 6 shows, it is more than eight times that level.

Table 4   **GDP per capita**

Area	AD1	1000	1500	1700	1820	1952	1995
Europe	$425	$400	$640	$870	$1,129	$4,374	$13,951
USA	400	400	400	600	1,260	10,645	23,377
India				531	531	609	1,568
China	450	450	600	600	600	537	3,196
Africa	400	400	400	400	400		1,221
World	425	420	545	604	673	2,268	5,194

Notes: In 1990 international dollars (see note 45). Data for Europe AD1 and 1500 based on Maddison (1999), using arithmetical average for Western Europe and the Rest of Europe. Data for USA AD1 to 1500 based on Maddison's (1999) estimate for North America. Data for Africa are assumed to be a straight line until 1820.
Sources: Maddison (1998, 1999).

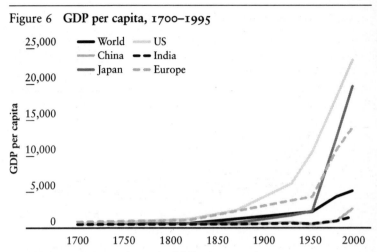

Figure 6   **GDP per capita, 1700–1995**

Note: GDP per capita in 1990 international dollars (see note 45).
Sources: Maddison (1998, 1999).

Acceleration of economic growth began around 1800 and has been dramatic in recent years. Basic necessities such as food are much more easily obtained than they were even a few decades ago. For instance, between the years 1897 to 1902 and 1992 to 1994, US retail prices of flour, bacon and potatoes relative to per capita income dropped by 92%, 87% and 80%, respectively.[46] Not only is food cheaper and the average person's annual income higher, but also workers spend fewer hours on the job. Between 1870 and 1992, average hours worked per person employed declined by 46%, 48% and 36% for the United States, France and Japan respectively. Ausubel and Grübler estimate that for the average British worker, total life hours worked declined from 124,000 in 1856 to 69,000 in 1981.[47] Because the average Briton lives longer and works fewer hours each year, the life hours worked by the average British worker have declined from 50% to 20% of his or her disposable life hours. In other words, the average person has more disposable time for leisure, hobbies and personal development.

Thus, trends in real wages measured in dollars per hour would show an even more dramatic improvement than the income growth shown in Figure 6. However, even these trends would substantially underestimate the true improvements in wages because methods to

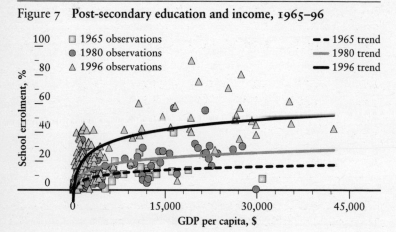

Figure 7   **Post-secondary education and income, 1965–96**

Note: School enrolment is the per cent of relevant population; GDP per capita is in 1995 dollars.
Source: World Bank (1999)

convert current dollars in one year to real dollars in another year are not robust when there has been a vast technological change between the two years. Goods and services available in the year 1950, for instance, were vastly different from those available in 1995. Personal computers, cell phones, VCRs and instant access to the Library of Congress's electronic catalogue, to mention a few, simply were not available in 1950. Today, for a few hundred dollars people can buy goods and services they could not buy for all the money in the world a generation or two ago.

Education and child labour

Figure 7 shows that the percentage of the eligible population enrolled in post-secondary education increased with time and with affluence across a range of countries.[48, 49] Table 5 shows long-term improvements in the levels of education for the United States, France, Japan, China and India, based on data from Maddison.[50]

Literacy has increased worldwide as well, rising for each of the ten countries shown in Figure 4.[51] Between 1970 and 1997, global illiteracy rates dropped from 45.8% to 25.6%. Complementing these increases are declines in the portion of the population aged 10 to 14

Table 5 **Education, average number of years**

Area	1820	1870	1913	1950	1973	1992
France			6.99	9.58	11.69	15.96
USA	1.75	3.92	7.86	11.27	14.58	18.04
Japan	1.50	1.50	5.36	9.11	12.09	14.87
India				1.35	2.60	5.55
China				1.60	4.09	8.93

Sources: Maddison (1998, 1999).

years who are working. Worldwide child labour measured this way has declined from 24.0% in 1960 to 12.6% in 1997.[52]

Political and economic freedom

In 1900, no country had universal adult suffrage; today virtually all do. Multiparty electoral systems were introduced in 113 countries in the quarter century following 1974.[53]

Economic freedom is also ascendant around the world. Gwartney and his co-workers have constructed an index of economic freedom that takes into consideration personal choice, protection of private property and freedom to use, exchange, or give property to another. According to this index, economic freedom increased in the 1990s in 98 of the 116 countries for which they had data. Their analysis indicates that the more economic freedom a country's population has, the higher its economic growth.[54] *See* Figure 8.

Human development index

While the above indicators make a strong case for a steady increase in many aspects of human well-being, it is possible to create a single indicator that incorporates a number of key measurements of well-being. The United Nations Development Programme has popularised this approach with its Human Development Index. This index is based on life expectancy, education and GDP per capita.[55]

According to the latest *Human Development Report*, the Human Development Index (HDI) has been going up for most countries.[56] This index is somewhat arbitrary and probably understates improvements

Figure 8   **Economic freedom rankings by quintiles, $**
           (for 116 countries)

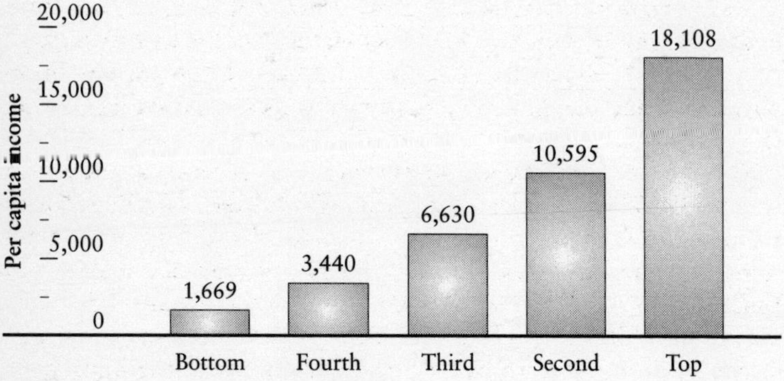

Source: Gwartney, Lawson and Samida (2000).

because it omits measurements of hunger and infant mortality. Nevertheless, the data show that:

All but one of the 101 countries for which data are available showed improvement in the HDI between 1975 and 1998. The exception, Zambia, had increased its HDI between 1975 and 1985 (due to longer life expectancy and higher literacy rates, despite a decline in GDP per capita) but by 1998, continuing declines in GDP per capita and lower life expectancy due to HIV/AIDS more than erased those gains. The presence of refugees may have contributed to these declines in Zambia.

Ten countries in Sub-Saharan Africa and thirteen in Eastern Europe and the former Soviet Union had lower HDIs in 1998 than in 1985 or 1990. The ten Sub-Saharan countries were all affected by HIV/AIDS and some also had declining GDP per capita. Of those, three were plagued by civil conflict or unrest (Democratic Republic of the Congo, South Africa and Burundi); at least two more chose sides and expended scarce resources in those conflicts (Zimbabwe and Namibia); and at least three (Zambia, Congo and Kenya) were contending with refugee populations.[57]

Of the 166 countries for which the World Resources Institute has data, only thirteen had lower life expectancies between 1995 and 2000 than between 1970 and 1975.[58] These included seven Eastern

European and former Soviet Union countries and six Sub-Saharan countries. GDP per capita has declined in eleven of these thirteen, at least since 1990.

In summary, the data indicate that human well-being has improved and continues to improve for the vast majority of the world's population. Over the past 10 to 15 years, however, well-being has been reduced in some Sub-Saharan, Eastern European and former Soviet Union nations.

One of the critical factors underlying these declines is insufficient wealth. HIV/AIDS is identified as the major cause of reductions in HDI in Sub-Saharan countries.[59] When AIDS first appeared, it resulted in almost certain death. Developed countries, particularly the United States, launched a massive assault on the disease. US deaths due to HIV/AIDS dropped from a high of 43,115 in 1995 to 13,210 in 1998.[60] In 1996, it was the eighth leading cause of death; by 1998 it had dropped off the worst-fifteen list. But similar improvement is unlikely to occur soon in Sub-Saharan countries because they cannot afford the cost of treatment unless it is subsidised by governments, charities or industry from the richer nations.

For the United States, I have constructed a similar index. Instead of education *per se*, I use literacy data, which are more readily available. The minimum value for each of the three components corresponds roughly to what it was around 1820, approximately the start of industrialisation. These are: 30 years for life expectancy, 73.7% for literacy and $1,350 (in 1992 dollars) for GDP per capita.[61] For the maximum values, I assume 85 years, 100% and $40,000 respectively, similar to what UNDP assumes.[62] My index assumes that literacy stays at 99% after 1970. This actually understates the level of improvement since it does not account for long-term increases in the educational level of the average American. Based on these assumptions, Figure 9 shows trends in the composite HDI and its individual components for the United States from 1870–1997. Despite minor fluctuations in the components, there has been a general improvement in overall human well-being in the United States during the twentieth century. Each component improved throughout the century except for literacy, which reached saturation around 1970.

Have gaps in human well-being widened?

While human well-being has improved continually over the past two centuries, it is often claimed that inequalities continue to grow

Figure 9   **Human Development Index, United States, 1850–1997**

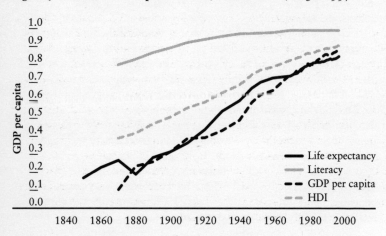

Sources: Life expectancy data: 1850–90, Haines (1994); 1900–70, Bureau of the Census (1975); 1971–97, various *Statistical Abstracts* including Bureau of the Census (1999). GDP per capita data: 1900–28, calculated from Bureau of the Census (1975); 1929–97, Bureau of Economic Analysis (1998), per Goklany (1999c, 68–9). Literacy data: Bureau of the Census (1975); Costa and Steckel (1997).

between the developed and developing nations. A typical observation is the following from the United Nations Development Programme's 1999 *Human Development Report*:

> Nearly 30 years ago the Pearson Commission began its report with the recognition that 'the widening gap between the developed and developing countries has become the central problem of our times.' But over the past three decades the income gap between the richest fifth and the poorest fifth has more than doubled. Narrowing the gaps between rich and poor ... should become explicit global goals ...[63]

As Figure 6 showed, there are wide – and, in many cases, growing – disparities in income between the richer and poorer countries. The gaps in per capita income between Western Europe and the United States and other regions have ballooned since 1700 and many people remain terribly poor.[64] According to the UNDP, 1.2 billion people, mainly in the developing world, live in 'absolute poverty' (defined as subsisting on less than one US dollar per day) and at least 35 nations had lower per capita incomes in 1998 than in 1975 (measured in real dollars).[65]

However, measurements that describe human well-being more directly than income do not show quite the same pattern. Yes, gaps in life expectancy and infant mortality between the more and less developed countries are substantial. However, these gaps have narrowed by 55% since the Second World War. The gap in life expectancy was 25.4 years in the 1950–1955 period but fell to 10.9 years in the 1995–2000 period, while the gap in infant mortality fell from 121 to 53 deaths per 1,000 live births.[66] In addition, as shown in Table 1 and Figure 1, food supplies per capita have increased. Hunger is less prevalent than it was 30 years ago and the number of people suffering from chronic undernourishment has declined in both absolute and relative terms.[67] Thus, while income inequalities have widened, in the aspects of human well-being that are truly critical – life expectancy, infant mortality, hunger – the world is far more equal.

Are rural residents better off?

Historically, as the currently developed countries embarked on modern economic growth, the welfare of urban dwellers generally lagged behind that of their rural compatriots.[68] Fogel notes that US cities with populations above 50,000 had twice the death rates of rural areas in the 1830s.[69] Evidently, overcrowding, lack of knowledge about hygiene and lack of safe water and sanitation made urban populations more susceptible to contagious diseases such as cholera, typhoid and tuberculosis. The image of urban suffering compared to a healthier rural life is reinforced in the mind of anyone who visits the overcrowded and polluted urban areas of the developing world, which give the impression that life in developing countries is worsening as cities grow.

In fact, however, urban residents are better off than rural ones in most developing countries. When measured by the United Nations' Human Development Index and its related Human Poverty Index, there is more progress and less deprivation in urban areas.[70] For instance, in Swaziland, the rural HDI is 35% below the urban level, reflecting less access to safe water, sanitation and public health services; lower rates of literacy; and higher rates of undernourishment. Figure 10 shows for 1990–96 the urban–rural divide for access to safe water and access to sanitation for some of today's more populous developing nations. In each case, rural residents have lower access.

Figure 10   **Access to sanitation and safe water, 1990–96**

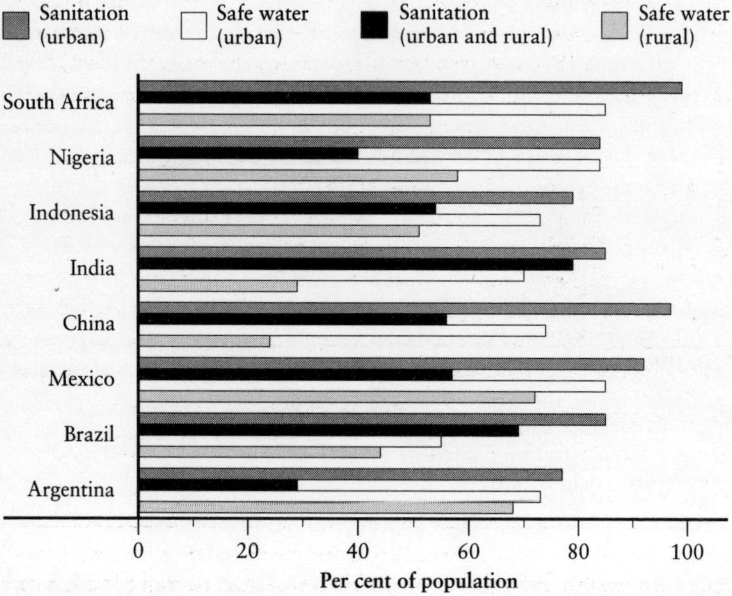

Source: World Resources Institute (1998).

The cycle of progress

We have seen that human welfare advanced more during the twentieth century than it did in all the rest of mankind's tenure on earth. I contend that this progress in human well-being was sustained, and perhaps even initiated, by a cycle composed of the mutually reinforcing, co-evolving forces of economic growth, technological change and free trade.

Technology increases food production through various mechanisms. It boosts yields through special seeds, mechanisation, judicious application of inputs such as fertilisers and lime, and reductions of losses to pests, spoilage and wastage. Use of this technology is closely linked to economic development because not everyone can afford it. One reason why poorer countries have lower cereal yields is that farmers cannot afford sufficient fertiliser and other yield-enhancing technologies.[71] Thus we see in Figure 11 that yields increase over time

Figure 11   **Cereal yield and income, 1961–97**

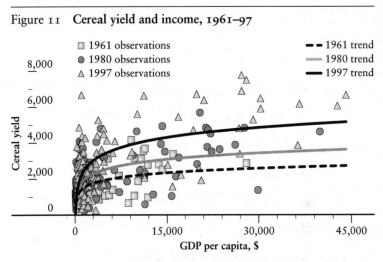

Note: Cereal yield data in kilogrammes per hectare; income is expressed as GDP per capita in 1995 dollars.
Source: World Bank (1999)

and with wealth.[72] Higher crop yields translate into more food. Even if food deficits exist, trade moves agricultural crops and products voluntarily from surplus to deficit areas, allowing developing countries like Afghanistan and Zimbabwe to reduce their food shortfalls.

Thus, global trade in conjunction with improved technology increases food security.[73] The infrastructure – ships, refrigerated trucks, roads and rails – that trade depends on, as well as the financial mechanisms that transfer money and hedge risks, are products of technology, capital and human resources. More food also means more healthy people who are less likely to succumb to infectious and parasitic diseases. That – along with capital and human resources targeted on improvements in medicine and public health[74] – has reduced mortality and increased life expectancy worldwide.[75] Hence, as populations become more affluent mortality decreases, as shown in Figure 5 for infant mortality, and life expectancy increases, as shown in Figure 3.[76] Thus, a wealthier population is a healthier population.

A healthier population is also wealthier because it is more productive.[77] Fogel estimates that the level of food supplies in eighteenth-century France were so low that the bottom 10% of the labour force could not generate the energy needed for regular work and the next

10% had enough energy for about half an hour of heavy work (or less than 3 hours of light work).[78]

Citing a United Nations study, Easterlin notes that when malaria was eradicated in Mymensingh (now in Bangladesh), crop yields increased 15% because farmers could spend more time and effort on cultivation.[79] In other areas elimination of seasonal malaria enabled farmers to plant a second crop. According to the World Bank, the near-eradication of malaria in Sri Lanka between 1947 and 1977 raised its national income by an estimated 9%.[80] A joint study by the Harvard University Center for International Development and the London School of Hygiene and Tropical Medicine estimated that if malaria had been eradicated in 1965, Africa's GDP would be 32% higher today.[81]

A healthier and longer-living population is also likely to invest more time and effort in developing its human capital, which contributes to the creation and diffusion of technology. It is not surprising that levels of education have gone up with life expectancy or that researchers today spend what at one period was literally a lifetime to acquire the skills and expertise necessary for careers in research.

In addition, several measures undertaken to improve public health provided a bonus in economic productivity. Draining swamps not only reduced malaria but also added to the agricultural land base.[82] The World Bank reported that an international programme to curtail river blindness, the Onchocersiasis Control Programme, a mixture of drug therapy and insecticide spraying, has protected 30 million people (including 9 million children) from the disease.[83] It is also freeing up 25 million hectares (60 million acres) of land for cultivation and settlement. Similarly, improved food supplies and nutrition by themselves may aid learning. This is one of the premises behind school meals programmes.[84]

Improvements specific to health, food and agriculture also benefit from a larger, more general cycle in which broad technological change, economic growth and global trade reinforce each other. Other technologies – invented for other reasons – have led to medical advances and improved productivity or reduced the environmental impacts of the food and agricultural sector. For example, computers, lasers and global positioning systems permit precision agriculture to optimise the timing and quantities of fertilisers, water and pesticides, increasing productivity while reducing environmental impacts. Plastics – essential for food packaging and preservation – also increase productivity of the food and agricultural sector. Transportation of every kind increases the ability to move inputs and outputs from farms to markets, and vice versa. Broad advances in physics and engineering have led to new or improved medical technologies, including electricity (without which virtually no present-day hospital or operating room could function), x-rays, nuclear magnetic resonance, lasers and refrigeration.

These specific impacts do not exhaust the benefits of broad economic growth, technological change and global trade. Technological change in general reinforces economic growth,[85] giving countries more resources to research and develop technological improvements and to increase education.[86]

As Figure 7 showed, the proportion of the eligible population enrolled in post-secondary schools increases with wealth. Anecdotal evidence reinforces the importance of wealth in developing human capital. Wealthy countries have the best education. An informal survey of fellow immigrants suggests that many of the most talented people from poorer countries end up in the universities and research establishments of the richer nations, not only because they expect a higher quality of education but because they anticipate job opportunities that will better use their education and talents. In 1993, for instance, ten of the richest (and most well-educated) countries accounted for 84% of global research and development and controlled more than 80% of the patents acquired in the United States and in developing countries.[87] Freer trade contributes directly to greater economic growth, helps disseminate new technologies and creates competitive pressures to invent and innovate.[88] As an example, trade accelerated the clean-up of automobile emissions in the United States because the threat of cleaner cars from imports advanced the introduction of catalytic converters in the 1970s.[89] By expanding competition, trade helps contain the costs of basic infrastructure, including water supply and sanitation systems. A vivid example of the importance of trade in improving human well-being comes from Iraq. Because of trade sanctions, Iraq is unable to operate and maintain its water, sanitation and electricity systems, resulting in significant public health problems.[90]

Without the additional food supplies obtained through trade, prices would be higher and levels of hunger and malnutrition would increase in developing countries. These countries would have had to increase their cereal production by 10% to make up the shortfall from the absence of any international trade in cereals.[91] The result would be higher food prices (which would price more poor people out of the market), greater cultivation of more marginal lands, or both.

In terms of income alone, trade raises income levels for both the poor and the rich.[92] Dollar and Kraay[93] also find that economic growth favours rich and poor equally, confirming analyses by Ravallion and Chen,[94] and Easterly and Rebelo.[95] Similarly, increased protection of property rights and fiscal discipline (defined as low government consumption) raise overall incomes without increasing inequality.[96]

Thus each link in the cycle – higher yields, increased food supplies, lower mortalities and higher life expectancies – is strengthened by the general forces of economic growth, technological change and trade. Qualitatively at least, this explains why all the figures for cereal yields (Figure 11), food supplies per capita (Figure 1), safe water (Figure 2), life expectancy (Figure 3) and post-secondary education (Figure 7) when plotted against per capita income look similar, and all look like mirror images of Figure 5 for infant mortality rates.

Conclusion

Since 1800, global population has increased about six-fold.[97] Manufacturing industries have increased 75 times in value[98, 99] and coal production has increased 500 times.[100] Overall, global economic product has multiplied more than 50-fold.[101, 102] Despite the environmental disruption that might have been caused by all this activity, the state of humanity has never been better. Specifically:

- In the last two centuries, the average person's life expectancy at birth has doubled, infant mortality is less than a third of what it used to be and real income has grown seven-fold. Food is more affordable, a child is less likely to go to bed hungry and a woman is far less likely to die in childbirth.
- Children are more likely to be in school than at work. People are more educated and freer to choose their rulers and express their views. They are more likely to live under the rule of law and are less fearful of being arbitrarily deprived of life or limb, freedom, property, wealth or other basic human rights. Not only is work less physically demanding, but people work fewer hours and have more leisure time and money to devote to optional pursuits.
- Although gaps between richer and poorer nations may be expanding in terms of per capita income, gaps in the critical aspects of human well-being (particularly life expectancy,

infant mortality, hunger and malnourishment, and literacy)
have for the most part shrunk over the past half-century.

- Developing nations on the whole have benefited from
knowledge and technology generated in developed countries.
With respect to the most critical indicators of human well-
being – life expectancy, infant mortality and hunger –
developing countries are better off than were developed
countries at equivalent levels of income. These improvements
have come from reducing death and disease due to inadequate
food supplies and to infectious and parasitic diseases such as
cholera, malaria, typhoid, diarrhoea, dysentery and other
water-related illnesses.

- The reductions in water-related diseases and diseases caused or
aggravated by inadequate food and nutrition have not yet run
their full course. Thus, improvements in infant mortality and
life expectancy in developing countries may continue,
shrinking the gap between developing and developed countries
for these indicators.

However, once the easy and relatively cheap improvements in
health and life expectancy have been captured, the gap may widen
again. Further improvements will come only through dealing with
non-traditional diseases such as AIDS and the diseases of affluence.
While the United States reduced deaths from HIV/AIDS by almost
70% between 1995 and 1998, treatment is unavailable to most in the
developing world. This illustrates not only the need for improved
technology but also the importance of economic growth as well as
trade in ideas and products.

*This chapter was adapted from a paper entitled 'Economic Growth and
the State of Humanity', originally published in April 2001 by PERC –
the Center for Free Market Environmentalism in Bozeman, Montana
(www.perc.org). Indur Goklany wrote it while he was a Julian Simon
Fellow at PERC, and the paper was published in Julian Simon's honour.
Tables and figures are © Indur M. Goklany and PERC 2001.*

3 Does it pay to be green?
Some historical perspectives

Pierre Desrochers

'Will it Pay?' then is, after all, the question usually put when any attempt is made to introduce a new product, or to utilise in a new way any of the residue material used in our popular industries.[1]

A widespread belief among contemporary writers on sustainability is that past economic development was characterised by wasteful practices. For example, Ernst Worrell writes: 'Historically, society and industry have operated as an open system, transforming resources to products or services and emitting wastes and pollutants to the environment at all stages of the life cycles.'[2] Bhaskar Nath, Luch Hens and David Pimentel similarly believe that 'it is hard to find any human activity or intervention for economic development that has been beneficial, benign or cost-free to the natural environment'.[3] In their bestseller *Natural Capitalism*, Paul Hawken, Amory Lovins and L. Hunter Lovins indict traditional capitalism as a 'financially profitable [but] nonsustainable aberration in human development'[4] rooted in wasteful practices that result in ecological strain, causing not only the loss of forests, topsoil, fisheries and freshwater but also 'poverty, hunger, malnutrition, rampant disease, crime, corruption, lawlessness, anarchy and refugee populations'.[5] In short, as Richard Florida and Derek Davison argue in a book sponsored by Resources for the Future: 'Since the dawn of the industrial age, the goals of economic growth and enhanced environmental quality have been at odds.'[6]

In recent years, however, many authors have documented numerous cases where the profit motive has led to so-called 'win-win' situations where firms improved their bottom line while reducing their environmental impact.[7] As the incentives behind such behaviour are as old as market economies, could it be that it has always paid to be green? This chapter provides historical evidence to make just such a case. The first three sections illustrate that pollution prevention, 'green' technologies and loop-closing, the main components of 'eco-efficiency,' were a reality long before they drew the attention of sustainable development theorists.[8] The final section discusses why it is now widely believed that past industrial development was characterised by a linear model of extraction, production and disposal.

Pollution prevention

The goal of 'pollution prevention' is to reduce pollution from existing plants and processes by implementing one or more of the seven following practices: 1) equipment modernisation and modification; 2) improved maintenance; 3) improved operation practices; 4) better inventory control; 5) process and/or product modification; 6) substitution of inputs; 7) in-process recycling.[9] Much evidence indicates that this behaviour has always been typical for competitive firms. Thus in his classic *On the Economy of Machinery and Manufacture*, Charles Babbage pointed out: 'Amongst the causes which tend to the cheap production of any article, and which are connected with the employment of additional capital, may be mentioned the care which is taken to prevent the absolute waste of any part of the raw material.'[10] The British authors of the *Descriptive Catalogue of the Collection Illustrating the Utilization of Waste Products* of the Bethnal Green Branch Museum[11] concurred with this observation two generations later:

> Few among the minor tendencies of industries are more worthy of note than that shown in the utilization of waste materials. As competition becomes sharper, manufacturers have to look more closely to those items which may make the slight difference between profit and loss, and convert useless products into those possessed of commercial value, which is the most apt illustration of Franklin's motto that 'a penny saved is twopence earned:' our manufacturers have not been slow to appreciate this truth, as is shown in more than one branch of trade. . .[12]

The German engineer Koller was to make similar comments at the turn of the century based on his observation of the Reich's industries: 'Competition is so keen that even with the most economical – and therefore the most rational – labour it is difficult to make manufacturing operations profitable, and it is therefore only by utilizing to the full every product which is handled that prosperity for all may be assured.'[13] Looking back to the middle of the nineteenth century, the American economist Rudolf Clemen wrote in 1927: 'The development of by-products in industry is one of the most outstanding phenomena in our economic life'[14] and that 'from the viewpoint of individual business, this manufacture of by-products has turned waste into such a source of revenue that in many cases the by-products have proved more profitable per pound than the main product.'[15]

He credited market forces entirely for this state of affairs by pointing out that the development of by-products was done simply in order to avoid being overwhelmed by the competition of other industries, or of other corporations within the same industry:

> Modern conditions make it almost impossible materially to cut
> production and distribution of expense for the majority of
> commodities; hence one of the most important opportunities for
> gaining competitive advantage, or even for enabling an industry or
> individual business to maintain its position in this new
> competition, is to reduce its manufacturing expense by creating
> new credits for products previously unmarketable ...[16]
>
> Indeed, the materials from which the by-products in nearly all
> industries are manufactured today were formerly partially or
> wholly wasted, and the change to intensive utilization of these
> materials for by-product manufacture has been brought about by
> the ever-increasing force of competition in American business,
> both between individual concerns within a single industry and
> among different ones.[17]

In the same era, Max Muspratt, a former president of the Federation of British Industries, summarised what he perceived to be typical industrial behaviour: 'In the days of my childhood, "waste not, want not" was a lesson inculcated upon all young people. Whether there was at once a suitable response in the nursery I am now too old to remember, but the same wise saying has had the constant consideration of every progressive manufacturer for at least a century.'[18] 'Pollution prevention' has obviously been around for a long time. As will now be illustrated, the same can be said of 'green' technologies.

Green technologies

The importance of technological change for environmental protection has been increasingly appreciated in recent years, mostly in studies and anecdotes on 'cleaner' or 'greener' technologies. Yet, if one agrees with Dyson Carter that the goal of most technological innovations has always been either to save time, lower costs, make a product last longer, do more or work better, then the environmentally beneficial impact of most innovations seems to be a given.[19] The fact that new technologies were essential in creating resources out of by-products was well understood by Peter Simmonds, who wrote in 1876: 'Modern science has pointed out the uses of many substances which were formerly regarded as offal, and thrown away; and the result is, that in England and on the Continent scarcely anything is entirely wasted.'[20] The Austro-Hungarian Archduke Rainer Ferdinand von Habsburg had made similar comments a few years earlier: 'An extensive and refined use made of the waste of materials of industry and housekeeping might be considered [a good] measure of the degree of industrial development and capability. It would also scarcely be possible to find in the processes of Manufacture and in Agriculture an instance which shows to the same extent the really creative force of Science.'[21] The authors of the *Descriptive Catalogue of the Collection Illustrating the Utilization of Waste Products* of the Bethnal Green Branch Museum also pointed out: 'One of the greatest benefits that Science can confer on man is the rendering useful those substances which being the refuse of manufactures are either got rid of at great expense, or when allowed to decompose produce disease and death.'[22] They added: 'A large number of such are now used in various ways which were formerly regarded as offal, and cast away, but many others still exist inviting the ingenuity of men of science to find for them useful applications.'[23]

Karl Marx, building on the work of Charles Babbage, also argued that one of the general requirements for the re-employment of industrial 'excretions' was 'improved machinery whereby materials, formerly useless in their prevailing form are put into a state fit for new production: scientific progress, particularly chemistry, which reveals the useful properties of such waste'.[24] Another radical European economist, John Hobson, made similar observations a few decades later:

New industrial arts owing their origin to scientific inventions and their practice to machinery arise for utilising waste products. Under 'waste products' we may include . . . the refuse of manufacturing processes which figured as 'waste' until some unsuspected use was found for it. Conspicuous examples of this economy are found in many trades. During the interval between great new inventions in machinery or in the application of power many of the principal improvements are of this order.[25]

The British economist Alfred Marshall also wrote during the same period that 'many of the most important advances of recent years have been due to the utilizing of what had been a waste product; but this has generally been due to a distinct invention, either chemical or mechanical'.[26] Another contemporary, Frederick Talbot, was even more explicit:

> It is distinctly interesting, if not actually amusing, to follow what may be described as the utilitarian conjugation of waste. It remains an incubus, if not an unmitigated nuisance, until the chemist, or some other keenly observant individual possessed of a fertile mind, comes along to rake it over and to indulge in experiments. Such efforts are often followed with ill-conceived amusement . . . In due course some definite conclusion is reached, and the fact becomes driven home that, if such-and-such a process be followed a particular spurned refuse can be utilised as raw material for the production of some specific article. Then scepticism and amusement give way to intense interest and speculative rumination. The new idea is submitted to the stern test of practical application upon a commercial basis, while the financial end of the proposal, which is the determining factor, is carefully weighed.[27]

As numerous examples illustrate,[28] this pattern was common to all industry, a point that Talbot summarised concisely: 'To relate all the fortunes which have been amassed from the commercialisation of what was once rejected and valueless would require a volume. Yet it is a story of fascinating romance and one difficult to parallel in the whole realm of human activity.'[29] As will now be illustrated, loop-closing – the idea that the by-products of one industry can become the valuable inputs of another – an idea hailed by many modern-day writers to be a form of 'new thinking', was also widespread during the last two centuries.

Loop-closing

The idea that firms should reduce their aggregate environmental impacts by turning waste into feedstock has been actively promoted in recent years by so-called 'industrial ecologists'[30] and 'natural capitalists'.[31] Once again, however, it can be argued that contemporary ideals are only trying to catch up with past practices. For numerous such illustrations, one can look at books devoted to industrial resource recovery that were written long before the advent of modern environmental consciousness and regulation. Countless other examples can also be found in ancient technical books dealing with specific kinds of waste, and in patent records, graduate dissertations and trade journals.[32] Indeed, the practice of industrial resource recovery between otherwise unrelated firms was deemed widespread by many past commentators. Simmonds thus observed:

> In every manufacturing process there is more or less waste of the
> raw material, which it is the province of others following after the
> original manufacturer to collect and utilise. This is done now,
> more or less, in almost every manufacture, but especially in the
> principal ones [of the United Kingdom] – cotton, wool, silk,
> leather, and iron.[33]

Some years later, the organisers of the waste exhibit of the Bethnal Green Branch Museum wrote that many ingenious individuals were busily devising 'means by which [the] rubbish may be worked up into a useful product' and that there were 'few . . . great manufactures now which have not one or more of these dependent industries attached to them'.[34] Following the First World War, Talbot wrote: 'The German, when he encounters a waste, does not throw it away or allow it to remain an incubus. Saturated with the principle that the residue from one process merely represents so much raw material for another line of endeavor, he at once sets to work to attempt to discover some use for refuse.'[35] A few years later, Kershaw replied to some criticisms of his attempt to cover, in one volume, the waste in all branches of manufacturing industry in the United Kingdom and the United States by pointing out: 'It is a mistake to imagine that our industries can be carried on efficiently in water-tight compartments, for the waste material or by-product of one manufacture is quite often the starting-point or raw material of another.'[36]

There is thus little ground to believe that widespread loop-closing is either an utopian goal or a modern idea. Yet, if contemporary thinking on sustainable development was so clearly anticipated by previous thinkers and practised by past industrialists, why is it now believed to be a radical departure from past behaviour? This issue will now be examined in more detail.

Economic development and the linear model of production

Why is it so widely believed today that 'eco-efficiency' is an epochal break from past practices? Assuming that the information provided in this essay describes accurately such past practices, the question is indeed a puzzling one. While there are no easy answers, a few hypotheses can be suggested.

The first is that while environmental, technology and business historians have in recent years shown increased interest in the past environmental behaviour of firms, most of them usually begin their inquiry assuming that by-product recovery did not make much economic sense. For example, environmental historian John Cumbler writes: 'Historically business has tended to look on the pollution costs of production as an external cost to be born by society in the form of dirtier water or air or depleted natural resources. Externalizing environmental costs encouraged economic expansion and employment by reducing costs to the manufacturer.'[37] As a result, the inquiries of these historians have often ignored the ideas of authors outlined in previous sections, namely, that the profit motive could lead to situations where firms improved their bottom line while reducing their environmental impact. Instead, historians focused their attention on Progressive Era governmental conservationists and proponents of 'scientific management', who widely believed in the obsolescence of laissez-faire and the urgent need to 'organise' society along 'scientific' lines.[38]

While it is true that many of these latter thinkers declared a 'war on waste' a century ago, they had comparatively little to say on industrial by-products recovery. For one thing, the conservation movement's political leadership was mostly concerned with the exploitation of raw materials. Thus when US governmental forest manager Gifford Pinchot ascribed 'preventing waste' as one of the three principal goals of the conservation movement, he was primarily referring to natural occurrences such as forest fires.[39]

For their part, advocates of scientific management who called for the creation of 'wealth from waste' through centralised scientific planning were primarily concerned with, on the one hand, the unnecessary duplication of work in the anarchic marketplace and, on the other, wasteful behaviour such as conspicuous consumption and luxury that diverted resources away from more pressing needs.[40] While some proponents of scientific management, such as Henry J. Spooner in his book *Wealth from Waste*, gave 'short accounts in simple language of how such unpromising substances as sweepings, scourings, dross, dregs, scum, scoriae, flue-dust, sediments, lees, offal, etc., etc. have been economically utilised,'[41] most of their effort was targeted towards such concepts as 'waste time', 'waste due to traditional methods in management' and the 'utilisation of waste land'.[42] Thus, for example, many authors viewed US reticence in adopting the metric system as a considerable source of waste. As Stuart Chase, now best remembered for having coined the expression 'New Deal', put it in *The Tragedy of Waste*:

> The American Metric Association has estimated that one year of school life for every American child could be saved if the decimal system of weights and measures replaced the pints and feet and acres and rods, the quires and reams, the bushels and pounds of the present immemorial usage. We confess it is with sorrow that we see a child enter upon this uncorrelated, illogical – almost mystical – desert of mathematics. And certainly, in later life, 50 per cent of all clerical labor dealing with weights and measures could be saved by the introduction of the metric system. The Metric Association puts the total loss at $800,000,000 a year, the equivalent of 400,000 man-power hours.[43]

Indeed, Chase argued that, viewed in the light of widespread industrial inefficiency, by-products were not a serious issue: 'On the whole ... This "garbage pail" aspect of waste – despite its prominence in the public mind – is, in our eyes, a minor matter. Compared with such losses as spring from the military establishment, super luxuries, unemployment, excess plant capacity, the retail store traffic, oil drilling, it is, relatively speaking, only a drop in the bucket.'[44]

Perhaps another reason why 'industrial loops' were not deemed prevalent in the past by proponents of central planning, and are indeed often believed to be absent from contemporary market economies, is that they spontaneously appear without any central authority being in charge and that few people have taken the time to study them in any depth. This argument becomes more plausible when one considers that the few research projects that have tracked them using a 'snowball' approach have documented sophisticated linkages. For example, in a fascinating study, Eric Schwarz and Karl Steininger chose a basic goods company in the Austrian province of Styria and followed the waste streams coming into the plant site as well as originating from it. For each new supplier and recipient thus identified the procedure was repeated until the geographic system boundary was reached. The result was the 'discovery' of a very sophisticated case of 'industrial symbiosis'.[45] These findings triggered further research in the Ruhr region of Germany, which resulted in qualitatively similar results.[46]

Perhaps part of the explanation also lies in the fact that most individuals are more familiar with municipal waste disposal practices than industrial behaviour towards by-products. For a number of reasons, ranging from 'city machine politics' to the fact that domestic waste has always been more difficult to collect and of a lesser 'quality' than industrial waste, municipal officials turned to a 'tax and bury' approach to waste long ago, a pattern that rapidly killed the entrepreneurial instincts of their administrators and employees. As Talbot pointed out:

> Ostensibly, [in the United Kingdom] we have the very finest
> machinery in existence for the reclamation of waste of every
> description – the municipal and civic authorities. But, as results
> have conclusively demonstrated, they are the least efficient
> institutions in that respect. The few cities which are able to point
> to great achievements in this field are the very exceptions which
> serve to confirm the rule . . . The system is responsible for this
> deplorable state of affairs. The average municipal engineer, even if
> anxious to excel in this province, finds himself hampered at every
> turn. He is not vested with sufficient authority or freedom to carry
> any carefully prepared scheme into operation without the sanction
> of this, or that, Committee which, as a rule, is notorious for its
> lack of practical knowledge, more particularly in all matters
> pertaining to the value of waste. Then the multiplicity of officials
> and their salaries reacts against every possibility of a scheme being
> turned into a financial success.[47]

One last possible explanation for industrial loops not being deemed prevalent is that over the years a number of policies have actually discouraged industrial resource recovery, most notably through the erection of various institutional barriers, transport cost discrimination against secondary materials, subsidies to the primary sector, 'set aside' programmes and minimum content laws.[48] Current environmental regulations, which are squarely based on the notion that industrial by-products are a nuisance to be destroyed rather than potentially valuable inputs, are a case in point. Indeed, in modern environmental statutory law the designation of a by-product as waste can often prevent further productive uses. Robert Frosch gives the following illustration:

> A characteristic tale from industry is illustrative of the problems facing those firms that attempt to use materials more efficiently. The corrosion coating of auto bodies is accomplished by passing the cars through a zinc phosphate bath. After a period of use, the bottom of the bath contains a slurry rich in zinc. At one plant, this slurry was for many years removed periodically when the tanks were cleaned and then sent to a zinc smelter, which processed it and put the resulting zinc metal back into the industry supply stream. In the course of regulatory actions not aimed at this material, the slurry became classified as a hazardous waste. When the smelter became acquainted with the regulations that would now apply, it refused to accept the material any longer. At the time this anecdote was told, the slurry was being sent to a landfill.[49]

Actually, it is now widely acknowledged that environmental statutes typically define pollution prevention in a way that excludes recycling and reclamation while often instituting pervasive biases against technological innovation.[50]

Conclusion

Virtually all contemporary experts on sustainability assume that traditional economic development was characterised by a linear approach in which materials and energy were extracted, processed, used and dumped in a linear flow into, through, and out of the economy. Much historical evidence, however, indicates that industrial resource recovery was much more widespread than is currently thought. To understand the basic error underlying current assessments of past practices, we must realise that our ancestors did not expand their economies by simply doing more of what they had already been doing, but by inventing new kinds of goods and services and by creating wealth out of what had hitherto been considered valueless things. It therefore seems fair to say that all of today's recyclable products were considered waste at one point in time, before value was created out of them through the use of human creativity and entrepreneurship. The market process is, of course, not perfect and some potential linkages certainly were and currently are overlooked on occasion. In the end, however, it may be that in today's economies, regulatory barriers and price-distorting subsidies are more serious obstacles to creating value out of by-products than traditional market incentives.

This chapter first appeared in the Journal of Private Enterprise, *vol. 17, no. 2, spring 1992, pp. 20–36. It is reproduced here by permission.*

Part Two
Unsustainable Development

4 Why Africa is poor

George B. N. Ayittey

'Instead of being exploited for the benefit of the people, Africa's mineral resources have been so mismanaged and plundered that they are now the source of our misery.'

UN Secretary-General Kofi Annan, at the OAU Summit in Lomé, July 2000

The African paradox

Africa's deteriorating economic situation is baffling. The continent's untapped mineral wealth is immense and its tourism potential enormous.[1] Yet, it is inexorably mired in steaming squalor, misery, deprivation and chaos. According to the *African Observer*: 'Four out of 10 Africans live in absolute poverty and recent evidence suggests that poverty is on the increase ... If Africa wants to reduce poverty by half over the next 15 years, it needs to attain and sustain an average annual growth rate of 7 per cent – an enormous task.'[2]

The African continent, consisting of 54 countries, is the least developed region of the Third World. In 1997, the PPP GNP per capita for Africa was $1,460, compared to $1,590 for South Asia, $3,170 for East Asia and $6,730 for Latin America.[3] Economic growth rates in Africa in the 1970s averaged only 4 to 5%, while Latin America recorded 6 and 7% growth rates. From 1986 to 1993 the continent's real GNP per capita declined 0.7%, while the average for the Third World increased by 2.7%. For all of Africa, real income per capita dropped by 14.6% from its level in 1965, making most Africans worse off than they were at independence.

African growth rates in the late 1990s – around 5% on average – were higher than the 2% growth rate of the early 1990s. But subtract an average population growth rate of 3% and that leaves miserly rates of growth of less than 2% in GDP per capita – woefully insufficient to have a substantial impact on poverty.

The real causes of Africa's crisis

Why is Africa in this state? Two schools of thought exist: the 'externalist' and the 'internalist'. Externalists ascribe Africa's woes to factors beyond Africa's control: Western colonialism and imperialism, the pernicious effects of the slave trade, racist conspiracy plots, exploitation by avaricious multinational corporations, an unjust international economic system, inadequate flows of foreign aid and deteriorating terms of trade. Internalists, on the other hand, lay the blame largely on the shoulders of the local systems of governance: excessive state intervention and associated corruption of institutions at all levels, from the police and judiciary to the highest branches of government.

In his book *The Africans*, African scholar and historian Professor Ali Mazrui claimed that almost everything that has gone wrong in Africa is the fault of Western colonialism and imperialism,[4] which: 'harmed indigenous technological development'[5] and caused the infrastructure (roads, railways and utilities) to collapse.[6] He even argued that, 'the political decay is partly a consequence of colonial institutions without cultural roots in Africa'.[7] Therefore, according to this externalist view, self-congratulatory Western assertions of contributing to Africa's modernisation are hollow: 'The West has contributed far less to Africa than Africa has contributed to the industrial civilization of the West,'[8] claimed Mazrui. In Mazrui's version of events, decay in law enforcement and mismanagement of funds were all the fault of Western colonialism,[9] which signal 'the slow death of an alien civilization'[10] and Africa's rebellion 'against westernization masquerading as modernity'.[11] Western institutions are doomed 'to grind to a standstill in Africa' or decay.

Many African leaders rigidly adhered to this externalist position. In fact, since independence in the sixties, African leaders, with few exceptions, attributed almost every African malaise to the operation or conspiracy of external agents. President Mobutu even blamed corruption on European colonialism. Asked who introduced corruption into Zaire, he retorted: 'European businessmen were the ones who said, "I sell you this thing for $1,000, but $200 will be for your (Swiss bank) account."'[12]

African leaders still point fingers at everyone else but themselves. As his country faced economic meltdown in 1999, Robert Mugabe refused to accept any blame: 'It is, he says, the fault of greedy Western powers, the IMF, the Asian financial crisis and the drought.'[13] The Chairman of Ghana's ruling NDC, Issifu Ali, decreed that whatever economic crisis the nation is going through has been caused by external factors, claiming that since 1982 the NDC had adopted pragmatic policies for the progress of Ghana but that the adverse macro-economic situation in Ghana was caused by 'global economic developments'.[14] Even Ghana's President, Jerry Rawlings, who executed corrupt former heads of state, also blamed the West for African corruption, saying it has 'a responsibility to curb the menace so as to promote good governance on the continent'.[15]

The internalists

For decades this externalist position held sway in African government circles and intellectual discourse. Naturally, its disciples comprise mostly African leaders, scholars and intellectual radicals. By the early 1980s, however, Africans were fed up with the colonialism/imperialism claptrap and the refusal of the leadership to take responsibility for its own failures. A new and angry generation of Africans emerged, who stressed the role of internal factors, including: misguided leadership, misgovernance, systemic corruption, capital flight, economic mismanagement, declining investment, collapsed infrastructure, decayed institutions, senseless civil wars, political tyranny, flagrant violations of human rights and military vandalism, among others. Internalists maintain that, while external factors have played a role, the internal factors have been more important in determining the current state of Africa. According to Nigerian novelist, Chinua Achebe:

> The trouble with Nigeria is simply and squarely a failure of leadership. There is nothing basically wrong with the Nigerian character. There is nothing wrong with the Nigerian land or climate or water or air or anything else. The Nigerian problem is the unwillingness or inability of its leaders to rise to the responsibility, to the challenge of personal example which are the hallmarks of true leadership. We have lost the twentieth century; are we bent on seeing that our children also lose the twenty-first? God forbid![16]

A scathing editorial in the *Ghana Drum* lamented:

> Many a time we have wondered if the so-called African leaders sometimes lack the capacity to think and understand the ramifications of their actions. After all the bloodshed in Rwanda you would think we have learnt a lesson but no! Idiocy of our

power-hungry leaders seems to triumph over pragmatism and common sense. The rationale for the current fighting defies any logic. The world must be getting tired of us, given our self-inflicted tragedies galore. We seem to lack any sense of urgency to handle problems in an expedient manner devoid of bloodshed. Lord Have Mercy![17]

Ghanaian Akobeng Eric claimed in a letter to the *Free Press* that: 'A big obstacle to economic growth in Africa is the tendency to put all blame, failures and shortcomings on outside forces. Progress might have been achieved if we had always tried first to remove the mote in our own eyes.'[18] Now, the people are angry about being betrayed.

In May 1995, thousands of Ghanaians, angry at deteriorating economic conditions in their country, marched through the streets of the capital city, Accra, to denounce the ruling regime of President Rawlings. In Zimbabwe, the people did not buy President Mugabe's claim that 'Britain, greedy Western powers, the IMF, the Asian financial crisis and the drought' were responsible for the country's economic mess. They rejected his request for constitutional revisions to give him more draconian powers in a referendum of 15 February 2000, handing him his first political defeat in twenty years of virtually unchallenged rule. In the presidential election of 10 March 2002 his party, ZANU-PF, retained its grip on the country only through wide-scale electoral fraud, intimidation and violence.

The ranks of 'internalists' now include UN Secretary-General, Kofi Annan. At the July 2000 Organisation of African Unity Summit in Lomé, he told African leaders that they were to blame for most of the continent's problems.[19] At an earlier press conference in London, he charged that, 'Billions of dollars of public funds continue to be stashed away by some African leaders – even while roads are crumbling, health systems have failed, school children have neither books nor desks nor teachers and phones do not work.'[20]

The vampire African state

Today, most Africans cite bad and corrupt leadership as the major cause of Africa's woes. The post-colonial leadership, with few exceptions, established defective political and economic systems in which enormous power was concentrated in the hands of the state and, ultimately, one individual. The political systems were one-man dictatorships and the economic systems were those of *dirigisme* – heavy state participation or direction of economic activity. The rationale behind the adoption of these systems is well known: the need for national unity, ideological aversion to capitalism, and the need to protect the newly independent African nation against foreign exploitation.

Over time, these systems metastasised into an ugly monstrosity, where government as it is generally recognised ceased to exist. Today 'government' as an entity is totally divorced from the people and is perceived by the ruling elite as a vehicle not to serve but to fleece the people. The African state has been reduced to a mafia-like bazaar, where anyone with an official designation can pillage at will. Thus, what exists in many African countries is a 'vampire' or 'pirate' state – a government hijacked by a phalanx of gangsters, thugs and crooks who use the instruments of the state to enrich themselves, their cronies and tribesmen. All others are excluded.

To understand why a rich country is rich and a poor country poor we need to examine how the rich in both countries make their money. In the United States the richest person is Bill Gates, with a personal fortune of around $70 billion (as of early 2002). He generated his wealth in the private sector, producing computer software, and as such has something to show for his wealth. By contrast, in Africa the richest people are heads of state and ministers, who accumulated their wealth by raking it off the backs of their suffering peasants. Quite often, the chief bandit is the head of state himself. This form of presidential banditry merely redistributes wealth and does not result in any net creation of wealth. In fact it destroys wealth, by discouraging investments in entrepreneurial activity and encouraging investments in 'rent-seeking' – where political entrepreneurs expend resources in an attempt to capture some of the president's *largesse*.

Consequently, a peculiar system of governance now pervades Africa where the primordial instinct of the ruling elite is to loot the national treasury, perpetuate itself in power and brutally suppress all dissent and opposition. Worse, the booty is not invested in Africa but in foreign banks. According to a UN estimate, in 1991 alone more than $200 billion in capital was siphoned out of Africa by the ruling elite – equivalent to more than half of Africa's total foreign debt (which stood at $320 billion in 1991). [21] In fact, every year, capital flight from Africa exceeds incoming foreign aid.

In Kenya, government officials have larger foreign bank accounts than business people. Estimates in 1995 suggested that individual holdings in foreign banks were larger than the country's entire foreign debt of about $6 billion in 1995.[22] Some have suggested that if politicians are serious about eradicating poverty, they should start by returning the money they have stolen.

To achieve its nefarious objectives of self-aggrandisement and self-perpetuation in power, the ruling elite takes over and subverts every key institution of government: the civil service, judiciary, military, media, banking. It even controls commissions, including the press/media commission, human rights commission, and commission on civic education, with lofty ideals that are supposed to be non-partisan and neutral. As a result, state institutions and commissions become paralysed, whilst laxity, ineptitude, indiscipline and unprofessionalism are able to flourish in the public sector.

African countries have police forces and judiciary systems but in many cases the police are themselves highway robbers and the judges crooks. According to *The Post Express*, based in Lagos, Nigeria, former Nigerian dictator General Sani Abacha 'is believed to have siphoned more than $8 billion of Nigeria's foreign exchange into fictitious accounts in European, Asian, American, Caribbean and Arab countries.'[23] When Olusegun Obasanjo was elected as Nigeria's president in 1999, he launched a highly public campaign against corruption and vowed to recover the loot stashed abroad by Abacha. By March 2000, government officials had declared that $709 million and another £144 million had been recovered from the Abachas and other top officials from Abacha's regime. But this recovered loot was itself quickly re-looted. When the Senate Public Accounts Committee looked more closely, it found only $6.8 million and £2.8 million in the Central Bank of Nigeria. Said Uti Akpan, a textiles trader in Lagos commented, 'What baffles me is that even the money recovered from Abacha has been stolen. If you recover money from a thief and you go back and steal the money, it means you are worse than the thief.'[24]

Since politics constitutes the gateway to fabulous wealth in Africa, the competition for political power has always been ferocious. Political defeat could mean exile, jail or starvation. Those who win power take over key state institutions and proceed to plunder the treasury. Key positions in these institutions are handed over to the president's tribesmen, cronies and loyal supporters – to serve their interests and not those of the people or the nation. Meritocracy, rule of law, property rights, transparency and administrative capacity vanish. Eventually, however, the vampire state implodes, sucking the country into a vortex of savage carnage and heinous destruction. This has been the fate so far of Liberia, Rwanda, Somalia, Sudan and Zaire. The process varies but its onset follows two predictable patterns.

First, those exploited by the vampire state are forced to remove themselves from the formal economy, either by leaving altogether, or by turning to smuggling, the underground economy and the black market. This deprives the state of tax revenue and foreign exchange. Over time, the formal economy progressively shrinks and the state finds it increasingly difficult to raise revenue as taxes are massively evaded, leading the ruling vampire elite to resort to printing money in order to inflate the economy.

Second, those excluded from the spoils of political power eventually rise up in a rebel insurgency or secede (such as Biafra in 1967). And it takes only a small band of determined rag-tag malcontents to plunge the country into mayhem. Back in 1981, Yoweri Museveni, the current President of Uganda, started out with only 27 men in a guerrilla campaign against Milton Obote. Charles Taylor, now the President of Liberia, set out with 150 rebels; the late Mohamed Farah Aidid of Somalia began with 200 rebels; and Paul Kagame of Rwanda set out with less than 250. Not a single African government in the post-colonial era has been able to crush a rebel insurgency.

Thus one word – power – explains why Africa is in the grip of a never-ending cycle of wanton chaos, horrific carnage, senseless civil wars and collapsing economies. It is the struggle for power, its monopolisation by one individual or group, and the subsequent refusal to relinquish or share it that causes so much destruction and misery. The adamant refusal of African despots and the ruling vampire elites to relinquish or share political power is what triggers an insurgency. In fact, the destruction of an African country, regardless of the professed ideology of its government, *always* begins with some dispute over the electoral process. Unwilling to relinquish or share political power, the ruling vampire elites block, sabotage or manipulate the electoral process to keep themselves in power. The blockage of the democratic process or the refusal to hold elections are what plunged Angola, Chad, Ethiopia, Mozambique, Somalia and Sudan into civil war. The manipulation of the electoral process by hardliners destroyed Rwanda (1993) and Sierra Leone (1992). The subversion of the electoral process in Liberia (1985) eventually set off a civil war in 1989 and instigated civil strife in Cameroon (1991), Congo (1992), Togo (1992), Kenya (1992) and Ivory Coast (2000). Finally, the annulment of electoral results by the military started Algeria's civil war (1992) and plunged Nigeria into political turmoil (1993).

For the latest instance of such shenanigans, witness the current crisis in Zimbabwe.

The internalist solution

Obviously, Africa's vampire state must be reformed. Power needs to be taken out of the hands of the elite and given to the people, where it belongs. This entails both political and economic reform: democratisation, market liberalisation, decentralisation or diffusion of power, and the adoption of power-sharing arrangements. The politics of exclusion must be replaced by the politics of inclusion. The senseless civil wars in Africa must end. In addition, state institutions must be reformed so that transparency, accountability and professionalism prevail. These reforms, in turn, will help establish in Africa an environment conductive to investment and economic activity.

Investment – both domestic and foreign – is the way out of Africa's economic miasma; it is the key to economic growth and poverty reduction. But Africa's environment of chaos, famine, diseases, civil wars, coups, dictatorships, social disorder, corruption and collapsed infrastructure repels foreign investment. Africa has remained so unattractive to foreign investors that, over the decades, official development assistance (or foreign aid) has replaced private capital as the primary source of development funding. Net foreign direct investment in Sub-Saharan Africa dropped dramatically from $1.22 billion in 1982 to $498 million in 1987. Even the French have become disillusioned: 'French direct investment in Sub-Saharan Africa ran at $1 billion a year between 1981 and 1983; by 1988 that had translated into a net outflow of more than $800 million a year.'[25]

The OECD noted that though private capital flows to developing countries over the period 1990–7 exceeded $600 billion, the flow to all of Sub-Saharan Africa barely amounted to $10 billion. Even then, of that total, fully $9 billion accrued to one country, South Africa – meaning that the other 49 countries and 560 million people of Sub-Saharan Africa attracted essentially no net new private capital during the greatest international investment boom ever witnessed.[26]

To turn Africa around, the abominable political and economic systems established by its post-colonial leaders must be dismantled and replaced by systems based on a market economy and the politics of inclusion. These alternative systems are not new to Africa. In fact, pre-colonial Africa was characterised by free enterprise, free markets and free trade. Moreover, the traditional African system of governance is of participatory democracy, as evidenced by the fabled village meeting. The importance of returning to and building upon Africa's own institutions has been subsumed in the new mantra 'African Renaissance'. But in spite of the rhetoric, the commitment to reform is trenchantly lacking. The ruling elite is simply not interested in real reform because it is unwilling to give up power. It undertakes only the minimal cosmetic reforms needed to keep World Bank loans and the dollars of Western aid flowing.

The resistance to reform

The resistance to reform in Africa has four key drivers: egomania and the cult of personality, political entrepreneurship, fear, and a combination of self-interest and intellectual opposition amongst the elite. Let's consider these in more detail:

First, egomaniacal African despots have created a cult of personality around themselves which gives them an air of invincibility and infallibility. Their nations' fortunes and destinies are very much tied up with their personalities. Accepting reform of any kind is an admission of failure or fallibility. Even if they accept reform, they do so reluctantly, trying everything possible to sabotage it so as to prove that any plan advocated by Western donors does not work. Thus Moi predicted that if Kenya established multiparty democracy, it would degenerate into tribal rivalry and strife. Indeed, since 1991, when Moi bowed to external donors and did institute his own version of multiparty 'democracy', more than 1,500 Kenyans have been killed – mostly Kikuyus but also Luos and Luhyas – and 300,000 have been displaced in ethnic clashes. In the words of Nairobi lawyer Gitobu Imanyara, 'We have a President who is determined to fulfil his prophecy that the country is not cohesive enough for multiparty democracy. His desire is to prove that he is right, even if it means destroying Kenya as a country.'[27]

A similar self-fulfilling prophecy was evident in Ghana. Commenting on the democratic system in his country before members of the African parliamentarians of the Commonwealth Parliamentary Association in 1999, President Rawlings of Ghana said: 'We tried it in our country, whether it is going to succeed or not is something I am not too sure of.'[28] Obviously, democracy cannot be expected to 'succeed' when the president implementing it does not even believe it will do so.

Second, state controls allow African leaders to extract resources to build personal fortunes and to dispense patronage to their political supporters. Occupying the presidency is a lucrative business. Abacha, Eyadema, Mobutu, Moi and the other kleptocrats amassed legendary personal fortunes. According to John Bearman, a London-based oil industry analyst, 'Abacha, the late head of state of Nigeria, increasingly monopolised the oil trade himself. There's no deal that does not go through the presidential villa.'[29] The business empires of African leaders would collapse if economic reform were to strip them of state controls. Further, economic liberalisation may also undermine their ability to maintain their political support base.

Likewise, the sycophants and supporters who benefit from a president's *largesse* are reluctant to give up their politically derived wealth. Typically, these people are drawn from the leaders' own tribes, lending a dangerous ethnicity element to the reform issue and creating inter-tribal rivalry: one tribe, fearing it may lose its dominant position in government, opposes multiparty democracy, while the other excluded tribes resort to violence to dislodge the ruling tribe from power. Thus in Rwanda, 'Habyarimana's embrace of reform was conspicuously half-hearted, a capitulation to foreign coercion. It was universally understood that the northwesterners, who depended on his power and on whom his power increasingly depended, would not readily surrender their percentage. While Habyarimana spoke publicly of a political opening, the *akazu* [the inner mafia-like core] tightened its grip on the machinery of the state.'[30]

Other supporters are simply bought: soldiers with fat pay cheques and perks; urban workers with cheap rice and sardines; students with free tuition and hefty allowances; and intellectuals, opposition leaders and lawyers with big government posts and Mercedes Benzes. Even when the head of state does contemplate stepping down, his supporters and lackeys fiercely resist any cutbacks in government *largesse* or any attempt to open up the political system.

Third, many of Africa's heads of state have their hands so steeped in blood and their pockets so full of booty that they are afraid that all their past gory misdeeds would be exposed were they to step down. So they cling to power at all costs, regardless of the consequences.

Finally, senior government officials, intellectuals, lecturers, teachers, editors and civil servants oppose reform for both intellectual reasons and reasons of self-interest. 'There have been numerous strikes against proposed sell offs of state enterprises as unions fear loss of jobs or reduced benefits. Student activists, academics and others have condemned both the theory and practice of privatization.'[31] Members of this class of the population benefit immensely from government subsidies and controls. They may have access to free government housing and medical care, and to government loans for the purchase of cars, refrigerators and even funeral expenses. They would also resist any cutbacks of such government largesse. In Guinea, 'Progress [on reform] was slow because civil servants and others with a stake in the past sought to preserve it. Dissatisfaction produced a series of coups, the latest in February 1996, when a group of soldiers dissatisfied about going without pay joined forces with others in the military who sought General Conte's ouster.'[32]

In Zambia, resistance to reform comes from within President Chiluba's own circle. Some clamour for the continued influence of state spending and patronage. As Mundia Sikatana, a Chiluba adviser and a founder of the Movement for Multiparty Democracy, explained, the government continues to provide vehicles and fuel to hundreds of civil servants. The government, said Sikatana, 'cannot abandon the old habits. The structural adjustment programme is not doing enough'.[33]

Other members of the elite class may oppose economic liberalisation on purely ideological grounds. Africa's intellectual community harbours a deep-seated aversion to capitalism or free markets. This attitude is a throwback from colonial days, when capitalism and colonialism were confused. African nationalist leaders reasoned that colonialism was evil and exploitative and since the colonialists were 'capitalists', therefore, capitalism too is evil and exploitative. The involvement of the World Bank, generally castigated by African intellectuals as a 'neocolonial institution', accentuates this bias against capitalism.

To skirt opposition from the elite, in the 1980s African governments opted for politically safe budget cuts: education, health care and road maintenance. Sub-Saharan African governments slashed spending on education by more than 50% in the 1980s while Guinea, Malawi, Tanzania, Zambia and Senegal cut education budgets by 18 to 25% during the late 1980s. Real per capita spending on health during the rest of the 1980s fell below the 1980 level in over half of Sub-Saharan African countries during the rest of the 1980s. In Zimbabwe, for example, President Robert Mugabe slashed spending on healthcare and education, while spending $3 million a day on the 11,000 troops he had sent to the Congo.[34]

There is some chicanery here. African governments constantly lament that Structural Adjustment Programmes (SAPs) hurt the poor. Of course, SAPs are bound to hurt the poor when these governments exempt the elites and shift the burden of adjustment disproportionately onto the rural poor, especially women and children. Worse, these cuts in social services and infrastructure have undermined economic reform efforts across Sub-Saharan Africa. Roads, schools, and telecommunications systems have fallen apart while rates of infant and child mortality, child malnutrition, primary school dropout, illiteracy and non-immunisation have all increased. The number of teachers has declined as salaries have failed to keep pace with inflation. Between 1999 and 2000, Zimbabwe experienced a mass exodus of doctors and nurses to neighbouring Botswana and South Africa.[35] Communicable diseases such as yellow fever, malaria and cholera reappeared with vengeance.

To compound the problem, the 'politically safe' budget cuts were often not enough to reduce budget deficits. With revenue collection systems in shambles, cash-strapped African governments resorted to printing money. This fuelled inflation and provoked demands for wage increases. Between 1986 and 1991, Ghana's money supply increased at an astonishing average rate of 43%. That created further problems, as civil servants, teachers, doctors and other government officials, unable to cope with rising costs of living, had to 'invent' ways of earning a living.

In sum, most African leaders are simply not interested in reform. Under pressure from external agencies, they implement only the bare minimum of cosmetic reforms to ensure continued flow of Western aid. Africans deride the posturing, tricks and acrobatics as 'Babangida Boogie': one step forward, three steps back, a sidekick, and a flip to land on a fat Swiss bank account. All much ado about nothing: 'One day Nigeria's Finance Minister, Anthony Ani, talks of mass privatisation. The next day privatisation is merely an option to be considered by some government committee. Lagos businessmen are appalled. "Just as we were beginning to move forward, this will set us back years," says a Lagos merchant banker.'[36]

Western culpability – the failure of foreign aid
In destroying their economies, African tyrants received much help from the West – not so much out of wilful intent or malice but out of sheer naiveté. In the post-colonial period, various Western governments, development agencies and multilateral financial institutions have provided generous assistance to support Africa's development efforts. According to the OECD, 'the net disbursement of official development assistance (ODA) adjusted for inflation between 1960 and

1997 amounted to roughly $400 billion. In absolute magnitude, this would be equivalent to almost six Marshall Aid Plans.'[37] According to Jennifer Whitaker:

> Even in 1965 almost 20% of the Western countries' development assistance went to Africa. In the 1980s, Africans, who are about 12% of the developing world's population, were receiving about 22% of the total, and the share per person was higher than anywhere else in the Third World – amounting to about $20, versus about $7 for Latin America and $5 for Asia.[38]

Yet, sadly, the conclusions of a 1989 World Bank report remain true today, 13 years later: 'Overall, Africans are almost as poor today as they were 30 years ago (at independence).'[39] The general consensus among African development analysts is that foreign aid programmes and multilateral lending to Africa have failed to spur economic growth, arrest Africa's economic atrophy, or promote democracy. The continent is littered with a multitude of black elephants (basilicas, grandiose monuments, grand conference halls and show airports) amid institutional decay, crumbling infrastructure and environmental degradation.

According to Doug Bandow of the Cato Institute in Washington DC, 'The United Nations declared in 1999 that 70 countries – all aid recipients – are now poorer than they were in 1980. An incredible 43 were worse off than in 1970s. Chaos, slaughter, poverty and ruin stalked Third World states, irrespective of how much foreign assistance they received.'[40]

The African countries that received the most aid – Liberia, Zaire and Somalia – have slid into virtual anarchy.[41] Another large Western aid recipient, Kenya, teeters on the brink of an economic collapse, whilst its government 'inflicts unspeakable abuses of human rights on its own citizens while aid pays the bills'.[42]

In a 1995 letter to US Secretary of State, Warren Christopher, the US House of Representative's International Relations Committee chairman, Republican Benjamin Gilman, and Lee H. Hamilton, a ranking Democratic member, wrote:

> Zaire under Mobutu represents perhaps the most egregious example of the misuse of US assistance resources. The US has given Mobutu nearly $1.5 billion in various forms of aid since Mobutu came to power in 1965. Mobutu claims that during the Cold War he and his fellow African autocrats were concerned with

fighting Soviet influence and were unable to concentrate on creating viable economic and political systems. The reality is that during this time Mr Mobutu was becoming one of the world's wealthiest individuals while the people of Zaire, a once-wealthy country, were pauperized.[43]

Somalia is probably the most execrable example of Western patronage gone berserk. Huge amounts of economic and disaster relief aid were dumped into Somalia, transforming the country into a graveyard of aid. But it was the massive inflow of food aid in the early 1980s that did much to shred the fabric of Somali society. Droughts and famines are not new to Africa, and most traditional societies have developed indigenous methods of coping. The flood of cheap food aid destroyed these methods and Somalia became more and more dependent on food imports. 'The share of food import in the total volume of food consumption rose from less than 33% on average for the 1970–9 period to over 63% during the 1980–4 period, which coincides with Western involvement in the Somalia economy and food-aid programs.'[44]

Nor has adjustment lending by multilateral institutions been successful in Africa. According to the United Nations Conference on Trade and Development (UNCTAD), 'Despite many years of policy reform, barely any country in the region has successfully completed its adjustment program with a return to sustained growth. Indeed, the path from adjustment to improved performance is, at best, a rough one and, at worst, a disappointing dead-end. Of the 15 countries identified as 'core adjusters' by the World Bank in 1993, only three (Lesotho, Nigeria and Uganda) are now classified by the IMF as "strong performers".'[45] The World Bank itself evaluated the performance of 29 African countries, all of whom had received more than $20 billion in funding from the Bank to sponsor SAPs over the period 1981 to 1991. Its report *Adjustment Lending in Sub-Saharan Africa*, released in 1993, concluded that only six of these had performed well: The Gambia, Burkina Faso, Ghana, Nigeria, Tanzania and Zimbabwe. Six out of 29 gives a failure rate in excess of 80%.[46] More distressing, the World Bank concluded, 'no African country has achieved a sound macro-economic policy stance'. Since then, the World Bank's list of 'success stories' has shrunk. The Gambia, Nigeria and Zimbabwe were struck off the list on account of political turmoil. And the World Bank's own Operations Evaluation Department noted in its December 1995 report that, 'although Ghana has been projected as a success story, prospects for satisfactory growth rates and poverty reduction are uncertain'.[47]

In 1998, the West began touting Guinea, Lesotho, Eritrea and Uganda as the new 'success stories' – but not for long. The conflict in eastern Guinea, the senseless Ethiopian–Eritrean war, the eruption of civil strife following an army takeover in Lesotho in 1998, and the eruption of civil wars in western and northern Uganda have eclipsed their stardom.

'The West's record of aid for Africa in the past decade [1980s] can only be characterised as one of failure,' declared Sir William Ryrie, executive vice-president of the International Finance Corporation, a World Bank subsidiary.[48] In a more general indictment, Nicholas Eberstadt wrote: 'Western aid today may be compromising economic progress in Africa and retarding its development of human capital ... Western aid directly underwrites current policies and practices; indeed, it may actually make possible some of the more injurious policies, which would be impossible to finance without external help.'[49]

Many Africans would agree. David Karanja, a former Kenyan MP, was blunt on the subject: 'In fact, foreign aid has done more harm to Africa than we care to admit. It has led to a situation where Africa has failed to set its own pace and direction of development free of external interference.'[50]

The reasons why Western aid programmes failed in Africa are many and familiar: Most aid programmes were crafted in Western capitals with little input from the people they were intended to benefit; aid was used to support grandiose, prestige projects with little economic value; and aid funds were sometimes looted, among other reasons. Western donors often exercised little prudence in backing wrong-headed projects. For example, Tanzania's ill-conceived *Ujaama* socialist experiment received much Western support. *The New York Times* reported that, 'at first, many Western aid donors, particularly in Scandinavia, gave enthusiastic backing to this socialist experiment, pouring an estimated $10 billion into Tanzania over 20 years. Yet today, as Mr Nyerere leaves the stage, the country's largely agricultural economy is in ruins, with its 26 million people eking out their living on a per capita income of slightly more than $200 a year, one of the lowest in the world.'[51]

The 1990 *World Development Report* by the World Bank noted that Tanzania's economy contracted an average of 0.5% a year between 1965 and 1988. Meanwhile, average personal consumption declined by a dramatic 43% between 1973 and 1988.[52] *The Economist* observed that for all the aid poured into the country, Tanzania only had pot-holed roads, decaying buildings, cracked pavements, demoralised clinics and universities, and a 1988 income per capita of $160 (lower than at independence in 1961) to show for it.[53]

Western donors often fail to make the fundamental distinction between 'African leaders or governments' and the 'African people', believing rather naively that they can help the African people by working with or forming 'partnerships' with African leaders and governments. Thus the Western approach to African problems has been 'leader-centred'. President Clinton epitomised this approach. During his historic visit to Africa in March 1998, Clinton hailed Presidents Laurent Kabila of Congo, Yoweri Museveni of Uganda, Paul Kagame of Rwanda, Meles Zenawi of Ethiopia and Isaiah Afwerki of Eritrea as the 'new leaders of Africa' and spoke fondly of the 'new African renaissance sweeping the continent' – Africans taking charge of their own backyard. But barely two months after his return to the United States, Ethiopia and Eritrea were at war and the rest of the 'new leaders' were pounding each other in the Congo conflict. As if the embarrassment of seeing its friends at war was not enough, the administration's other African 'partners in development' have turned out to be crocodile reformers and crackpot democrats.

The mistake the West often makes is investing its faith in some 'Abraham Lincoln' figure who will transform his African society. Of course it would be desirable to have democratic African countries, based on the free market system. But these are the outcomes of often long and arduous processes. By focusing almost exclusively on the outcomes, Western leaders set themselves up to be duped by hucksters, who preach democracy and free enterprise, not out of conviction but because that is the key that unlocks the floodgates of Western aid.

President Daniel arap Moi of Kenya is well adept at this game. His version of the 'Babangida Boogie' was succinctly described by *The Economist*:

> Over the past few years, Kenya has performed a curious mating ritual with its aid donors. The steps are: One, Kenya wins its yearly pledges of foreign aid. Two, the government begins to misbehave, backtracking on economic reform and behaving in an authoritarian manner. Three, a new meeting of donor countries looms with exasperated foreign governments preparing their sharp rebukes. Four, Kenya pulls a placatory rabbit out of the hat. Five,

the donors are mollified and aid is pledged. The whole dance then
starts again.[54]

Four years later it wrote: 'Kenya's government knows precisely
when it can resist donors' demands, when to use charm, when to cry
"neo-colonialism" and when to make promises of reform – promises
it will break when the new loans are obtained and the donors' backs
are turned.'[55]

The problem is the 'enabling role' played by the West. Accordingly,
the democratisation process in Africa has been stalled by political chicanery, strong-arm tactics and suffocating acrobatics. In 1990, only 4
of the 54 African countries were democratic. This tiny number grew
to 14 in 1995 and remained stuck there: Botswana, Benin, Cape Verde
Islands, Central African Republic, Madagascar, Malawi, Mali, Mau-
ritius, Namibia, Sao Tome & Principe, Senegal, Seychelles, South
Africa and Zambia. Since then, there have been some reversals in
Congo (Brazzaville) and Sierra Leone, which saw their democratic experiment brutally terminated in 1997. Thus, political tyranny is still
the order of the day in most of Africa.

Incumbent autocrats appoint their own Electoral Commissioners,
empanel a fawning coterie of sycophants to write the constitution,
massively pad the voter's register and hold fraudulent elections to return themselves to power. For example, President Gnassingbe
Eyadema of Togo, who has ruled for more than 32 years, stood for
re-election on 21 June 1998. His Kabye tribesmen who pack the
army, the police and the bureaucracy, fudged the electoral rolls, and
intimidated and denied opposition politicians access to the state-run
media. Still, when it appeared that Eyadema was losing, paramilitary
police halted the vote count, and burned the ballot boxes, as well as
the offices of Togo's main opposition leader, Gilchrist Olympio. President Eyadema was then declared the winner. The West protested;
the European Union suspended aid. A few months later, normal relations were restored and EU aid resumed. Exactly the same Western
response was evident regarding Kenya in 1991, Ghana in 1992,
Nigeria in 1993 and Niger in 1997.

The Western leader-centred approach to Africa's problems must be
replaced with one that places more emphasis on institution-building
or processes. Leaders come and go but institutions endure. Four are
critical: 1. An independent central bank, vital for monetary and economic stability, as well as to stanch capital flight. Evidence from Russia, Nigeria and many other African countries shows that massive

amounts of capital could not have been transferred abroad without the connivance of central bank officials. 2. An independent judiciary, crucial for the establishment of rule of law, protection of property and an end to rapacious plunder with impunity. 3. An independent and free media, to facilitate the free flow of information, to expose criminal wrongdoing before too late, to disseminate ideas and promote home-grown solutions to the country's problems. 4. A neutral and professional armed or security forces, to protect life and property and ensure law and order. These institutions are established by civil society, not leaders. Since these institutions would effectively limit the leaders' own power or the arbitrariness with which it is exercised, an implicit conflict of interest is involved if African leaders are asked to establish them.

Conclusion

The causes of Africa's crises or poverty have little to do with artificial colonial borders, American imperialism, racism or the alleged inferiority of the African people. They have more to do with bad leadership and the enabling role played by the West.

The centralisation of both economic and political power and the absence of mechanisms for the peaceful transfer of that power leads to a struggle over political power which degenerates into civil strife or war. Chaos and carnage ensue. Infrastructure is destroyed. Food production and delivery are disrupted. Thousands are dislocated and flee, becoming internal refugees and placing severe strains on the social systems of the resident population. Food supplies run out. Starvation looms.

The Western media bombards the international community with horrific pictures of rail-thin famine victims. Unable to bear the horror, the conscience of the international community is stirred to mount eleventh-hour humanitarian rescue missions. Foreign relief workers parachute into the disaster zone, dispensing high-protein biscuits, blankets and portable toilets at hastily erected refugee camps. Refugees are rehabilitated, repatriated and even airlifted. At the least sign of complication or trouble, the mission bogs down and is abandoned. That is, until another vampire African state implodes and the same macabre ritual is repeated year after year. It seems nothing – absolutely nothing – has been learnt by any side from the meltdowns of Somalia, Liberia or Rwanda.

The real tragedy of Africa is that most of its leaders don't use their heads. Even more tragic is the fact that the Western donors who, gushing with noble humanitarianism, set out to help the African people, don't use theirs either. As long as the politics of exclusion is practised in Africa, more states will collapse and the West will be obliged to go to the rescue.

5 Unsustainable development, Latin style

Fabiano Pegurier and Gilberto Salgado

In 1900, Latin America (all the countries on the continent of America south of the United States) had a population of about 70 million; today that population stands at over 500 million. In 1900, per capita income in the region was approximately 14% that of the US; this rose during the early part of the century but fell again and today it is probably lower than it was in 1900.[1] This chapter focuses on the most critical factors shaping the course of the last 50 years of the region's economic development, especially the rise of government intervention and inflation, as well as subsequent reforms.

Import-Substitution Industrialisation (ISI)

After the Second World War, the governments of Latin American countries adopted deliberate measures intended to reduce their dependence on the export of primary goods. The justification for such policies came from a belief that income from the sale of primary exports would not grow in proportion to the increase in the income of the wealthiest countries.[2] It was argued that the terms of trade between agricultural and manufactured products had a secular tendency to deteriorate and that this was a structural problem. In other words, countries reliant on exports of agricultural products would inevitably grow less quickly than countries whose main exports were manufactured goods. To get out of this bind, developing countries were advised to adopt measures to promote Import-Substitution Industrialisation, or ISI.

ISI proponents disputed the argument put forward by classical economists that market-driven specialisation, comparative advantage (in international trade) and domestic savings were the engines of growth. Indeed, according to one variant, no matter how much domestic saving occurred, investment would be structurally limited by the lack of foreign exchange required to import the necessary raw materials and intermediate products. Specialisation, even if accompanied by some gains in productivity, would not lead to development, but to deeper specialisation, and the gains would accrue entirely to the more advanced countries.

The prevailing view was that of the United Nations' Economic Commission for Latin America (ECLA), under the direction of Raúl Prebisch. According to this view, known as 'structuralist', Latin America needed significant government intervention in order to develop. In particular, structuralists argued that government should promote industrialisation through the protection of the domestic manufacturing sector from foreign competition, thus reserving scarce foreign exchange for essential purposes only.

It is worth bearing in mind that structuralists and other proponents of ISI promoted a particular form of industrialisation. Critics of ISI policies did not argue that industrialisation was not desirable – they simply questioned the methods chosen by the supporters of ISI. This is why a major participant in these debates, Professor Gottfried Haberler, would often quite deliberately refer to ISI not as Import-Substitution Industrialisation but as 'the policy of extreme protection'.[3]

Aiming at ISI, Latin American governments adopted import restrictions, exchange controls, limits on the export of products 'needed' by the domestic manufacturing sector, and financial subsidies to certain industries. They also often became directly involved in import-substituting production. In addition, governments kept local currencies generally overvalued, which hurt primary exports, lowered incomes in rural areas and made agricultural products more abundant and cheaper domestically. This amounted to an additional subsidy to industry, as it simultaneously stimulated migration to urban areas and kept the price of food low, reducing industry's labour costs.

The impact of ISI policies

These policies had several undesirable consequences. The artificially low prices of imported intermediate products and capital goods helped make industry more capital intensive (and less labour intensive) than it need have been. The expectation that a dynamic industrial sector would generate enough jobs to absorb workers displaced from the rural areas was unfounded. Income inequality was aggravated and the breakneck speed of industrialisation was accompanied by the creation of gigantic urban slums. Also, the high level of trade protection, combined with the scarcity of foreign exchange, made it strategically profitable to import obsolete and highly polluting equipment.

Since the export sector was hurt by the overvalued exchange rate and the misdirection of resources to industry (which consequently had less incentive to compete in foreign markets even if it were able to), export revenues dwindled, with at least two significant consequences. First, it restricted the amount of foreign exchange available for imports, decreasing the flexibility of local demand for imported goods and making Latin American countries more, rather than less, vulnerable to eventual unfavourable changes in the terms of trade. Since the industrialisation drive could not be kept alive by indefinitely increasing trade deficits, the need for foreign direct investment as a source of foreign currency became crucial. This was a rather ironic unintended consequence, as it ran counter to the driving idea that national industry should supersede the need for reliance on foreign producers.

Second, the ailing export sector had the effect of reducing government revenues, which had depended heavily on high taxes on exported products. That in turn placed a heavy burden on the public budget, as government expenses had been growing with the policies that increased direct and indirect interference in the economy, including a large bureaucracy, overstaffed public enterprises and nationalised industries. The result was greater pressure on governments to print money to cover their deficits, fuelling inflation. Fiscal imbalance became characteristic of Latin American countries, especially Argentina, Brazil, Chile, Uruguay, Colombia, Peru and Venezuela, during this period.[4]

In the early 1960s, the economic imbalances caused by industrial protectionism and the associated complete neglect of agriculture became obvious. The initial stimulus to economic growth that ISI helped promote could not be sustained and manufacturing output grew at half the rate it had in the 1950s. However, the initial apparent effectiveness of ISI policies increased hopes for their eventual success and undermined the prospects for those who sought other paths to economic growth. This led to costly dependence on continued government support and to the formation of pressure groups to maintain these privileges. In most cases, the narrow goal of helping industries to become self-sufficient and self-sustaining turned into a distant hope.

Tariffs were increased, as more and more sectors needed some form of government support to protect them from foreign competition.[5] In 1962, manufacturing output represented 32% of Argentina's GDP, but only 3.2% of its exports. Other Latin American countries following ISI policies showed similar ratios: Brazil (26% and 3.2%); Chile (29% and 3.7%); Colombia (17% and 3.5%).[6]

In the mid-1960s, beginning with Chile, Brazil and Colombia, most Latin American countries started to change their policies. Gradual devaluations became the rule, export subsidies were widely adopted and some reasonably successful attempts were made at reducing fiscal deficits and controlling inflation. These measures allowed growth to occur at a faster pace by the end of the 1960s, and Latin America's GDP per capita grew at an average of 3.4% in 1965–70, against 2% in 1960–5. Even Mexico, whose average annual per capita GDP growth was 4% in the first half of the decade, managed to increase the pace to 4.4% in the second half.

It is instructive to look at the contrasting patterns of growth in Peru and Colombia. From 1950 to 1965, Peru was a relatively open economy, with virtually no deliberate industrial policy, and from 1960–5 GDP per capita grew at an average rate of around 3% – far faster than the regional average. In the late 1960s, Peru's government adopted heavy-handed industrial protection and growth in GDP per capita almost stagnated, with growth during the 1970s averaging only 0.8%. Colombia, on the other hand, grew more slowly than the regional average in 1950–65, but as it started to reduce the level of protection and to promote exports, output responded and GDP per capita went from an average of 1.3% in 1960–5 to 3.0% in 1965–70 and 3.6% during the 1970s.[7]

Besides support for export promotion, which was eventually favoured by structuralist thinkers, the 1960s and 1970s saw defences of regionalised trade as a means to broaden the scope of ISI.[8] The Andean Pact of 1969, which included Bolivia, Chile, Colombia, Ecuador, Peru and, later, Venezuela, may have been the foremost achievement in this context. Despite a reduction in the very highest marginal rates – which began in the mid-1960s – tariffs remained very high and unequal towards goods from countries outside these accords.

During the late 1960s and the 1970s, Brazil, Mexico and Colombia promoted exports through subsidies. Despite some significant increases in exports, however, such programmes did not have substantive effects on the structure of their economies.[9] Moreover, the region as a whole performed dismally during this period. Between

1965 and 1980, exports *fell* by an average of 1% per year in Latin America, while they *grew* by an average of 10% per year in the 'Asian Tigers', which included South Korea and Taiwan. Many different factors have been suggested to explain this difference.[10] Abnormally high tariffs hurt potential exports that required imported inputs. Local substitutes, when available, were rarely affordable or up to standard. Indeed, a primordial problem in countries attempting to create new industries (and support existing ones) is the lack of relevant skills of the local labour force. ISI did nothing to increase the cost-effectiveness of local labour. On the contrary, decades of high protection were a cause of uncompetitive wages.

Regardless of how they were promoted, investments in Latin America tended to yield a low return. In part this was because the economies of the region have been very heavily regulated. Not only have incentives been distorted – the rules and regulations themselves have often been contradictory and impermanent.

Finally, the promotion of exports was not a particularly measured attempt to generate foreign exchange. Unlike East Asian policy, subsidies were not usually conditioned on results or set to expire within definite time periods. The policies that gave governments discretionary power to set very uneven tariffs eventually also allowed for the arbitrary disbursing of subsidies to chosen sectors. There was no real quest for efficiency. Instead, as had happened with protectionist measures for industry, support for exports became the source of rent through wasteful privilege-seeking activities.

ISI led to an endless stream of unintended consequences. The policies made income distribution more unequal and the long-run level of growth was lower than would have been the case if there had been fewer interventions in the market. More importantly, ISI caused huge silent disruptions in people's lives. Massive migrations from rural areas may have helped boost the growth of the manufacturing sector temporarily. But without the ISI's market-distorting policies many of those migrants would probably have continued to live where they were respected, working on activities they had already mastered, instead of moving into cities to live anonymously in slums, looking for work in unfamiliar trades. Similarly disturbing is the evidence that these masses have fallen prey to populist politicians responsible for some of the worst calamities ever to afflict their lives.

Inflation

High inflation has been one of the main problems in Latin American countries during the last 50 years. The issue is particularly serious because governments of the region have been engaged in the promotion of growth, and policies so oriented. As Haberler has said, even if such policies were acceptable on other grounds, '[they] cannot be justified if [they have] to be financed by rapid inflation since the resulting growth invariably proves unsustainable'.[11] The basic problem has been the enduring tendency for governments to spend beyond their means, eventually financing their deficits through monetary expansion. In most countries, stabilisation plans have been periodically implemented, but no plan that failed to deal with overspending was ever successful.

In the 1950s and 1960s, Argentina, Brazil, Chile and Uruguay were the countries with particularly high inflation rates. The worst case may have been that of Brazil, where inflation approached 100% in 1963. Between 1964 and 1966, military-led Brazil adopted a largely successful programme that contained and brought down accelerating inflation. The government concentrated its efforts on deficit reduction, but it also adopted less orthodox means, such as a wage policy, to help break the inflationary memory of the system. Inflation rates fell significantly, providing the basis for the subsequent 'Brazilian miracle' years (1967–74) of very high growth and increased productivity.

The oil crisis of 1973 put pressure on these governments to devalue their currencies and established a tendency for real wages to fall, in order for the shock to be absorbed.[12] But many governments were committed to growth and thought that they could avoid the adjustment, hoping, instead, to take advantage of the high liquidity of international financial markets. Indeed, due to the extraordinary revenues of oil-exporting countries, commercial banks became a major source of capital for developing nations, which allowed fiscal policies to become even more expansive than usual. Governments used foreign exchange reserves to intervene in currency markets in an attempt to keep inflation under control, by keeping fiscal deficits down and financing rising imports. Nevertheless, inflationary pressures increased.

At the end of the 1970s and the beginning of the 1980s, the world went through a second oil crisis. The consequent rise in international interest rates, and the slowdown in economic activities, hurt Latin American exports. With dollar revenues declining and foreign debt service payments rising, Latin American indebtedness rose at an unsustainable average of 20% a year. Between 1973 and 1982, the real dollar value of foreign debt grew sevenfold; as a percentage of GDP it rose from 19% in 1975 to 46% in 1982.[13]

The debt crisis and the 'lost decade'

In 1982, after a decade of borrowing to finance huge increases in government expenditures, Mexico, despite being an oil exporter, was unable to meet its obligations to foreign creditors. As a result, new credit to the region became extremely limited.[14] It was the beginning of the 'debt crisis'. Accustomed from years of heavy protectionism to direct production and local consumption, Latin American countries had no recourse but to reduce imports and stimulate exports, and many responded with sharp currency devaluations.[15] Governments sought to finance themselves with credit from domestic commercial banks, which led to a rise in interest rates, with a deleterious effect on private investment. This reinforced the tendency for declining economic activity and hurt revenues further. It became impossible to service the external debt or to finance public debt without inflating the money supply.[16] The pressure on domestic prices mounted and high inflation became an endemic problem. Most affected was Bolivia, where the consumer price index, CPI, rose on average by 2692.4% per year during 1981–5. During the same period, Argentina's CPI rose on average by 382%, Brazil's by 153.9% and Peru's by 104.9%. The IMF index of consumer price inflation for non-oil-exporting developing countries in the Western hemisphere went from 38.7% in the 1970s to 95.9% in 1980–4 and to 163.6% in 1984–5.[17]

The impact on growth was dramatic. The 1980s became known as 'the lost decade', though perhaps the period should be extended to include the 1970s. Average gross domestic product per capita for the region fell by 0.9% in 1970–80, 1.5% in 1980–5, and 0.2% in 1985–90. In the 1990s, the region's average gross domestic product grew by a modest 1.2%.

Besides the huge nominal devaluations in exchange rates, efforts to reduce imports and increase exports included enhanced use of traditional ISI measures. The adoption of higher tariffs and the broadening of the scope of import licences and quotas became standard responses. Despite significant achievements, these efforts were insufficient to generate the resources needed to service the debt and protracted negotiations took place, involving multilateral institutions and foreign commercial banks.

In the mid-1980s several adjustment plans were implemented, including three whose failures had significant consequences for future transformations in the region.[18] In Argentina and Brazil, the plans placed almost exclusive emphasis on inertia – the element in price inflation related to the generalised indexation of the economies. A relatively modest effort to control the fiscal deficit took place in the early stages of Argentina's 'Austral Plan'. Such effort was not even envisaged in Brazil's 'Cruzado Plan'. In Peru, the 'APRA Plan' actually stimulated demand. These plans failed miserably because they concentrated on the elimination of the symptoms of inflation rather than its causes. In the process, they fostered major intrusions and disruptions in private activities. An important share of professional local economists saw in them the occasion to promote a concerted increase in government participation in the economy. But their failure changed perceptions about the importance of fiscally responsible management and the ineffectiveness of attributing to the private sector ills that are of the government's own making.

Reforms

By contrast, in the late 1970s Chile's government decided to free prices, eliminate quotas and tariffs, free interest rates, eliminate credit controls, free the flow of foreign capital, and reduce the share of the public sector in production.[19, 20] These policies were vehemently attacked by economists of structuralist conviction. But after a period of difficulty, due to macroeconomic mismanagement and the onset of the debt crisis, the economy began to grow rapidly. These pro-market policies, initiated under the military rule of General Pinochet, were continued by the democratically elected Aylwin government, which was inaugurated in 1989. The policies were even backed by some of their former critics.

Several factors combined to encourage other countries of the region to adopt market-oriented reforms in the late 1980s and the 1990s. Among them were the Chilean experience, the fiasco of heterodox stabilisation programmes in the mid-1980s, the perception of the 'Asian Tigers' as comprising basically unhampered market economies and the encouragement of multilateral institutions, both financially and through studies showing the benefits of liberalisation.[21]

In the mid-1980s, several countries started to use the secondary market to rescue their sovereign debt. This strategy gained impetus in 1988, as Chile used debt capitalisation to pay for the privatisation of state enterprises. Starting in 1989, countries used an important American initiative – the Brady Plan – to negotiate with foreign banks ways of reducing and rescheduling debt payments. Bolivia, Chile and Mexico were among the countries that opted for using the secondary market; Argentina, Brazil, Costa Rica, Mexico, Uruguay and Venezuela reduced their debts with the help of the Brady Plan.

Debt renegotiations and financial support from multilateral institutions, conditional on reforms, were instrumental in changing policy and institutions and set Latin American countries on the path to liberalisation. Among the most aggressive reformers were countries in such dire situations that they had little to lose from radically changing course, such as Argentina and Peru, as well as the early reformers, Chile and Bolivia. Several distortions were addressed. A more favourable macroeconomic environment was achieved through greater fiscal restraint and increased revenues from the privatisation of previously burdensome companies. The sale of major state-owned telecommunications, transport, mining and steel enterprises, for instance, and the regulation of newly competitive sectors were important achievements, since earlier market-oriented reforms had not even addressed privatisation.

With respect to trade liberalisation, according to the Inter-American Development Bank 'average tariffs fell from close to 50% in 1985 to around 10 % in 1996, and maximum tariffs fell from an average of 84% to just 41%. By 1996, non-tariff barriers affected only 6% of imports, while in the pre-reform period they affected 38%.'[22] Lower tariffs and the end of export subsidies caused the miserable failure of industries that had been protected for as many as 30 to 35 years, under the assumption that they would eventually become competitive. The auto parts industry in Brazil is one of the most remarkable cases.

Since 1994, when Brazil tamed hyperinflation (2,489% in 1993), the average growth rate of the consumer price index for the region (including the Caribbean) has fallen dramatically, from 25.8% in 1995 to 6.3% in 2001.[23] Ecuador, with inflation approaching 40% in 2001, was practically the only country significantly removed from the single-digit rate. But the country has now replaced its currency with the US dollar, and inflation should drop to single-digit levels in 2002; indeed, most of that 40% occurred prior to the May 2001 change.

Some persisting problems

It would seem that, after 40 years of growth promotion, Latin American governments have finally become more interested in creating a market-friendly environment conducive to sustainable development. That path, however, is not yet clear.

The continued existence of powerful interest groups makes it unlikely that fundamental reforms will be approved without meaningful popular support. In such an environment, it is doubtful that politicians will have the courage to reduce government interventions in labour markets or promote fiscal reforms that would reduce distortions without in some way balancing these by creating more privileges for those with vested interests. It is therefore unfortunate that there is so little appreciation among Latin Americans of the close relationship between free markets, the rule of law and economic growth. The enormous popular support for detailed, costly and inflexible labour legislation illustrates the barriers to meaningful reform. Labour laws are much less flexible in Latin America than in East Asia, for instance. This is the case even though a large proportion of the Latin American population is outside the formal labour market and does not have access to the 'protection ensured' by labour legislation. Of course, it is the labour laws themselves that have to a large extent led to this problem of economic exclusion. Nevertheless, questions are rarely raised in the media or other public fora as to why governments are able to place themselves between an unemployed person and a job; or why they are able to prevent a person from accepting the most favourable employment package he or she can find.

Few can appreciate the extent to which the rule of law and the principle of administrative decentralisation have been compromised in the name of stimulating growth and combating inflation. Latin Americans have become accustomed to their rights as individuals being assaulted in the name of the greater good. During the nonsensical stabilisation plans of the 1980s, which were focused exclusively on price controls, people of all social classes responded with tremendous intensity to the call forcibly to prevent exchanges at freely agreed terms.

With respect to foreign trade, the prevailing mentality sees tariff reductions as the 'price' that must be paid in order to obtain access to foreign markets. Tariffs are never portrayed as an artificial restriction on the choices of local producers and consumers. The protectionism of more developed countries encourages that distorted view, as such policies are interpreted not so much as resulting from well-organised privilege-seeking, but as a means to defend 'the interest' and 'the jobs' of those countries. The appropriate response in Latin America, according to the President of Brazil's House of Representatives, is to 'do the same, and protect ours'.[24]

Although there is at least a modest understanding that interest groups are active in the region, seeking the rents available from government control, people do not seem to understand why they exist. Indeed the conventional view is quite topsy-turvy. Whereas the underlying reason for such rent-seeking is the labyrinthine system of rules and restrictions imposed by government, which enables discretionary disbursements of favours by officials of the state, the public simply equates the seekers of special favours with 'rapacious entrepreneurs'. This is tragic because true entrepreneurship and the free market, *a system founded on the rule of law*, are the solution to Latin America's troubles, not the problem.

A closely related issue is corruption. It is not generally appreciated (in Latin America or elsewhere) that corruption is a symptom of other, underlying problems, and that there are ways of organising society that are more conducive to low levels of corruption than others. On one level, the emphasis on corruption is misplaced because in some nations the size of the bureaucracy and the scope and complexity of regulations are such that without corruption there might be no economic activity at all. Excessive bureaucracy operates as a major barrier to potential entrepreneurship.[25] On another level, the emphasis on corruption *per se* is misplaced to the extent that it betrays disregard for the source of large-scale corruption, which is to be found in governments with enormous powers to promote and to discourage, to take and to give. This is not to belittle the fact that enormous resources are wasted every year on account of corruption and that these resources are exceptionally scarce in Latin America. The point is that if one's concern is the efficient use of resources and the encouragement of economic growth, then one should not focus primarily on corruption itself. Rather, one should focus on the underlying problems: the size of the state and the number of rules and regulations it promulgates.

Significant progress has been made to reduce both fiscal and external imbalances. But continued improvements in economic performance depend on additional progress along these lines. While it is certainly exciting that inflation has in recent years been the lowest since the Second World War, it is worrying that some of the other foundations for continued progress are not as sound as might be desirable.

A leading concern is the serious current account problems facing many countries. This makes them vulnerable to a reduction in foreign direct investment or to a rise in the spread of their international bonds. Domestic savings are crucial to economic development and can help overcome current account vulnerability. But Latin America traditionally has had a very low level of domestic savings (in part because of the high levels of inflation and the consequent uncertainty about the future value of savings). So it is important that, at the very least, governments balance their budgets. Yet despite recent efforts to avoid macroeconomic imbalances, in 2000 the region had a (simple average) deficit of over 2% of GDP, with a projected deficit of over 3% of GDP for 2001.[26] If we consider that taxes tend to be already high in the countries with greater fiscal problems, that situation is not sustainable without significant crowding out of private investment by the financing needs of government. It is unlikely that private savings will grow significantly in such a scenario. A virtuous circle with higher levels of savings and income leading to even higher levels of savings and income cannot be counted on just yet.[27]

A 1999 study by Arthur Andersen showed that, of 28 countries surveyed, only 6 charged taxes on gross revenues, but of those 5 were from South America (Argentina, Bolivia, Brazil, Colombia and Venezuela).[28] Taxing revenues rather than profits discourages local economic activity – it is effectively a tax on production. In Brazil, 25% of all revenues come from highly distorting cumulative taxes. High taxes on production, especially if they are cumulative, stimulate imports and discourage exports. That is certainly harmful to countries that seek to grow through trade.

There is, however, reason for hope. By 2005 the countries of the region should become integrated into a single Free Trade Area of the Americas (FTAA). That could encourage many countries to adopt more sensible domestic policies and introduce important institutional reforms.

6 The Soviet experiment: lessons for development

Charles N. Steele

For most of the twentieth century, central economic planning was regarded as a path to rapid economic growth. It was also seen as a means of avoiding pitfalls of capitalistic development, such as pollution and income inequality. Despite these commonly held views, central planning has proved to be an unsustainable system everywhere it has been tried. The experience of the USSR provides a useful case study.

The Soviet system was widely promoted as a superior way of coordinating economic activity compared to the market system. In reality, knowledge and incentive problems led the Soviet system to waste resources and provide poorly for citizens. Such growth as the Soviet system generated came primarily from increasing the amount of resources used, rather than increasing efficiency of resource use as occurs in market economies. The costs of the system, in terms of wasted resources and environmental degradation, were immense and the benefits, in terms of better living standards for the average citizen, were inferior to those of market economies. The subsequent performance of the transition countries of the former Soviet Union (FSU) has been chequered, held back by a strong state sector, incomplete reform and corruption.

This chapter surveys development in the Soviet Union. It begins by outlining the theory and practice of Soviet central planning, and shows why central planning failed as an economic development strategy. The chapter also analyses the consequences of a necessary condition for central economic planning – concentrated political power – and discusses how these political and economic features of the system generated environmental and human catastrophe.

If sustainability is defined as the ability of a system to provide an acceptable standard of living for citizens, whilst simultaneously ensuring that environmental problems are adequately addressed, central planning is not sustainable. The Soviet system should be regarded as a model of how not to develop.

The theory and practice of Soviet planning

The Soviet Union was one of the great experiments in economic development – a grand, tragic, failed experiment. The poor performance of the system is directly attributable to the inability of central planners rationally to allocate resources. This in turn is a consequence of the lack of private property rights and markets, which meant the planners were unable to acquire coherent information about what should be produced by whom, with what, when and how.

In a market system, the voluntary exchange of private property leads to the emergence of prices. These prices then act as a signal to entrepreneurs, who identify goods that might be offered for sale. When the entrepreneurs are correct about their estimates, they produce and sell goods that people want at a price they are willing to pay and they make a profit. When they are incorrect, they make a loss; if they continue to make losses, they go out of business. The system therefore favours entrepreneurs who are better at gathering information and using it to coordinate production. It is, to use the current jargon, a self-ordering and self-correcting system.

By contrast, the incentive structure of the Soviet system led to the persistence of 'obvious' mistakes, causing unnecessary waste as well as both human and environmental destruction.

Unfortunately, the Soviet system has been widely adopted as a model for development both by less developed countries and by international agencies such as the World Bank. The result has been development failure and a perpetuation of misery and poverty. The victims of the Soviet model are far more numerous than the Soviet citizenry (which itself numbered nearly 300 million at the height of the system) and the citizens of the Soviet client states in Eastern Europe. Given this legacy, and the continuing calls in some quarters for increased central planning in order to promote 'sustainable development', it is important to understand the Soviet system and why it failed.[1]

This section outlines several key aspects of the Soviet system. The first thing to recognise is that central planning, as it is supposed to work in theory, cannot function, and that the reality of the system diverged from how it was supposed to operate.

The theory
In principle, the system was supposed to substitute rational planning, by experts, for the alleged vagaries of allocation by prices in markets. In place of market allocation, the system used what was called 'materials balance planning'. While some of the specifics of the system changed over time, the basic model remained the same. The system was hierarchical, with production decisions made at the top and handed down through the system as orders. At the same time, information regarding production capacities and goal attainment were to be passed back up through the system from below.[2]

Under materials balance planning, initial objectives for output were set by the state planning agency, Gosplan, in line with 'guidelines' (orders) handed down from the communist party. These objectives specified kinds and targeted quantities of various outputs, in line with the goals of the Soviet leadership. These targets were then passed down to the level of various economic ministries and sub-ministries (e.g. ferrous metals, machine building, agricultural) where they were augmented with further detail and passed down to the level of the state owned enterprises (SOEs) in the form of output quotas. Each SOE, in turn, was to estimate the inputs it would need in order to fulfil its quota. This information was then passed back up through the system, to be assembled by the planners into an overall plan. Armed with the lists of proposed outputs and required inputs, the central planners attempted to calculate the total production needed to achieve the planned outputs, that is, to achieve a feasible plan. Since there are multiple ways to produce most goods, there are, in principle, multiple feasible plans – the objective of the planners would then be to select the lowest-cost (in terms of resource use) of these. The resulting plan specified planned production, including production quotas for each SOE.

The practice
While such a system might in theory be expected to coordinate production well, in practice it was plagued by flaws that the Soviet planners were unable to overcome. These flaws, which are inherent in the system and not amenable to correction, were essentially twofold:

First, planners were unable to generate feasible plans. The enormous task of coordinating all production for an entire economy is simply beyond the ability of a central planning agency. Calculating a balanced plan, in which sufficient inputs were produced to permit production of the planned final output, proved impossible, and in fact no plan ever successfully achieved a 'materials balance'. Attempts at *ex ante* coordination of the entire economy led to chronic shortages of inputs throughout Soviet industry. This, in turn, led to hoarding of inputs by SOEs, an unusual degree of vertical integration, as enterprises attempted to produce their own inputs, and the development of an unofficial economy in which inputs were traded among firms desperate to meet their official output quotas. Also, when a shortage of some particular input became apparent, the planners often responded by allocating the supplies to the most politically powerful sectors (e.g. military and heavy industry) and cutting allocations to less favoured ones – typically those which produced such things as consumer goods, housing and medical infrastructure.

Second, planners found themselves unable rationally to calculate factor costs. They were thus unable to identify the most efficient way of producing any particular output. Given that there are multiple ways of producing most goods, and that these differ in terms of resource requirements, the question arose as to what was the lowest-cost set of (sub) plans. In the absence of market prices, it proved impossible to compare the values of inputs in alternative uses, and hence Soviet industry was plagued with persistent waste. For example, Soviet petroleum extraction techniques used more inputs to extract less crude oil, for a given quality of deposit, than did Western techniques. Such wastefulness was harmful both to economic development and environmental quality.

The absence of a measure of cost and value generated a related problem. In order to ensure that managers and workers followed the plan, those at the top of the hierarchy used a combination of terror and rewards to induce compliance. Of the latter, the payment of bonuses to managers and workers for successful fulfilment of the plan was particularly important in ensuring obedience. But the lack of market prices to indicate value made the determination of success or failure problematic. When market indicators are not available, how does one measure success or failure? This 'success indicator problem' hindered the attempts by planners to direct the economy throughout the existence of the USSR.

The obvious solution to the problem is to measure output in terms of physical characteristics, including both quantity and quality. Unfortunately, it was not possible for planners to know, much less to specify, the minimum quality characteristics required for each good in order to make the overall plan feasible. For example, in assigning quotas for sheet steel, the plan would assign tonnage to be produced but would necessarily leave some dimensions unspecified – in practice, these included such things as gauge, chemical composition and heat treatment. SOEs then produced output in such a way as to increase the likelihood of achieving quotas, that is, by cutting corners on un-specified margins. Monitoring and specifying these unspecified margins proved impossible. Hence, much of the output of the Soviet economy was of poor quality, or even useless, even though it seemed on paper to represent successful production. As a result, a substantial portion of Soviet output is thought to have been 'negative value added', that is, less valuable than the resources and labour that went into its making.

The perverse incentive effects of central planning

Closely related to these difficulties are the incentives that were gener-ated downstream from the planners. At the levels of industrial min-istries, sub-ministries and SOEs, the first concern was to satisfy the central authorities above, in order to avoid punishment and earn bonuses for attainment of targets. This had several detrimental effects on behaviour. It was in the interest of the managers and workers of an SOE that the planners should underestimate the enterprises' produc-tive capacity and overestimate its input needs – this would ensure lower, more easily attainable quotas, and greater likelihood of suffi-cient resources. As a result, the system generated strong incentives for misreporting, and much of the information that was passed through the system was intentionally false. Coupled with the success indicator problem, this meant that the central authorities had no real under-standing of the economy's performance.

Also, enterprise managers had little incentive to invest in innova-tive, resource-saving technology, since to do so would increase plant capacity or reduce input requirements. The former effect would lead to higher quotas for the plant, while the latter would imply lower input allocations; neither of these was in the interest of managers or workers, whose primary objective was to earn bonuses as easily as possible. This contrasts with the incentive of a capitalist firm to de-velop resource-saving technologies in order to reduce costs and thereby increase profits. Such innovations are a primary means of con-serving resources and avoiding pollution.[3] The lack of innovation plagued Soviet industry, which used more resources and generated more pollution per unit of output, compared to Western industry. This failure to innovate persisted despite the extremely high quality of physical science and theoretical engineering in the Soviet Union, attesting to the strength of the perverse incentives of the system.

Another effect of the system was to generate severe 'commons problems'. All productive property was officially owned by the state, and in principle all decisions concerning its use were made by the planners. In practice, it was impossible for the central planners closely to monitor the use of raw resources and other inputs. Thus many resources were 'open access', waiting to be grabbed by anyone on the spot. This sometimes resulted in destructive competition for resources, or in diversion of assets to private uses. Examples include the hauling away of Black Sea resort beachfront sand for construction purposes, and the mass diversion of water from the Aral Sea for cotton irrigation, resulting in the destruction of the one of the Soviet Union's largest fishing industries.[4]

Such commons problems are, at heart, competition for unassigned or poorly assigned resources. These occur in every economy, but were particularly severe in the Soviet Union. Again, this is inherent in the system. Under a system of private property, with legal institutions for the enforcement of property rights and contracts, agents can generally avoid such wasteful competitions. But under central planning, with official ownership by the state, much property becomes de facto open access. Furthermore, in another triumph of a priori constructivist reasoning over reality, there existed in the Soviet Union no good formal mechanisms for adjudicating subsequent disputes – on the grounds that such disputes were in principle impossible if the system functioned correctly.

A final unintended result of the system was the development of a second, unofficial economy alongside the official planned one. The unfeasibility of the plan, and the low quality of much of what was produced, meant that SOEs often found themselves without adequate inputs for meeting their assigned quotas. One common response was to engage in market trading with other firms for inputs. This trading was outside of the plan, and while it was, strictly speaking, illegal, it was pervasive. The result was a shadow market economy for inputs. Similarly, black market trading was extremely common in the areas of consumer goods and services – particularly services – sectors that received short shrift in the official planning. Given the poor functioning of the official system, people had little choice but to develop and rely on such unofficial and extralegal activities.

One effect was to make shadow activity seem commonplace and acceptable, a normal part of life. This has very likely been an important 'cultural' factor in the explosive growth of shadow activity and corruption following the demise of the Soviet Union.[5] Regardless, it is well understood that an unofficial market system offers far less in terms of gains than does one in which individual rights and contracts receive official legal protection. The central planning system proved unable to avoid the need for markets, and at the same time undercut markets' potential efficiency by forcing them into the shadows. In doing so it also encouraged a general attitude of cynicism and a belief that deception is a normal part of day-to-day life.

Mobilising resources as a development strategy

Despite these problems, the Soviet economy was able to produce a sort of growth, which by some measures was spectacular, and was able to sustain itself for nearly 70 years. Growth rates in terms of physical units of output were often impressive (although such measures do not control for quality, nor for value, as discussed above). Although reported production levels must be taken cautiously, since everyone in the system had incentives to overstate success, apparent Soviet performance was sufficiently impressive to ensure the Soviet system was seen as the best strategy for rapid economic development. This belief is still given credence by some, which is unfortunate because the sort of growth the Soviet system was able to generate seems particularly unsustainable – indeed it is detrimental to real sustainable development.

Industrial output clearly expanded enormously over the course of Soviet history. However, we now know that the primary engine of this growth was the increased use of resources. Under such a strategy, growth must slow as resources become more scarce. And once all resources have been mobilised, growth must cease.[6] This is exactly what happened in the Soviet Union: growth gradually slowed and then the economy went into decline, as the natural barriers to this strategy were reached. Socialism – both as it was attempted in the Soviet Union and in any other form – is ultimately unsustainable.

By contrast, growth in Western capitalist economies originates predominantly from *improved* use of resources, rather than *increased* use of resources. These improvements come from innovations in technology, in human capital, in methods of organisation, and in institutions. Capitalist growth is fundamentally knowledge-based rather than resource-based. It is, therefore, not constrained by the physical availability of resources. Knowledge-based resources generate more output, and more valuable output, from given resources, and in this sense are resource-conserving; quite the opposite of what is observed under socialist growth. Industrial production in the Soviet Union on average required at least twice the input per unit of output, compared to that of the West.[7]

The economist Paul Romer has observed that if technical knowledge develops at a sufficiently rapid rate *and* is successfully brought to bear on economic problems, there seems no obvious limit to economic growth.[8] The Soviet system did invest heavily in scientific and technical research; it just didn't apply the research effectively. The problem is that innovative advances are often specific to a particular firm or industry and they typically require experimentation and learning, through a process of trial and error. Such innovations are far more likely to occur in a system of decentralised decision making, in which all stakeholders in the economy have control over their particular productive assets, than in an economy where central authorities direct everything.

In addition, the theory that development and growth are resource-driven led to some of the worst excesses of Soviet terror. The leading reason behind the collectivisation of agriculture was the desire to extract a 'surplus' for investment in industry. The theory was that the application of resources, embodied as physical capital and applied to industry, would be the engine of growth. The resulting 'dekulakisation' (1928–1933) resulted in the premature deaths, through execution and enforced famine, of millions of peasants.[9] The collectivisation of agriculture was successful inasmuch as it enabled the central planners to squeeze a surplus from the peasantry to fund industrial expansion. But even if the resulting production increases constituted real growth, which is questionable, it is impossible to consider such a bloodstained strategy a reasonable model for development.

Unfortunately, the apparent success of the Soviet approach in generating growth reinforced the notion that development comes primarily from investing heavily in industry and that this can be most effectively done by a central authority. Accordingly, until recent times poor attention has been paid to the role of economic systems, the incentives they generate, and their underlying institutions. The idea persists that failure of a country to develop is primarily a matter of insufficient capital. International agencies such as the World Bank continue to base development strategies on this notion, even though it is now discredited both empirically and theoretically.[10]

If it is a mistake to think that economic development is primarily a matter of investment, it is even more unfortunate that the belief persists that economic development can be directed from the top down. As noted above, truly sustainable development can only occur through individuals applying their own knowledge of local circumstances, conditions, opportunities, needs and interests. Central economic planning has no way of taking this into account.

The politics of Soviet central planning and development

Another fact of the Soviet system was the unconstrained power of the state and the destructive use of this power. These characteristics were not coincidental to central economic planning – they were inherent in it. If a centrally planned system is to function at all, planners must hold sufficient power to enforce compliance with the plan. In a system where nearly all of the productive assets were assigned to the state, the state's authority would necessarily be of tremendous scope and power. This is both a prerequisite for and a consequence of central planning – for the greater the state's control over the productive assets, the greater its control over the lives of the citizens.

In the Soviet Union, the leaders' attempt to take total control was by design and implemented from the start. The rationale was that rapid economic and social development required strong direction from the top down. In principle, the purpose was to achieve an advanced, developed socialist state, for the well-being of the proletariat. In practice, what emerged was a system run for the personal benefit of the decision-makers at the top.

This was not simply a matter of ill intent or bad luck; a perpetual problem of *all* forms of government is how to constrain officials from using power to pursue their own private interests, and to generate incentives for them to act in the public's interest. This is a problem for which there is still no satisfactory solution, but the best results seem to come from strict constitutional constraints on the power of officials, combined with the ability of the citizenry to select and remove officials via mechanisms such as democratic voting procedures.

However, a necessary part of central economic planning is a lack of such constraints on the state. This was particularly true in the case of the Soviet state, which was established in order to remake society in its entirety. The lack of constraint led to a system that was run for the benefit of the small minority that held power. This manifested itself in several related ways: in the kinds and qualities of goods and services produced; in the use of terror and oppression; in the persistence of extreme environmental externalities; in the absence of any liability of the leadership for the negative consequences of its actions and in the absence of legal recourse for those citizens victimised by it.

Soviet production plans exhibited a strong bias in favour of goods preferred by leaders, at the expense of goods and services that would raise standards of living for the citizenry. In particular, military goods and heavy industry were emphasised, since leaders saw these as enhancing their hold on power. Consumer goods and services received less emphasis in the plans. Furthermore, when, during the implementation of plans, shortages arose in some input, officials tended to reallocate available supplies from the less favoured consumer industries to the more favoured military-industrial sectors. As a result, a particularly large proportion of the USSR's production went to things that had little to contribute to general living standards or real development.

The lack of constraints on government power also contributed directly to the use of terror and oppression. The use of terror as an economic and political tool included executions and concentration camps, and resulted in perhaps 25 million deaths of Soviet citizens. This use of terror generated a climate of fear that pervaded society at all levels, affecting personal relationships and stifling the development of civil society (which was officially discouraged by the state, which sought to shape cultural and social relations as well as political and economic ones). The consequent effects on public attitudes are likely one of the many factors responsible for the poorer transition performance of the former Soviet republics, compared with the Central European transition countries. The widespread use of terror was, in part, a consequence of the system. The system was established without internal checks and mechanisms to constrain the leadership – such an environment favoured those who had the greatest aptitude and willingness to employ ruthlessness, a sort of natural selection for tyrants. The system was designed this way from the start, of course, with Lenin's intentional establishment of an all-powerful dictatorship. This institutional environment of unconstrained power naturally led to systematic brutality and totalitarianism.

Measuring the effects of the Soviet system

Official Soviet estimates proclaimed high annual growth rates, exceeding 10% in the 1950s, and remaining above 3.5% through 1985.

In fact, these figures are believed to be largely fabrications.[11] In the late 1980s, Soviet economists Khanin and Selyunin re-estimated growth rates, and found them to be much lower. Their work suggests that overall growth averaged at most perhaps 3.5%.[12] They also detected a sharp decline in growth rates beginning in about 1960, and falling below 1% after 1975. It is likely that the Soviet economy was actually shrinking in the last years of the union; one estimate for Russia gives a growth rate of minus 4% for 1990.[13] The estimating of these numbers remains a matter of controversy. Regardless, Aslund suggests that a best guess is that by the mid 1980s, per capita GNP in the Soviet bloc was at most one third that of the United States.[14] OECD figures for Russia, probably the most prosperous Soviet republic, indicate a per capita GDP of 38% of that of the United States for 1990.[15] This places the Soviet Union among the lower-middle-income countries in World Bank classifications, rather than among the high-income developed countries.

Aggregate income statistics only begin to tell the story. The Soviet economy was heavily weighted towards military development, which consumed as much as 25% of output.[16] The structure of the Soviet economy placed too much emphasis on heavy industry, and left services underdeveloped, helping to suppress living standards.[17] Civilians faced chronic and growing housing shortages throughout the existence of the USSR.

The environmental consequences of central planning

One alleged benefit of central economic planning is that central planners will take into account negative externalities, such as environmental pollution, which would be ignored by private decision-makers in a market economy. The notion is that central planners, acting for the public good, will consider *all* effects of economic activity, and not simply their own personal benefit.[18] In fact, Soviet central authorities appear to have based their decisions primarily on their own perceived benefits.

Although on paper Soviet environmental regulations were extremely stringent, enforcement was practically non-existent. The reason for this is that neither planners nor managers bore liability for harms imposed on the public, so they had little incentive to reduce them. In addition, central planners lacked good knowledge of local conditions and the effects of the actions they ordered: there was no reliable mechanism for transmitting to them information on environmental disruption, nor did they have any strong incentive to rectify such problems if they learnt of them. Because the negative consequences of production plans, including pollution, were borne by local citizens, not by central authorities, they were effectively ignored.

The result was some of the most persistent and destructive instances of environmental disruption observed anywhere, ever. These included extreme cases of chronic air pollution, contamination of water and ground resources by hazardous chemical and radioactive wastes, desiccation of inland seas and massive desertification.

In 1989, over 70% of surface water in the USSR was considered polluted, compared with roughly 10% for the United States.[19] Common contaminants included metals, dioxin, petroleum, pesticides and human waste, and resulted from untreated industrial, agricultural and residential sources. Air pollution was likewise appalling. An analysis of 125 major Soviet cities found that air pollution was ten times higher than the maximum permissible norms, with consequential negative effects to public health.[20] In the 1970s and 1980s, the incidence of cancer grew explosively, with the rate of lung cancer growing at three times that of the United States.[21] In combination with an underfunded and underdeveloped healthcare system,[22] this environmental degradation took a human toll that is reflected in declining life expectancies from the 1960s onward (particularly for males) and third-world rates of infant mortality.[23] Soviet industry was also probably the major source of Arctic air pollution.[24] The overall picture is not one of development, but of callous indifference to human well-being.

Soviet central planners also exhibited favouritism for grandiose development projects, which frequently proved disastrous for both people and the environment. Included among these was the development of a major cotton industry in the Central Asian republics. This was achieved by diverting all inflows of the Aral Sea into irrigation. With essentially no inflows, the Aral Sea contracted to about one fifth its original size and salinity tripled, causing the collapse of what had been a very productive fishery, as well as microclimate changes and dust storms, which damaged natural flora and fauna in the region.[25] The intensive cotton monoculture also had direct side-effects, including salinisation and destruction of topsoil, which undermined productivity of both cotton and food crops, as well as contamination of drinking water supplies with agricultural chemicals. The result was tragic, if predictable: increasing regional rates of cancer and infant mortality, lower life expectancies, and – eventually – falling cotton output.[26]

A similar episode, on a smaller scale, affected the Caspian Sea, where a large gulf, the Kara Bogaz Gol, was dammed and desiccated in a failed attempt to extract minerals, resulting in destructive dust storms. In the Belarusian Republic, attempts to drain the massive Pripyat Marsh in order to develop agricultural land generated poor-quality land at the cost of the destruction of environmentally important wetlands.[27] These failed projects illustrate the consequences of a system in which far-removed planners act on maximal vision and minimal information, unconstrained by the rights of those for whom they claim to act. They seek prosperity and development, but generate waste and suffering.

Despite the claims of proponents, placing control of the economy in the hands of central authorities seems to have exacerbated, rather than ameliorated, environmental disruption. This is completely understandable, when one considers the lack of constraints and absence of good information facing planners. It is inherent in the system of central planning.

Abrogation of individual rights

Closely related to the above is the lack of legal recourse for those victimised by the system. Soviet citizens experienced a variety of injuries – from terror and oppression, through substandard consumer goods and services, to environmental degradation. Whether the harms inflicted were intentional, as in the case of terror, or accidental, as in the case of environmental disruptions, citizens had little opportunity to seek redress. Conversely, leadership bore little liability for its actions. This is an unsurprising result, an implication of the absence of constraints on power needed for central planning to function. Without liability, leaders were able to get away with behaviour that seems completely irresponsible. The Chernobyl nuclear disaster of 1986 provides a number of examples. The RMBK-type reactors in use in Chernobyl were designed and built without containment domes – standard safety equipment in the West.[28] Such equipment could have reduced the damage done by the accident, but was not included because it would have contributed nothing to the operation of the plant and was primarily for the protection of those living in the vicinity. The response and subsequent actions of the authorities in Moscow was irresponsible and callous. First, they ordered brigades of clean-up workers into the power plant without adequate protection, subjecting them to near certain illness and death. Second, in their efforts to cover up the extent of the accident, the authorities permitted the 1 May Labour Day parade in Kiev to go ahead as planned, assuring participants that the situation was safe – even as windblown contaminants were settling on the city. While abuse of power and irresponsible behaviour occur in any system, the institutions of central planning – particularly the centralisation of power – lead to an excess of such problems. The inherent difficulty of suing government, as opposed to private violators, made it extremely difficult for victims to receive justice for wrongs done. And this in turn made it more likely that such wrongs would occur in the first place.

These political consequences are not, strictly speaking, the results of central planning *per se*. Similar effects can be seen wherever there is concentrated, unconstrained political power and lack of protection for the rights of the individual. However, poorly constrained government is inherent in central economic planning, with its system-wide hierarchical decision-making and enforcement.

Soviet development of nuclear power is a history of the sacrifice of human well-being in the name of development. Soviet reactor design ignored safety measures standard in the West.[29] Once again, planners bore no liability for risks imposed on the public, hence there was little incentive to incorporate devices to reduce these risks. The catastrophe at Chernobyl was a consequence. So too was the less well-known accident at Kyshtym (near Chelyabinsk) in 1957, which resulted in the evacuation of more than 10,000 people and the contamination of approximately 900 square kilometres of land. Inattention to nuclear safety included widespread improper discarding of nuclear wastes, such as in an unprotected dump near Ust-Kamenogorsk in Kazakhstan, and even open-air dumping in Lake Karachay, near Chelyabinsk.[30] These actions were again reflected in above-average cancer rates for people living in the afflicted areas.

The human toll of the system was not entirely unintentional, of course. Soviet use of terror as a normal day-to-day tool of policy was brought to its pinnacle by Stalin, but its use began from the start of the Bolshevik Revolution, and continued until the demise of the Union. The numbers are, again, difficult to calculate. It is likely that the number of civilians killed in the course of imposing policy exceeded 20 million.[31] Countless more were deported to Siberia and Central Asia, often to prison camps. Much of the labour used in developing the Soviet economy was essentially slave labour, with individuals forced to work in horribly inhumane conditions.[32] Additionally, the system exacted a toll on all members of society, in the form of lack of freedom,

and the constant fear of arbitrary punishment. The ever-present threat of terror prevented the development of civic culture, and led to widespread cynicism and apathy as a way of life.

In sum, the Soviet experiment with central planning was a disastrous failure in a number of dimensions. It gave a poor level of economic development. It sacrificed its citizens and their interests for the benefit of the planners, and generated a bloated military and an inefficient, environmentally disruptive industrial structure. It permitted politically powerful elites to use the state for their own purposes, to callously ignore individual rights and to employ terror on a massive scale. This legacy of inadequate development, environmental disruption, totalitarianism, and a dispirited citizenry is directly attributable to the political and economic institutions of the system.

Lessons for development – the dangers of central planning

Central planning in the USSR resulted in a seemingly endless stream of contradictions. It generated rapid 'development', of a sort, through the establishment of a large industrial and military infrastructure. Some of this even 'trickled down' to the citizens, particularly in terms of such things as literacy, electrification and access to free health care (although this last fell badly into decay over the course of time). But it also generated excessive pollution, waste and environmental degradation, which took a measurable toll on human health. Meanwhile, much of the development was channelled into non-productive or even counterproductive areas, particularly the enormous post-war military infrastructure. It also did immense harm to public attitudes and civic culture, and established the seeds for widespread corruption, all of which have undermined the ability of the post-Soviet transition countries to develop the informal institutions of trust and cooperation on which the formal institutions of market development depend.

The Soviet experience clearly highlights the danger of central planning as a development strategy. These dangers are twofold: economic and political. From the economic standpoint, central planning does not deliver rapid development. Whilst it can deliver large-scale industrialisation and can mobilise huge amounts of resources, it is unable to acquire and utilise dispersed information, so it does not, indeed cannot, mobilise those resources rationally or efficiently. The resulting economic structure is wasteful and unsustainable, and much of the output reduces rather than adds value. Worse, there is no systematic feedback to correct such mistakes, so they persist and compound one another, leading to a cycle of destruction.

In addition, attempts at central planning inevitably lead to hierarchical political structures, with an extreme concentration of power at the top. Whilst all political systems are subject to corruption and abuse, Soviet-type systems are particularly subject to systematic abuses of individual rights. Such systems end up serving the interests of politically powerful elites, to the detriment of the people they are designed to serve. Again, the message for those thinking about policies for sustainable development is to avoid establishing agencies and institutions that would be subject to capture and exploitation by elites and special interests.

More generally, decision-makers considering strategies for sustainable development should be extremely wary of establishing systems that rely on the judgement of central planners in place of the dispersed decisions of individuals operating within frameworks of property rights and the rule of law. In a well-functioning market system, actors have both the incentive and knowledge to minimise waste and harm, and to maximise the value of economic production. Under a properly constrained political system, agents – both public and private – are liable for injuries; this reduces the likelihood of abuse of others, whether intentional (such as torture) or inadvertent (such as pollution). In the words of Winston Churchill, 'Democracy is the worst form of government yet invented except for all the others.' Whilst a market system with democratic government may not be without problems, at least it provides mechanisms for resolving these problems. Central planning does not.

Part Three

Global Governance

7 Green accounting

Martín Krause

Whether I decide to be a soccer fan, an opera expert or a religious mystic is not a matter I need to coordinate with others; it is the kind of decision that I can take by myself. Think about it and you will find a large number of other decisions that do not require coordination with other people. Indeed, most decisions regarding *consumption* are best made by the individual doing the consuming. But when we make decisions regarding what and how we are to *produce*, very often we benefit from coordinating our activities with those of others.

To explain this process and to elucidate the elemental laws of economics, classical economists used the example of Robinson Crusoe. Like the soccer fan, Crusoe needed only to consider the effects of his actions on himself when he arrived on his desert island. When Man Friday comes into the picture, however, the situation changes. Crusoe's decisions must now take his new companion into account. Among the good things that can happen in such a situation is one that Adam Smith viewed as the cornerstone of human progress: the division of labour. This allows for the division of tasks, resources and time and enables each individual to exploit his or her comparative advantage arising from his or her different abilities. Thus, Crusoe gets the food and Man Friday the water. This division of labour brings about improved satisfaction of human needs and wants, whatever those may be (in the case of Crusoe and Man Friday, there is now more food and more water for both).

In order for humans to enjoy the benefits of this division of labour, their actions must be coordinated. It would be useless for Crusoe to concentrate on obtaining food and for Man Friday to do the same with regard to water unless they were able mutually to benefit. The question therefore arises: how should this coordination be achieved?

The answer is, of course, dependent on a previous question: how *can* such coordination be achieved? (it would be pointless to state which options 'should' be used if those options are not achievable in the first place). Two 'pure' alternatives are regularly offered. The first was made famous by Adam Smith in *The Wealth of Nations* as the 'invisible hand' of the market. This is a spontaneous order, wherein coordination is based on the voluntary exchange of property among individuals in a free society. The second is based on command and control, on power and social engineering, planning and political decisions. Of course there are many shades of grey in between, but the two main ideas, markets and planning, are always there to different degrees. This is true in many different fields of activity: in morals and culture, in companies and sports teams, in currencies and arts.

One such field in which these alternatives are suggested is that of natural resources and the environment. This is an area where both consumption and production decisions may have effects on others, and so one in which the actions of human beings require coordination. The question again is: how should this coordination be achieved? Under the conceptual framework previously described, the two options, markets and planning, should be considered and evaluated. This chapter is an attempt to describe such an endeavour. The motive for so doing is that in many instances one option (markets) is usually disregarded in order to consider only different instances of the other (planning). This tendency is exemplified by the initiatives at the United Nations to introduce so-called 'green accounting' or, more formally, a system of integrated environmental and economic national accounting.

The problem we face today is how to use the planet's natural resources in a sustainable way. In other words, to use resources in a way that – according to the Brundtland Report definition of 'sustainable development' – ensures on the one hand that the needs of the present generation are met, whilst on the other that sufficient resources remain to enable future generations to meet their needs.[1]

It should be noted, though, that the word 'resource' implies a valuation – a subjective valuation for an individual. The planet is full of 'matter', but not all of it is a resource for us, nor is all of it necessary to produce a 'natural equilibrium' (if such a thing exists or even could exist). Some of this matter, in excess, can even be a danger to life – as one could say of lava or carbon dioxide, for example. The subjective nature of resource valuation means that in order for resource exploitation to be effectively coordinated there must at the same time be coordination of the different criteria used to establish what a resource is. That, of course, makes the problem much more complex. If we were in unanimous agreement about what is and what is not a resource, as well as who is entitled to which resources, then coordination would merely be a matter of assigning engineers to design the best allocation system. But when something is a resource for some and not for others, or even is a nuisance for a few, a different approach is required.

Some argue that the solution to this conundrum is improved central planning – incorporating more fully all the possible determinants of human desire and happiness. (Although explicit philosophical justification is rarely, if ever, given, proponents presumably support such central planning on the grounds that it will create the best of all possible worlds – maximising human happiness.) Others disagree. Again we come back to the conflict: should decisions be left to individuals acting in the market, or should the planners decide?

Measuring the unmeasurable

How, then, do you measure happiness? This question has vexed philosophers, psychologists and economists for centuries without ever producing a satisfactory answer. In an attempt to overcome the inherently subjective nature of happiness and produce an objective measure of human welfare, neoclassical economists developed a range of different indexes of economic performance. The presumption behind this approach is that a higher level of economic development means a better satisfaction of human needs. Since its invention by Simon Kuznets in the 1940s (and subsequent adoption by the UN), Gross National Product (GNP) has reigned supreme as an indicator of the economic performance of a country. As Herman Kahn points out:

> Even many who accept the desirability of economic affluence and technological achievement have qualms about using the common measure of such progress – GNP (gross national product) per capita. Indeed, almost any *explicit* use of this index has become discredited in some academic and intellectual circles. *Explicit* is emphasized because, despite its many theoretical and practical defects, practically everybody includes GNP per capita in any serious judgment about a nation's economic affluence, technological advancement, and ability to produce for culturally desirable purposes. Furthermore, governments everywhere try to increase it. Even the zero-growth movement uses the GNP concept, if only negatively.[2]

Though there have been critics of GNP as a measurement of progress, such criticism has focused on the form – not the fundamentals – of the concept. Recently, the focus has been on 'greening' the national accounts by adding factors representing such things as the depletion of the natural capital stock. According to a recent United Nations Environment Programme (UNEP) report:

> Green accounting addresses the shortcoming of traditional national accounting, known as the System of National Accounts (SNA). Green accounting is based on the concept that a proper assessment of a country's income and wealth needs to account for the contributions of activities made by all sectors of the economy and their impact on resource depletion and degradation. Traditional SNA ignores the value of resources (on and in the ground) as well as the value of environmental degradation. Therefore, it gives a false impression of income and wealth and often leads policy-makers to ignore or destroy the environment to further economic development. Incorporating the real value of natural resources as well as their depletion and degradation allows for better allocation of priorities, thereby helping to address the causes of current major environmental problems including the over-exploitation of natural resources such as forests.[3]

Such adjustments hardly represent a revolution. Indeed, they do little more than tinker at the edges with a very dubious idea – which for years was the preferred tool to implement vain and failed attempts to plan the economy. As the ecologist Hazel Henderson says:

> Historical and current evaluation tools used to measure industrial 'success', deeply rooted in macroeconomic models, are now obsolete from perspectives of global equity and human development, as well as those of the global environment and resource management.[4]

and

> Since Earth Day 1970, environmentalists have challenged economists' definitions of progress, wealth, and development – pointing out that economic theories and models short-change Nature as well as future generations. They highlight absurdities of GNP accounting such as in Alaska, which posted gains after the

Exxon Valdez oil spill because the additional costs of the clean-up are added to GNP instead of being subtracted (as environmentalists advocate). GNP ignores the value of clear water, fish and pristine, scenic environments like Prince William Sound.[5]

The author quotes *The Economist*:

conventional statistics of economic growth are ... particularly blind to the environment. National income accounts (Gross National Product) take no notice of the value of natural resources: a country that cut down all its trees, sold them as wood chips and gambled away the money ... would appear from its national accounts to have got richer in terms of GNP per person. Equally, they show measures to tackle pollution as bonuses, not burdens ... It would be easier for politicians to talk rationally about effects of sensible environmental policies on growth if governments agreed to remove some of these oddities from the way they keep their economic books.[6]

Starting in the sixties, there have been several attempts to create new indexes, measuring such quantities as 'Basic Human Needs' or 'Material Quality of Life' or the 'Measure of Economic Welfare' (developed by economists James Tobin and William Nordhaus). In 1989 the president of Venezuela organised a meeting entitled 'Towards New Ways to Measure Development', which recommended the inclusion of the degree of literacy or life expectation. Likewise, the Organization for Economic Co-operation and Development (OECD) has developed its Environmental Indicators to complement the information in national accounts.[7] In May 1989 the OECD Council called for the development of a means of integrating the process of economic and environmental decision-making. This concept was supported at the G-7 summit meeting in Paris in July of the same year. The G-7 meeting in July of the following year declared, 'we encourage the OECD to speed up its most useful work on the economy and the environment. Of particular importance are the development of environmental indicators and the design of market approaches to be used in order to achieve environmental goals.' Nevertheless, the OECD-designed indicators are a long way from the planning ambitions of the UN.

Green national accounting

The most developed and complete attempt at an alternative to national accounts – and the one with the highest likelihood of being implemented – is without a doubt the one developed by the UN under the name 'Integrated System of Environmental and Economic Accounts' (IEEA). The United Nations Statistical Division is coordinating the development of this 'all-encompassing and integrated' green accounting system.

The IEEA originated at a series of seminars organised by the UNEP and the World Bank during the 1980s. At these seminars, two main approaches were considered: The first was to create separate 'satellite' accounts alongside the traditional national accounts, to capture changes in natural resources but not to integrate them within the framework of the traditional SNA. The second was to integrate the measures with the traditional SNA – although this would be limited to easily valued resources (such as oil, coal and timber) and would not include other environmental aspects, such as pollution.

During the 1990s, some Latin American countries such as Colombia and Mexico experimented with IEEA, although in parallel to the traditional SNA. The UN expect that the IEAA might eventually replace the SNA altogether.

From the green accounting of the IEEA it is expected that new indicators will be developed to replace the traditional GNP or GDP. One such indicator is the Eco-Domestic Product (EDP), under which certain activities – such as the extraction and export of minerals – would be accounted for differently than they are under GDP/GNP. So, for example, in conventional national accounting, when a country increases its exports of minerals this counts as an increase in GDP. Under EDP, the decline in the stock of natural resources would show up as a negative figure, reducing the gain from the production and export of the mineral.

The UNEP report states that such an indicator 'would serve as an aid to policy setting and enable more informed decision-making regarding resource allocation and economic development'. But decision-making by whom? Not the mineral companies making investment decisions – they already know their cost of capital and are able to evaluate individual projects based on the likely flow of revenues. No, UNEP means decision-making by government. Government officials would use the information to impose restrictions on the activities of private individuals and companies, such as restricting the production of a specific mineral through taxation or quotas.

One problem with EDP is that it amounts to double-counting. When a company buys a piece of land, which it believes to contain mineral deposits, the cost of that purchase shows as an expenditure on the company accounts. In order to make the purchase, the company will use resources that could have been deployed elsewhere. The investment will therefore affect the profitability of the company. If it is a good investment it will increase profits – and hence show as an increase in GDP. If it is a bad investment it will reduce profits – and hence show as a reduction in GDP. Either way, the cost of the investment already shows on the GDP, so to include separately the depletion of the mineral reserves that result from exploiting the investment amounts to counting that depletion twice: once as the amortised cost of capital associated with the purchase, and again as a reduction in the stock of resources.

Because EDP double-counts the sunk costs of capital investment, any additional taxation of mining based on EDP would amount to double taxation of mineral extraction. The result would be an increase in the cost of minerals and all the downstream activities that are reliant upon it. Economic actors would, perversely, be encouraged to substitute non-mineral resources. So, oil from fish and other marine animals might be used in place of crude oil, encouraging more rapid depletion of these species. Of course, environmentalists might argue that fish and whales should also be included in EDP, in which case the effect on consumption of each resource would depend on the level of restrictions (quotas, taxes) attached to each, as well as their substitutability.

If all natural resources were taxed, there would be a bias in favour of using human labour as a substitute. So, instead of using chemical pesticides (including so-called 'organic' pesticides such as copper sulphate and *bacillus thuringiensis*), which require the use of natural resources, there would be an incentive to go back to manual removal of insects and weeds. Miners would become redundant but some would obtain jobs as manual labourers on farms. The number of low-value-added activities, such as weeding, would increase. Meanwhile, the number of high-value-added activities, such as identifying and developing new medicines capable of reducing child mortality, would decrease. Generally speaking, the economic effect of implementing EDP would be negative.

This leads to something of a paradox: EDP is justified on the grounds that it will increase overall human satisfaction and well-being. But inasmuch as human satisfaction is more dependent on the actual level of economic activity than on the amount of natural resources remaining (either in an individual country or on the Earth as a whole), the immediate result of implementing EDP will be to reduce human satisfaction and well-being.

EDP would also be constrained by the fact that it is dependent on a static conceptualisation of what is a resource. In reality, the nature of resources changes over time. During the nineteenth century, whale oil was an important fuel, especially for lighting, and an entire industry grew up around the hunting and processing of oil-rich whales, such as Blues and Greys. So large was this industry that it threatened to wipe out the entire population of these magnificent creatures.[8] When crude oil was discovered and methods for extracting and refining it developed, it largely replaced whale oil, saving these whales from extinction. In rich countries, oil has been replaced by distributed electricity as the dominant source of energy for lighting, though oil remains important in this context in poor countries.

What would have happened if, on the grounds that oil is a depletable resource, the United States had regulated the use of its crude oil reserves at the end of the nineteenth century – imposing a hefty tax on it, for example? The cost of using paraffin derived from crude oil would have been high compared to whale oil, so the hunt for whales would have continued for longer before finally ceasing. Almost certainly the number of Blues and Greys would be lower than it is today. (This presumes that the US would not have attempted to impose restrictions on the hunting of whales outside its territorial boundaries.) In addition, the cost of other refined products, such as octane and diesel, would have been high compared to other countries, so making them less attractive as a fuel for transport. This would have discouraged the development of the US automobile industry. Perhaps Henry Ford would never have invented the automobile production line. For transport, people would have relied for longer on horses, which would have continued to foul the streets in greater quantities. Generally things would have been slower and less efficient.

If similar restrictions had been placed on the use of crude oil by countries around the world, economic growth in the past century would certainly have been slower than it has been and the toll on human life would have been great. Of course, opponents of modern civilisation will argue that without oil the two world wars might never have taken place, or that they would have been less severe. But consider another counterfactual: Perhaps, in the absence of abundant, cheap gasoline, the drive to produce nuclear power would have been more intense with less concern placed on its adverse consequences.

Germany might have won the Second World War by detonating atom bombs over New York and Washington DC. Of course, all of this is a flight of fancy, but it is not entirely far-fetched. Ideas have consequences and this particular idea might have had many negative ones.

In their bid to construct a system of green national accounts, officials have so far mostly addressed resources, such as minerals, for which there are established markets and visible prices. Those prices fulfil a very important role: they are indicators of the future availability *and* the future valuation of a resource. They also create incentives to act on that information. If one resource is being replaced by another, or its supply is increasing, its price will be falling, increasing the incentive to consume it. If, on the other hand, demand for a resource is increasing or its supply falling, its price will be rising, reducing the incentive to consume it and so creating incentives to find and develop alternative resources. Many decisions will be made on the basis of such information, with some people speculating a future scarcity, others a future surplus, and losers learning from winners as they compare profits and losses.

The price system, as Friedrich Hayek showed,[9] relays information not only on the physical availability of a resource but, more importantly, on the valuation consumers and producers make about it. It is true, as the UN report observes, that in some countries 'traditional SNA ignores the value of resources (on and in the ground) as well as the value of environmental degradation', giving a 'false impression of income and wealth'. And, as the UN also says, 'incorporating the real value of natural resources as well as their depletion and degradation allows for better allocation of priorities, thereby helping to address the causes of current major environmental problems including the over-exploitation of natural resources such as forests'. But that is a task government officials cannot do because they cannot know the valuations placed on these things by individuals. By contrast, such valuations *can* be expressed through markets: where there are clearly defined property rights and people are free to contract for the purchase and sale of such rights, individuals express their valuations through their choices about what to buy and sell. And the SNA incorporates the subsequent choices.

Accounting without prices

Prices arise from free exchanges of property between two parties. That is, a price is the ratio of exchange between two owned things. The existence of prices therefore requires two conditions: 1) freedom to make contracts for those exchanges and (2) property rights that may be legally enforceable. The absence of either requirement precludes the existence of a price system.

In the absence of prices we are faced with two possibilities, which again shows the planning versus markets dilemma. The 'market' solution is to remove the barriers to exchanges and allow for the creation of property rights. Prices will then emerge, acting as a guide to individuals' choices with regard to the future use of resources. Some may show concern about the decisions individuals make and demand an alternative 'planning' solution. But government officials are individuals as well and can make the same – and worse – mistakes. At least property owners are rewarded if they make proper use of a resource, taking care of it or multiplying it, and are punished if they do not. Government officials, in contrast, rarely suffer personally for the losses their decisions bring about.

In order to try to make 'planning' more effective, people have searched for replacements to prices that may give government officials appropriate information on which to base decisions. It is this second option that is being pursued by the UNEP. But new and insurmountable problems are created by this approach.

First of all, physical accounting must take place, and that is no small endeavour. This is what the UN says:

> Nature is composed of biological assets (produced and wild),
> water and soil surfaces with their ecosystems, underground assets
> and air. Attention must be paid to living beings (animals and
> plants) and their natural environment. Therefore, all animals and
> plants associated with the natural environment and their living
> conditions should be supervised. Including cattle and other
> animals controlled by man, as well as wild animals, agricultural
> plants and trees as well as wild ones.[10]

It is immediately clear that the task for the 'environmental accountant' is unachievable. First, we do not know – even within an order of magnitude – how many species of plant and animals there are on the planet, let alone how many there are of individual species, nor by inference their rate of depletion.[11] Physical accounting then looks like an idea that may rapidly become ridiculous: Should all doves be counted? And what about their stock changes from year to year? What about cockroaches? Are they a 'resource' to be counted or should GDP accounts include the production of 'roach killers' instead? This last example shows the need to incorporate valuations into the accounting process. But how will the connection between physical units and the valuations of individuals be made?

As we have already noted, consumers reveal their preferences through their decisions to buy and sell. Perhaps inspired by this fact, one of the first proposals by the UN was to poll consumers, asking them how much money they would be willing to spend on various environmental amenities:

> A direct valuation of benefits (or losses) related to the economic functions of the environment is usually only possible by asking people about the monetary value of those functions. This method (contingent or conditional valuation) starts from the assumption that those polled have enough information with regard to the benefits in monetary terms.[12]

The UN's proposal also includes the use of data related to the cost of pollution or the expenditures needed to comply with certain regulations. As an example of the first case it mentions 'the valuation of a reduction in air quality' and suggests that 'Each person could be asked what annual amount they would be willing to pay in order to avoid such a change in quality.'[13]

The UN further explains that

> The method used for estimating the costs for non-market goods was *contingent valuation* by applying the *willingness-to-pay approach*. Here consumers were asked how much they were prepared to pay for a better or healthier environment. Another approach was to use a questionnaire, where people were asked to what extent they would reduce their consumption in order to achieve fewer environmental hazards.[14]

But there is a big difference between a decision in the marketplace and an opinion given to a pollster. When someone buys or sells in a market, the transaction has a direct cost to the decision-maker as well as an opportunity cost in the form of the alternative decisions that could have been made. No such costs are associated with a poll; just giving an answer to a questioner has no cost, direct or opportunity. Anyone can see the difference between answering a request about how much money one would be willing to pay to have clean air and actually issuing a cheque for that same amount.[15]

Other environmentalists try to go even further. Ecologist Hazel Henderson says that 'the data on externalities and social costs would have to be developed by more realistic disciplines: thermodynamics, biology, systems and chaos models and ecology'.[16] In reality, this approach would almost guarantee complete 'chaos' in the management of resources.

In Argentina, the Fundación Vida Silvestre (Wildlife Foundation) supports a 'political criteria', stating that 'A new methodology needs to be created in order to value natural resources and their contribution to the economy. In such a valuation process government agencies, scientific institutions, universities and NGOs should participate.'[17] But one can only imagine the degree of political activity and lobbying that such a proposal would bring. Ironically, the supporters of EDP emphasise the importance of political activity, implying that this will be a positive force:

Tremendous political activity on the part of the global citizens of every nation will be needed to force these priorities onto politicians and other leaders in business and academe, unions, and other social groups. The more we have better social and economic indicators to provide better feedback on our current course, the sooner political will can be mustered for the necessary shift in policies.[18]

No wonder they are having trouble constructing a reliable green accounting system. The Chief of Division for Input-Output Analyses at Germany's Federal Statistical Office is quoted as saying that 'it was easy to develop concepts, but difficult to implement them ... Focusing on the most important environmental problems caused certain difficulties, since it was not easy to make a list of priorities. It was possible that some problems were not recognized because they were thought to be minor, but under closer scrutiny it transpired that they could cause major monetary losses.'[19]

In the end, the problems stem from the intention to plan the activities of people. Again, as Hayek has said, it is not a matter of the existence of planning or not but a question of who does the planning: government officials with the difficulties they find or individuals guided by the price system which makes use of widely dispersed information of such a kind that it may not even be available in a form that allows its transfer to government decision-makers. To the proponents of EDP, society is something that needs to be guided by a central planner. And planners need feedback in order effectively to implement their plan; hence the need to develop instruments such as green accounting. Hazel Henderson reiterates this idea quite clearly:

> In fact, trying to run a complex society on a single indicator like the Gross National Product is literally like trying to fly a 747 with only one gauge on the instrument panel. There would be nothing there to tell you whether the wing flaps were up or down, whether the fuel tank was full or what the altitude was. In effect, you'd be flying blind. Or imagine if your doctor, when giving you a check up, did no more than check your blood pressure![20]

The problem with this perspective, however, is that society is nothing like a jetliner, with its unique destination and clear need for a pilot. A society is composed of hundreds of thousands, or indeed millions, of individuals, each one of them unique, with different needs, wishes and capabilities and, therefore, different destinations. A free society in fact more resembles the entire transportation system, where people can choose not only the destination, but also the time of departure and the mode of transport.

Extending the market

The lack of property rights and consequent lack of prices for natural assets not only causes problems for green accountants, it also results in what is called 'the tragedy of the commons'[21] – or perhaps more accurately, the tragedy of open access. This is a situation that arises when there is no clear assignment of benefits and costs to individual users of a resource. As a result, each user has an incentive to use as much of the resource as possible. When the resource becomes scarce (which might happen, for example, when the number of users increases or when technology reduces the private cost of exploitation), depletion occurs because the benefits of exploitation are private whilst the costs are shared with all the other users. By contrast, the owners of property rights become 'protectors' of the assets they own. But in order for such a right to exist it must be possible to exclude non-owners from its use, and its predation.

The history of Argentina shows a clear example of this. Spanish explorers brought horses and cows to the now famous 'pampas' and in this favourable environment large numbers of wild herds of these animals grew – until one of the first local industries was established:

leather. Tanneries were set up and cattle were chased and killed over the pampas for their skin alone, leaving the remains to be consumed by predators. In this situation of open access, cattle were being killed by predators at such a rate that in the early nineteenth century, in an attempt to save the endangered species, Viceroy Arredondo tried to control the tanneries. Historian Félix de Azara estimates there were 48 million head of cattle in the Pampas in 1700 but by 1800 only 6 million remained.[22] The lack of property over cattle did not allow for the existence of 'protectors' – someone who would not only try to get leather from cattle but also would have an incentive to encourage the animals to reproduce and thereby ensure a future supply. Establishing property rights came up against some difficult problems: cattle is a moving resource, so even if the borders between different pieces of land could have been clearly marked, the cattle would not have respected them. However, with the introduction of barbed wire, property rights in cattle could be enforced and cattle ceased to be an endangered species in Argentina. Actually, the idea that cows could be an endangered species would now make many Argentines laugh, no doubt unaware that this was the case in their country just 200 years ago.

Once property rights are established, the benefits and costs of managing a resource fall with the owner who, therefore, has an incentive to protect his or her resources in order to preserve and enhance their value. Of course property rights do not eliminate error from decision-making, but they do bring a powerful motivation to learn from past mistakes. If owners do not learn from their mistakes and those of others, the resource may decline in value, or they may lose control of it. Also, because owners can enforce their rights through the courts, they do not need tremendous political action in order to act. Political and other collective actions suffer from 'free-rider' problems, making them difficult and costly. By contrast, the courts are typically cheaper and quicker, so using them rather than the political process reduces the cost of acting and increases the likelihood that decisions will be made in a timely and effective manner.

True, setting up property rights over some kinds of resources is not an easy matter – whales and the atmosphere spring to mind. But the creativity of humans should not be underestimated: we are now able to farm almost any kind of animal, from crocodiles to shrimp, and those that cannot be farmed, such as elephants, can be raised in protected environments. One only has to look at the small rivers traversing the city of Buenos Aires, or even the large Rio de la Plata, to see that the rivers' present owner, the government, is not a good protector. Several are so polluted that no creatures are able to survive in them. All are too polluted for city dwellers to bathe safely during the long hot summers. To the casual observer, it seems difficult to assign property rights to courses of water. But there are already several examples of such systems in common law countries. In the western United States, where water is very scarce, rights to water were apportioned on a first-in-time basis. As a result, private owners value and hence conserve scarce water supplies. Meanwhile, in England and Wales, riparian owners are entitled to water that is of undiminished quality and so are able to sue polluters. Anglers in the UK, who value water quality because of its impact on the fish they prize, have taken thousands of actions against polluters and thereby kept the rivers far cleaner than otherwise they would have been.[23] Argentinian property rights legislation does in fact allow private ownership of small ponds of water, as long as they are part of a single property. Clearly, it would not be difficult to allow riparian owners to enjoy property rights over streams and rivers. Such rights would enable them to act in defence of the resource, something that can now only be done through the political system.

Argentine authorities complain that the different uses of water make it difficult to plan the use of the resource. But it is this very plurality of interests that make the property rights approach interesting. As Terry Anderson and Don Leal explain:

> If all polluters who use an estuary for waste disposal are held
> strictly liable for the cost of their pollution, they have an incentive
> to consider the costs and benefits of their actions. Under these
> circumstances, the market process, with liability enforced by the
> courts, forces polluters to weigh the costs of abating pollution
> against the potential damage costs. If it is less expensive to abate
> pollution than to face the liability, then polluters will do so; if it is
> not, the other asset owners will be compensated. Of course, this
> assumes that polluters can be identified and that damages can be
> assessed, but these are the same assumptions that are necessary if
> government regulations or fines are to effectively control
> pollution.[24]

Of course there will be situations where there is a large number of polluters or parties affected by pollution, which make it difficult to assign responsibilities. But there have already been some interesting experiences with market-like arrangements, such as tradable pollution permits, which have been shown to be more efficient than traditional regulations – leading to more rapid environmental improvement at lower cost.[25] Meanwhile, tort law remains open to all other instances where the polluter can be identified (with tracing technologies extending the possibilities of assigning responsibilities).

Conclusions

Central planning has been extensively tested during the twentieth century and has consistently failed to produce economic benefits.[26] Attempts to make central planning function more effectively by accounting for inputs and outputs made little difference to the effectiveness of Soviet and other systems. So what reason do we have to believe that green national accounts will make central planning of the environment any more effective?

Curiously enough, the recipe for green accounting and environmental planning does not come from old-fashioned socialist writers but from the very heart of mainstream neoclassical economics. The argument is advanced following what is called 'market failure theory' and the supposed inability of market institutions to solve problems that have the characteristics of 'public goods' or, in this case, bads.

There is not space in this chapter to discuss the detail of the neoclassical theory of market failure but it is worth considering the case of the lighthouse. Paul Samuelson, in his influential textbook on economics, gave the lighthouse as the classic example of a public good. Lighthouses, it was suggested, would not be supplied privately because there was no means by which the owners could be compensated for the supply of the beneficial warning light they give to ships. However, Ronald Coase, in his seminal article on the subject in the *Journal of Law and Economics*, pointed out that in England, lighthouses had been run privately for over a century, the owners earning their keep from a toll charged at ports.[27] Thus it is clear that public goods can be supplied privately – if only one has the imagination to construct the appropriate institutions.

Suffice it to say that after the disastrous results of economic planning in the former socialist countries and in existing developing countries, the burden of proof should lie on the planners to show they can outperform property rights, markets and the rule of law in the protection of the environment. And while they are doing this, it would not be a bad idea if they were to redirect all the efforts and budgets currently dedicated to green accounting towards the analysis of ways to develop property rights where they currently do not exist.

8 Environmental protection and the WTO

Alan Oxley

In November 2001, the 142 members of the World Trade Organization (WTO) agreed to launch a new trade round. The Doha Development Round should be good news for trade liberalisation and world economic growth. The WTO membership is now committed to policies which will speed recovery from recession and which will support growth in the developing world. The anti-globalisation movement has, at least for the moment, had the wind taken out of its sails. In the aftermath of September 11, the agreement at Doha, Qatar, to continue to build global economic interdependence is a reaffirmation by the nations of the civilised world of their intention to continue to cooperate for the common good of all.

There are, however, few successes in life that come without strings attached, and the string in this case was the mainstreaming of the environment as an agenda item in the new trade round. Most members of the WTO – especially developing countries – did not want environment to be negotiated in the Round. So why did they agree? After the debacle of Seattle and in the wake of the then pending economic downturn following September 11, Robert Zoellick, the US trade negotiator, was under enormous pressure to make Doha a success. Meanwhile, Pascal Lamy, his counterpart from the European Commission, made it clear that he 'had to have something' on the environment to deliver to the European Union (EU). Lamy had been telling everyone that the EU would not accept anything less and Zoellick knew this. So Zoellick brokered a deal.

The deal is that the environment issue of immediate interest to the EU – 'clarifying conflict between the provisions of the WTO and MEAs [Multilateral Environment Agreements]' – would in the first instance be studied and then, at their meeting in 2003, WTO Ministers would decide whether or not to negotiate changes to WTO rules. One wonders if negotiators understood the opportunity this gives the EU to exert dramatic leverage at the 2003 meeting. The issues on which the EU has historically been most reluctant to move – agriculture and garments and textiles – are issues of the greatest importance to developing countries. So it is easy to imagine progress on those issues being held hostage by the EU, at the 2003 meeting, to commitments to negotiate rule changes on environmental issues. Adding to these woes, a recent decision by the Appellate Body of the WTO 'court'[1] upheld the use of trade sanctions by the United States, enabling the United States to require importers to comply with domestic US environmental standards. This potentially creates an important precedent for the wider use of trade sanctions to coerce other nations to comply with the environmental standards of rich countries, such as the United States, Japan or EU, and legitimises new grounds to protect uncompetitive industries.

What is at stake?

The international trading system operates according to rules spelt out in the General Agreement on Tariffs and Trade (GATT) and applied by the World Trade Organization (WTO). In general the GATT/WTO system has enabled a flourishing of international trade, with enormous benefits in terms of improved efficiency of resource use and increased wealth in all trading nations. So far, rich countries have benefited more from the WTO than have poor countries. This is not because the system is rigged against poor countries, as some have claimed. Rich countries do not 'exploit' poor countries through trade. Trade is voluntary: if someone in a poor country sells something to someone in a rich country it is because both believe they will gain in the process.[2] However, poor countries continue to impose and to face higher tariffs than do rich countries, especially on agricultural and textile products. As a result, people in these countries are unable to gain as much from engaging in international trade as they would if they faced fewer restrictions. The question is: will these barriers be lowered, or will the system flounder under the weight of protectionist interests and environmentalist pressure?

GATT rules enable trade restrictions to be imposed for the protection of human health and/or the environment but limit the circumstances under which these may be applied. Specifically, Article XX of the GATT allows some such restrictions, subject to stringent tests.[3] Historically, trade restrictions were generally not permitted under Article XX if they related only to the methods by which a good was produced but not to the qualities of the product itself.[4]

However, a recent decision by the Appellate Body of the WTO's dispute settlement system indicates that WTO members may be able to impose restrictions on imports based upon the way those imports are produced under certain circumstances.[5] Those circumstances are: (a) that doing so is necessary for environmental protection or the conservation of natural resources; (b) that the importing country has attempted to negotiate a bilateral or multilateral agreement involving the country of export to achieve the environmental/conservation measure without the imposition of sanctions, but that this has failed; (c) that the sanctions imposed conform with the basic precepts of the WTO, namely fairness and non-discrimination. This case is discussed in greater detail below.

The EU seeks to legitimise the imposition of trade sanctions that are based on the way goods are produced. To achieve this end, it is employing a multi-component strategy. One key component is its support for the elaboration of numerous multilateral environmental agreements (MEAs) containing trade provisions.[6] A second, reinforcing component is its attempt to obtain an agreement that would assert the primacy of MEAs over trade rules enforced by the WTO. A third component is the attempt to introduce the Precautionary Principle into international law in general and trade law in particular. If successful, the trade provisions of MEAs would for many goods replace the WTO rules, whilst for other goods, nations would be able to impose essentially arbitrary restrictions on trade. The consequences for the WTO and for liberalisation of international trade more generally could be devastating.

Clarifying the WTO rules as they affect MEAs

In at least three significant MEAs, parties are obliged to use trade sanctions to enforce the specified environmental objectives and are required to ban trade in certain goods with countries that are not parties to the MEAs. These MEAs are: the Convention on International Trade in Endangered Species (CITES), the Montreal Protocol on Ozone Depleting Substances, and the Basel Convention on Transboundary Movements in Hazardous Waste.

It is, to say the least, morally and legally dubious to negotiate international treaties that impose penalties on non-parties. The United Nations Charter decrees it a breach of the doctrine of national sovereignty. At the UN Conference on Environment and Development (the Rio 'Earth' Summit) in 1992, Ministers declared that trade sanctions should not be used to enforce environmental goals.[7,8] UN meetings are not known for the wisdom of their declarations but in this case the Ministers got it right: trade sanctions are poor environment policy. Government measures to secure protection of the environment should aim to impact on the source of the environmental degradation. Usually this is the point of production or consumption. Trade is almost never the cause of degradation. Trying to secure an environmental result with a trade ban is an extremely inefficient and consequently ineffective method.[9, 10]

However, this did not dissuade the World Wildlife Fund from promoting trade bans ostensibly to protect endangered species. Under CITES, trade in species listed on Appendix 2 requires the prior approval of the CITES Secretariat. Meanwhile, trade in species and products derived therefrom and listed on Appendix 1 is effectively banned (except, for example, antiques, such as nineteenth-century carved ivory, which require a permit). The fact that these bans have in most cases had little impact on the species they supposedly protect, except in cases where they have been harmful,[11] does not deter WWF and other more radical organisations from pushing to keep them in place.[12] Nor did these facts deter Greenpeace from promoting a ban on trade in 'hazardous waste' under the Basel Convention. The Basel Convention requires industrialised nations to permit exports of specified materials only if they consider and approve the waste management policies of the importing countries.[13] Under a Ban Amendment being sought by Greenpeace and its affiliates in the Basel Action Network, Basel would ban completely trade in other proscribed materials.[14] As such, Basel injects into international law a view of the developing world reminiscent of the European colonial period, a view that still permeates the mindset of European NGOs, i.e. that the interests of developing countries are better understood and managed by the developed world. Greenpeace, for example, is currently pressuring the Dutch Government to exercise its rights under the Basel Convention to ban the export of ships to India for breaking, because Greenpeace considers the pollution caused by the Indian ship-breaking industry to be unacceptable.[15]

Like CITES, the Basel Convention has had all manner of bad consequences, which, even from the perspective of the colonial interventionist with an eye for eco-imperialism, should make one wary of promoting it as a model for future trade relations.[16] For example, restrictions on the export of used lead to India have undermined the formal lead recycling industry in that country with perverse environmental consequences. The formal recycling industry, which operates under strict environmental and health and safety regulations, requires high throughput of lead. Because of the relatively low levels of lead use locally, the industry requires imported lead in order to operate at a profit. The restriction on exports of used lead to India has led to the closure of a number of formal-sector lead recycling facilities, which became unprofitable. As a result, more of the locally produced waste lead is now recycled by the informal sector. These are unregulated backyard operations, which typically cause contamination of water and air, with adverse health consequences.[17]

What is the conflict?

The potential conflict between these MEAs and the WTO arises from the fact that the WTO rules bar members from imposing their own policies extraterritorially under the threat of trade bans and bar WTO members from discriminating amongst each other in their trade policies. In contrast, the MEAs say 'we will not trade with you unless you apply our policies and standards'.

In principle, a member of the WTO that is not a party to an MEA might secure a ruling from the WTO that another member has acted illegally under WTO rules by restricting trade in accordance with the terms of the MEA. During the past decade, various environmental groups have pressed for an amendment to the WTO rules that would remove the right of any WTO member to take such a case. The EU has now joined them in this cause.

No such case has so far been lodged within the WTO. No member has yet had sufficient reason to do so. The application of trade measures in MEAs has not imperilled a commercially significant amount of trade. Nor is any environmental interest significantly advanced by the trade bans. They are relatively ineffectual. Indeed, the MEAs in question were recently reviewed in a series of case studies by the UN Conference on Trade and Development (UNCTAD), which reported that in no case had trade bans secured the environmental purpose of the MEAs.[18]

Why does the conflict matter?

So, if this is not a matter of practical importance, why not do as the EU proposes and remove the irritant by having the WTO legitimise the trade provisions in a formal agreement? Two good reasons: First, a fundamental issue of principle is at stake. Second, the EU is driving environmental and regulatory policy in a direction that will significantly disadvantage businesses both inside and outside the EU.

The issue of principle is that such a result would legitimise discriminatory trade provisions and undermine the core values that have made the GATT/WTO an outstanding success. The GATT/WTO is arguably the most successful international institution that has ever been developed. It has led to a global trading based on clear, non-discriminatory rules, and reciprocal reductions in tariffs and other trade barriers. This has encouraged trade to flourish and has laid the foundations for a sustained period of economic growth enveloping more people than ever before in the world's history. The WTO system has just embraced China, giving the world's most populous country a stronger stake in the global economy. As a result, China is now more actively engaged in the international community – and on more friendly and positive terms – than it has ever been. As Bob Zoellick himself has said on many occasions, the global system of economic interdependence, based on free markets, is fundamental to global peace and security.

The WTO rules have worked because they respect the sovereignty of every WTO member. Non-discrimination is guaranteed by these rules, which are accepted and applied in common by every member, rich or poor, large or small. If the principle is established that one member, or a sub-set of members, can impose its own conditions for trading with other members of the WTO, the fundamental principle that sustains the whole WTO legal structure will fail.

Unwitting support from Washington

That is the long answer to the question 'why not clean up this problem the way the EU proposes?' The short answer is even simpler: it is the wrong solution. Why don't environmental groups accept the principles set down by the UN and stop proposing trade sanctions in MEAs? It is not the WTO rules which need changing; it is the habit of environmentalists to push for trade bans in multilateral environmental agreements – and the habit of environment ministers negotiating the agreements of accepting the bans – that should be changed.

One reason is that, as fundamental as this issue is, the conflict between the trade measures in MEAs and the WTO rules has never attracted as much attention in Washington as it has in Brussels. The argument that there is something wrong with trade sanctions has little traction in DC. A trade sanction is a traditional weapon for US interest groups and has been attractive to Congress. US Administrations have been forced to defend several trade sanctions demanded by environmental NGOs, mandated in law by Congress, and triggered by environmental NGOs through litigation in the US courts. Some of these sanctions are well known – the bans on imports of tuna from countries that do not mandate fishing methods which reduced the incidental kill of dolphins and, more recently, bans on imports of shrimp where the incidental kill of turtles was not minimised. Most of the US restrictions were struck down after complaints in the WTO by countries whose trade was affected (*see* discussion of *Shrimp–Turtle* on page 136 below). The EU itself lodged one of the complaints against the tuna bans. The EU has always maintained that unilateral trade sanctions are unacceptable, but that trade sanctions maintained by a group of countries, such as through an MEA, are legitimate.

In addition, the United States is not a party to the Basel Convention, which is the most egregious offender against WTO principles. It is understandable that policymakers in Washington would pay little attention to a Convention to which the United States was not a party. But it leaves a large blind spot.

However, there is a policy interest in Washington which results in a sympathetic hearing for the EU approach. The collaboration between protectionist interests and environmental lobbyists over the last decade, first against the GATT over the tuna/dolphin rulings, and second (and more significantly) in the campaign against NAFTA, have made respectable the idea that no trade agreement is any good unless it provides for extraterritorial reach with regard to environmental policy. This idea is now part of the basic position of the protectionists in Congress, giving perhaps unintended support to the EU position. Green groups such as WWF and Greenpeace understand that this position reinforces their global interest in protecting the MEAs that they have sponsored – CITES and Basel respectively. However, other US-based environmental groups see themselves as acting in accord with the older American tradition of supporting trade sanctions, in this case to see them used to force their preferred environmental policies on other countries.

What ultimately matters in Washington is, however, how many

votes in Congress are locked into the position that environment has to be linked to trade. That the WTO might well be poisoned in the process does not rate in that situation. The focus in Washington is, always, on how many votes they have. This political calculus can only be challenged when it can be shown that other US interests are threatened as a consequence, and the negotiation in January 2001 of the Biosafety Protocol, which restricts trade in certain GMOs, has done just that.

EU trade bans on GMOs

Strongly supported by Greenpeace – as part of that group's wider campaign to ban genetically modified organisms (GMOs) – the Biosafety Protocol was driven politically by the EU. In contrast to the MEAs so far discussed, the Biosafety Protocol does not mandate trade sanctions. But it creates other significant conflicts with WTO rules. It gives importing countries absolute discretion to ban imports of living products which are genetically modified (including potentially all manner of grains, seeds, fruit and vegetables). By invoking versions of the Precautionary Principle, which are laid down in the Protocol, importers may impose a ban simply because they have not carried out tests that satisfy them of the safety of the products to be imported. The fact that nothing is perfectly safe, or that the items to be imported may be significantly safer than other conventionally produced food items that are regularly imported, is irrelevant. The Protocol is predicated exclusively on the way the products are produced.

By contrast, WTO rules allow members to restrict imports to protect human health, and animal plant health and safety, but oblige members, when challenged, to demonstrate that such restrictions are based on scientific evidence, or at least a risk assessment. The United States has already had experience with EU efforts to evade this obligation.

In 1985, the European Commission decided to ban hormones used for animal growth promotion, on the basis that 'their safety has not been conclusively proven'. This ban was instituted in spite of the fact that the EC's own official inquiry into the effects of growth promotion hormones had given the all-clear to the three natural hormones (progesterone, testosterone and oestradiol) and had not yet reported on the two synthetics under investigation. The decision seems to have been motivated primarily by a highly vocal campaign by consumer organisations, which sought to ban all hormones.[19]

There is no scientific evidence that such meat can be distinguished from that of other cows, or that it is a threat to human health. The United States brought a case against the EU at the WTO, which it won. The EU appealed the decision and the Appellate Body upheld the earlier decision, ruling that in the absence of any scientific evidence to the contrary, the EU bans were illegal. Incidentally, in the same case, the Appellate Body also narrowly construed the 'Precautionary Principle' as at most justifying emergency restrictions pending a risk assessment or new scientific evidence. In a subsequent case, the WTO narrowed this further by specifying that such a risk assessment should be carried out in a timely manner. Thus did the WTO attempt to bring even the unwieldy Precautionary Principle within the rule of law.

To see how the Biosafety Protocol might impact on trade, consider a case where the EU and Canada are parties both to the Biosafety Protocol and the WTO. The EU bans imports of GMO oilseed from Canada. Canada challenges the EU under the terms of the WTO rules requiring demonstration of the science or risk assessment which supposedly justifies the ban. The EU replies that under the Biosafety Protocol it does not need to provide scientific justification and that under international treaty interpretation the Biosafety Protocol post-dates the WTO Agreement and, therefore, trumps EU obligations under the WTO. If the case went to the WTO Dispute Panel, there is a strong chance the result would run against Canada.

It is no accident that this conflict exists between the Biosafety Protocol and the WTO. The promoters of this Protocol[20] were fully aware it would conflict with the WTO rules. Before the WTO Seattle Ministerial meeting, the consumer-lobbying organisation Public Citizen advocated completion of the Biosafety Protocol so that there would be a basis to undermine the science-based approach in WTO agreements.[21] During the Biosafety negotiations some countries wanted a clause in the Protocol stating that WTO rights would be unaffected by accession to the Protocol. The EU refused point blank to accept the proposal. Today, EU officials point to the Biosafety Protocol and its articulation of the Precautionary Principle as a standard which should be followed and applied elsewhere.

The Clinton Administration was actively involved in the negotiation of the Biosafety Protocol. Aware of the dangers it posed to global arrangements for trade in GMOs, the Administration worked actively to soften it. However, the Administration did not have the final card to play in the negotiations over the treaty – change it or we will not go along – because as a non-ratifier of the Convention on Biological Diversity it could not sign the agreement.[22]

In this case, officials were aware that the United States's interests were not fully protected by non-signature. The EU might not be able to invoke biosafety provisions against the United States, which currently cannot and probably will not ratify the Convention, but it could in the case of other countries, both developing and developed. The result would be fragmentation of global markets for many key GMO products. For every WTO member that adhered to the Biosafety Protocol, the science-based regime of the WTO and its international authority to regulate global trade in the category of GMOs covered by the Protocol would be correspondingly diminished.

The Protocol is an important precedent for the EU to build its case to restrict trade in response to consumer or protectionist pressure, and to ban imports without scientific justification.

Wider EU policy interests

The EU has signalled the direction in which it wants trade policy to move – towards wider use of trade sanctions to enforce its own regulations extraterritorially. Meanwhile, its own regulatory policy has been gradually moving towards that of a Hegelian bureaucracy, in which administrative officials have wide powers of discretion to construct and enforce new regulations. Through this combination of measures, the EU will perpetuate old interests and create powerful new interests dependent upon the use of trade sanctions for protection. A key element in this strategy is the implementation of the 'Precautionary Principle'.

The Precautionary Principle

The EU has stated that it wants to see a wider application of the Precautionary Principle (by this it means its version, recalling that there is no agreed version of 'the' principle).[23] As noted above in the context of the Biosafety Protocol, the Precautionary Principle (PP) enables the imposition of essentially arbitrary restrictions on economic activity. In the context of trade, the Precautionary Principle is antithetical to the science-based, rule-driven system of the WTO.

The impact of wide application of the PP by the EU can be seen by considering what might happen to GMOs. The EU could use the PP to deny access of GMO products to the open, global international trading system. Trade in GMOs would then always be subject to case-by-case approvals for imports. Within a couple of decades, most food products are likely to have GMO variants or contain GMO elements.

If the EU gets its way, international markets in foodstuffs will be highly regulated and access to the EU will be heavily restricted. The benefits of GMOs will be denied to EU consumers and producers. Worse, food producers outside the EU will be less likely to adopt GMOs because of the costs of obtaining access to the EU. This will reduce returns on investment in GMOs, slowing down their development. The knock-on effects for those in developing countries – where the potential benefits from GMOs in terms of increased yields and ability to withstand extreme conditions are likely to be highest – would be severe.

More general application of the Precautionary Principle would slow the development of a whole slew of technologies, from lifesaving drugs to more fuel-efficient automobiles, with adverse consequences for pretty much everyone (even the environmentalists pushing for the use of the PP).

Basing regulation on the Precautionary Principle requires officials to be invested with executive powers. This is because the version of the Principle favoured by the EU is not based on technical or scientific standards – it is essentially an excuse for arbitrary intervention. So it can only be administered by officials through the political exercise of executive discretion. Indeed, EU officials have praised the fact that they are able to use the Precautionary Principle as a means of over-ruling the advice of their scientific committees in order to ban substances that are of clear benefit to commerce and consumers, and have not been shown to cause any harm.

Integrated Product Policy
In the lead up to Doha, EU officials also indicated that they wanted WTO rules to be altered so that trade can be restricted on the basis of the environmental impact of the way in which products are produced and processed. In March 2000, the EU issued a paper on 'Integrated Product Policy' (IPP). This reported the intention of the European Commission to apply regulations for whole-of-life cycle product management across the EU. It referred to a draft directive that was being developed as a model. This is the Directive on the Disposal of Waste Electronic and Electrical Equipment (WEEE), which in turn is based on the 1994 Directive on Packaging and Packaging Waste. Under the WEEE Directive, every producer and major importer of every electrical and electronic product would be responsible for disposal and recycling of the product at the end of its product life.[24]

The proposal is of course economic lunacy. (The Packaging and

Packaging Waste Directive, which set in place a similar scheme for the collection and recycling of waste packaging, costs EU consumers billions of dollars per year.) It is also essentially unworkable because – even more than for packaged goods – a large proportion of electrical goods are imported from outside the EU. That means the only way it would have any chance of working would be if imports were subject to the same cost burdens as domestically produced products. One effect of this policy is clear: the EU will diminish the global competitiveness of every industry regulated in this way. This is – in part – why the EU wants to amend the WTO rules to permit government-mandated 'eco-labels'.

The eco-label will be the certification that whole-of-life cycle regulations are being followed.[25] As well as verifying that manufacturers have committed to dispose of the product, there will be related or companion obligations to meet, in various ways, the costs of all the perceived polluting impacts of the production and use of the product. To ensure that imported products, which do not have to bear the extra cost of whole-of-life cycle management, do not have a cost advantage in the market over domestic products, the imported product will not be allowed to be sold unless it qualifies for the eco-label.

Whilst voluntary eco-labels are permissible under WTO rules, mandatory eco-labels of this sort almost certainly would not be. The EU therefore wants a change to WTO rules to enable it to mandate that products be eco-labelled. This would undermine the generally accepted WTO principle that trade restrictions based on production and process methods are not permissible. If the WTO gets into the business of ruling on how a product is made, this would be a slippery slope indeed. Labour rights, animal rights, religious freedom, women's rights, any number of the elements of what is perceived to constitute comparative advantage in any economy, can be picked out to justify denial of entry of a product into a market. However the recent decision in the trade dispute over US sanctions against imports of shrimp raises the possibility that in some circumstances trade might be controlled on such grounds (see below).

This goes to the heart of how the WTO succeeds. Trade between people in different countries occurs for a number of reasons, including the perceived quality of the goods produced in specific places. But a fundamental driver of much international trade is the principle of comparative advantage – that relative costs of production vary from country to country. Trade agreements work best when the rules are primarily focused on liberalising access to markets. If countries want to improve the environment (or any other sphere of activity, such as respect for human rights, or compliance with labour standards) through international action, they should do so by negotiating policies and measures to that end, in a purpose-built international agreement through which each member commits to apply those measures in national law. If multilateral trade laws are used to enforce non-trade purposes, their capacity to serve their trade end and to benefit the common good is lost. (This may not apply to issues that are primarily trade-related, such as international trade in knowledge-based products, where there are potentially large externalities from the trade itself.)

The well-established position is that the WTO cannot get into the business of ruling on the legitimacy of how a product is made. In the first place, it does not have the technical competence to deal with non-trade issues, as shown by its handling of the *Shrimp–Turtle* trade dispute (see below). Second, if it did get into this business, it would become the focus of every political, religious or ideological interest group within the metropolitan powers. Any of the rights of the various interest groups would become issues used to justify denial of entry of a product into a market. International trade would become, as it was in the interwar period, highly politicised. In such a situation, commercial interests would be quick to use the cover of the environment, labour rights or religious freedom in order to secure protection against imports, and those commercial interests would be prepared to provide financial support for these causes. Just such an alliance was manifest in the campaigns within the United States, against the WTO, which preceded the Seattle Ministerial meeting in December 1999 and culminated in massive street demonstrations.[26]

The strategic implications of EU policy

If the EU secured the principle that the trade provisions of MEAs were legitimate instruments that the WTO should sanctify, it could then set about creating new MEAs to lay down its preferred environmental standards. It could propose an MEA on application of the Precautionary Principle. It could propose an MEA on eco-labelling and whole-of-life cycle product management. It could, more generally, argue that actions taken by countries to protect the environment warrant trade restrictions to enforce them and that, as a matter of principle, the WTO should respect such restrictions.

There is already a major new multilateral environment agreement that the EU might seek to legitimise in this way. It is the Kyoto Protocol to the UN Framework Convention on Climate Change. Parties listed in Annex B of the Protocol – most are industrialised economies – are required to reduce emissions of greenhouses gases, particularly carbon dioxide, by an average of 5% below 1990 levels by 2008–12. To achieve the targets, industrialised economies will have to impose taxes on energy consumption, particularly of carbon-based fuels. This will significantly reduce their competitiveness compared with countries that do not increase their energy costs in this way. The cost impact of 'whole-of-life cycle' management is likely to be very low in comparison.

According to the Kyoto Protocol, developing countries are not obliged to reduce emissions. The United States has said it will not accept the Protocol if developing countries do not have comparable obligations.

A recent study indicated that the costs of complying with Kyoto to European economies could be huge. The UK and Germany in particular might face reductions in GDP of up to 5% by 2010.[27] It is hard to believe that the EU, disadvantaged by self-imposed carbon taxes, would not invoke a right to restrict trade on environmental grounds to protect itself against the competitive advantage of industries in the United States and other countries not so burdened by high energy costs – there will certainly be strong pressure from European business on the EU to do so. If the EU will contemplate using trade leverage through eco-labelling, which mandates adherence to its preferred methods of production and processing, why would it not tie access to its markets to requirements that developing countries adopt the CO_2 emission reduction programmes which it applies at home?

The acceptance, therefore, by the trade ministers at Doha of the EU's demand to include the environment in the negotiating round is a significant breakthrough by the EU in a long-term campaign to secure new rights to use trade sanctions to achieve environmental and other non-trade objectives, including the protection of European industry and agriculture from international competition.

Shrimp–Turtle

The EU did not get all that it wanted at Doha, but conclusion in October of the *Shrimp–Turtle* dispute creates some of the grounds to use trade sanctions to enforce environmental standards that the EU has been seeking.

Shrimp–Turtle began in 1996, when India, Pakistan, Malaysia and Thailand launched a case against a trade ban imposed by the United States on shrimp imported from Thailand on the grounds that its shrimp boats did not use the Turtle Excluder Devices (TEDs) mandated by US legislation on American shrimp trawlers. The initial Disputes Panel which considered Thailand's complaint against the US import ban ruled that the US measures were so much at odds with WTO principles – it described them as a threat to the multilateral trading system – that they should be disallowed. The United States appealed and the Appellate Body over-ruled the Panel, arguing that the measures were legitimate and important environmental objectives, justified because they related to national measures to conserve exhaustible natural resources, as described in Article XX(g) of the GATT.

The Appellate Body made no case that the circumstances that the United States faced were extreme, and ignored the widely recognised and fundamental principle that countries have a sovereign right to determine their domestic policies and not be coerced through the threat of trade sanctions. The Appellate Body deliberately elected not to address whether or not the United States was entitled to assert extraterritorial reach when invoking the terms of Article XX. The United States was clear about this. It was banning shrimp imports in order to force other countries which did not use Turtle Excluder Devices when they fished for shrimp to do so, in accordance with the requirements that the United States imposed on US shrimp boats.

By remaining silent on this point, the Appellate Body has opened up the possibility that WTO members may impose production and processing methods in the jurisdiction of other countries. This has far-reaching implications. Until *Shrimp–Turtle*, the vast majority of WTO members would have refused to accept there was any right to assert jurisdiction under Article XX in the territory of another member. Although the WTO does not officially follow precedent, the Dispute Panel and Appellate Body regularly refer to earlier cases in justifying their decisions. It is possible that the aberrant *Shrimp–Turtle* decision will therefore influence future decisions. The implications of this for world trade could be dramatic. Economically powerful countries now have grounds to impose their political will with trade sanctions upon countries which are economically dependent on uninterrupted access to their markets.

Ruling on environment policy, poorly

In *Shrimp–Turtle* the WTO Dispute Panel and the Appellate Body assumed the competence to assess the environmental importance and effectiveness of the US measures.[28] In so doing they demonstrated incapacity in understanding and lack of expertise in handling technical material. The terms of Article XX(g), with which they justified the US measures, addressed conservation. They declared that the international community had agreed (in CITES) that migratory turtles were in danger of extinction, but they did not demonstrate that the US measures would be effective conservation measures. They judged the US measures for their preservation value (would it save turtle lives?), not their conservation value (would it conserve the species?).

The scientific evidence before the Panel supported the preservation value of the US measures, but did not concur on the conservation value. There was significant evidence that the measures might have little conservation impact, since restricting trade in shrimp from the complainant countries (Thailand, Malaysia and the Philippines) would have little effect. The United States was not a significant shrimp export market for them. There was no conclusive evidence that forcing the Asian countries to reduce the incidental kill of turtles in their waters had a related impact on the conservation of turtles in US waters. There was no agreement among experts that turtles in US waters migrated regularly to the waters of the complainants. Neither the Panel nor the Appellate Body sought to define 'sustainable development', the term in the preamble to the WTO Agreement to which they pointed as a relevant objective for US measures invoked under Article XX. The meaning of the term 'sustainable development' is in fact strongly contested. Some argue that it is synonymous with preserving the environment, regardless of other considerations. Others maintain that it means balancing conservation with economic development. The Appellate Body's findings suggest the former meaning was the one employed by the Panel, and this is a significant point. In determining, as it did, that the sustainable development objective is the preferred trade objective, this approach meant that a different outcome was achieved than if sustainable development had been understood to mean a balanced pursuit of environment and economic goals.

The Appellate Body quoted extensively from the 1992 UN Conference on Environment and Development and the WTO Committee on Trade and Environment to demonstrate that sustainable development was endorsed by the international community as a legitimate goal, but ignored the leading conclusions of both bodies that trade measures should not (except as a last resort) be used for environmental management. Article XII of the Rio Declaration explicitly states that 'Unilateral actions to deal with environmental challenges outside the jurisdiction of the importing country should be avoided'.[29] This was ignored. The Rio principles on trade and environment allowed the possibility of unilateral action, but effectively categorise this as a last resort. The Appellate Body did not consider whether the US measures could be so characterised. In fact, on the basis of the evidence before the Panel it plainly was not a last resort. US law mandated a wide series of alternative activities to preserve turtles.

Having elected to decide if the US measures were necessary to conserve the environment by examining the environmental impacts of the US policies, the Appellate Body (and the Panel to some extent as well) demonstrated that it did not have the technical competence to address this question. This result is extremely serious. The Appellate Body has placed the WTO in the business of determining environmental policy for the members of the WTO, despite the repeated refusal of the membership, confirmed by Ministers in 1996, to entertain any such outcome. Aside from the fact they have demonstrated plainly that the WTO system is not capable of working competently on that subject, it has set a worrying precedent for any future decisions by the WTO disputes system when it is next asked, as it assuredly will be, to assess the propriety, the necessity and the effectiveness of any policy measure, not according to its legitimacy in relation to the international trade responsibilities of the WTO, but within its own particular policy parameters.

Ignoring policy preferences of WTO members
The most striking thing about the disputes process rulings in the *Shrimp–Turtle* case is that the Appellate Body interpreted the WTO rules in such a way that ignored positions and principles that member states of the WTO had consciously considered and rejected in WTO fora. *Shrimp–Turtle* is a revolution in WTO jurisprudence. WTO members have renounced unilateral trade sanctions, and commended multilateral conventions without discriminatory trade provisions as the preferred instrument for multilateral measures to advance international objectives concerning trade and the environment. They have rejected suggestions that trade should be restricted on the basis of the methods of production and processing. Their governments at Head of Government level at the UN Conference on Environment and Development firmly stated that unilateral trade

restrictions with extraterritorial reach should be avoided, and that respect for national sovereignty should be the fundamental guiding principle in international endeavours to improve the environment.[30] The Appellate Body has taken upon itself to determine that, through WTO provisions which have not been so interpreted for half a century, members of the WTO meant otherwise.

The Appellate Body ruling also lays grounds for the EU to restrict imports from the United States and other countries for not restricting CO_2 emissions according to the Kyoto Protocol.

Conclusions

If all multilateral environmental agreements were unambiguously beneficial to mankind – or merely unambiguously beneficial to the environment – it would be difficult to object to the clarification of the rules of the WTO that the EU is seeking. But the reality is that not all MEAs are unambiguously beneficial either to mankind or the environment. Indeed, there is a considerable body of work indicating that most MEAs are at best inefficient means to achieve environmental objectives and at worst actually harmful both to man and the environment. MEAs that contain trade sanctions seem to be particularly ineffective, inefficient and even counterproductive.

The result, therefore, of such a 'clarification' of the WTO rules would be to weaken the pro-trade, rule-based system of international trade governed by the WTO, all in the pursuit of poor environment policy. This is bad news for business and the global economy. It is bad news for developing countries and it is bad news for the environment.

The EU's agenda reflects the disposition in the EU's institutions (the Commission, the Council and the Parliament) towards centralised command and control, rather than free-market policies and the subsidiarity principle, as the means of improving the environment. The EU also uses environmental policy as a means of imposing costs on foreign producers, who have no formal representation in the EU. Such policies inevitably impact on trade and WTO rules threaten to impede their use. This is why both the EU and leading environmental NGOs want the WTO rules to be changed.

The greater efficiency of the subsidiarity principle and of encouraging free-market forces to serve public policy interests applies to environment policy as much as to any other area. It is why the free-market systems of the West increased prosperity and raised social and environmental standards, while the command and control of the communist systems destroyed both physical and social capital and degraded the environment.

Environment officials have a choice. It has been repeatedly demonstrated that trade sanctions make for poor environment policy. The approach preferred by the international community for international action to improve the environment, endorsed by Ministers at the 1992 UN Rio Summit on Environment and Development, is to seek international agreement among governments to take common action, negotiate international agreements, and implement the commitments in national law. This approach respects the national sovereignty of each government, so that the merits of individual agreements are subject to the democratic processes in each member state. The Rio Summit of 1992 specifically abjured the use of trade sanctions as enforcement mechanisms in MEAs.[31]

The trade and environment issue must now be put back on track. Respect for national sovereignty must be restored as a key principle underpinning the WTO rules. Use of trade sanctions to secure extraterritorial compliance with national environment standards must be rejected as fundamentally contrary to the *modus operandi* of the WTO.

If this does not occur, global markets will be divided, with new instruments applied for protectionist purposes, and environment policies will be developed which are intended as much to punish business as to improve the environment. Increasingly poor and ineffective environment policy will be the result. The opportunity presented by the Doha Development Round of multilateral trade negotiations to deliver the benefits of greater prosperity to the developing world will be severely undermined.

Part Four

Climate Change and Energy

9 A climate of uncertainty in the greenhouse century

Robert C. Balling Jr

The climate of the Earth has always been in a state of change, ranging from long periods when the planet was nearly covered by ice to warm periods with no ice caps whatsoever. Millions of years ago, the dinosaurs roamed an Earth nearly devoid of ice and snow, while only a few thousands of years ago, woolly mammoths ranged across a North American continent, half of which was covered by a mile of ice. These natural ebbs and flows in the global climate system are closely tied to variations in the Earth's orbit around the Sun, changes in the output of the Sun, periods of unusually high or low volcanic activity, and/or substantial changes in oceanic circulation.

We know about these natural climate variations from research on ice cores, tree rings, ancient pollen spores and fossil records, all of which tell us the same story: Climate is highly variable, climate can change rapidly, and we should not expect the climate of our day to persist over long periods of time. Research also tells us that climate change has occurred many times on a grand scale during the history of the Earth without any interference from human activities.

Despite this rich understanding of the climate history over the past five billion years of Earth's existence, we have recently witnessed the emergence of global climate change as one of the pre-eminent environmental issues of the day. The 9 April 2001 issue of *Time* magazine contained a cover story about global warming, and the final page of the issue was a letter to US President Bush signed by Jimmy Carter, John Glenn, George Soros, Jane Goodall, Harrison Ford, Mikhail Gorbachev, Walter Cronkite, J. Craig Venter, Edward O. Wilson and Stephen Hawking, stating in the first sentence that 'No challenge we face is more momentous than the threat of global climate change.' Up

until 11 September 2001 this viewpoint was shared by many environmentalists and policymakers, and despite the more immediate and serious threat posed by terrorism, the global warming 'threat' is still
very much in the minds of scientists and policymakers around the
world.

The invention of the global warming scare

The global warming issue had been smouldering in climatology for
nearly a century, but in a matter of a few months in 1988 it went from
the stacks in the science library to front-page news throughout the
world. During the late spring and early summer of 1988, much of the
United States was suffering through an exceptional drought and stifling heat. On 23 June of that year, Dr James Hansen, then director of
NASA's Goddard Institute for Space Studies, told a US Senate hearing
on climate change that the world was warmer than at any time in the
instrumental period (the past 150 or so years) and that at least some
part of the warming was related to the build-up of greenhouse gases.
In a much repeated and often misunderstood phrase, Hansen told the
committee that he was '99 percent certain' that observed increase in
global temperature was related to a global greenhouse effect enhanced
by a variety of human activities, most notably the burning of fossil
fuels.

Global warming was a leading news story for many months in
1988, fuelled only further by September's wildfires in Yellowstone
Park (and throughout the western United States) and Hurricane
Gilbert's devastation from the Yucatán to Texas. Throw in a few other
calamities from other parts of the world, including a record-breaking
windstorm in southern England, and by the end of 1988 the global
warming scare had shifted into a high gear.

Acting in response to this scare, the UN quickly formed an 'Intergovernmental Panel on Climate Change' (IPCC). Soon-to-be US Vice
President Al Gore took a leadership role in the global warming cru-
sade (even publishing *Earth in the Balance* in 1992). Practically every
environmental group on the planet climbed on board the global
warming bandwagon. The media took any unusual weather event as
convincing evidence of global warming, and on it went.

Momentum for the global warming scare became so great over
such a short period of time that the ongoing debate regarding many
key scientific questions and uncertainties was nearly squashed by the
calls to 'do something' about the problem. This momentum would re-

ceive a boost each January, as we learnt that the previous year had been one of the warmest, if not *the* warmest, year on record. That momentum, quite unlike anything seen for any other environmental issue, continues to drive the global warming scare into the 21st century. And while the tragic events of 11 September 2001 may have deflated the importance of the perceived global warming crisis, countries throughout the world continue to push global warming as a centrepiece environmental issue.

The global warming debate entered the new millennium with many scientists and policymakers worldwide believing that without a substantial slow-down or reduction in the consumption of fossil fuels, we will soon witness a significant increase in planetary temperature, a rise in sea level, the melting of icecaps and alpine glaciers, and an increase in droughts, floods and severe storms.

But while some folks see a global warming apocalypse over the horizon, other scientists do not believe that warming is inevitable or that policy actions would significantly impact variations and trends in the global climate system. Furthermore, literally thousands of experiments have been conducted throughout the world which show that elevated levels of atmospheric carbon dioxide (CO_2) cause virtually all plants to increase their photosynthetic rates, water-use efficiency and resistance to drought and other stresses. The spectrum of opinion runs from seeing CO_2 as a curse threatening the climate system at one end to hailing it as an inadvertent blessing from the Industrial Revolution at the other. The 'heated debate' is likely to go on for many years and uncovering the fact amidst the fiction in such a complicated scientific, political, economic and social area is a major challenge in itself.

How reliable are predictions of climate change?

The concentration of atmospheric CO_2 has increased from around 280 ppmv (parts per million by volume) at the beginning of the Industrial Revolution to approximately 370 ppmv in 2001, and the consumption of fossil fuels appears to be the largest contributor to this upward trend. At present, approximately 20% of CO_2 emission comes from the United States, leading to the popular observation that a relatively small number of people (approximately 5% of the global population) contribute disproportionately to the build-up of CO_2. But in the first few decades of this new century CO_2 emissions from developing countries are expected to rise substantially, thereby lowering the proportion of global emissions emanating from the United States (the United States accounted for nearly half of global fossil-fuel CO_2 emissions in the late 1940s). Humans are currently adding over six billion tons of carbon to the atmosphere each year, thereby overwhelming the climate's carbon budgeting system and allowing the atmospheric CO_2 concentration to increase on a global scale.

Other human activities release assorted gases into the atmosphere which also have the ability to trap heat energy that would otherwise escape into space. These other greenhouse gases include methane, nitrous oxide, and various chlorofluorocarbons, and each of these gases has its own unique geography of emissions. For example, rice paddy agriculture in southeastern Asia is a leading contributor to the global increase in methane. Humans are engaged in activities throughout the world that slightly alter the composition of the global atmosphere; however, even these relatively small changes to the gaseous mixture we call air can produce substantial changes to the climate.

For more than a hundred years, climate scientists have calculated that a doubling of the concentration of these many greenhouse gases (expressed as CO_2 equivalents) would raise the planetary temperature by up to 6°C (10.8°F). The naturally occurring greenhouse gases (water vapour is by far the most important of these) act as a thermal blanket and maintain a mean atmospheric temperature 30°C (86°F) to 35°C (95°F) above the planetary temperature we would experience in the absence of these critical gases. The CO_2 and other greenhouse gases increase in atmospheric concentration and absorb heat energy (infra-red radiation) given off by the surface of the Earth. The addition of these greenhouse gases alone should warm the Earth, but a water-vapour feedback mechanism nearly triples the overall warming effect. Basically, as the planetary temperature rises in response to higher concentrations of greenhouse gases, more water is evaporated into the atmosphere, and the increased concentration of water vapour drives the global temperature further upward.

Today, sophisticated global climate models, which are giant computer programs designed to simulate the laws of physics that control the atmosphere, continue to show that a doubling of greenhouse gas concentrations would force the global temperature to rise from between 1°C (1.8°F) to as much as 6°C (10.8°F). Furthermore, these models predict that a warmer world will have an invigorated hydrological cycle leading to an increase in precipitation at most locations across the globe.

There is no doubt that the prediction for higher global temperatures and precipitation levels, given higher concentrations of greenhouse gases, is solidly grounded in the underlying physics that govern the climate system. These are fairly basic principles in the atmospheric sciences that have been known for over a century. Moreover, the prediction for warming comes from numerical climate models developed in major research laboratories in many nations, employing hundreds of the world's leading atmospheric scientists.

But the prediction is not without significant uncertainties. Climate models poorly represent cloud processes that could be critical in determining the overall energy balance of the Earth-atmosphere system. Additional high cloud cover in response to global warming would create a positive feedback effect, leading to even higher temperatures. However, any increase in low cloud cover would act to cool the Earth, putting a natural brake on the greenhouse effect. Today's models are not able to resolve critical questions regarding how the global cloud patterns will respond to higher temperatures, and as a result it is difficult to make predictions for future temperature increases with any great confidence.

When the cloud patterns are not well modelled, then neither are the precipitation patterns, which in turn produce problems for the accuracy of the simulated surface hydrology. And without an adequate representation of soil moisture patterns, the models cannot accurately predict the surface energy balance, including the calculation of the near-surface air temperatures. Furthermore, a shortcoming of numerical climate models is that they fail accurately to account for the relationship between the ocean and the atmosphere, which is especially critical for a planet on which land cover is less than 30% of the total global surface area. The numerical models also poorly simulate snow and ice processes, have poor, if any, biological routines, and often require significant flux adjustments (fudge factors) to keep from drifting into unrealistic climate states. One of the greatest uncertainties in model construction is the representation of water vapour levels in the middle atmosphere in the subtropical latitudes. These are known to be critical in maintaining the radiation balance of the planet.

Despite these many uncertainties, the models are fabulous achievements in the atmospheric and computing sciences, and their prediction for global warming, given a build-up of greenhouse gases, should not be taken lightly. The exact amount of warming that will occur as a result of mankind's emissions of greenhouse gases remains unknown but current models, along with those simpler models that have been used for over a century, universally show some level of global warming.

Figure 12 **Thermometer-based annual global temperature anomalies, 1900–2001[1]**

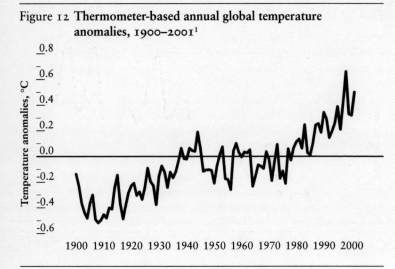

Observed climate changes

Given the long-standing prediction for global warming with increasing concentrations of greenhouse gases, it is logical for empirical scientists to examine the temperature record of the Earth to determine if warming has in fact occurred during the period of greenhouse gas build-up. Thermometer-based temperature records from land and sea have been assembled for as much of the Earth as possible,[2] and, indeed, the record shows a linear warming of 0.68°C (1.22°F) over the period 1900–2001. Furthermore, the warming has accelerated in recent decades (Figure 12).

Scientists have noted that warming has occurred in most areas of the world, with the greatest warming occurring in high-latitude land areas of the northern hemisphere, in winter, and at night.[3] While interpretations vary on how to assemble these records and calculate the global temperature, the inescapable fact emerges that the thermometer-based near-surface air temperature record shows statistically significant warming over the past century, with the warmest years occurring in the most recent decades. At first glance, the warming anticipated from model simulations is similarly reflected by the historical temperature record from thermometers around the world. Analyses of global precipitation patterns are far less certain, although some evidence certainly exists to suggest a slight increase in global precipitation over the past century.

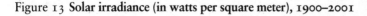

Figure 13 **Solar irradiance (in watts per square meter), 1900–2001**

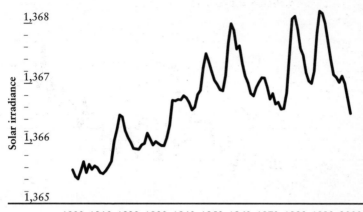

Attributing the observed surface warming to changes in atmospheric chemistry is compounded by many factors. First, as noted earlier, the climate system fluctuates naturally, even without any external forcing, and the observed warming is not outside the bounds of natural fluctuations seen repeatedly in the long-term reconstructions of the global temperature. Also, much of the Earth experienced a 'Little Ice Age' from approximately AD 1450 to AD 1850, and the recent warming may be nothing more than a natural recovery from this unusually cool period.

Second, the irradiance from the Sun has varied through the past century with a distinctive upward trend (Figure 13) from 1900 to 1960. Many scientists believe that much of the observed warming prior to the 1970s can be ascribed to increasing output from the Sun and not to the build-up of greenhouse gases.[4] A more careful inspection of the near-surface global air temperatures (Figure 12) reveals substantial warming from 1910 to 1940, and that warming coincides nicely with the increasing output of the Sun.

Third, volcanic eruptions and the El Niño/Southern Oscillation (ENSO) patterns exert significant influence on the climate system, producing a non-greenhouse forcing on planetary temperature. The periodic disruption to global temperature caused by volcanoes and ENSO complicates any search for the greenhouse 'fingerprint' in the records.

Fourth, the thermometer measurements themselves are compromised by local influences (e.g., urban effects), the uneven distribution of the thermometer network, and changes through time in instrumentation and recording practices. We have few, if any, actual temperature records from huge parts of the planet, including much of the South Pacific. Nonetheless, and despite an endless number of criticisms of the thermometer-based near-surface air temperature record, there is compelling evidence that the global temperature has increased on a planetary scale over the past century, and the warming near the surface has accelerated in recent decades.

With the models predicting warming, consequent on a build-up of greenhouse gases, and thermometer-based records of the world also showing warming, it would seem that any debate on the global warming subject would be one-sided. However, global temperature measurements made from space call into question the recent planetary warming seen in the thermometer records.[5] Sounding units aboard polar-orbiting satellites measure microwave emissions from the low atmosphere that are directly related to the temperature of the atmosphere from approximately 1,500m (4,947ft) to 8,500m (28,024ft). The polar orbits provide true global coverage as the Earth rotates underneath the satellites that carry the measuring devices. Unlike the near-surface air temperature record that shows warming over the past few decades (Figure 12), the satellite-based observations show no warming whatsoever from 1979 to 2001 (Figure 14), in spite of the very warm El Niño year of 1998. The thermometer-based record and the satellite-based record are well correlated, showing that their annual measurements are similar, but over time the surface record has a significant upward trend while the satellite record has no trend whatsoever.

Obviously, scientists and policymakers want to know which of these two trends is correct, and are therefore searching for other means of estimating global temperature. Twice a day at hundreds of locations around the world balloons are launched through the atmosphere to measure vertical profiles of temperature, wind and moisture. When the balloon-based measurements are averaged globally for the same 1,500-m to 8,500-m layer measured by the satellites, the two records are nearly identical in terms of variations and overall linear trend (both show no warming from 1979 to the near present). This finding leads to an argument that the Earth is simply not warming, despite the trend seen in the near-surface thermometer record. However, measurements from these same balloons made close to the ground are similar to the thermometer-based temperatures, and show approxi-

Figure 14 **Satellite-based monthly global temperature anomalies,
January 1979–November 2001**

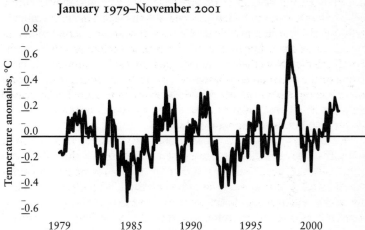

mately the same upward trend. This dilemma has been the focus of
many scientific articles and reviews, and most scientists now agree
that the surface *has* been warming over the past few decades, but that
the low atmosphere is not warming at all.[6]

These differently derived temperature trends represent anything
but a 'draw' in the greenhouse debate. The numerical models of climate used to simulate the response to higher concentrations of greenhouse gases suggest that the low atmosphere should be warming faster
than the surface, and that is clearly not the case. The observed temperature trends – warming at the surface and no warming in the low
atmosphere – are simply not consistent with model expectations,
given the build-up of greenhouse gases. Volcanic activity, El Niño
events, and even instrumentation changes have all been suggested as
causes for the differential warming between the surface and the lower
atmosphere, but the answer to this critical matter remains elusive and
a major focus of scientific inquiry.

While climatologists have struggled in their attempts directly to
link any trends in global temperatures with the build-up of greenhouse gases, other patterns in the climate system have been even more
difficult to reconcile.

Precipitation levels are generally increasing in most parts of the
world, and the pattern is broadly consistent with the predictions from

the numerical models.[7] In the United States and Australia, there is some evidence that heavy precipitation has increased slightly, but the pattern has not been verified in other areas studied to date. Droughts continue to plague different parts of the Earth each year, but most scientists are unwilling to attribute drought patterns to changes in greenhouse gas concentration.

Analyses of tropical cyclones, mid-latitude cyclones and/or tornado activity have generally led to the conclusion that no discernible trends in these events are apparent in the historical records. The most recent UN Intergovernmental Panel on Climate Change report concludes that 'No systematic changes in the frequency of tornadoes, thunder days, or hail events are evident in the limited areas analysed' and that 'changes globally in tropical and extra-tropical storm intensity and frequency are dominated by inter-decadal and multi-decadal variations, with no significant trends evident over the 20th century'.[8]

These conclusions from the scientific community fly in the face of the popularised visions of the greenhouse world that inevitably include images of more severe storms and increased climate variability in the coming decades.

Observed changes in climate over the past few decades include (a) warming at the surface particularly at night, in mid-to-high latitudes over land, and during the winter; (b) no warming in the lower troposphere on a global scale; (c) a general increase in precipitation; and (d) no change in extreme events or climate variability. Whatever changes have occurred fall well within the natural variability of the climate system and are difficult to ascribe to the increase in greenhouse gas concentrations.

Some of the changes are broadly consistent with numerical climate model predictions for a build-up of greenhouse gases, others are not. The lack of warming in the lower troposphere, as measured by satellites and balloons, remains as a major contradiction to expectations from the model simulations, and will likely be the focus of intense research over the next decade.

Complicating effects

The inability clearly to isolate global or regional climate signals related to the build-up of greenhouse gases is further compounded by other anthropogenic forcings of the climate system. Burning fossil fuel undoubtedly produces CO_2 that collects in the global atmosphere, but it also produces sulphur dioxide (SO_2). The SO_2 enters the atmosphere and quickly transforms to sulphate aerosols that have a wide-spread cooling effect by: (a) reflecting incoming sunlight back to space; (b) brightening clouds; and (c) making clouds last longer. Unlike CO_2, which mixes fairly evenly throughout the entire atmosphere, the sulphur aerosols are short-lived in the atmosphere, thereby producing a regional pattern of high concentrations near major industrial emission sources and low concentrations throughout the rest of the world. This regional structure complicates the ability to model correctly the thermal effects of the sulphur load in the atmosphere. But to date all models show a cooling in areas of elevated sulphur concentrations, though they differ in terms of the magnitude of the cooling.

Humans have degraded drylands throughout the arid and semi-arid portions of all major land masses, and this degradation has resulted in an increase in mineral aerosols in many parts of the world. This appears to have a cooling effect that may be important at the global scale, although significant uncertainties remain as to the magnitude of this cooling. Also, various chlorofluorocarbons deplete ozone in the high atmosphere, which results in a significant cooling at the surface. Again, uncertainties abound in terms of the magnitude of this cooling.

Fossil fuel soot, biomass burning, changes in surface reflectivity caused by land-use patterns, and contrails from high-flying aircraft are all considerations in 'predicting' future climate, and yet to date the scale of these effects on the climate system remain unknown and vary considerably from model to model.

Noted climate modeller James Hansen (the same fellow who was '99% certain' in 1988) and colleagues concluded that 'The forcings that drive long-term climate change are not known with an accuracy sufficient to define future climate change.'[9] Hansen suggests that even with perfect models and perfect data, climatologists would continue to struggle in an attempt to 'predict' climate changes for the next century, given the uncertainties regarding the forcings of climate that will be operating 50 to 100 years from now. Overall, the models definitely predict warming in the years to come, but one must appreciate the many uncertainties associated with the prediction.

Hopeless policy

Uncertainties regarding the future of the Earth's climate will remain for many decades to come. Given these uncertainties, many scientists and policymakers believe that we should cut back on greenhouse gas emissions and avoid conducting an unknown and largely irreversible experiment on the global atmosphere.

The argument that we have only one atmosphere and should there-fore avoid making substantial changes to its composition that may significantly alter the 'normal' climate system is certainly a compelling one. To that end, the governments of many nations have expressed their grave concern over the threat of global warming and have signed (but not necessarily ratified) the Kyoto Protocol. The Protocol in essence requires that the world return to a level of anthropogenic emission of greenhouse gases equivalent to such emissions in 1990, with the bulk of the reduction coming from the developed nations that have been large emitters for many decades.

Under Kyoto, the United States is required to reduce emissions to 7% below 1990 levels. However, US emissions of greenhouse gases are currently 13% above 1990 levels; emissions of CO_2 are rising quickly (due in no small part to the electrical demand of the Internet), and US President Bush has largely withdrawn from the Kyoto process. The concerns of the Bush administration include uncertainties regard-ing global warming science and the near-certain negative impact the Kyoto Protocol would have on the US economy. While greenhouse ad-vocates cry out that we cannot chance our only atmosphere to some global experiment on the effect of elevated greenhouse gas concentra-tions, opponents in the United States are unwilling to risk their only economy on the outcome of implementing the Kyoto Protocol.

One of the startling facts regarding the Kyoto Protocol is that its implementation with full participation would have a trivial impact on the climate system. The goal of the Protocol is to stabilise *emissions* of CO_2, not the atmospheric *concentration* of CO_2 (and of course the other greenhouse gases). Even if emissions could be stabilised at 1990 levels, six billion tons of carbon would be added to the atmosphere an-nually by human activities. That carbon would build up in the atmos-phere and a doubling of CO_2 would still occur near the middle of this century. If the Protocol went into effect today, and greenhouse gas emissions suddenly returned to their 1990 levels and remained at that level every year from now until 2050, the entire exercise would 'spare' the Earth only a few hundredths of a degree of warming. Similar ob-servations have been made by no less a figure than global warming protagonist Tom Wigley. Wigley, a major figure in greenhouse policy circles, is a senior scientist at the National Center for Atmospheric Re-search (NCAR) in Boulder, Colorado, director of NCAR's Consor-tium for the Application of Climate Impact Assessments, and was head of the Climate Research Unit in Norwich, England, which is responsible for assembling and analysing thermometer-based temperature records from throughout the world. Wigley carefully analysed the climate impact of the Kyoto Protocol and concluded that 'the influence of the Protocol would, therefore, be undetectable for many decades'.[10]

The fact that the Kyoto Protocol would have such a small climate impact is not altogether bad news in many circles. Leaders of the IPCC remind us that the Kyoto Protocol is a framework convention that will lead the way to future international agreements aimed at stabilising concentrations of greenhouse gases below 'dangerous' levels. Defining and defending a 'dangerous' concentration in this context may be the biggest fight in the greenhouse in the years to come.

Others, particularly those involved in the fossil fuel industry (especially those in the coal industries), may argue that the Kyoto Protocol will not impact climate, and that there is therefore no need to rush into any implementation that would hurt their enterprise or the economies that depend on their products. These same leaders might be quick to point out that James Hansen recently argued in the *Proceedings of the National Academy of Sciences* that 'rapid warming in recent decades has been driven mainly by non-CO_2 greenhouse gases (GHGs), such as chlorofluorocarbons, methane (CH_4), and dinitrogen monoxide (N_2O), not by the products of fossil fuel burning'.[11] Not only will the Kyoto Protocol have little climatic effect, but it may be firing at the wrong target.

Environmentalists are naturally drawn into the seductiveness of a potential global disaster brought about by the build-up of greenhouse gases emanating largely – at present – from the world's most developed nations. However, they also realise that policies aimed at substantially reducing greenhouse gas emissions are expensive and that these same policies will likely have a trivial impact on climate. We have only limited funds for environmental issues, and relatively simple cost/benefit analyses reveal that spending money on the global warming issue produces few, if any, benefits. Money targeted at global warming is not available for other environmental issues (often local issues) where real return on investment is far more certain.

The global warming 'crisis' dropped quickly from the radar screen of public concern during a few short minutes on the morning of 11 September 2001. But as time goes on, the global warming issue will again find a place in the public consciousness; the greenhouse momentum built up during the 1990s is simply too great for this environmental issue to suddenly vanish for good. Hopefully, cooler heads will prevail in the future, policymakers will base their decisions on climatic and economic facts, not hype and hysteria, and the complexities of the issue will replace the simplistic presentations which suggest that the planet is warming, greenhouse gases are increasing in concentration, and the two must be linked. As we have seen, there is much more to the story, and what might appear to be promising policy options may in fact be useless in impacting the global climate system. Stay tuned ... the greenhouse debate has taken some time off, but it will certainly be with us all in the years to come.

10 Energy for sustainable development

Robert L. Bradley Jr

E nergy from hydrocarbons (coal, oil, gas) has contributed hugely to the economic development of the world. But some argue that a hydrocarbon-based energy economy is inherently unsustainable and have called for extreme restrictions on the use of hydrocarbons, as well as the promotion of alternatives. How might the world move towards a more sustainable energy future? Would alternatives to hydrocarbons be more sustainable? The facts show that hydrocarbon energy is becoming ever more sustainable both economically and environmentally. This chapter presents these facts and then makes the case that the *real* energy sustainability issue is intervention by the state, which has entrapped 1.6 billion persons in energy poverty.

Energy: the master resource

Energy has been called the *master resource*. As Julian Simon explained,

> Energy is the master resource, because energy enables us to
> convert one material into another. As natural scientists continue to
> learn more about the transformation of materials from one form
> to another with the aid of energy, energy will be even more
> important. Therefore, if the cost of usable energy is low enough,
> all other important resources can be made plentiful.[1]

The modern energy era has contributed to the decline of child labour and slavery, the emancipation of women, industrialisation, and, ultimately, the deferral of death.[2] Going forward, the Brundtland Commission stated,

Energy is necessary for daily survival. Future development crucially depends on its long-term availability in increasing quantities from sources that are dependable, safe, and environmentally sound.[3]

Increasing use of affordable energy was considered an anathema in the earlier days of the modern environmental movement. 'Sustainability' once meant curtailing energy use to reduce the human imprint on the environment. 'Environmental deterioration and energy consumption go hand-in-hand,' argued Paul Ehrlich and Anne Ehrlich in 1974.[4] During this period, both the Ehrlichs and John Holdren argued for an energy transfer from developed to the underdeveloped nations, combined with fundamental lifestyle changes, to stretch scarce energy resources.[5] High taxes on hydrocarbon fuels, they argued, could be used to discourage consumption in developed countries and, at the same time, fund Third World growth.

Since then, however, developed countries have become even more dependent on modern, reliable energy. Electricity in the Internet age must be especially regular and dependable. New uses of electricity are increasing overall consumption even as efficiency gains reduce energy consumption per application. Consumers and voters consider higher energy prices a problem, not a means to a greater good.[6,7]

Even many mainstream environmentalists who question the sustainability of the modern hydrocarbon-based energy economy now acknowledge the benefits of affordable and plentiful energy for both sides of the economic divide. 'A reliable and affordable supply of energy,' John Holdren recently stated, 'is absolutely critical to maintaining and expanding economic prosperity where such prosperity already exists and to creating it where it does not.'[8] In their 1996 book *Betrayal of Science and Reason*, the Ehrlichs warned against 'taking action on the basis of worst-case prognoses' by imposing fuel rationing and high energy taxes.[9]

Tragically, most of the world's poorest people continue to be denied access to high-quality, low-cost energy. Wood and dung account for approximately 25% of domestic energy consumption in China, but in most of Asia (including India, the second most populous country in the world), the proportion is over 75%.[10] The situation in Africa is similar. Proponents of 'renewable' energy euphemistically refer to wood and dung as 'biomass' and suggest that these old technologies might be desirable alternatives to coal, oil, gas and electricity. In reality, primitive biomass is highly polluting,[11] inefficient, expensive[12] and toxic.[13]

Availability, flexibility and affordability

What sources of energy will be most available, affordable and flexible in the future? Pessimistic hyperbole aside, hydrocarbons (coal, oil and natural gas) are an *expanding*, not depleting, resource.[14] The world's proved reserves of crude oil are fifteen times greater today than they were when such oil statistics began to be recorded over a half century ago. World natural gas reserves are five times greater than they were in the mid-1960s. Coal reserves are four times greater than originally estimated half a century ago and twice as great as all of the known oil and gas reserves combined on an energy-equivalent basis.[15]

New members of the hydrocarbon family are being commercialised. In Venezuela, tar-like oil is being upgraded into a power plant feedstock called Orimulsion.[16] Estimated reserves of this so-called 'fourth fossil fuel' are greater than the global supply of crude oil on an energy-equivalent basis. New technology is also commercialising the vast quantities of oil sands of Alberta, Canada. In addition, drilling and refining innovations are enabling us to tap previously inaccessible or uneconomic reserves in remote onshore and offshore areas – all outside of the Middle East.[17]

Technology is also increasing the *flexibility* of hydrocarbons. Processes now exist to convert stranded (unmarketable) natural gas reserves into petrol and diesel for motor vehicles. While such resource substitution does not increase the aggregate supply of hydrocarbons, it does increase the amount that is economically recoverable. As the technology of hydrocarbon improvement and substitution develops, the *enhanced* hydrocarbon age may replace the hydrocarbon age as a new energy era later this century and even far beyond.

The hydrocarbon age is still young in physical terms. A working group of the Intergovernmental Panel on Climate Change (IPCC) calculated that total cumulative world consumption of hydrocarbons constituted only 1.4% of what is estimated to remain.

This abundance explains why energy economists have yet to see a 'depletion signal' nearly two centuries into the mineral-fuel age. One possible explanation, proposed by Thomas Gold, is that super-abundant hydrocarbons exist deep in the earth and are slowly seeping towards the drill bit.[18] A more conventional explanation is that the ultimate resources, human ingenuity and financial capital, are not depletable but expanding, and it is these resources that are driving the discovery of new reserves and new ways of extracting, processing and consuming current reserves of hydrocarbons.[19]

The increasing abundance of hydrocarbons has led to increasing affordability, whether measured in terms of inflation-adjusted prices or work-time pricing (the amount of time it takes the average labourer to purchase a unit of energy). Today, the average labourer in the United States can purchase both a tank of petrol and several days of residential electricity in about three hours of work time. In 1940, the same purchase of 15 gallons of petrol and 100 kilowatt-hours of electricity required ten hours of labour. But consumers have reason to desire still lower prices for the record quantities of energy they are now purchasing.[20]

Environmental quality

Much opposition to the modern hydrocarbon-based economy is driven by a belief that the extraction, processing, distribution and consumption of hydrocarbons are environmentally damaging. This opposition has focused on damage to air quality in particular, but hydrocarbons have other environmental impacts, including effects on agriculture and forestry.

Air quality

For centuries, the burning of wood and coal made cities across the world unpleasant places to live. Over the course of the past half-century, however, most major cities in developed countries have seen declining levels of air pollution.[21] This is especially true of cities where the major pollutants were smoke and sulphur dioxide. London now has lower levels of air pollution than at any time since the sixteenth century.[22] Factories and power stations have either moved out of the cities or switched to less polluting production processes. Domestic users have switched from wood and coal to natural gas and electricity as the primary sources of heat. This is not to say that air pollution from the burning of hydrocarbons has been eliminated, nor that it cannot be improved; low-level ozone and to a lesser extent carbon monoxide and soot (mostly from older diesel vehicles) remain problems in many cities. But the environmental impact of hydrocarbon consumption in developed countries is declining even while its use is increasing.

In developing countries, the story is somewhat different. There, urban air pollution is in many cases becoming worse. Industrialisation tends to result in an increase in pollution in the short term, followed by a reduction in pollution once a certain level of development is achieved – at average incomes of about $5,000 (1985 US dollars).[23,24]

But even this is misleading because it is based on measures of 'pollution' that apply in developed countries. Circumstances in developing countries are very different. The worst air pollution in the world results from burning dung, wood and coal in poorly flued domestic fires.[25] People in poor countries are often able to adopt less polluting technologies (such as more efficient stoves) at very low-income levels.[26] In this respect, it could be argued that environmental quality improves more or less linearly with improvements in income. However, the switch to more efficient wood stoves is only one step along the road to high-quality, low-pollution energy – and one that is hampered by certain cultural factors.[27] In this context, grid electricity, even from the dirtiest source – uncontrolled coal-fired plants – would probably be an environmental improvement for the 1.6 billion people currently denied this luxury.

Agriculture
Energy, and in particular hydrocarbon-derived energy, has contributed to agricultural intensification in many countries, enabling the production of chemical fertilisers and synthetic pesticides, as well as the mechanisation of agricultural processes (preparing, planting and harvesting crops; milking cattle; battery farming of chickens and pigs). In addition, it has enabled longer-term food storage (through large-scale processing, packaging and refrigeration), as well as the economical transportation of foods over long distances.[28]

The positive results from reliance on hydrocarbons include significant increases in yields (more than doubling for many cereal crops over the past century) and reductions in waste (as a result of better storage and transportation). Thus, more people are now fed using less land than would have been required without the use of hydrocarbon-derived energy. Despite the fact that the amount of cropland per capita has been almost halved, daily food supplies per capita (in Kcal/capita/day) have increased 23% from 1961 to 1997, and the real price of food commodities has declined 75% since 1950.[29] Thus, notwithstanding a 40% increase in population between the early 1970s and mid-1990s, the number of chronically malnourished people in developing countries dropped from 920 million to less than 800 million (or from 35% to 19% of their population) during the same period.[30]

The negative results of reliance on hydrocarbons have included: eutrophication of some streams and rivers as a result of excessive use of nitrogen fertilisers; reductions in some farmland species, including certain bird species; and land degradation (soil erosion, salinisation) in some poorly managed and sensitive areas. However, these negative consequences have been magnified by government subsidies (either for production or irrigation) and/or inappropriate systems of ownership[31] and are thus not directly attributable to energy use *per se*.

Notwithstanding the excessive conversion of land in Europe, the United States and elsewhere as a result of subsidies, the loss of farmland species must be balanced against the likely larger benefits of reduced conversion of wetland and forest that would have occurred had not fossil fuel use increased agricultural productivity.[32] High levels of shifting ('slash and burn') agriculture have a far more serious impact on biodiversity than more efficient sedentary agriculture.[33]

Had it not been for technological progress in the food and agricultural sector, feeding the world's population at 1961 productivity levels would have required an additional 1,040 million hectares (Mha) of cropland beyond the 1,510 Mha of cropland actually used in 1997.[34] Such progress also helped reverse centuries of deforestation in the richer nations.[35] Between 1980 and 1995, for instance, forest cover increased by about 20 Mha in the developed countries.[36]

Forestry, fuel-wood and biomass energy generation
As with agriculture, forestry has benefited from hydrocarbons and hydrocarbon energy in the form of fertiliser, pesticide, harvesting technologies, transport and processing. The result has been a significant increase in forestry yields and a partial shift in production from northern Europe and Canada to South America and South-east Asia, where costs of production are lower because the climate is better suited to rapid plant growth.

While the conversion of natural forest to plantation forest has in many cases had a negative impact on species diversity, the intensive forestry that is made possible by hydrocarbon-based energy reduces pressure on non-plantation forests by supplying higher levels of wood and wood fibre at lower cost.[37] If the same amount of wood were to be produced less intensively, the impact on biodiversity would be far more extreme.

As countries develop, the use of wood and dung for fuel tends to decline relative to coal, oil, gas and electricity (which is mostly produced using hydrocarbons, nuclear, or hydro), with significant environmental advantages in terms of reduced exposure to the toxic by-products of poorly flued wood and dung fires.[38] Despite the serious environmental consequences of the production and burning of biomass, there has recently been a surge in support for the use of wood and other organic material to generate energy because of its putative benefits in terms of reduced climate change impact.

The impact of such wood/biomass systems on biodiversity is a contentious issue. To produce energy from biomass requires the expenditure of significant amounts of energy in order to produce and apply fertiliser, to prepare the soil, and to plant, water, harvest and transport the crops.[39] The ecological effects of biomass energy production vary widely depending upon the ecosystem being displaced. If perennial biomass production displaces existing farming operations, such production may be ecologically beneficial.[40] However, given the likely increase in global demand for food crops, as populations and wealth increase, this seems a very unlikely outcome. The more probable alternative is that biomass crop production would displace previously undisturbed forests, wetlands and plains.[41]

Climate change

In spite of – or perhaps because of – improvements in the overall environmental profile of hydrocarbon energy, some critics have begun to focus on the threat of climate change from hydrocarbon-related greenhouse gas (GHG) emissions as a justification for severely regulating the use of hydrocarbons beyond traditional pollution control. There is insufficient space in this chapter to address the scientific concerns relating to global warming. However, many consequences of climate change are *not* expected to be harmful. Indeed, leading economists analysing their impact note that there are likely to be many ecological and social benefits of a moderately warmer and wetter world, not to mention the benefits of longer growing seasons and a fertilisation effect of higher carbon dioxide (CO_2) concentrations on plants and agriculture.[42] Economists also factor in the scientific evidence that weather extremes are not increasing,[43] the rate of growth of GHGs has slowed,[44] and the greenhouse warming is favourably distributed toward higher minimum temperatures (a reduced diurnal cycle).[45] A disproportionate amount of the warming is also 'dead warming', where higher below-freezing temperatures are recorded. Greenhouse physics, as well as the statistical records, point toward manmade warming occurring in the coldest and driest air masses, predominantly during winter Siberian and Alaskan nights.[46]

While warmer and wetter are trends in the positive direction, sea level rise from the human influence on climate is not. Yet even this concern has moderated. The Intergovernmental Panel on Climate Change (IPCC) reduced its estimate of sea level rise from the human influence on climate as new information became available. The sea level rise forecast made in the IPCC's 1990 report was reduced by 25% in 1995, and by a further 2% in their 2001 report.[47] Some evidence suggests that the sea level rise of the twentieth century has been greater than in the nineteenth century, although 'no significant acceleration in the rate of sea level rise during the twentieth century has been detected'.[48]

The global warming scare has led two European-based oil majors, BP and Royal Dutch Shell, to trumpet their diversification into renewable energy in general and into solar energy in particular. Meanwhile, the two companies' aggressive hunt for oil around the world and their investments in cleaner petrol are making the petroleum age more sustainable, not less. BP, having reconsidered its 'Beyond Petroleum' moniker, is poised to help develop the Arctic National Wildlife Reserve.[49] Shell has offered an alternative scenario whereby the market share of renewable energies catches up to hydrocarbons and nuclear by the middle of this century, but reality suggests otherwise. Shell's own highly publicised multi-year global budget for renewable energy – $500 million thus far (2002) and a further $500 million to $1 billion by the year 2007 – is a fraction of their budget for developing oil and gas fields in the Gulf of Mexico alone.[50]

Security enhancement

Supply security is another dimension of energy sustainability. Oil import security became a major issue in the world's largest economies as a result of the supply shocks of 1973 and 1979, caused by the intergovernmental oil cartel, OPEC, which choked supply in order to increase state revenue. Almost three decades later environmentalists cite dependence on Middle Eastern oil as a second reason (after climate change) to move beyond the petroleum era.[51]

However, the worst effects of the first oil 'crisis' in 1973 were caused not by OPEC but by price and allocation regulation by the US government. Shortages have not reappeared in the decades since because retail prices have been free to rise to limit demand in response to diminished supply.

The amount of oil that a country imports is not an indicator of its 'energy security'. Petroleum prices are set in a globally interconnected market by worldwide supply relative to demand. A supply cutback or oil embargo anywhere affects countries that supply all of their own oil (Britain), none of their oil (Japan), or half their oil (the United States). Government programmes to reduce consumption (such as Britain's sizeable petrol tax) or to stockpile supply (such as the Strategic Petroleum Reserve in the United States) are costly taxpayer responses to the 'improved' security.

The market offers self-help alternatives for energy users who face supply and price risks. In the 1970s and 1980s, futures markets were established for crude oil and oil products, where prices and supply could be locked in for months or even years. Natural gas followed in the 1980s and electricity products in the 1990s. Internet trading of energy commodities has increased transparency and improved opportunities for price and supply hedging. Mandating fuel diversity for its own sake or stockpiling oil are not necessary. Market demand and competition will continue to drive improvements in the future.

Energy hyperbole

Alarmism has presaged the call for a new energy future of renewables, hydrogen-based fuel cells, electric vehicles and distributed generation. Should we take this call seriously?

Environmentalists who advocate 'renewable energy' in general actually *oppose* many specific projects.[52] They have turned against the kingpin of renewable energy, hydropower, because of concerns about fish migration and loss of habitat. They have blocked wind and geothermal projects in sensitive areas. Some have questioned the viability of solar farms and biomass projects on the grounds that these are too land intensive for the (limited) energy that they produce. Their concern over the role of CO_2 emissions on global climate fails to square with the fact that virtually carbon-free hydropower and nuclear power, which they also oppose vehemently, produces 240 times more power globally than grid wind and solar combined.[53] The reality is that we are moving away from the 'renewable' energy era of wood, waste, water, sun and wind. Energy carriers that are more intensive, portable and reliable – coal, oil and natural gas – have replaced those energy sources in developed countries and are poised to do the same in developing countries.

Will fuel cells and electric cars – technologies that have received a great deal of attention in recent years – be commercially viable in the decades ahead? The fuel cell was invented in 1839, and subsequent attempts to commercialise it have repeatedly failed. While possible future breakthroughs in fuel cell technology cannot be dismissed, it would take a courageous venture capitalist to bet on a technology with such a dismal past. The electric car, on the other hand, dominated US transportation until Henry Ford's internal combustion engine entered mass production after the turn of the last century. It seems unlikely that electric cars will replace the petrol-powered automobiles in our lifetime and, even if they did, such vehicles would probably still rely on hydrocarbon-based electricity.

What about 'distributed energy?' Again, the past is being sold to us as the future. In most developed countries, isolated plants housed in the buildings that they electrified were displaced in the mid-twentieth century by large central station plants that economically served whole business and residential districts. Reduced waste and more reliable service brought an end to the 'distributed generation' era.[54] Mini-generators are still common in houses and apartments in developing countries but only because of the failure of governments in those countries to allow private companies to supply high-quality grid electricity to consumers. One only need compare two Indian cities – Bombay and Delhi. Bombay receives its power from a private company, which was set up before the government got into the electricity supply business. Power-outages are rare, and few people have any need for back-up generation. Delhi, by contrast, receives its electricity from a government-run company and power-outages are common. This is especially true during the long hot (40°C or more) summer months when demand for air conditioning rises dramatically. As a consequence, Delhi's wealthier citizens typically have diesel-powered generators that provide back-up energy and contribute to the city's unpleasant smog.[55]

Problems and improvement

Real energy problems stem primarily from acts of government, not acts of the market or of God. The electricity shortages that California experienced between May 2000 and June 2001 had the same cause as the petrol lines during the First and Second World Wars, and during the 1970s in the United States: retail price controls. Regional petrol price spikes experienced in the United States in the summer of 2001 were caused by clean air requirements that required different areas to use different blends of motor fuel ('boutique' fuels).[56]

Not all energy problems are caused by 'government failure' but the most pronounced aberrations generally are. Since most energies are commodities, they will be periodically subject to price swings. Often these swings favour consumers – unregulated energy markets are generally buyers' markets – but at times supply constraints can increase prices above historical or customary levels. Market processes then come into play to bring prices back to normal levels, except when tax policies (such as in Europe for motor fuel) make prices permanently high. In free markets, the cure for high prices is competition.

Poverty – the *real* energy sustainability issue

The threat to continued energy progress – or energy sustainability – is not depletion, pollution, or anthropogenic global cooling or warming. Activist government policies that increase prices and/or reduce reliability are the real threat for those still awaiting modern energy and for those who are more reliant on energy than ever before.

The major challenge for energy sustainability in the new century is *eradicating energy poverty*. The World Energy Council estimates that 1.6 billion people – one fourth of the global population – still do not have access to electricity and other modern forms of energy.[57] These individuals consequently suffer from acute smoke inhalation, subsistence productivity and unsanitary living conditions. A study by the United Nations and the World Energy Council estimated that 2 million premature deaths per year occur from primitive biomass pollution alone.[58]

Regional energy poverty amid global plenty is the direct result of economic statism whereby a paucity of private property rights, hampered market exchange and poor legal institutions have stymied human ingenuity and progress.[59] In such settings, people can often be the problem rather than the solution. This is far different from in market settings, where the statistics show that the hypothetical average person is simultaneously increasing energy and reducing pollution.

Damages from climate change are particularly acute for the most vulnerable regions of the world that have the least ability to cope with weather extremes or adapt to new climatic circumstances over the longer term. Poverty magnifies the damage caused by extreme weather events (events that have not been linked to the human influence on climate).

Thus it is poverty, not weather/climate events themselves, that is the primary sustainability issue, and poverty eradication the major policy imperative. If climate change policies divert resources that otherwise could be used to improve living standards – say introduce clean water and electricity – economic and thus environmental sustainability may worsen in the short run.[60] The policy implication is clear. According to Sarewitz and Pielke, 'The moral imperative should be not to prevent human disruption of the environment but to ameliorate the social and political conditions that lead people to behave in environmentally disruptive ways.'[61]

The same may be true if climate change policies reduce energy availability or affordability for populations that are industrialising. International trade restrictions (such as sanctions) that pose as enforcement mechanisms for global climate-change regulations are also a potential threat to living standards.[62] Any of these policies could halt 'no regrets' GHG reduction initiatives that wealthy nations are following to a large extent.

Climate change policies for the developing world should be designed to pass a short-run poverty sustainability test. Will the policies make energy expansion less likely? Will such policies make energy more expensive or less reliable? And, finally, will the policy hinder the most critical task of moving statist economies toward sustainability via the institutions of private property, voluntary exchange and the rule of law?

Equally, policy proposals should be also judged under a 'health-is-wealth' standard in both developed and undeveloped countries alike. Regulatory programmes intended to promote health through the perceived mitigation of manmade climate change must overcome a health loss that intrinsically occurs when private sector wealth is lost through taxation or regulatory burdens.[63] This 'opportunity cost' element of the cost/benefit equation is another barrier to moving directly from a scientific finding of a human impact on climate to an activist public policy intended to mitigate climate change.

Conclusion

Across-the-board improvements in hydrocarbon energies, coupled with environmental and economic problems with the leading alternatives to hydrocarbons, are expected to increase the combined market share of oil, gas, Orimulsion and coal in the coming decades. The International Energy Agency predicts that fossil fuels will account for 90% of the world's primary energy mix by 2020, up slightly from the share accounted for by these sources in 1997.[64] The US Energy Information Administration also predicts that the market share for hydrocarbons will rise relative to renewables and nuclear in the next twenty years.[65] In the longer term, the future of the hydrocarbon era looks bright, as new forms of hydrocarbons commercially vie with each other to best meet people's needs.

Energy policy is becoming more focused on expanding energy reserves and infrastructure to keep up with demand growth. Gone is the assumption that supply will always be there, despite a variety of government disincentives, until politically favoured energy alternatives can emerge. Environmentalist critics of hydrocarbons have retreated to the position that affordable, available energy is a prerequisite to policy reform.

The mantra of reducing overall energy usage has become less politically and intellectually tenable over time. Hydrocarbon energies are at the centre of today's consumer-driven technology revolution. More importantly, an estimated 1.6 billion people still do not have access to electricity and other modern forms of energy, leaving them impoverished and physically at risk.[66] This mass of humanity would benefit economically and environmentally from grid electricity. Expensive, intermittent distributed generation from solar power may be necessary for remote locations receiving electricity for the first time, but this is likely to be no more than a bridge to conventional power generation. Wealthy societies may be able to afford public sector forays to support exotic energy technologies, but consumers around the world desire plentiful and affordable energy to improve their lives.

The good news is that hydrocarbons are plentiful and their use is becoming cleaner and more 'sustainable' over time. The bad news is that the obsession with renewables and energy efficiency to meet growing demand[67] over the past 25 years has diverted sizeable resources away from more productive uses. In order to move towards a more sustainable energy future, it is of critical importance that governments around the world get out of the energy business and leave it to self-interested market participants. The new sustainability agenda should be to privatise indigenous resources and energy infrastructure, uphold property rights and the rule of law, and otherwise leave the provision of energy to the market.

Part Five

Resources

11 Do conservation conventions conserve?

Jonathan H. Adler

The conservation of biological diversity – or simply 'biodiversity'[1] – has emerged as one of the most important international environmental issues. The extent of biodiversity loss is unknown, but the fact that species and habitat are disappearing is quite certain. Human activity has accelerated the rate of species extinction substantially. Even if the world does not face an extinction 'crisis' that threatens human survival, the danger to many species, and biological diversity more broadly, is real and worthy of concern.

For decades, governments and international organisations have sought to stem the loss of biodiversity through the adoption of international agreements. The 1973 Convention on International Trade in Endangered Species (CITES) was the first multilateral agreement to address concerns about biological diversity. More recently, over 180 governments entered into the Convention on Biological Diversity (CBD). This was soon followed by an international protocol on 'biosafety', which provides for the regulation of transgenic crops. This chapter assesses the extent to which these conservation conventions can be expected to stem the loss of species and the decline in biological diversity.

The threat to biodiversity

The loss of biological diversity is a serious environmental concern. 'We – the human species – have been dependent on other species since the beginning of our time.'[2] Non-human species provide sources of food, clothing and shelter, not to mention satisfaction and pleasure. Estimates of species loss vary greatly but there is broad agreement that the current rate of loss is substantially higher today than at any time in human history and that human activities contribute directly and indirectly both to the decline in biodiversity and to the extinction of individual species.

Species extinction and the decline in biological diversity, while inter-related, should not be confused with one another. Biological diversity consists in not only the multitude of different species but also the genetic differences within given species and populations. The extinction of individual species reduces global biodiversity. So does the extirpation of distinct populations of species, the elimination of species from a given area, or the reduction of genetic diversity within a given population of a species. Thus, widespread species extinction is not a necessary precondition for the substantial biodiversity loss.

Estimates of the total number of species on the planet vary from 3 to 111 million,[3] though most conventional estimates place the number between 5 and 15 million.[4] As many as 15,000 new species are identified and described each year,[5] yet fewer than 2 million plant and animal species have been recorded to date.[6] It is generally accepted that a substantial percentage of birds, mammals and plants have been identified. This is not the case with other orders of species, however, such as insects, nematodes and bacteria.[7] To date, efforts to determine the precise number of plant and animal species on the earth have been 'surprisingly fruitless'.[8] Several new initiatives are underway, however, which could greatly expand human knowledge about the species with which we share the Earth.

Although there is little hard data to indicate *which* species are threatened, conservationists estimate that approximately 11% of mammals and birds are threatened with extinction around the world and presume that a similar percentage of other types of species may be threatened as well.[9]

Current extinction rates are no more certain. Recent studies have estimated extinction rates as being anywhere between 10% and less than 1% of species per decade.[10] Activist groups trumpet the high-end estimates. The Worldwatch Institute, for example, cites loss estimates of approximately 50,000 species *per year*.[11] The ecologist Norman Myers presented a similarly catastrophic assessment – 40,000 species per year – in his 1979 book *The Sinking Ark*.[12] While the precise rate of species extinction is uncertain, these more extreme estimates are highly speculative – and highly unlikely. In the early 1980s, ecologists Thomas Lovejoy and Paul Ehrlich estimated that at least 15 to 20% of all species would be gone by the year 2000 – predictions that almost certainly did not come to pass.[13]

Because of the difficulties in estimating the number of species that might become extinct, many choose to quantify estimates of species loss in relation to the background rate of extinction. A commonly cited estimate is that 'terrestrial species are vanishing one hundred times faster than before the arrival of humans'.[14] The *Global Biodiversity Outlook*, published by the CBD Secretariat, similarly estimates that the current rate of extinction is at least 100 to 200 times the natural background rate.[15] If these estimates are accurate, less than 1% of all species will become extinct over the next 50 years. Such an extinction rate is unfortunate – and may well justify concerted international action – but it is a far cry from disaster.

Despite the high estimates, we know of only about 1,000 extinctions that have taken place in the last four centuries.[16] According to Ross D.E. MacPhee of the American Museum of Natural History, 'No well-investigated group of animals shows a pattern of loss that is consistent with greatly heightened extinction rates.'[17] But the small number of recorded extinctions could be the result of poor knowledge about the number and distribution of species around the globe. Data from IUCN indicates that the rate of documented extinctions increased rapidly from the year 1600 until the middle of the twentieth century.[18] In contrast to estimates of species extinction rates, however, the rate of documented extinctions appears to have slowed since the 1930s.[19] This does not mean that the rate of species extinction has declined, though, because the criteria for declaring a species to be extinct are quite conservative, and there is no way for scientists to determine the precise rate of extinction for the countless species that have yet to be identified and catalogued.

In sum, species extinction and biodiversity loss are real concerns, but predictions of imminent ecological collapse due to species loss lack an empirical basis and are implausible. Human activity has increased the rate of extinction and the loss of biodiversity, though it is uncertain by how much. The relative lack of knowledge about the overall number of species, and their distribution, is a barrier to more accurate estimates.

The causes of biodiversity loss

Whether or not conventional extinction estimates are accurate, there is a general consensus that human activity threatens many species around the globe. Over one-third of documented animal extinctions were due to habitat destruction.[20] Saving biodiversity requires protecting plant and animal species in their native habitat – what is called *in situ* conservation.[21] *Ex situ* conservation through zoos, gene banks, and the like can complement *in situ* conservation, but it is no substitute. Protecting habitat is also the most important step in preventing the extinction of species from the wild. Degradation and loss of habitat are, however, not the only causes of species extinction and biodiversity decline. The introduction of exotic species and hunting are also leading causes.[22]

Most habitat loss is caused by human conversion of land to other uses.[23] 'In particular, conversion of land to agriculture is the single greatest agent of habitat conversion, and associated displacement of species and increasing stress on biological diversity.'[24] Since 1980, net agricultural land worldwide increased by over 4%, or 200 million hectares.[25] Low crop yields and increasing human populations create substantial pressure to clear land for crops. In Sub-Saharan Africa, for example, the use of land for agriculture and livestock poses a substantial threat to biodiversity.[26] In much of the continent '[p]overty is so intense that all land with agricultural potential will be exploited and even that with very little potential will be put to use – even if that use is unsustainable,' notes Rowan Martin, a noted conservationist actively involved in the development of community-based conservation programmes in southern Africa.[27]

Species are not evenly distributed across the planet. As a general rule, the level of species 'richness' or diversity increases towards the equator.[28] There also appear to be 'hot spots', which are particularly rich in species. Tropical forests, for example, typically contain a greater abundance of species than temperate forests or grasslands. Thus, the destruction or degradation of tropical forests and other habitats that are particularly rich in species can impose a substantial toll on biodiversity. Forest cover in many developed countries is stable or increasing. In stark contrast, deforestation of tropical forests, particularly in developing nations, is substantial and appears to be on the rise.[29] Between 1980 and 1995, net forest cover declined by 180 million hectares worldwide and by 200 million hectares in developing nations.[30] (Net forest cover actually *increased* in developed nations by approximately 20 million hectares over the period.[31])

Most of the loss of forest cover in developing nations is driven by the need to clear land for agriculture, and is exacerbated by poor land tenure regimes and government subsidies.[32] While some blame commercial timber harvesting for deforestation, Roger A. Sedjo of Resources for the Future notes that 'forestlands that are commercially

harvested typically remain as forestlands'.[33] The Food and Agriculture Organization (FAO) reports that '[n]atural forests are arguably
the single most important repository of terrestrial biological diversity'.[34] Tropical deforestation is expected to have a substantial impact
on species survival rates as forest habitat houses an estimated 60% of
the world's terrestrial biodiversity.[35]

The introduction of exotic species is also a substantial threat, not
least because it can contribute to the deterioration of habitat. Habitat
invasion by exotic species is generally considered the second leading
threat to endangered species, behind habitat loss due to human conversion.[36] By some estimates, up to 20% of endangered vertebrate
species are threatened by exotic species.[37] While the introduction of
species from one part of the world to another as crops or livestock can
bring tremendous benefits, the occasional introduction of biologically
invasive species has had substantial adverse consequences for many
native species.

While invasions of exotic species and other threats to biodiversity
will remain important, habitat loss is likely to be the greatest threat in
coming decades. Global population hit an estimated 6 billion in
1999.[38] At present, global population increases by 1 billion people
every 12 to 13 years. While many expect this rate of increase to slow,
most analysts believe that there could be approximately 10 billion
people on the planet by 2050.[39] Increased population will mean more
mouths to feed, and that will require increased agricultural production. Increased wealth in the developing world will also spur demand
for greater caloric and nutritional intake, pushing up agricultural demand further still.[40] An estimated one in five people in developing nations suffers from chronic undernourishment. For these reasons,
global demand for basic agricultural commodities, such as wheat,
maize and rice, will increase by 40% by 2020, or 1.3% per year, according to estimates by the International Food Policy Research Institute.[41]

Over the past several decades, global food availability has kept
pace with the increase in agricultural demand.[42] Yet the explosion in
agricultural productivity unleashed by the 'green revolution' may be
reaching its limits as annual increases in agricultural productivity appear to have been slipping. Cereal yields per hectare rose 2.2% per
year in the late 1960s and 1970s, but only 1.5% per year in the 1980s
and early 1990s, and rates of increase may fall even further.[43] Unless
agricultural productivity increases substantially, this will mean
putting thousands, if not millions, of additional hectares under plough

– and consequently losing thousands, if not millions, of hectares of species habitat. Thus, a failure to enhance per-acre agricultural productivity will have severe consequences for global and regional biological diversity.

The threat to species, particularly charismatic megafauna such as elephants, rhinos, pandas and tigers, from poaching and commercial exploitation receives abundant media attention. In particular, there has been a tendency to blame international trade in animal parts (ivory, rhino horn, tiger penis) for the demise of these species. However, 'there have been remarkably few, if any, species extinctions that can be attributed to exploitation for international trade'.[44] Charismatic megafauna in particular compete directly with people for land use, often posing a threat to human well-being, if not life itself (tigers and lions kill animals, including humans; elephants and rhinos eat vast quantities of cellulose). So if the value of the land is higher in an alternative use, such as farming, than in conserving species, the locals will kill the animals. Even when species loss has been attributed to commercial exploitation, as with the passenger pigeon, the likelihood is that they would have disappeared due to other causes, such as habitat destruction or degradation.[45]

Given that the greatest cause of species extinction today is loss of habitat, the key to conservation of biodiversity is to increase the conservation of undeveloped land and other habitat. This, in turn, requires increasing the value of land when it is in an undeveloped state, and reducing the economic pressures that drive land conversion. Conservation demands policies and institutional reforms that promote these processes. By contrast, most international treaties relating to conservation of biodiversity focus on regulatory responses. We now consider the role of these treaties.

The Convention on International Trade in Endangered Species

The Convention on International Trade in Endangered Species (CITES) is among the oldest multilateral environmental agreements. It is also one of the most controversial. Agreed in 1973 by 80 nations, it came into force two years later. Today 158 nations are parties to the Convention. As the name suggests, CITES focuses on the threat to wildlife from international trade in species. By its own terms, it does nothing to address habitat loss and degradation, domestic consumption, or other threats to wildlife or their habitat. In some cases, CITES may make habitat conservation more difficult.

The primary function of CITES is to identify endangered and threatened species and restrict international trade in such species and products derived from them. Species 'protected' by CITES are placed in one of three appendices. Those 'threatened with extinction' are listed in Appendix I. Trade in Appendix I species is generally prohibited in all but the most exceptional circumstances. Species that are not threatened with extinction, but that nonetheless might be imperilled if trade is not restricted, are placed on Appendix II. Export of Appendix II species is controlled through a permitting system. Appendix III contains those species that have protected status in at least one country that is a party to CITES and that has asked for controls on trade in that species. Unlike listing under the US Endangered Species Act, the CITES listing process is more political than scientific.

Over 33,000 species have been listed on the three appendices since the inception of CITES. The CITES Secretariat proudly proclaims that 'not one species protected by CITES has become extinct as a result of trade since the Convention entered into force'.[46] This is faint praise, for it is well acknowledged that many species have become extinct in the decades since CITES entered into force. CITES has done little, if anything, to stem this tide. In fact, it is doubtful whether CITES has ever helped any species in danger of extinction. There are startlingly few populations of species that have recovered while they were listed on CITES. This should not be surprising, as CITES does absolutely nothing to address the primary causes of species extinction. The wildlife trade is rarely a major threat to the survival of a species. This does not mean CITES has been without effect. Quite to the contrary, in some cases, CITES has undermined species conservation. As Jon Hutton and Barnabas Dickson of Africa Resources Trust explain: 'By restricting trade in wild species, and so limiting the benefits that humans can derive from them, CITES has actually reduced the incentive to maintain wildlife habitat.'[47]

In the 1960s, there were an estimated 70,000 black rhino in Africa, yet their numbers were already in decline. Demand for rhino horn from Asia was encouraging widespread hunting, and the black rhino was listed on Appendix I in 1975. Yet black rhino populations continued to plummet. By 1991, the IUCN Species Survival Commission African Rhino Specialist Group estimated there were fewer than 3,500 black rhino left in Africa.[48] In just five years, from 1987 to 1992, Zimbabwe's black rhino population fell by over 75% (1,750 to 430).[49] The Appendix I listing merely drove the trade in rhino horn underground, and prices soared. The economic demand for rhino horn remained and poaching increased.

Faced with the failure of the CITES Appendix I listing, some southern African governments successfully sought a relisting of the black rhino onto Appendix II so as to allow trade in live rhino specimens. This trade, albeit modest, provides some economic incentive for rhino conservation. Live rhinos are auctioned to private landowners, generating much-needed funds for habitat protection and conservation. The downlisting of South African white rhino populations in 1994 had similarly positive effects on conservation.

While CITES did little to protect rhino populations, for species such as the leopard and the African elephant an Appendix I listing likely caused more harm than good. The prohibition on trade greatly reduced the economic value of the species to local communities, thereby reducing local incentives to engage in and cooperate with conservation efforts. At the same time, the leopard and elephant listings did nothing to reduce the costs of living near such species. To people living in the wealthy nations of the North, leopards and elephants are majestic creatures – charismatic megafauna – but to rural villagers and farmers in the poor nations of the South they can be giant pests, trampling crops, preying on livestock, and generally competing for land. Appendix I listing failed to discourage the poisoning and shooting of leopards or the clearing of vital habitat to make room for cows and ploughs. Rather, 'landholders came to see [the leopard] not as an asset and something to conserve, but as a nuisance to be exterminated'.[50] Only once a limited export of leopards was allowed did they become an asset for landowners.

In the 1980s elephant populations in much of Sub-Saharan Africa were declining rapidly, despite the creation of wildlife preserves and strict controls on hunting. In East Africa especially, poaching was rampant. In southern Africa, on the other hand, elephant populations were stable or increasing. Governments in the South opposed the Appendix I listing for fear the resulting trade restrictions would eliminate elephant-related revenue. The African elephant was listed nonetheless. The listing of African elephants did nothing to reduce crop damage caused by elephants or otherwise endear them to African peasants. Nor did it appear to reduce the demand for ivory; the ivory trade was merely driven underground.[51] Indeed, insofar as the Appendix I listing reduced the legal supply of ivory, it increased black market ivory prices, thereby increasing the incentive for poaching.

Sustainable utilisation is the key for many species' survival. Yet the structure of CITES is hostile to sustainable utilisation. Its primary mechanisms – trade restrictions – reduce the economic value upon which sustainable utilisation may depend. Commercial utilisation of species, even through eco-tourism or safari hunting, can provide a substantial economic incentive for conservation. 'If people can benefit from wildlife, they have an incentive to maintain wild habitat and not to convert it to other uses such as agriculture.'[52] As wildlife becomes more valuable, private landowners will invest more in its protection. As Grahame Webb found in the case of crocodiles, legal trade in a species can 'be a significant deterrent to illegal trade, which is now markedly reduced around the world'.[53] Where wildlife does not have value, there may be few viable conservation options. Secure land tenure, local control of or proprietary rights in wildlife, and the opportunity to create economic value in wildlife are key elements in sustainable utilisation. Trade restrictions are not.

The Convention on Biological Diversity (CBD)

Nearly twenty years after the adoption of CITES, United Nations representatives agreed upon a new convention to address the loss of species: the Convention on Biological Diversity (CBD). The CBD was initially signed at the United Nations Earth Summit in Rio de Janeiro in 1992. As of March 2002, 183 nations are parties to the Convention. An additional five nations, including the United States, have signed, but not ratified, the CBD.

The CBD is a framework convention with three stated objectives: 1) 'the conservation of biological diversity'; 2) 'the sustainable use of its components'; and 3) 'the fair and equitable sharing of the benefits arising out of the utilization of genetic resources'. To these ends, the CBD contains a range of provisions intended to promote the conservation of biological diversity and limit the environmental impacts of human development. Like many environmental treaties, the CBD explicitly endorses a precautionary approach to the protection of biodiversity. The preamble to the Convention states, 'where there is a threat of significant reduction or loss of biological diversity, *lack of full scientific certainty should not be used as a reason for postponing measures to avoid or minimize such a threat*' (my emphasis). In this regard, the CBD echoes Agenda 21, the Rio Declaration, and other international calls for adoption of the precautionary principle in environmental policy.[54]

The CBD imposes numerous broad obligations upon its signatories, though as yet there is no enforcement mechanism. The CBD obligates parties to develop 'national strategies, plans or programs' for the conservation of biodiversity, which shall include, among other things: a) 'a system of protected areas,' such as parks or reserves with protective buffer zones, managed to ensure 'conservation and sustainable use'; b) 'measures for the recovery and rehabilitation of threatened species,' including the reintroduction of species into their native range; and c) measures to 'facilitate access to genetic resources for environmentally sound uses' and the transfer of advanced technologies to other nations. In addition to developing 'national strategies', CBD parties are to engage in efforts to 'prevent the introduction of, control or eradicate those alien species which threaten ecosystems, habitats or species'. Under Article 8(j), parties are also instructed to 'respect ... indigenous knowledge' and 'encourage ... equitable sharing' of the benefits of biological resources.

Different countries interpret these obligations in different ways. As with most framework conventions, negotiators from member countries seek to clarify the ambiguous language, and have done so at a series of COP – Conference of the Parties – meetings. In April 2002, for instance, negotiators at the Sixth COP meeting drafted voluntary guidelines on access to genetic resources and benefit sharing. For many countries, however, it seems that the CBD is merely another potential source of foreign assistance for government bureaucracies.

The CBD's emphasis on the need for governments to establish official 'protected areas' is misguided. Substantial amounts of land are already in officially designated 'protected areas' around the globe, but such designations have done little to prevent the continued loss or degradation of habitat and ecosystems. Most nations lack sufficient resources to establish, demarcate, defend and manage wildlife preserves on a scale sufficient to stem the loss of biological diversity. Even in wealthy nations, such as the United States, national parks, wildlife refuges and other protected areas fail to safeguard ecological resources, due to persistent political mismanagement and rent-seeking.[55] In poorer nations, the prospect of protecting biological diversity through a series of government-owned and managed protected areas is even more bleak. As a recent report by IUCN and Future Harvest found, agricultural production threatens habitat and biodiversity in approximately half of all the major wildlife preserves in the world.[56] The officially 'protected' nature of these areas has had little effect. The creation of protected areas can be quite controversial as well, as it often results in the economic – or even physical – dislocation of local communities.[57] 'Local people often view wild animals as pests who destroy crops, raid granaries, and sometimes cause loss of life.'[58] Though well intentioned, the creation of protected areas through government fiat can increase local opposition to conservation, further hampering efforts to increase biodiversity, particularly in remote areas.

More promising would be efforts to increase the value of habitat and undeveloped land through various forms of commercial utilisation. One possibility is the creation of local game preserves that can provide hunting and eco-tourism opportunities. As noted above, those species most subject to poaching and illegal hunting can typically be managed for commercial gain, funding species conservation in the process. Community-based management efforts have shown substantial progress in conserving species and the ecosystems upon which they depend, largely by giving local peoples an economic incentive to care for and protect natural resources.[59]

Another possibility actively promoted by some CBD proponents is bioprospecting. Bioprospecting agreements have the potential to promote the sustainable utilisation of biological resources by encouraging pharmaceutical and biotechnology companies to contract with local communities or governments to fund habitat conservation in return for access to genetic resources. Perhaps the most prominent example of how bioprospecting for genetic resources can provide economic incentives for conservation is the 1991 INBio-Merck agreement in Costa Rica.[60] Under the terms of the agreement, Merck & Company, a pharmaceutical firm, agreed to pay the Instituto Nacional de Biodiversidad (INBio), a non-profit foundation, $1 million in return for several thousand plant, insect and soil samples collected by INBio – in the Costa Rican rainforest. Merck received exclusive rights to the use of the samples collected by INBio, while INBio and the Costa Rican Ministry of Natural Resources were guaranteed a portion of any royalties from pharmaceuticals or other products developed from the samples. With these funds, INBio and the Costa Rican government can fund additional conservation efforts. Merck also supplied INBio with substantial amounts of technical equipment to assist in sample collection and testing.

The Merck-INBio agreement has been almost universally heralded as a model for the sustainable utilisation of biodiversity. To be sure, this arrangement has provided substantial funds for conservation and has helped to spur additional bioprospecting agreements. Nevertheless, funding mechanisms based upon the potential value of genetic material found in undeveloped areas are likely to be of only limited value because once the prospecting has taken place, the primary economic need for the land in question is greatly reduced. The original Merck-INBio agreement was for only two years. The promise of a share of royalties is, in a sense, the promise of a lottery ticket. The potential payoff is quite large, but the chances of a payoff are actually quite slim. In addition, gene banks and the like can serve as *ex situ* catalogues for genetic information without providing much incentive for *in situ* conservation. Bioprospecting can certainly help fund conservation efforts, but it is no panacea.

While two articles of the CBD – Articles 15 and 16 – focus on access to genetic resources and the transfer of technology, it is not clear that CBD implementation will further profitable bioprospecting agreements. It is not even clear whether the CBD – or any international agreement – is necessary for private firms to enter into prospecting agreements with local communities. The Merck-INBio deal was inked before CBD negotiations were concluded. Economic and legal institutions in the host country, particularly a legal system in which contracts can be entered into and enforced, are more important than an international agreement. Indeed, there is some concern within the biotechnology industry that the CBD will lead to international standards that hamper bioprospecting agreements. This would only reduce the role of such agreements in biodiversity conservation. In May 2002, the *New York Times* reported that in some countries the CBD is spawning 'paralyzing biological bureaucracies' that are obstructing bioprospecting and other conservation efforts.[61]

The CBD's emphasis on the sustainable utilisation of biological resources represents a step forward for international environmental agreements. Insofar as the Convention can spur greater reliance upon economic incentives and community-based management to promote conservation efforts, it will enhance global efforts to stem the loss of biodiversity. Yet insofar as the Convention promotes greater government control of natural resources, hampers profitable bioprospecting agreements, and limits conservation through commercial use of biological resources, it will retard future progress.

The Cartagena Protocol on Biosafety

Whilst the net effect of the CBD on biodiversity conservation is unclear, the effect of the Cartagena Protocol on Biosafety is not. Although the Protocol espouses the need to protect biodiversity, insofar

as it impacts biological diversity, it is likely to undermine habitat conservation efforts, particularly in those parts of the world in which
such conservation is most needed. For imperilled species, there is
nothing 'safe' about the Biosafety Protocol.

Under Article 19 of the CBD, parties to the Convention were to
'consider the need for and modalities of a protocol' regulating 'the
safe transfer, handling and use of any living modified organism resulting from biotechnology that may have an adverse effect' on biological
diversity. In particular, parties were entreated to determine when 'advance informed agreement' is necessary before genetically engineered
organisms or GMO-derived products are imported to one country
from another.

The final Protocol language, agreed on 29 January 2000 in Montreal, establishes an international framework for the regulation of all
'living modified organisms' (LMOs) 'that may have adverse effects on
the conservation and sustainable use of biodiversity, taking also into
account risks to human health'. While not as stringent as some environmental activists and negotiators demanded, the Protocol text creates mechanisms whereby national governments will be able to
restrict, or even prohibit, the importation of LMOs, such as genetically engineered crops. The Protocol's terms may allow government
authorities to restrict the import of foodstuffs as well. The Protocol
also requires the labelling of bulk shipments of LMOs – also known
as genetically modified organisms or 'GMOs' – intended to be used
for food, feed or processing. Such shipments must bear a label that
says they 'may contain' LMOs. These provisions could have a substantial impact on the diffusion of agricultural biotechnology, particularly in developing nations.

The primary mechanism for limiting the importation of genetically
modified crops in the Protocol is a set of provisions for 'advance informed agreement'. These provisions make the first shipment of any
LMO intended to be planted as a crop or otherwise released into the
environment conditional upon the approval of the importing country.
Technically, once the importing nation is notified of the intended shipment, it is supposed to respond within 90 days, acknowledging the
notification, and provide an answer within 270 days, indicating
whether or not it approves of the import. Yet there is no provision in
the Protocol to enforce this time limitation, and an importing nation's
failure to respond does 'not imply ... consent' to the shipment. 'Cooperative procedures and institutional mechanisms to promote compliance' are to be agreed upon at a later date.

The advance informed agreement provisions of the Protocol embrace the precautionary principle advocated by environmental activists. They provide that 'lack of scientific certainty due to insufficient relevant scientific information and knowledge regarding the extent of the potential adverse effects' of an LMO 'shall not prevent' the importing nation from limiting transboundary shipments. These provisions are reinforced by the statement in the preamble 'reaffirming the precautionary approach' to environmental regulation 'contained in Principle 15 of the Rio Declaration on Environment and Development'.[62] The importing nation may also take into account 'socio-economic considerations arising from the impact of living modified organisms' in making its determination. In other words, parties to the Protocol can effectively bar the importation of genetically modified crops irrespective of whether there is *any* scientific basis for the refusal.

During the Protocol negotiations, an Indian agricultural scientist who teaches in the United States released a petition of scientists endorsing 'the use of recombinant DNA [rDNA] as a potent tool for the achievement of a productive and sustainable agricultural system'.[63] Echoing a wealth of scientific literature on the likely benefits of agricultural biotechnology, the proclamation declared that rDNA techniques are a 'powerful and safe means for the modification of organisms' that 'can contribute substantially in enhancing quality of life by improving agriculture, health care and the environment'.[64] Just one week earlier, *Science* published research documenting the successful creation of vitamin A-enhanced rice.[65] This so-called 'golden rice' was immediately hailed as a 'major advance in global nutrition' because vitamin A deficiency, which can cause blindness and other ills, affects up to 250 million children worldwide.[66]

The broad scientific support for expanded use of rDNA techniques to engineer more productive, nutritious and environmentally benign crops is, however, not reflected in the text and structure of the Biosafety Protocol. While the scientific community generally supports advances in biotechnology, environmental activists charge that the spread of LMOs could pose untold threats to human health or the environment. As written, the Protocol could inhibit the spread of genetically engineered crops, particularly to those nations that need agricultural biotechnology to increase agricultural productivity. Parties to the Protocol will be able to bar importation of modified crop varieties for valid scientific reasons, questionable economic reasons, or no reason at all. Henry Miller and Gregory Conko explain:

> Rather than creating a uniform, predictable, and scientifically
> sound framework for effectively managing legitimate risks, the
> biosafety protocol establishes an ill-defined global regulatory
> process that permits overly risk-averse regulators to hide behind
> the precautionary principle in delaying or deferring approvals.[67]

In addition, the Protocol could expand opportunities for economic
interest groups to erect trade barriers to competing agricultural products under the guise of environmental protection.[68]

As noted above, the stated purpose of the Biosafety Protocol is to
establish safeguards against potential 'adverse effects on the conservation and sustainable use of biological diversity'. Yet the Biosafety Protocol may well retard, rather than advance, the protection of
biodiversity. The Protocol's operative provisions will do little, if anything, to promote or enhance habitat conservation. Worse, the net effect of the Protocol could actually be to *increase* risks to biodiversity
by making it more difficult for farmers to feed a growing global population without clearing more species habitat.

Population growth and economic development are rapidly increasing the demand for food in much of the developing world. This creates
a trade-off between increasing agricultural productivity and reducing
the threat to biodiversity from land conversion. Meeting global food
needs can be achieved either by clearing more land for agriculture or
enhancing the productivity of existing agricultural lands. Increasing
agricultural productivity a scant 1.4% per year from 1993 to 2050,
which may be necessary to meet global food needs, would produce an
overall increase in agricultural output of 121%.[69] To achieve this
same increase through the use of more cropland alone would probably require increasing the amount of cropland by *more than* 121%, or
over 1,700 million hectares.[70] If anything, this is a conservative estimate, as it does not fully account for the diminishing marginal returns
that are likely as less productive lands are converted to agricultural
use. It also does not include the conversion of land to other agricultural uses, such as pasture.

If gains in agricultural productivity do not outpace the rising demand for agricultural production, biodiversity will suffer, as forests
are cleared and grasslands are ploughed to make room for crops. As
environmental analyst Indur Goklany explains, the difference between an average annual increase in agricultural productivity of 1%
and 1.5% between 1993 and 2050 is 'the difference between convert-
ing 368 Mha [million hectares] of habitat (globally) to new cropland

or reducing cropland by 77 Mha'.[71] By Goklany's estimates, to protect biodiversity from the encroachment of agriculture, annual increases in agricultural productivity worldwide must exceed 1.4%. Even these estimates may be a bit optimistic. In some parts of the world, such as Sub-Saharan Africa, it may be necessary to achieve an annual productivity increase of 1.8% to 3% to avoid clearing habitat for cropland.[72]

Genetically engineered crops are likely to play an integral role in increasing the productivity of existing croplands and thereby reducing pressures on species habitat – if their use is not stifled by an overly burdensome regulatory regime. A scientific panel convened by the World Bank and Consultative Group on International Agricultural Research (CGIAR) concluded that genetic engineering could increase agricultural yields by as much as 25%.[73] Early transgenic harvests in the developing world show promising results, such as a modified rice variety with increased yields of 5 to 15%.[74] Corn and cotton engineered to produce a natural pesticide has increased crop productivity as well.[75] Even delaying ripening in fruits and vegetables could substantially enhance food supplies, as post-harvest and end-use losses are estimated to be as high as 47% in some countries.[76]

The negative impacts of a protocol on habitat conservation will be felt most in Sub-Saharan Africa. 'The African continent, more than any other, urgently needs agricultural biotechnology, including transgenic crops, to improve food production,' notes Kenyan biotechnologist Florence Wambugu.[77] Indeed, the agricultural biotechnology revolution is potentially even more valuable for some developing countries than the original 'green revolution', because the use of transgenic crops will not require the same costly inputs that many 'green revolution' techniques do.[78] Without the contribution of new generations of genetically modified crops, it will be immensely difficult to meet the rising food demands of the world's peoples and still preserve large areas of undeveloped habitat. Even if the use of genetically engineered crops allows for the further intensification of agricultural production, which has environmental impacts of its own, these impacts pose a lesser threat to biodiversity than the unabated loss of native habitat throughout the world; 'the environmental costs of expanding the area tilled are enormously greater than those of increasing yield'.[79]

While the Biosafety Protocol will likely retard efforts to protect habitat from the encroachment of agriculture, some hope that the Protocol will help to reduce other ecological risks from the introduction of LMOs. One prominent concern is that the introduction of

LMOs into the broader environment could disrupt local ecosystems. The introduction of non-indigenous animal and plant species, ranging from the brown tree snake in Pacific regions to Zebra mussels in North America and feral cats in New Zealand, has had a significant impact on biodiversity and is a substantial contributor to species extinction.

The introduction of exotic species into new environments is a legitimate concern. The Biosafety Protocol, however, is ill equipped to address it. There is no basis for presuming that LMOs pose a distinct threat of ecosystem invasion. The National Academy of Sciences noted that 'a mutation made by traditional techniques may be accompanied by many unknown mutations'.[80] The 1992 report of the National Biotechnology Policy Board reached the same conclusion that 'biotechnology processes tend to reduce risk because they are more predictable'.[81] The additional precision offered by rDNA techniques utilised in GMOs, however, makes the introduction of a new 'pest' species less likely, as it reduces the chances of inadvertently transferring unwanted genetic traits from one species to another.[82] Moreover, most scientists believe that those genes introduced to transgenic crops 'in fact decrease their fitness in the wild'.[83] In other words, good crops make bad weeds. Existing regulatory measures may well be insufficient to prevent the introduction of invasive exotic species, yet a protocol focusing on biotechnology does little to remedy this problem. Consider that in 1998, 27.8 million hectares were planted with genetically modified crops around the world, albeit concentrated in just a handful of countries. One year later, such crops covered 39.9 million hectares. Yet despite the millions of acres planted, most in plots with extensive oversight systems, there is scant evidence that transgenic crops are having any adverse environmental effect. [84]

> This remarkable record of safety for crop plants would indicate that either (1) the risks to the environment are low; (2) the extensive field testing prior to commercial use and the institutional assessments and decisions on which plants or varieties to grow as crops have been sound; and/or (3) the management practices in place have been adequate to mitigate any risks inherent with plants.[85]

Any of these conclusions would suggest that a biosafety protocol is unnecessary. Similarly, there has yet to be a single indication of any health risk from any genetically engineered food product commercially available in the United States.[86]

While the Biosafety Protocol is unlikely to increase the protection of rural environments in developing countries, it could well retard the use and development of genetically engineered crops. The more uncertain and costly the regulatory structure becomes, the more research and investment will steer clear of biotechnology. According to former Food and Drug Administration official Henry Miller, '[u]nnecessary governmental scrutiny in the form of case-by-case reviews will cause delays in the testing of biotechnological products, increase the potential for corruption and markedly inhibit the diffusion of this useful technology to the developing world'.[87] An overemphasis on the potential risks of using agricultural biotechnology ignores the equal, if not far greater, risks of doing without such advances. 'For the world's developing countries, one of the greatest risks of genetic engineering is not being able to use this technology at all.'[88]

Conclusion

Habitat loss around the world poses a real threat to biodiversity. Lack of advances in agricultural production, the world's burgeoning population, and the consequent increased demand for food production will accelerate this trend. If the parties to the Convention on Biological Diversity want to arrest this trend, their efforts would be better spent building institutional capacities for habitat conservation.[89] A global regulatory regime for biotechnology will not do much to stem the loss of biological diversity. If anything it could make this real problem worse.

Sustainable utilisation of wildlife will be necessary to ensure the continued survival of many species. This is true not only for those species that have substantial economic value, such as elephants, rhinos, leopards, and other charismatic megafauna. Protecting such species in the wild necessarily entails protecting the habitat upon which they depend. This not only benefits the charismatic megafauna – the species for which tourists and hunters will pay handsomely to photograph or shoot. It also benefits the other species that rely upon the same or similar habitat.

Insofar as wildlife management can be more profitable than traditional ranching or agriculture, it can also reduce the economic pressure to clear additional habitat elsewhere. In southern Africa, wildlife management is the highest-value use for most non-arable land.[90] Thus, where landowners have had proprietary rights in wildlife in developing nations, the land devoted to habitat has expanded. From

1975 to 1990, private landowners in Zimbabwe nearly doubled the amount of land devoted to wildlife, largely due to the ability to manage wildlife for profit. [91]

Indeed, prior to the recent political unrest, the amount of private land managed for wildlife in Zimbabwe was more than double the area of Zimbabwe's national parks.[92] Where land is not privately owned, the extension of quasi-property rights in wildlife to rural communities has also led to increased wildlife populations and greater habitat for species. 'In the developing world, wildlife is competing with humankind for limited resources. Denying wildlife a commercial value denies it the opportunity to compete successfully with alternative land use practices.'[93]

Both the sustainable utilisation of wildlife and increased agricultural productivity depend, in large part, upon liberal economic and legal institutions. Secure land tenure, economic liberty, and the rule of law are essential elements of an institutional environment in which conservation can thrive. This is borne out empirically: as economic liberty and the rule of law improve, agricultural productivity increases and rates of deforestation decline.[94] Both measures correlate more strongly with economic and legal institutions than they do with rates of population growth.[95] This should not be surprising, as there is ample evidence that 'environmental quality and economic growth rates are greater in regimes where property rights are well defined than in regimes where property rights are poorly defined.'[96]

The conservation of biological diversity is possible. Meeting this challenge requires greater attention to institutional reform than to the adoption of international conventions. Insofar as the CBD encourages sustainable utilisation and eschews regulatory measures that suppress the commercial value of wildlife and habitat, it could help conservation efforts turn the corner. Insofar as the Biosafety Protocol suppresses increases in agricultural productivity and CITES prevents conservation through use, these conventions will not advance conservation. Without reform and redirection, the conservation conventions themselves could be the greatest threat to conservation.

Portions of this article are adapted from 'The Cartagena Protocol and Biological Diversity: Biosafe or Bio-Sorry?', (2000), 12 Georgetown International Environmental Law Review, *761.*

12 Forest conservation and development: the role of institutions

Douglas Southgate

Reflection on all the hard work that has been done over the years for forests and other species-rich habitats in the developing world is bound to induce a certain amount of frustration. Successes have been achieved in a number of settings. However, deforestation throughout the tropics continues at a very rapid pace. Clearly, the conservation strategies employed to date have not been entirely appropriate and effective.

Ideas about what can be done to save biodiverse habitats in the tropics have come and gone with great frequency. The first conservation efforts, some dating to the early twentieth century, involved replicating natural reserves of the North American or European kind in Africa, Asia and Latin America. By the 1980s, the shortcomings of this approach had become all too apparent. As a rule, the underfunded park services of poor countries were finding it severely challenging to compel respect for park boundaries among local populations, which quite often had been evicted to create nature reserves in the first place. Escape from the predicament of 'paper parks' seemed to come in the form of integrated conservation and development projects (ICDPs), which are known in some places as initiatives for community-based natural resource management (CBNRM). These involve the promotion of economic activities that are environmentally sound as well as remunerative for local communities, quite often in buffer zones surrounding officially designated reserves. Almost from the beginning, the difficulties of designing and successfully implementing ICDPs were recognized.[1] With time, awareness of these difficulties has increased, so much so that at least some conservation organisations currently are demonstrating a keen interest in seeing what can be salvaged of the national park model.

The scholarly literature has not always been a source of consistent guidance about solutions to tropical deforestation. For example, initial enthusiasm for ICDPs was fuelled by a two-page article published in a prestigious scientific journal less than a year after Francisco ('Chico') Mendes, a union leader in the Brazilian Amazon who advocated using forests for the sustainable harvesting of rubber and other non-timber products, was murdered by two young cattle ranchers. The article described a case study, carried out in northeastern Peru, that appeared to demonstrate that environmentally sound extraction of non-timber products can be much more rewarding than either logging or clearing the forest to make way for crop and livestock production.[2] Although the case study's investigators acknowledged some of its limitations,[3,4] the conclusion that 'without question, the sustainable exploitation of non-wood forest resources represents the most immediate and profitable method for integrating the use and conservation of Amazon forests'[5] strengthened the impulse that Mendes's murder had created for ICDPs during the late 1980s and early 1990s. Further research has revealed that the harvesting of non-timber products never has been very remunerative, at least for forest dwellers, and is unlikely to become so. Thus it would be risky if the future of tropical forests were to hinge on the promotion of this activity.[6]

No less than writings in other fields, the economic literature has been enlivened by active debate over the driving forces of tropical deforestation. This debate continues to this day; not even the firm conviction of the Brundtland Commission that rural poverty and environmental degradation are mutually reinforcing[7] has escaped critical scrutiny. It has been shown, for example, that the well-to-do (e.g. soya bean farmers colonising the Brazilian Amazon) are sometimes responsible for tropical deforestation, and it is not unheard of for deforestation to occur as living standards rise in the countryside.[8]

If initiatives aimed at forest conservation are less successful than many would like them to be, it is not because unambiguous findings in the economic literature are being ignored. Such findings are few and far between, which is only to be expected when we realise that deforestation happens mainly for one reason here and for an entirely different reason there. The literature addresses various causes and, at the end of the day, offers no panacea. However, a recurring theme of economic analysis is institutional – the nature of individual or local control of forest resources.

Property rights and resource development

For most economists, the case for strong property rights could hardly be more compelling. For one thing, the lack of formal ownership makes it impossible for land to be used as collateral for a loan. As a result, there is no access to the bank credit that often is needed to undertake land improvements, including the application of conservation measures. Furthermore, resource users who enjoy all the prerogatives of ownership avoid the sort of insecurity that impedes resource conservation, which usually yields returns only with the passage of time.

Statistical evidence that attenuated property rights help to accelerate the clearing of tree-covered land in the tropics has been accumulating for at least ten years. It has been found, for example, that agricultural colonists in the Amazonian lowlands of eastern Ecuador are especially likely to deforest parcels that have not been adjudicated.[9] One reason for doing so is to strengthen informal agricultural use rights, which predominate in the institutional vacuum that characterises many agricultural frontiers. In a more recent study, a cause-and-effect relationship has been found between the lack of formal land tenure, on the one hand, and deforestation, on the other, in a cross-section of tropical countries.[10]

The linkage between secure ownership and forest conservation should not be exaggerated. Research carried out in Brazil highlights the circumstances under which incentives for land-use conversion are overpowering, certainly more potent than the incentives to conserve forests through property rights in tree-covered land. In particular, the returns to 'mining' an ecosystem, first by extracting timber and then by farming and ranching in a depletive fashion, greatly exceed the returns to ecosystem management in previously inaccessible areas where roads are being constructed and land is cheap.[11] Mining dominates management in these areas regardless of the ownership regime.[12]

It is also true that strengthening property rights does not eliminate all discrepancies between the interests of resource users and those of society as a whole. For example, even an agricultural colonist with secure property rights will neglect biodiversity loss and other environmental impacts of land-use conversion entirely. Where environmental values are not internalised, decisions about the replacement of forests with cropland or pasture will be based solely on clearing costs and the relative commercial returns of forestry and agriculture. This is a classic externality problem, or market failure.[13]

Another feature of ownership is that its benefits are never achieved for free. To adjudicate and to enforce property rights, scarce talents and capacities for administration and policing are required. These talents and capacities are in particularly short supply in the tree-covered hinterlands of Africa, Asia and Latin America. At an extreme, no attempt at all is made to establish property rights, which brings about a state of 'open access'. A resource owned by no-one – that is, a resource that anyone can use in any way and at any time that he or she wishes – tends to be depleted. This is because any positive value of the resource (i.e. any difference between the value of whatever can be extracted, on the one hand, and extraction costs, on the other) represents a clear signal to a competitive group of users to increase exploitation of the resource. Thus exploitation increases up to the point where the value of the open-access resource is dissipated entirely. Examples of this outcome include excessive fishing on the high seas, where no sovereign nation has a claim, and excessive grazing of pastures that no-one happens to own.

Between open access at one extreme, and private properties owned by individual firms and people at the other, institutional options exist. Among these is common property – a form of resource tenure in which a group, not an individual agent, is the owner. This turns out to be a ubiquitous arrangement in the forests of Africa, Asia and Latin America.

The common property option

From a purely economic standpoint, common property, like any tenurial arrangement, involves a balancing of two categories of costs. The first category comprises all the expense and effort involved in the establishment and maintenance of property rights, the second has to do with negotiations within the ownership-group over the internal management regime – that is, rules of access to be obeyed by all members of the group. With private property, in which all ownership is vested in individuals, the second category of cost can be said to be negligible,[14] while the first category, as mentioned already, is often very sizeable. With common property, defining ownership is less troublesome. However, there has to be more bargaining among members of the group holding property rights over the management regime. This bargaining is costly, sometimes very costly.

Whether common property makes more sense than private property or vice versa depends on the relative magnitudes of the two categories of costs, as well as on the value of resources. Nobel laureate and economic historian Douglass North contends that, over time, the expense of administering private ownership has fallen relative to the scarcity value of the resources. In addition, individual ties to local communities that traditionally have owned and managed common properties have weakened. As a result, individual claims on resources have proliferated, more often than not displacing group claims.[15] Before the invention of barbed wire, for example, establishing private ranches in drier parts of the western United States was infeasible. This is because grassland values compared poorly with the cost of demarcating property lines with fences made entirely of wood, which locally was in very short supply. But once barbed wire became available, vast sections of the open range were incorporated into private ranches.[16]

While the finding of North and other economic historians of a general tendency towards private property is hard to dispute, circumstances still exist under which the benefits of privatisation, which include improved capture of resource values as well as the avoidance of transaction costs, are outweighed by the costs of the same. For example, access remains entirely open to environmental resources of vital importance, including the air we breathe. Likewise, common property is a viable option in many settings. In particular, it makes sense where natural resources have local value, where this value does not compare all that well with the expense of apportioning resources among individual agents, and where these agents find it fairly easy to strike a bargain concerning the internal management regime.

As Elinor Ostrom and her collaborators have shown, these circumstances are far from rare in the developing world, including with regards to its forests.[17] They find that the prospects for common property are good where local groups perceive, or can be brought to understand, that forests are important, commercially or otherwise, and that the benefits of resource protection exceed the costs. Another facilitating factor is a history of local collective action, which creates a legacy of trust that keeps transactions costs to a minimum. It is also helpful for the forest not to be very large. Otherwise, one supposes, the scarcity value of forest resources does not compare favourably with the cost of warding off interlopers and monitoring group members' compliance with the internal management regime.

Why common property can fail

The findings of Ostrom and others who carry out systematic empirical investigation that is well grounded in economic theory demonstrate that there is space in the world for tree-covered common properties. However, their research also makes clear that group tenure is not a universally superior, or even universally viable, option. For example, common property is difficult to establish where local populations have little prior experience of collective action, as is the case along agricultural frontiers populated primarily by recent migrants. Since people such as these have little or no reason to trust one another, the trouble and expense of bargaining over an internal management regime usually turn out to be prohibitive. Also, market circumstances can change in ways that are detrimental to the arrangement. Similarly, governments can undermine group tenure in various ways.

Before turning to the impacts of government policy, which feature prominently in analyses of the breakdown of common property, the challenge posed by problematical market conditions merits examination. This challenge was clear in the case of extractive reserves – areas set aside for groups engaged in the harvesting of non-timber products – which Chico Mendes and others advocated during the 1980s and early 1990s. As indicated above, there are a few tropical forests where non-timber extraction is commercially viable. In the floodplains of the River Amazon and its major tributaries, for example, useful species, like *aguaje*, are not too widely dispersed and access to major urban markets, such as Belém and Manaus, is relatively good.[18] But in most places, the earnings associated with the harvesting of non-timber products are much more modest. A case in point is the collection of vegetable ivory, a palm product used to make buttons; in northwestern Ecuador the daily returns captured by individuals who harvest this commodity are no better than the opportunity cost of unskilled rural labour.[19] The same has been true of rubber tapping and other forms of non-timber extraction in the Amazon Basin, both now and in the past.[20]

The commercial prospects of using tree-covered common properties for other purposes are no better. Sustainable management of tropical forests that are sources of timber turns out not to be very profitable.[21] Neither does nature-based tourism hold much promise, mainly because – aside from a few unique places, like Costa Rica's Monteverde Cloud Forest Biological Preserve – sites with tourism potential have little or no scarcity value.[22]

Especially unpromising from a business standpoint are efforts to make use of the biodiversity that is a primary characteristic of tropical forests. Among others, Mark Plotkin, an ethnobotanist, has painstakingly documented what indigenous shamans in places like the American tropics know about skin rash treatments, the curare extract used as a muscle relaxant, and other medicines derived from jungle plants.[23] However, economic analysis does not indicate that the biological inputs to pharmaceutical research are of great value. The most widely cited study indicates that, as locations for the collection of specimens to be used in biomedical investigation, most tropical forests are worth a dollar or two per hectare; even the most valuable sites, which feature unusual endemism and also are under severe threat, are worth no more than $20 per hectare.[24]

Needless to say, commercial values are not all encompassing, especially for people dwelling in tree-covered hinterlands whose contacts with outside markets are sporadic. For them, goods and services obtained from the forest and consumed locally – including food, livestock fodder and medicinal plants – can be of fundamental importance. When this is so, local interest in conserving forested common properties that do not appear to yield much marketable output tends to be quite strong. Nevertheless, this interest is not always decisive, particularly if – as Poteete and Ostrom emphasise – community-level institutions are being undermined by public policy and the interventions of governmental agencies.[25]

The subversion of local institutions happens in various ways. Sometimes, the assault on common property is direct and obvious, involving official usurpation or displacement. However, group tenure also perishes due to the suffocating effects of national policy. Put in place ostensibly to protect local communities and their members, accumulating laws and regulations complicate decision-making at the local level, quite often to the detriment of the natural environment.

Direct, frontal attacks on local institutions were obvious during the era of European colonialism. But in the middle of the twentieth century the source of subversion shifted to national capitals in the developing world. Nationalisation of Nepal's village (*panchayat*) forests in 1958 is illustrative in this regard. Apparently failing to distinguish between open access (to repeat, the complete absence of ownership) and common property, officials in Kathmandu decided that all tree-covered land needed to be taken over by the government. Had the public sector actually spent money on management and controlling access, environmental benefits might have accrued, although the injustice of taking village resources without compensation would have had to be redressed. But management never occurred. Neither was access controlled. Accordingly, all the results of nationalisation were negative. Forests in which villagers previously had some sort of ownership stake – imperfect though it might have been – were converted into a truly open access resource, one that villagers had virtually no reason to conserve.[26]

As recent events in Zimbabwe suggest, direct usurpation of local institutions is not entirely a thing of the past. However, it is much more common nowadays for subversion, which is often unintentional, to take an indirect form. This is certainly true in Ecuador, where group tenure has been officially recognised since passage of the 1937 *Comunas* Law. Interestingly, few communities in the northwestern part of the country have relinquished common property, even though the 1994 Agrarian Law made it possible for them to do so. The economic sense of this decision has to do with the returns of managing forests in large, unified parcels, as opposed to the 50-hectare plots traditionally awarded to the beneficiaries of land distribution initiatives. Nevertheless, forestry returns have been diminished, in part because the 1937 Law obliges every *comuna* to replace its entire governing *cabildo* annually. The discontinuity in local leadership that this creates has exposed forest communities to business practices that are unfair, uncompetitive, or both. Accusations that community leaders have been bribed to accept logging agreements that stipulate low prices and weak environmental controls are common in northwestern Ecuador. Although specific evidence of local malfeasance is difficult to come by, it is undeniable that stumpage values are very low in the region, averaging just a few dollars per cubic metre of standing timber.[27] As a rule, logging takes place with little or no attention paid to containing environmental damage.

The deleterious impacts of giving local communities control over the resources that surround them while simultaneously interfering with their internal governance and limiting their decision-making prerogatives are no less clear in El Salvador than in Ecuador. Traditional group tenure, of the sort recognised by Ecuador's *Comunas* Law, had absolutely no legal status in El Salvador for nearly a hundred years. In 1882, as coffee production and exports were starting to take off, El Salvador abolished common property. The enlargement of private estates that ensued provoked conflict in the countryside, which intensified during the twentieth century. Several thousand people were massacred during a peasant uprising in the 1930s. And in October 1979, after several years of mounting violence, a group of reform-minded military officers seized power. Shortly afterwards, they stated their commitment to achieving a 'new economic and social order' by means of comprehensive agrarian reform and related measures.[28]

The reform programme, announced in March 1980, specifically targeted the economic base of El Salvador's rural elite. A limit of 150 hectares was placed on what any single individual could own, with land in excess of this limit subject to state expropriation. To make sure that former owners did not gradually reacquire the land lost because of agrarian reform, expropriated tracts were assigned to cooperative associations, which were forbidden to sell their holdings.[29]

In the following years, agrarian reform was impeded by political corruption and instability, not to mention a bloody civil war. In addition, economic conditions were inauspicious, a sharp, global recession driving down prices for coffee and other commodities. Of the 320 cooperatives that had been created in 1980 and 1981, 28 were already defunct by 1982 and another 21 were in danger of abandonment.[30] A truer test of their viability was to come after peace accords were signed, in 1992.

By and large, the performance of cooperatives in recent years has been disappointing. Although these entities possess one-fifth of all the prime farmland in El Salvador, which is the most densely populated country on the American mainland, approximately 25% of these holdings were not being cultivated during the middle 1990s.[31] In part, poor performance is the result of political interference during the early 1980s, such as favouritism for members of the ruling political party.[32] But this is not the entire story. Restrictions on the choices that cooperatives were allowed to make, which again were put in place to preempt the reversal of agrarian reform, prevented cooperatives from taking full advantage of commercial opportunities. Flatly prohibiting the sale of cooperative land foreclosed access to financial markets, which discouraged the sort of investment needed to enhance or to maintain farm productivity.[33] Commercial viability was further impaired by laws and regulations influencing cooperative governance; these interfered with the sort of quick decision-making required for success in the marketplace.

There is one other way that public policy militates against the success of community-level resource management, which is its subsidisation of goods and services that substitute for the output of common properties. This is often a problem for rural communities attempting to manage traditional irrigation systems. Needless to say, convincing farmer-members to pay for operational and maintenance expenses and capital amortisation is next to impossible if water tariffs in competing public systems do not fully cover these costs. By the same token, it is beyond the realm of possibility under these circumstances to raise tariffs to a sufficiently high level to finance the conservation of forested upper watersheds, even though this may be required to avoid shortages of irrigation water.[34]

Local institutions and environmental values

At times, the scholarly debate over community-level institutions for resource management in the developing world has been polemical. Often passionate, defenders of common property get particularly exercised when no distinction is made between tenurial arrangement and open access.

Economists are largely responsible for the confusion. Significantly, the very title of the article that contained a seminal analysis of the over-exploitation of resources owned by no-one contained the term 'common property', not 'open access' or some other synonym.[35] Nearly half a century after this mistake, misuse of vocabulary still occurs. In some, though by no means all, textbooks on economic development and environmental economics, common property takes the blame for what are really problems of open access.

Along with Daniel Bromley, Elinor Ostrom deserves much credit for bringing clarity to the debate over local institutions for natural resource management, including appropriate care in the definition of key terms and variables. Rarely if ever do serious analysts mischaracterise common property; as a result, light is being shed on the circumstances under which it is a satisfactory – even the best possible – way to resolve ownership issues. As indicated earlier in this chapter, group tenure, which by definition involves development and adherence to an internal management regime, can be a superior alternative not only to open access but also to private property. That is, members of the group can find that their respective shares of internalised resource values and transaction costs are superior to what each of them would receive if resources were divided among private holdings. The latter rewards, of course, would be diminished by the costs of establishing and enforcing a regime of private property.

If common property can be – not necessarily is, but can be – a viable or desirable arrangement, the question remains why any outsider should care. Obviously, a simple sense of justice or altruism is offended when collective action by local communities in the developing world, which more often than not have experienced historical marginalisation, is thwarted. However, there is another consequence of suppressing local institutions, which is the creation of an institutional vacuum that can have far-reaching environmental impacts.

The environmental pay-offs that can arise when local institutions are reinforced, not suppressed, are evident in northern Guatemala, where tree-covered land is being cleared very rapidly. It turns out that forests are under the least threat in the *Zona de Uso Múltiple* (ZUM), where the national government has awarded 25-year concessions for sustainable timber management to thirteen communities and two private firms. The annual deforestation rate in the ZUM is just 0.2%, which is comparable to natural forest loss caused by storms and lightning fires and not greatly above measurement error. The annual rate in nearby national parks is twice as high – 0.4%.[36]

Along with encouraging better management of timber resources, recognising the ownership rights of forest-dwelling communities can create environmental benefits of international significance. This possibility is illustrated by an agreement still being negotiated that involves fifteen communities of Mayans, all belonging to the *Asociación Oxlajú Tzuul Tag'a Maya Q'eqchi'*, who have migrated in recent years to northern Guatemala. Under the terms of the agreement, these communities will receive pipes, pumps and other machinery needed to extract groundwater for drinking purposes. In exchange for this machinery, which has a combined value of $857,500, the indigenous communities, which achieved legal recognition only after the peace accords that brought an end to Guatemala's long civil war were signed in 1996, will agree to maintain tree cover on approximately half their holdings, which total 30,000 hectares or so. Dividing the total expense by half this area yields $57.17 per hectare, which by the standards of many projects is not a great amount to spend for the sake of forest conservation.[37]

The success of community forestry concessions in northern Guatemala and the possibilities raised by the agreement to protect forests in return for potable water machinery indicate the sort of environmental conservation that can result if local institutions exist. Or perhaps the lesson is best expressed negatively – environmental benefits can never be captured if there are no such institutions, as was the case in northern Guatemala before the peace accords were signed. In an institutional vacuum, any outside agency or group hoping to conserve biodiverse forests would have to bargain individually with the thousands of families that have settled in the region. The combined cost of reaching and monitoring all these agreements would be huge, much larger in all likelihood than the benefits of conservation.

Avoiding the suppression of local institutions, then, is not just a matter of social justice. Keeping these viable is a necessary condition for securing environmental gains, gains of significance beyond the local level. Healthy institutions may not be sufficient. But the price that is paid around the world if local communities are routinely disenfranchised needs to be universally recognised.

13 Sustainable development and marine fisheries

Michael De Alessi

World fishery production today is more than six times what it was half a century ago. Since 1960, the quantity of fish destined for direct human consumption has more than tripled and now stands at around 90 million tons per year.[1] Estimates put total world capture fisheries and aquaculture production (which includes all marine fish harvests) at 125 million tons for 1999, up from 113 million tons in 1995.[2] But this apparently rosy picture belies some worrying facts: the recent increase in production has come primarily from aquaculture; after decades of steady increases, capture fishery numbers now fluctuate around 90 million tons per year. More disturbingly, stocks of some important commercial fish are severely depleted and many of those are *not* recovering.

If one considered only the plight of the Atlantic cod, it would be tempting to agree with the World Wildlife Fund's (WWF) 1996 claim that 'Without a doubt we have exceeded the limits of the seas.'[3] Cod is one of the most fecund fish (an average female produces 1 million eggs) and has been a staple of many diets for centuries. Once one of the world's richest fishing grounds, cod are so scarce today in New England and Atlantic Canada that they are close to commercial extinction.[4] However, many other fisheries are healthy, and recent evidence indicates that even those that have been depleted may be remarkably resilient.[5]

This chapter considers why some fish stocks have been depleted while others have not. It assesses the various attempts that have been made to improve fisheries management and provides insights into which kinds of institutions lead to sustainable management of stocks.

Sustainable fishing

The notion of sustainability flows directly from the biological sciences, especially the study of natural populations of animals such as fish and wildlife. For most of the twentieth century, fisheries science focused on determining the 'maximum sustainable yield' (MSY); that is, the largest harvest that could be taken year on year from a specific population of fish. This calculation involved not only estimates of growth and fecundity but also of the size of base population needed to maintain stocks.

Unfortunately, due both to the great uncertainties involved in estimating fish populations and – perhaps more importantly – to political gamesmanship,[6] fish populations have been decimated in the name of MSY. As a result, the concept has fallen out of favour. But while the 'maximum' part has been maligned, 'sustainability' remains the holy grail of fisheries management for everyone from biologists to conservationists to some environmentalists.

Of course, without appropriate definition, sustainability is ambiguous and can be used – as was MSY – to justify good, bad and even ugly policies. For the purposes of this chapter, sustainability is taken to mean *an activity or a population of a species that is resilient over time*. It is important to consider sustainability of both populations *and* activities for two reasons. First, especially in the developing world, wildlife and fisheries will not be conserved unless the people who depend on them for food and sustenance also prosper. (Anyone worried about where their next meal will come from will hardly be too concerned about the effects of their catches on the long-term health of a particular fish population.) Second, the concern of this book is with sustainable *development*, so activities that benefit people must be given due consideration.

Conservation and development are often presumed to be diametrically opposed to one another. Having made this presumption, some argue that the environment must be sacrificed for development. Others argue that development must be foregone in order to preserve the environment. But these prescriptions are misguided because the underlying presumption is incorrect. While there are certainly many examples of environmental degradation resulting from development, there are also many examples of environmental improvement and economic development being mutually supportive. Indeed, development and the wealth that it creates are in many respects the environment's best friend.[7]

It is also important to distinguish environmental change from environmental degradation – modern environmentalists often confuse the two, seeing all change as detrimental.[8] In reality, change is the norm and must be embraced as an inevitable part of the sustainability of a system. And while individual fish species are certainly important, it is the resilience of the marine environment as a whole, as well as the resilience of the human activities that depend upon it, that merit the greatest concern.

Decentralising control over resources

There is no single answer as to how best to conserve the ocean's resources. However, experience shows that when people are given the opportunity to conserve marine resources, they generally do so.[9] To give people that opportunity, however, there must be a dramatic shift in the way fisheries are managed, away from many current regimes that all too often encourage depletion of resources and wasting of time, effort and capital. Resource conservation is not happenstance; it is a rational response to a given situation.

In most countries, the political solution to overharvesting of resources has been the imposition of regulatory controls on fishers and other resource users. As the above discussion suggests, these controls have largely failed to stem the overharvesting of important oceanic and terrestrial species. The problem with such regulations is their failure to constrain the incentives that traditional resource users have to harvest resources. Therefore, limiting the number of days a fisher may put to sea induces him to invest in more equipment, so that on those few days he is at sea he is able to pull in just as many fish as he did before. Meanwhile, nationalising wildlife and creating 'national parks' to separate local people from this wildlife actually encourages the rural poor to poach animals – especially if they pose a threat to their families or livelihoods.

Some nations have, however, demonstrated the promise of an approach, which, at its core, recognises the role of economic incentives in conservation and sustainable development. These nations, notably those in the South Pacific for marine resources[10] and southern Africa for wildlife,[11] have attempted to decentralise control over resources – effectively making the users the owners of the resources. Sceptics cry out that the fox is in the henhouse, but this is simply not the case. Resource users with a proprietary interest in the resources they rely upon for their livelihood will naturally strive to both protect and even enhance these resources over time. We now consider how this system works in more detail.

Property rights

Property rights essentially define who has the right to do what with a resource. Economists who study natural resources have demonstrated the fundamental importance of property rights institutions to conservation and sustainable use. The allocation of property rights sets the rules of the game. There are, broadly, three types of allocation rules for resources:

- Open access (no-one has any property rights);
- Government ownership;
- Private ownership (property rights are held by individuals or groups).

Any attempt to exert control over resources is an attempt to define property rights. When property rights are not well defined, or cannot be readily enforced, a situation approximating that of open access pertains. Under open access, scarce natural resources tend to suffer from what Garret Hardin termed 'the tragedy of the commons'.[12] When it is impossible legally to exclude others from utilising a resource, users will tend to behave as though the resource is non-renewable, taking as much as possible as soon as possible, regardless of the impact on the stock. This does not cause problems when the resource is plentiful and harvests are small,[13] but as the pressure grows, so does the potential for depletion. In a system of open access to a valuable resource with low harvesting costs, there are no rewards for restraint, and then, as Hardin described, 'ruin is the destination toward which all men rush'.

Property rights encourage particular users to consider the harms and benefits they cause because they determine whether the future effects of their current behaviour (either positive or negative) will be borne by the owner. As economist Harold Demsetz put it, 'A primary function of property rights is that of guiding incentives to achieve a greater internalization of externalities.'[14] Thus, as property rights become better defined, resource stewardship becomes more attractive and, equally, owners bear more of the costs of rapacious behaviour.

Clearly defined and readily enforceable private property rights to marine resources are rare. However, those few examples that do exist strongly support the arguments of theorists who have promoted private property rights in the oceans as a means to improve resource management.[15]

If a resource is held privately, then the owners have incentives to protect, conserve and husband resources. Formally, a resource is deemed to be privately owned when property rights over the resource are well defined and readily enforceable by an identifiable set of residual claimants. The crucial determinant for whether or not a resource is really privately owned, however, is whether the welfare of those making decisions about its use is tied to the economic consequences of their decisions.[16]

It is the lack of private property rights, not economic development or 'greed', that leads to environmental degradation. The reason that development and environment have often been viewed as diametrically opposed is that private property rights – which would have been a bulwark against environmental degradation – have so often been trampled by the state in the name of economic development.

The creation and evolution of property rights

Whether private rights develop depends not only on the value of resources and the costs of monitoring them but also on the political costs of creating those rights.[17] The process can be mutually reinforcing; as resources become more valuable, owners invest more in creating, monitoring and enforcing private ownership rights, which in turn make resources more valuable, and so on.

An early example of the development of private property rights concerned the trade in beaver pelts and the Montagne Indians in North America.[18] Prior to the arrival of the settlers, beavers were plentiful and not highly valued by the Montagne, so they did not bother to impose any restrictions on harvesting them. But with the rise of the fur trade, the value of beaver pelts increased rapidly and suddenly the beavers became susceptible to depletion. The Montagne responded by rapidly developing a system for allocating certain areas to specific families who could then benefit from conserving the beaver. As beaver were the only resource valuable enough to warrant this kind of protection there were no other harvest restrictions imposed on these territories. Other people were free to roam across them and were even free to kill and eat the beaver as long as they left the pelt behind. Thus, the trade in beaver pelts was 'sustainably developed'.

Another exemplary case study is the American West at the end of the nineteenth century. Much like the oceans not so long ago, few could imagine depleting its vast resources. But as the West was settled, its water and grassy lands became progressively more scarce and more valuable. Research by economists Terry Anderson and P.J. Hill showed that, as the rights to these resources became more valuable, more effort went into enforcing private property rights, and therefore into innovation and resource conservation.[19]

Defining private property by physical barriers was desirable, but there were too few raw materials, so livestock intermingled and monitoring was difficult. However, frontier entrepreneurs soon developed branding systems to identify individual animals, and cattlemen's associations were formed to standardise and register these brands, allowing cattlemen to define and enforce ownership over a valuable, roaming resource. Then, in the 1870s, another innovation came along that radically altered the frontier landscape: barbed wire. Barbed wire was an inexpensive and effective means of marking territory, excluding interlopers and keeping in livestock. It made it easier to enclose property and exert private ownership, and illustrates how private property rights encourage innovation.

Responses to depletion

Unfortunately, the most common response to open access and depletion has been government intervention, which has meant that ingenuity and innovation have focused on circumventing restrictions, rather than on conserving or even enhancing resources. For the fisheries, these restrictions are, typically, limits on fishing gear, effort and seasons. Yet so many variables influence harvest levels that regulators cannot hope to keep up. As seasons are shortened, fishers might respond with larger nets. As larger nets are restricted, more horsepower may take up the slack, and so on. One of the more extreme examples was the Alaskan halibut fishery, where the primary limitation was the length of the fishing season. As the season shortened, larger boats, larger nets, and technologies such as fish-finding sonar began to appear. Before long, a season that was once months long was down to two days, *with no discernible reduction in the total harvests.*

The halibut story is an extreme one, but the plot is common around the world. Political battles are inevitably fought over pieces of a pie that never gets bigger. Instead of investing in efforts to enlarge the pie, resources are devoted to attempts to grab a bigger share at someone else's expense. Moving resource allocations out of the political arena, however, turns a zero-sum game into a positive one.

While government control may define who has the right to fish, it fails to internalise the effects that harvesters have on the resource, and so it has generally failed to conserve marine resources, let alone help to provide a leg up to those in developing countries that depend on the marine environment for sustenance. Fortunately, however, many subsistence-fishing communities are already familiar with one form of private property – common property.

Common property rights

Private individual property rights offer the greatest rewards for conservation to their owners, but are also the most costly to define and enforce. Thus, in some instances, private communal property may be optimal, depending on the resource and the costs of monitoring and enforcing rules and excluding outsiders. Private communal property rights may range from nearly open access to a strict system of controls and rules, but essentially they define the rights shared by the members of a group with exclusive access to a resource.[20]

Margaret McKean and Elinor Ostrom provide an explanation for the existence of private communal rights: 'Common property regimes are a way of privatizing the rights to something without dividing it into pieces ... Historically, common property regimes have evolved in places where the demand on a resource is too great to tolerate open access, so property rights in resources have to be created, but some other factor makes it impossible or undesirable to parcel the resource itself.'[21] An example cited by McKean and Ostrom is a very large, forested area where edible flora and fauna are patchily distributed.

Private communal rights may not be easily transferable, but the welfare of either the individual or group is tied directly to the health of the resource, thereby generating incentives for conservation and sustainable use.[22] However, limits on transferability of communal property may lead to problems of transition, as transferability bolsters resilience in the face of pressure from outsiders. If out-transfers are not possible, pressure from outsiders for access often leads to expropriation, either of the resource itself or of the right of access to it.

In many cases common property regimes are not legally recognised, but as long as they are enforceable they can be workable. In the Maine lobster fishery, for example, lobstermen formed 'harbour gangs' to mark territories and turn away outsiders.[23] As a result, lobstermen in these gangs have higher catches, larger lobsters and larger incomes than lobstermen who fish outside controlled areas. Some of these common access rights have now even been legally recognised by the state of Maine.

Unfortunately, in most places around the world, not only does the legal system not recognise common property rights, it is often biased against them. In fact, many legal systems favour individual property at the expense of common property. Ostrom notes finally that 'When resources that were previously controlled by local participants have been nationalized, state control has usually proved to be less effective and efficient than control by those directly affected, if not disastrous in its consequences.'[24]

Common property rights arise when parcelling is difficult and/or the return from doing so is low. Otherwise, as resources grow in value and/or monitoring becomes cheaper, private property rights become increasingly attractive.[25] Common property rights are emphasised in this paper because of their prevalence in developing countries, and because in many places where individual rights to resources are too expensive to enforce, they may afford an opportunity for private property rights to gain a foothold, to the benefit of both people and wildlife.

Examples of common property rights
• Coral reefs
Coral reefs in the South Pacific suffer widely from destructive fishing practices such as fishing with dynamite or cyanide.[26] However, such practices are often proscribed in places where fishing rights are securely owned, most often by a village, clan or community. Biologist Robert Johannes has studied coral reef conservation throughout the Pacific and found village control over local marine resources to be the surest indicator of reef health.[27]

Reef tenure typically extends from the beach to the outer edge of the reef, sometimes even miles out to sea.[28] These reefs are valuable assets to the community and so are fiercely protected. In Fiji some communities employ fish wardens to watch over the reefs. In Johannes's study of Palauan fishers, he found community-managed fisheries employing closed seasons and areas, abiding by size limits and even imposing quotas to ensure conservation.[29]

The experience of much of the Philippines offers a dramatic contrast. Most of the common property regimes there were destroyed by the Spanish Conquest. Today, fishing over the reefs is nearly open access and many reefs are dead or deteriorating. The WWF's Hong Kong office looked into the problem of cyanide fishing and found that reef fisheries in Southeast Asia 'work in a sustainable way only in those few places where the rights to fish a particular reef are clearly established'.[30]

In many of these island communities, secure tenure has also led to initiatives such as giant clam farming, redress for coastal pollution and the development of ecotourism ventures, none of which would have been possible without a healthy environment and the income derived from well-defined property rights. And because of those secure property rights, development centres on a healthy environment.

• Japanese cooperatives
Another formal communal arrangement exists in Japan, where in many places Fishery Cooperative Associations (FCAs) hold the rights to coastal marine resources and impose strict conservation measures on their members. As a result, coastal marine resources in Japan are generally healthy. Cooperative ownership in Japan is so strong that FCAs have even been able to block polluting coastal developments by asserting the primacy of their fishing rights. As Kenneth Ruddle and Tomoya Akimichi note, 'Because fisheries rights have a legal status equal to land ownership under Japanese law, ... a private developer must ... either purchase all of the fisheries rights ... or compensate for any reduction in the quality of the rights.' [31]
These cooperatives are, however, not purely private endeavours, since they receive significant government subsidies (as do most Japanese farmers). But they do demonstrate the emphatic link between exclusive control and the stewardship of marine resources.

• Oysters in Maryland and Washington states
Much like the Atlantic cod of New England, the oyster fishery in Chesapeake, Maryland, was once a great industry and oysters were a staple of the local diet. Sadly, despite more than a century of warnings, oyster stocks in the Chesapeake have declined precipitously. In 1891, William Brooks, a scientist and Maryland Oyster Commissioner, declared that 'all who are familiar with the subject have long been aware that our present system [of open access] can have only one result – extermination'.[32] Brooks recommended the creation of privately owned oyster beds, in order to encourage oyster cultivation and stewardship. But regulation was chosen instead. As stocks continued to decline over time, the Maryland government continued to increase its involvement in the fishery, presenting us with a dramatic case of regulatory failure. It has been said that Maryland has passed more legislation dealing with oysters than any other issue. Restrictions on technology were (and still are) so severe that the skipjacks plying certain Maryland oyster beds are the only commercial fishers in the

United States still powered by sail. In recent years disease has also played a part in the continued decline of the Chesapeake oyster, but even before this new threat, oyster harvests were well below 1% of what they once were.

In marked contrast to public oyster beds in Maryland, oyster beds in Washington state may be owned 'fee simple'[33] – completely privately, and with a title to prove it, just like a house. As a result, harvests of oysters in Washington state look very different from those in Maryland. Additionally, the oysters are harvested by relatively modern means and the beds are often seeded from high-tech hatcheries financed by the oyster growers. Private rights not only allowed oyster growers to protect their beds from over-harvesting, they also enabled their industry to develop; to invest in enhancement projects, to invest in biological research, and even to stop pollution. [34]

Individual Transferable Quotas (ITQs)

Although the benefits and feasibility of private ownership are most readily apparent for sedentary species like oysters, they may also be perfectly applicable to more far-ranging species. Many countries are attempting to improve fisheries management by introducing some limited forms of private ownership into the fisheries, frequently by creating a quasi-property right called an Individual Transferable Quota (ITQ). ITQs grant a right to harvest a certain percentage of a Total Allowable Catch (TAC) of fish in a given year and can be bought or sold. Over time, ITQs may also offer a real opportunity to move towards the private ownership of marine resources. Within the past two decades they have been introduced in New Zealand, Iceland, Australia, the United States and Canada. Some developing countries, most notably Namibia, are also beginning to experiment with such systems.[35]

Although they are not really private rights, ITQs can be a tremendous step in the right direction. In contrast to regulation-based controls, they provide positive conservation incentives for those harvesting resources, because the health of the fishery is capitalised into the value of the quota. In other words, the brighter the prospects for future harvests, the higher the value of ITQs, allowing ITQ owners to gain now from steps they take to ensure the long-term health of the fishery. Some banks are even beginning to accept ITQs as collateral, improving access to the fishery by making loans easier to secure for new entrants.

ITQs in New Zealand

Until the introduction of ITQs, fisheries management in New Zealand followed a familiar pattern. Since 1960 the government had condoned free entry into the fisheries and subsidised development, with predictable results; depletion of fish stocks and over-investment in boats, nets and other technologies. The deplorable state of many inshore fisheries, combined with the importance of fish to the New Zealand economy, forced a rethink of past policies. The result was the Fisheries Act of 1983, which consolidated previous legislation and set out both to improve resource conservation and to increase economic returns from the fisheries. This led to the creation of tradeable quotas for some of the deep-water fisheries and, in 1986, the introduction of ITQs for all significant commercial finfish species with the creation of the Quota Management System (QMS).

Today, following numerous improvements, the programme appears to have been tremendously successful. Fish stocks are generally healthy, the fisheries receive no subsidies, capacity in the fishing industry has been reduced voluntarily (some quota owners bought out others and retired redundant equipment – especially in the deep-water fisheries), and there has been an increase in investment in scientific research into the fisheries.[36] The New Zealand Ministry of Agriculture's Philip Major described a remarkable transformation in attitudes after the creation of the ITQ system: 'It's the first group of fishers I've ever encountered who turned down the chance to take more fish.'[37]

It has been suggested that ITQs will result in the consolidation of the industry and the elimination of the small-scale fisher. While there has been some consolidation in New Zealand, especially in capital-intensive deep-water fisheries, the total numbers of vessels, full-time employees, and quota owners all increased from 1986 to 1996.[38] Of course, one reason for this is that limits have been placed on the percentage of the overall quota any one fisher may own, ranging from a limit of 45% in a given area for species such as hoki and orange roughy to 10% for rock lobster. While such limits may not make economic sense, in the short term they serve to quell objections from those who fear excessive concentration and make it politically easier to shift from open access to a system of privately owned ITQs.

The New Zealand quota system seems to be moving closer and closer to a real system of privately owned fisheries. In the orange roughy fishery, for example, quota owners in 1991 formed the Exploratory Fishing Company (ORH 3B) Ltd, in large part to fund management science and research.[39] Similarly, the owners of scallop ITQs formed the Challenger Scallop Enhancement Company Ltd, which manages the fishery. Through contracts, the company levies money for research, enhancement (a vigorous reseeding programme), monitoring, and enforcement both of ITQ allocations and daily catch limits.[40] They have even contracted with other fleets and owners to ameliorate multispecies effects of other fisheries (in particular, the dredge oyster fishery and the inshore finfish fishery) on habitat and productivity.[41]

Once again, when property rights in marine resources are clearly defined and readily enforceable, development proceeds along a path that is truly sustainable.

Overcoming the political nature of ITQs

This evolution from political allocation to private ownership is a very important aspect of some ITQ systems. The New Zealand system is the most notable in this respect and has gone the furthest, but the Icelandic system has also gradually moved in the same direction. In many other places, however, ITQs have been explicitly set up in a manner that prevents them from evolving into stronger rights. For example, the IFQ (Individual Fishing Quota) programme in Alaska (an ITQ-type system which successfully ameliorated the 48-hour halibut derby mentioned earlier) specifically states that IFQs are not private property rights and that they can be taken away without compensation at any time. Such threats of expropriation undermine the credibility of the IFQs as secure, long-term investments, and strike at the very reason why ITQs have had some measure of success in the first place.

As long as an ITQ system remains politically managed, it will be susceptible to many of the pitfalls discussed earlier, limiting the impetus for innovation and sound resource enhancement. It also discourages the exploration of alternative systems for managing resources – such as setting up a scheme under which rights are created in a particular area, rather than for a particular species.

These potential pitfalls highlight the importance of giving careful consideration to the structure of the rights being created before an ITQ system is implemented. The central lesson from New Zealand's experience should always be borne in mind: the more an ITQ resembles a private right, the greater is the likelihood that the system itself will adapt and evolve into a system of real private rights, which commensurately have the strongest possible incentives for conservation and sustainable development. The creation of such secure, private-like rights can even help overcome political opposition from powerful groups with emotive and, in many cases, morally and legally justified claims. In New Zealand, the Maoris claimed a significant portion of the fisheries under the Treaty of Waitangi. This claim was settled amicably and the Maoris now own the largest fishing company in New Zealand.

Aquaculture

While the world fish catch has remained relatively stable in recent years, aquaculture production has grown dramatically. In fact, it is primarily responsible for the 20-million-ton growth in world fish production over the last decade.[42] In 1991, world aquaculture production was approximately 13 million metric tons, double what it was seven years earlier.[43] By 1999, that number had jumped to almost 33 million metric tons.[44]

The reason for these increases is that aquaculture facilities have allowed entrepreneurs to set up private enclosures that 'fence' parts of the sea (or even transport it onto land). A fish not harvested today will be there tomorrow, normal rates of mortality notwithstanding. Private ownership has invigorated entrepreneurs to tinker, experiment and innovate and, even more importantly, has encouraged others to innovate as well. In this, the experience of aquaculture mirrors that of the cattle ranches in the American West: it was not landowners in the West who invented barbed wire, but entrepreneurs who sought to develop new markets and products. Of course, aquaculture is not without its problems. Most aquaculture (approximately two-thirds) occurs near the coast or in shallow estuaries, where pollution from outside sources can cripple the operation. In addition, intensive aquaculture in these areas can produce significant amounts of organic pollution, which can reduce levels of oxygen in the water and increase quick-growing algae harmful to marine life. There is also growing concern over the use of antibiotics in aquaculture.

It is worth noting, however, that pollution and environmental degradation generally occur where property rights have not been appropriately defined and/or are not readily enforceable. Government subsidies and incentives to expropriate coastal areas for aquaculture often further undermine near-shore conservation efforts. In Thailand, for example, aquaculture is heavily subsidised and in many cases farms are built in areas that were previously managed much more sustainably by a system of customary tenure.[45] In Malaysia, the Land Acquisition Act was amended in 1991 to allow the state to appropriate land for any reason deemed beneficial to economic development, including the construction of fishponds. In Ecuador, bribes, corrupt government partnerships and land expropriation are common because 'by law, coastal beaches, salt water marshes, and everything else below the high tide line is a national patrimony'.[46] Not only shrimp farms but also city slums regularly invade these areas, even in national ecological preserves.[47] Alfredo Quarto, a director of the Mangrove Action Project, has pointed out that the main reason why shrimp farmers choose to clear mangrove forests is that they are usually government owned.[48] In other words, government-sanctioned open access and expropriation of common property rights are really to blame for coastal habitat destruction in places like Thailand and Ecuador.

Barriers to the sustainable development of marine fisheries

One major reason that Japanese cooperatives have been so successful is that they have been recognised by law, which allows them both to defend their rights in court and develop ways of accommodating out-transfers. Unfortunately, in most places around the world, not only does the legal system not recognise private communal rights, it is often biased against them. McKean and Ostrom note that 'Some [common property regimes] may have disappeared naturally as communities opted for other arrangements, particularly in the face of technological and economic change, but in most instances common property regimes seem to have been legislated out of existence.'[49]

This was certainly the case in the Pacific Northwest, where Native Americans had developed complicated arrangements, both within and between tribes, to manage their salmon fisheries.[50] They relied heavily on fixed nets and weirs along the riverbank, but were careful to allow plenty of fish to pass in order to maintain the spawning runs and ensure a future supply. According to Robert Higgs, 'Indian regulation of the fishery, though varying from tribe to tribe, rested on the enforcement of clearly understood property rights. In some cases these rights rested in the tribe as a whole; in other cases in families or individuals.'[51] But as the numbers and power of settlers increased, these property rights were quickly expropriated by force.

Legal recognition of communal rights would go a long way towards resolving this problem, but unfortunately, especially in developing countries, expropriation is the norm. This may explain much of the current emphasis that many policymakers place on maintaining small fishing communities and their 'cherished way of life'. Barring legal recognition, sentiment seems to be the next best alternative. Unfortunately, this may do more harm than good, as it tends to work towards entrenching the status quo. Property rights institutions, including communal ones, are constantly evolving, and while some communities may choose to maintain a certain way of life, others may not. Empowering people with the property rights to protect their environment is a powerful tool for sustainable development. On the other hand, legislating stasis is bad policy.

Opposition to private rights is often justified by arguing that fisheries are a 'public' resource and that any move in the direction of privatising them will prevent 'the public' from benefiting from the resource. But such arguments are based on prejudice – not reason. If it is agreed that the greatest public benefit is likely to result from maintaining both a healthy resource and a healthy and prosperous populace, the available evidence suggests that, generally speaking, private ownership is superior to open access. Maintaining open access may appeal to egalitarian values but is likely to lead to a depleted 'wasteland'. By contrast, a shift to private ownership is more likely to ensure access to a valuable, plentiful resource. Therefore, in the interests of 'the public' and of sustainable development, marine resources should be privatised wherever possible.

Conclusions

A shift towards private solutions to marine conservation problems would almost certainly lead to better stewardship of marine resources and, as such, must be considered a necessary part of 'sustainable development'. With marine resources privatised, innovation would no longer be about finding ways to fish more quickly; it would be about protecting those resources.

There is, of course, no single answer as to what sort of private ownership schemes might develop – if given the chance. In fisheries where there is great uncertainty and large catch fluctuations, there would no doubt be more risk sharing and group ownership schemes – from village common property regimes (as occur in the South Pacific) to fishing companies made up of ITQ owners (as in New Zealand). In other places, advanced technologies, many of which already exist, might be used to define and protect private property in the oceans, just as branding and barbed wire did in the frontier American West.[52]

While new technologies can help define and enforce property

rights, their availability must not blind one to the overarching importance of institutions. As the discussion of common property regimes
above has demonstrated, in many places appropriate institutions already exist, though we may not understand them as such. It is worth
remembering the words of the anthropologist John Cordell:

> It is one thing to contemplate the inshore sea from land's end as a
> stranger, to observe an apparently empty, featureless, open
> accessed expanse of water. The image in a fisher's mind is
> something very different. Seascapes are blanketed with history and
> imbued with names, myths, and legends, and elaborate territories
> that sometimes become exclusive provinces partitioned with
> traditional rights and owners much like property on land.[53]

People the world over will continue to try to improve their lot,
whether or not the environment suffers. Fortunately, the success of attempts to marry conservation with development in countries from
Palau to New Zealand points to the only workable solution. By recognising and encouraging more private property rights and by allowing
conservation and commerce peacefully to coexist, both people *and* the
environment will be better off – in other words, there will be sustainable development.

14 'Desertification' – international conventions and private solutions in Sub-Saharan Africa

Mary Tiffen and Michael Mortimore

International policy and even scientific debate has been characterised by widespread confusion over the meaning of and, therefore, the causes of, drought, desertification, deforestation, degradation and development. The respective roles of man and of climatic variation (which is largely uncontrollable by human action) have been at the heart of the misunderstandings. This chapter briefly reviews the debates which led up to the Convention to Combat Desertification (CCD) in 1996, and the lack of official action which followed. It then examines the rainfall variations and trends with which farmers in Sub-Saharan Africa (SSA) have had to contend.

A second challenge facing these farmers has been population growth, relatively slow in rural areas but rapid in urban areas, transforming local food markets. The success of farmers in keeping up with local demand is demonstrated by the record of per capita food imports, which appear more affected by a country's exchange rate policy than by its rainfall. The adaptations and innovation by which farmers in areas with low and erratic rainfall have met market needs and maintained their own livelihoods is illustrated by some case studies. It is concluded that the CCD misunderstood the needs and underestimated the abilities of African farmers. National and international policies need to be redirected in order to create an environment which supports rather than frustrates African entrepreneurs, whether as small farmers, traders or businessmen and women.

The conventions

The great Sahel drought which culminated in the widespread famine of 1972–4 had a pivotal significance in the evolution of national and international dryland development policy. It was perceived at the time, in official circles, as a crisis in five different areas:[1]

- Drought – technically viable indigenous systems of production quite suddenly came to be seen as maladaptive and necessitating new technical or management solutions.
- Food scarcity – persistent dependency on food aid continued through the 1980s in the francophone Sahelian countries, casting doubt on the region's ability to feed itself.
- Overstocking – the massive mortality among livestock holdings convinced some that the populations exceeded the levels supportable.
- Degradation – the effects of drought were easily confused with 'desertification': 'overcultivation' (or 'soil mining'), 'overgrazing' (or pasture degradation), 'deforestation' (or removal of woodland) and – it was assumed – 'overpopulation', as discussed later.
- 'Coping' – a disaster that affected the viability of the crop and livestock sectors was believed to be the underlying cause of increased poverty, asset losses and extensive out-migration.

What many saw as a collapse of livelihoods across the region led to calls for massive interventions by governments and donors to save the natural resources from further destruction. Earlier pessimistic assessments had been made of degradation in Africa,[2] but the 1972–4 droughts provoked a sandstorm of literature surrounding the UN Conference on Desertification in 1977. Human activities were blamed:

> Desertification is the diminution or destruction of the biological potential of the land, and can lead ultimately to desert-like conditions ... Over-exploitation gives rise to degradation of vegetation, soil and water ... [3]

The Conference approved a Plan of Action to Combat Desertification (the PACD), which was coordinated by the Desertification Branch of the United Nations Environment Programme (UNEP), as the basis for national plans. Although global in its scope, the sheer size of the African drylands ensured their prominence. About 36–43% of Africa (depending on the definition used) is dryland. Of this, the heart is the semi-arid zone, where crops and livestock are of equal importance. This area contained in the 1970s about a third of the human and cattle populations of Africa, and about a quarter of its sheep and goats.[4]

Desertification was thus used to justify central policies, interventions in smallholders' management of their natural resources and spending by aid donors and development agencies on the grounds that 'People are the producers of desertification.'[5] Time-hallowed associations between population growth, overexploitation and degradation were repeated in the literature; and assessments continued to make extensive use of approximations and assumptions.[6] The struggles of the Desertification Branch of UNEP to mobilise funds for the PACD in the face of scepticism and controversies surrounding the history, definition and operation of the term 'desertification', the extent of the affected area and the institutional dynamic have been well documented.[7] The criticisms resulted in a new definition of desertification for the Earth Summit in 1992:

> Desertification means land degradation in arid, semi-arid and sub-humid areas resulting from various factors, including climatic variations and human activities.[8]

This became the basis of the UN Convention to Combat Desertification (CCD), which came into effect on 26 December 1996. Although climatic variation was now acknowledged as a contributing cause, the activities which followed the signing of the convention continued to advocate programmes and projects to reform farmers' and pastoralists' practices (though participation and institutional issues were elevated in the rhetoric). The focus of the Convention is the preparation of national plans for furtherance of the 'combat'.[9] However, the Intergovernmental Negotiating Committee was soon complaining of difficulties in attracting the necessary finance,[10] in spite of the fact that the CCD was ratified by the European Union, in 1997,[11] and by the US Senate in 2001.[12] The various national and international action plans put forward thus remain paper documents. Meanwhile, according to the October 2001 newsletter of the Convention to Combat Desertification, the fourth meeting to review implementation 'did not enable well-defined conclusions'.[13]

More recently a 'Global Drylands Partnership' has been set up to address drylands issues. It includes the Canadian International Development Agency, the UNDP's Office to combat desertification and drought (UNSO) and several major environmental NGOs. So far it has published online four Challenge Papers, which 'question many of the underlying assumptions (some of which are incorrect) that frequently inform programme designs and interventions in the drylands'. However, while emphasising a variety of situations, the Partnership continues to perpetuate without documentation statements such as 'the vicious circle of poverty and environmental degradation' (in *Poverty and the Drylands)* and the 'population pressures, social changes ... exploitative agricultural and grazing practices ...' etc. which 'degrade 20% of the world's drylands' (in *Vulnerability and adaptation to climate change in the drylands*). Accepting the 20% figure at face value suggests that 80% have met the challenges of rainfall variability and population growth with relative success, and the same paper acknowledges 'the knowledge and initiative of the dryland people themselves', but says that 'success stories are more the exception than the norm'. The underlying message, though, remains continued deterioration, increasing poverty, and lack of knowledge, requiring interventions by governments and agencies.

There is still a need, therefore, to define more carefully the nature of the challenge facing people in drylands SSA, to identify the responses that they have already made, and the policies which enable relatively successful adaptation, and which could help to alleviate the undoubted poverty from which many of their people suffer. The remedies are different depending on whether we are looking at ignorant degrading activities, or at partly successful efforts to sustain livelihoods for more people in the face of unfavourable rainfall trends. The argument of this paper is that rainfall plays a more important part than is normally acknowledged, and that people have responded rationally to the challenge of periods of diminished rainfall which have coincided with periods of high population growth.

Definitions

Warren and Khogali have suggested restricting the term 'dryland degradation' to degradation 'brought about mainly by inappropriate land use under delicate environmental conditions', and using the term 'desiccation' for natural drying out over decades.[14] This assists clearer thinking, though there are practical difficulties in separating the effects of each out and measuring their impact.

Unsustainable cultivation techniques or grazing practices, or care-less cutting of trees for fuel etc., often occur in patches, rather than on a wide front. They may also be temporary, remedied to a greater or lesser extent after a few years when people recognise they have a prob-lem. The indicators of desertification vary over time as well as space.[15] Measurement after a series of dry seasons can mislead, since with the return of more humid weather natural vegetation, crop yields and livestock numbers can recover – and there are periods of dry or humid conditions (see Figures 15 and 16). Sorting out the human and natural causes of what is measured is also difficult, since vegetation dies from lack of rain as well as 'overgrazing', leading to bare soil and erosion. Some soil phenomena are partly due to natural factors. The Loess Plateau in China has perplexed soil scientists for decades.[16] The human element comes into play when water is badly managed, but the problems of irrigated drylands, more extensive in Asia than Africa, are not at the forefront of the desertification debates.

Thus measurement presents a technical challenge, and it does not necessarily lead to clear identification of causes. Crop yields can fall because the cost of inputs has risen in relation to outputs, because of reduced water availability to plants (which affects their ability to take up nutrients), because of the depletion of soil nutrients or the deterio-ration of other valuable soil characteristics, or because of soil loss due to erosion. The required remedial measures will obviously differ.

There is the further problem of definition. Vegetation measure-ments usually relate to the natural vegetation. However, over time, in all countries, large areas have gradually been cleared in order to cre-ate farms. They may retain some, but not all, of the natural species as part of their farms. They also may introduce new species. Maize is now grown in countries far from its place of origin in the Americas; the Australian eucalyptus is everywhere; and the Indian neem pro-vides shade in Nigerian towns. The question is whether such activities should be regarded as degradation, deforestation, or development. Should degradation be measured by the underlying productivity of the soil in years of 'normal' rainfall, regardless of the type of biomass produced?

Dessication and rainfall characteristics in SSA

The reference to 'normal' rainfall brings us to the heart of the prob-lem. In semi-arid Africa farmers cope with great variation in rainfall from year to year, sometimes apparently coupled with underlying cy-

Figure 15 **Rainfall at Kano Farm, Nigeria, 1916–2001**

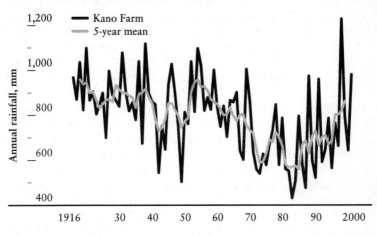

cles of more or less humid conditions about which we know very little. The few stations that have recorded measurements for as long as
80 years show this annual variability and conflicting evidence on
trends and cycles.[17] Figure 15 gives the annual seasonal rainfall
(May–October) and the five-year seasonal running mean at Kano
Farm, Nigeria, for the period 1916–2001. The annual totals demonstrate the risks farmers have to take into account. The five-year running mean shows that in this Sahelian region, the 1950s were a period
of relatively high rainfall. This was followed by a decline, which was
particularly steep from the mid-1960s to the mid-1970s, followed by
a slight recovery and then another dip in the early 1980s. This pattern,
which was fairly similar across the Sahel,[18] led to fears of what we are
terming 'desiccation'. However, now that we can extend the Kano
data to 2001, it looks as if there might have been a recovery since the
late 1980s. Data from Maradi in Niger and Diourbel in Senegal shows
the same upward direction in the 1990s, but less clearly, since we do
not have the figures for the last two years. The droughts of 1972 and
1984 had all the greater impact on livelihoods and ability to buy food
because farmers had been unable to rebuild grain stores and livestock
herds after immediately preceding poor seasons. Official concern
about drought and desertification coincides with the rainfall decline.

The rainfall record in East Africa shows a different pattern. There was no long decline around the period 1965–85, but some tendency towards a cyclical pattern which differs as between the two cropping seasons of October to December and March to May.[19] Figure 16 gives the data for Makindu station, in Makueni District, Kenya, for the period 1904–97. With good water conservation tactics, farmers in this area can get some maize from 250–300 mm of rainfall per season, provided the rainfall is well distributed. Figure 16 shows that they do not always get this minimum. Sequences of several poor seasons may make them dependent on assistance, from which they need time to recover.

Long-term rainfall data collected from a farm in the southern region of Zambia, which has been owned by the same family since the 1920s, shows similar variability. Periods of higher and lower rainfall could be detected, but no clear downward trend. The extremely low rainfall resulting in the drought of 1992 had been matched in 1923–4. The 1991–2 rains came after a decade of lower rainfall, somewhat worse than that of the 1920s.[20]

Rainfall accounts for a large proportion of variability of crop output, for some of the deaths and southward shifts of some native species, for the lowering of groundwater levels and the reduced availability of surface water. Lack of water and forage will lead to deaths of domestic livestock. Periods of poor rainfall make it more difficult for farmers to maintain good cultivation practices (death of oxen for ploughing and first weeding, lack of manure, lack of money to buy fertiliser, etc.). In fact, what is amazing when we look at the record of crop and livestock production in these areas is how farmers have continued to cope with rainfall variability, to adapt to it, and to recover.

There is the question of whether human actions have led to rainfall change. Some changes in climate may be caused by a rise in atmospheric concentrations of greenhouse gases, though the extent of this effect is contested.[21] Most concern has focused on the burning of fossil fuels, though changes in land use and particularly deforestation may also be important – but even then the main concern is the tropical humid forests,[22] which are outside the CCD's area of interest.[23] The likely effects on rainfall will differ regionally. A detailed study for the Food and Agriculture Organization (FAO) of the potential impact of global climate change on Nigeria under various scenarios found that temperature increases were likely, but would not necessarily affect crop productivity. The south of the country was expected to benefit from global change. In semi-arid northern Nigeria the effects were more uncertain – there *might* be reduced growing periods. Furthermore, the study pointed out that, 'higher technology levels under rain-

Figure 16 **Rainfall at Makindu, Makueni District, Kenya, 1904–97**

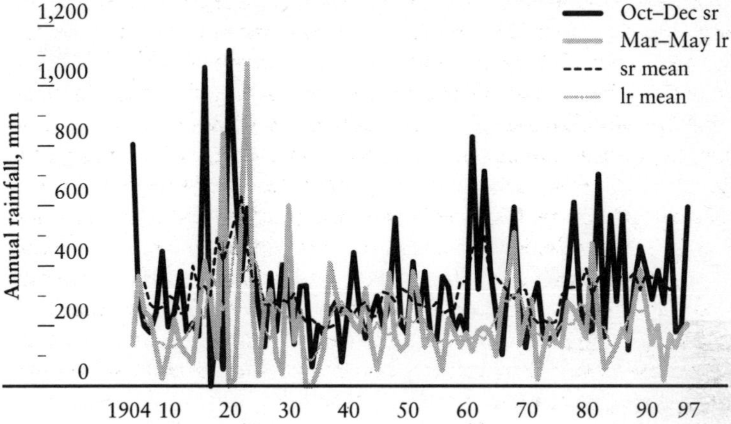

fed conditions cannot compensate for reductions in the length of the growing period ... if this occurs'. The study therefore called for climate monitoring and attentive preparedness, in view of the uncertainties.[24] The uncertainties are well illustrated in the rainfall for Kano in Figure 15.

Population growth, urbanisation and degradation

The main driver of degradation, in the view of pessimists, is overexploitation of resources due to population growth, and the associated growth in domestic livestock. Certainly, population growth in SSA has been very rapid. However, it started from a low base. In some areas, for several decades after 1960, rural growth could be accommodated by clearing new land for cultivation. Where people have moved to drier zones they are exposed to greater crop risks, for which they try to compensate by diversifying family income sources and using livestock as a buffer. In other areas, all nearby cultivable land was already occupied by the 1960s and in these areas rural population growth has been slower, as many young families have either migrated to towns or, in some cases, found new farmland at a considerable distance. As a result, though average farm size has diminished on inheritance, it has not done so as fast as if there had been no out-migration. There has, however,

Table 6 **Rural and urban population in three districts, and densities/km²**

	Total	Ur*a*	% urban	Average density	Rural density
Nigeria (Kano Province in 1952, Kano and Jigawa States, 1991)					
1952	3,396,350	335,707	14	79	77
1991	8,685,995	2,516,706	30	200	118[b]
					169[c]
Niger (Département de Maradi)					
1960 (estimate)	561,000	13,500	2	13	13
1977	949,747	44,459	5	23	22
1988	1,389,443	110,739	8	35	33
Senegal (Région de Diourbel)					
1960 (estimate)	261,000	n.a.	n.a.	60	n.a.
1976	423,038	117,761	28	97	70
1988	620,197	259,973	42	142	94

Source: Census data and analysis in Tiffen (2001) and Barry et al. (2000)
a Urban population in Nigeria and Niger defined as settlements over 5,000 in 1952 and 1960, and over 20,000 in later years. Urban population in Diourbel includes Touba Mosquée, a city without urban administrative status which has continued its rapid expansion since 1988.
b Jigawa.
c Kano.

been a remarkable spurt in urbanisation, so that those remaining on the farms have fed an increasing proportion off-farm. The change in rural and urban populations and the growth of the urban market for products that the semi-arid areas can produce – grains, pulses, livestock – are illustrated in Table 6. In northern Nigeria a tenth of the Kano area population in 1952 lived in towns of over 5,000 people; in 1991 nearly 30% were in towns of over 20,000. In Senegal, the urban drift is even more pronounced. It has been less marked in Niger, in the Department of Maradi, where population density is much lower, and where the option of starting a new farm in unclaimed bush was until recently still open, at least in its northern districts.

If, as the proponents of desertification argue, farm productivity is going down, then food imports per capita must rise to fill the gap. They have not done so in Nigeria, where the Naira has been progressively devalued since the 1980s. In Senegal, various pricing policies have discouraged farm investments and favoured imported rice,[25] but food imports per head have fallen since the devaluation of the Senegalese currency, the FCFA, in January 1994. In both countries, as Figure 17 suggests, food imports are more strongly related to a misaligned currency than to droughts (which should produce sudden rises in specific years) or degradation (which should show a steady upward trend in imports). In Nigeria, while the Kano area imports some southern foods such as yams, considerable amounts of northern maize, cowpeas and livestock continue to be sent south.[26]

Evidence of adaptiveness

The decline in food imports supports evidence of the adaptiveness of farmers found in many case studies. Despite rainfall variability and decline in average farm size, farmers have risen to the opportunities presented by market growth. This is illustrated by case studies made by Drylands Research, in cooperation with teams of national researchers, but other studies have found similar results.

Makueni District, Kenya

Makueni District was scantily inhabited until 1948, when the colonial government moved people from what were then degraded hillsides in the north of Machakos District, caused, it was believed, by overpopulation and overexploitation.[27] Some 2,000 families were resettled in Makueni,[28] at a cost to government of £148 per family (which can probably be multiplied by 20 or 25 to get the present-day equivalent). After 1960 the government lost control and thousands flowed into former uninhabited Crown land to establish new farms. The population rose from 190,631 in 1948 to 670,359 in 1989. They too invested time and money, but their own. The houses were constructed with an earth wall and grass thatch. An agricultural officer reckoned on 100 poles, 80 bundles of grass and 130 days labour per family for collection and construction.[29] By 1998, 40% of the families we interviewed in a sample of four villages had replaced thatch with corrugated iron (which enables the roof to harvest rainwater) and 13% had stone or brick walls.[30] Ox ploughs were in use by 40%; the numbers had been higher but many families had lost oxen to disease. In three of the four villages all farmers had fenced

232   *Sustainable Development*

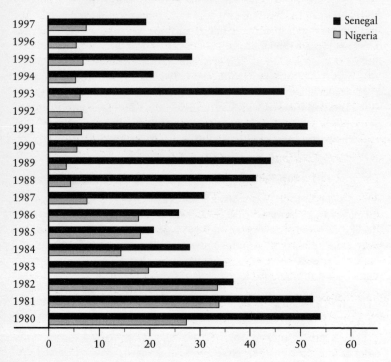

Figure 17 **Food imports per capita, in constant 1995 US $, Nigeria and Senegal, 1980–97**

Source: Constructed from World Bank Africa Database, 2000

their holdings. All farmers had over the years constructed cut-off drains, *fanya ju* terracing,[31] or grass strips to conserve soil and water, to a good standard. Construction of cut-off drains and terracing per farm took 93 to 245 man days, costing between US$230 and $600 at the exchange rate in 1998, being highest in the longer established villages.[32] All farmers had planted fruit trees, varying from 3 to 200, which required digging a large planting pit, purchasing manure, and watering during establishment.[33]

It is clear that the creation of new farms requires considerable private investment, which does not appear in national accounts. The Kenyan Government's policy of recognising and registering private rights in both grazing and cropland has provided security, but deeds are not risked to take loans because of the vagaries of rainfall.[34] Interfamily transfers are much more important than loans in providing money for farm improvements, education, or consumption needs.[35] Makueni now has large areas of conserved farmland instead of dry bush. Should we term this change development or degradation?

Given the uncertain rainfall, farmers regard it as extremely important to educate their children, so that some of them might be successful in the ever-more competitive and lucrative urban and non-farm labour markets. Primary schooling for both sexes is universal. Education costs parents, but educated children are expected to, and do, assist them.[36] Farmers were asked to name the three most important investments they had made for their overall welfare in the last ten years. The top five were terracing, planting trees, clearing bush (for cropping), house building and education.[37]

Makueni's grain production statistics are not very reliable[38] but show the expected great variation from year to year in the 1990s, with an average production of just over 200 kg per head of grains and pulses and no evidence of any downward trend in production. There were years when families without a member in paid employment needed help to buy food, and appreciated limited aid from government.[39] Temporary school feeding programmes helped them keep their children at school. This poor district is generally in the top five for Kenya Primary School Leaving Certificate results.[40] In other years people have been able to sell grains. There are farms in which insufficient manure is applied to replace nutrients,[41] but people blame the effects of livestock diseases on their holdings rather than on this.[42] The veterinary service is one of many government departments with inadequate budgets, and conditions in the district have not been such as to attract private sector vets, though there are now more shops selling veterinary supplies. Makueni presents a complex story which belies any simple desertification explanation.[43]

Maradi Department, Niger

Maradi Department, like Makueni, still had land available for settlement in 1960. The adjustments farmers had to make to their farming practices, as land became more scarce and fallowing impractical, took time. By 1999 there had been an increase in manuring, and in the use of artificial fertilisers when it was cost-effective, particularly in the more crowded southern districts. Figure 18 shows the contrasting trends in yields between a southern village in Madarounfa Arrondissement, where land has become scarce, and drier Dakoro in the

Table 7 **Year of acquisition of new capital equipment**

	Plough oxen	Ox cart	Heavy plough	Light plough	Bicycle	Motor cycle
To 1994	1	8	10	4	2	0
1995 onwards	18	9	2	34	6	4

Source: Hamadou, 2000

north, where production can still be expanded by taking in more land.

Analysis of soils and farmer practices showed that farmers knew how to recover fertility, but not all had access to sufficient manure, and chemical fertilisers at current prices had become less cost-effective.[44] Nevertheless, the crisis predicted after studies in the 1970s did not occur. Departmental records show continued increases in production. Despite population growth, the district produces enough grain and pulses to meet its own needs and to sell to Nigeria, except in drought years. However, as in most places, wealth is unequally distributed, and while some farmers are able to invest, expand and prosper, others are reliant on various forms of non-farm income to make a poor living.[45] Investment is the key to producing more, and is affected by the level of farm profits, which in turn depend partly on factors such as government management of the currency. The devaluation of the FCFA in 1994 prompted an increase in investments, as shown in Table 7.

The source of capital is mainly livestock and crop sales. Internal family flows from the contributions of educated children are less important than in Kenya. Many fewer children are sent to school in Niger, partly because the education, in French from day 1 and geared to qualifying for secondary education, presents greater risks of failure and has less practical benefits than its Kenyan equivalent. Hence, the many young men who go to Nigeria for spells of work, or trade, or Koranic study, are unable to access the better-paying jobs that demand literacy at least in Hausa, the lingua franca on both sides of the border. They go there to save their families the cost of supporting them in the dry season, and hope to return with enough to marry.[46]

The Kano area of Nigeria and Diourbel Department, Senegal
In Kano and in Diourbel, all cultivable land had already been claimed by specific families by 1960. Here, as in most of West Africa, custom

Figure 18 **Millet yields/ha in Madarounfa and Dakoro Arrondissements, 1979–96**

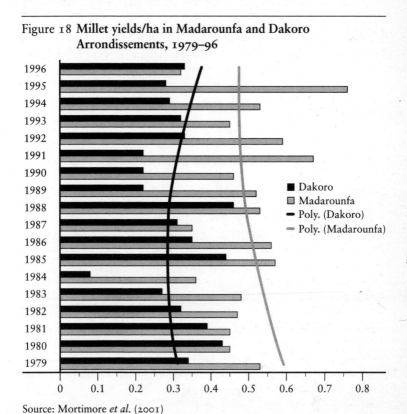

Source: Mortimore *et al.* (2001)

protected the rights of the cultivator to the fruits of his work and his investments in land, but, as in Kenya, owner-like rights did not extend to fenced grazing. As land becomes more scarce, so the rights of the farmer extend to exclusive use of his crop residues, the weeds in his fallow land, and the wild trees on it that he protects.[47]

In northern Nigeria there has been considerable investment in agricultural intensification, often greatest on the smallest farms.[48] As the meat market has grown with urbanisation, fattening of sheep, goats and cattle has become common. The animals are kept in pens for a great part of the year, and fed on nutritious groundnut hay and cowpeas, and the residues of maize, sorghum, millet etc. These may be produced on the farm, or purchased.[49] Grass, weeds and tree brows are also collected. Fattening requires considerably more labour than herding, and feeding and watering has to continue during the busy cropping season, when animals have to be kept off crops. In an extensive Sahelian farming system, livestock in the farming season took only 20 units of labour compared with farming tasks that peaked at 280 units in one week. In an intensive system, livestock care took 30 to 70 units in some weeks, when crops were taking 80 to 160 units.[50]

Many examples can be given of careful selection and crossing of local and research-bred varieties to adapt crops to lower rainfall and to particular niches.[51] Farmers in northern Nigeria have also invested heavily over the last twenty years in oxen and ploughs, and have switched on a large scale to cultivating maize, which has become more important in farming systems which were previously geared to millet and sorghum. They have also coped with the vagaries of the market, with prices at times strongly affected by inflation, or sudden devaluation, and changes of policy in regard to wheat imports, etc. However, while nominal prices for the main grains and pulses have been driven higher and higher by inflation, the real prices have mainly been on a downward trend since the 1970s, apart from sudden rises connected with severe drought years.[52] This does not suggest failure to meet rising urban demands, especially in view of the import record shown in Figure 17.

As regards tree cover, the evidence is that farmers husband resources rationally when wood becomes more scarce. The first stage is careful clearing, to preserve useful species – known as *défrichement amelioré*, as observed in Maradi. The next is careful preservation of useful species, and use of coppicing and pruning to obtain fuel, now more or less universal in northern Nigeria.[53] Finally comes planting species specifically for fuel, common in Kenya.[54] We had a nice illustration of the differences in view of the causes of degradation in a workshop in Senegal. There was a relative absence in the area of middle-aged *faidherbia albida*, a tree useful for improving soil fertility.[55] The academics were inclined to blame poor extension advice, which at one time advocated deep ploughing and the removal of all trees. The farmers present insisted they had always valued and preserved this tree, but many young ones had died in the droughts of the 1970s and 1980s. They had always preferred the light plough, which is more manoeuvrable.

Farming in Diourbel, Senegal, has been more subject to government intervention than in Nigeria. There was a government-fuelled investment boom in farm equipment and inputs in the 1960s and early 1970s, whereby farmers were compelled to join cooperatives and market their products through these at controlled prices, and credit was both subsidised and expected to be used for all inputs. Groundnut prices were deliberately kept below world levels to cream off as much as possible for the state and its growing number of employees. The system eventually crashed as growing expenses and corruption in parastatals encountered falling world prices at the end of the 1970s.[56] Millet was not an attractive alternative crop, as decades of imported broken rice at low and sometimes subsidised prices made this the preferred food both of urban people and rural people with a millet deficit. However, since the 1980s farmers have responded to the growing urban market for meat by fattening sheep and cattle. Their chief investments are now directed towards livestock, not crops. Groundnuts remain important in their farming system, however, as they are valued for their contribution to family food, fodder for livestock and cash from sales. Soil studies show that farmers know how to maintain fertility, and do so on fields close to their homes by applying manure, though outer fields may lack sufficient inputs now that the groundnut–fertiliser price relationship is unattractive.[57] Indeed, at current prices, the livestock once universally condemned for causing degradation is the key not only to raising soil fertility levels, but also income levels!

As in Kenya, farmers in Diourbel need to encourage their sons to obtain non-farm jobs. They do not see the education system (which is basically similar to that of Niger) as the route to this. A large proportion of their investment goes on what are termed ceremonies – the gifts and expenditures which sustain both family and religious networks. The latter are particularly important in Senegal, where most farmers are now linked to the Mouride brotherhood, which amongst other achievements finances a network of informal trading not only in Dakar but all over the world. There can be few tourists in Europe, the United States or South Africa who have not encountered a Senegalese hawker on the beach or pavement. Farmers at our workshop saw this as the best hope for their sons. Their investments have also created a new city in the region, the Mouride headquarters of Touba, and they have financed many quarters of Dakar.[58] The achievements of informal unrecorded urban investment in West Africa have been as neglected as farm investments. One estimate in the 1990s put them at $300 billion.[59]

Conclusion

Desiccation has occurred in SSA, sometimes over a number of years, with temporary ill effects on vegetative cover, erosion and other components of the natual environment. Unfortunately, we do not well understand all of the influences on rainfall trends. There may or may not now be an upturn in West Africa – there is insufficient evidence as yet. The impact of global warming on crop production will vary from place to place, in some cases being positive, in others negative. Hence, farmers may have to be even more adaptive in the future than at present.

Degradation of soils by mistreatment has not occurred as widely or as permanently as feared. In general farmers know the remedies, but they are not always economic or feasible given the risks, which include animal disease as well as the price relationship between fertiliser and marketed crops. What is needed are actions that make investment in farms more attractive – maintaining a stable currency, at a reasonable exchange rate, maintaining and if possible developing the public infrastructures that give access to markets and which act on the farm–gate prices of both inputs and outputs, maintaining those government services where externalities mean private sector provision may be handicapped (for example, in animal health). Ensuring that government services are relevant and give value for money (which parents judge keenly in relation to schooling) will benefit not only farmers but also the growing numbers trying to earn a living in towns. There is a symbiosis between prosperous and growing towns providing employment, and prosperous agriculture. Farmers in northern Nigeria have recently experienced a fall in their goat sales as urban disruptions (both of the socio-political variety and those caused by failures of electricity, petrol supplies, telecommunications and other factors) reduce urban incomes. [60]

In general, the government services listed above do not coincide with the desertification agenda. Naturally, it helps farmers if they are given information on new technologies that are practical and economically efficient. Research and dissemination are useful government provisions, but more fundamental is to ensure that economic policies give farmers the incentive, the security and the means to invest. It helps if they can also access written information. Bjorn Lomborg, the 'skeptical environmentalist', agrees with the pessimists that Sub-Saharan Africa trails the world in many economic and social indicators, for which he blames political and economic failures.[61] Some resource degradation can indeed be the result of human error, but where policies have been even moderately facilitating, case studies show that African farmers can conserve and improve.[62] They need not lectures but encouragement.

15 Water – can property rights and markets replace conflict?

Roger Bate

According to the UN, 2.7 billion people will face severe water shortages by 2025 and it warns that there may be wars over water. Already, many disputes in the Middle East concern water. Former President Anwar Sadat of Egypt claimed in 1979 that 'the only matter that could take Egypt to war again is water'.[1] Where peace is achieved in the region, there is often much emphasis on the resolution of water conflicts.[2] Hydrology and politics are strongly linked.

The availability of fresh water varies widely from country to country across the globe. In 1995, Canada had over 105,000 cubic metres of fresh water per person; Tunisia had only 500, Algeria 625 and South Africa 1,400. In semi-arid and arid regions, quantitative water scarcity is a serious concern. Precipitation is typically low and unevenly distributed, while evapotranspiration is high. Water scarcity is thus related to climate and is exacerbated by misuse, inefficiency, increasing populations and economic development. In these regions, pollution often constitutes an additional problem, but even if the pollution problem were resolved, water scarcity would remain. In other parts of the world, where rainfall is abundant and evapotranspiration low, water scarcity still exists but is more typically a matter of quality than quantity. In North America, agricultural pollution alone is estimated to cost $9 billion a year.[3] However, water quality is an even bigger problem in low-income countries. According to the World Bank, poor-quality water is responsible for around 3 million deaths a year in low-income countries, mostly from diseases such as dysentery, diarrhoea, hepatitis and cholera.[4] Industrial pollution is also a major problem in low-income countries.[5]

When a commodity is scarce, conflicts often arise over its use. This is especially true of commodities that are essential for human survival, such as water. Governance in general can be seen as an attempt to resolve such conflicts through the construction of allocation schemes. Methods of water allocation range from highly centralised governmental control,[6] to communal allocation with internal self-regulation,[7] to private markets enforced by communal reputation and ostracism and/or national law.[8]

This chapter discusses alternative allocation mechanisms for water and evaluates their relative success in ensuring stable, high-quality supplies at low cost to society. It also provides insights into what schemes might most successfully be employed in the future, especially considering the risk of international conflict.

Water allocation by central government

In most semi-arid countries, water has been allocated by centralised government administration. The track record of such schemes has not been impressive. Despite growing water scarcity and the high costs of hydraulic infrastructure, 'water is typically underpriced and used wastefully, the infrastructure is frequently poorly conceived, built and operated, and delivery is often unreliable'.[9] At the same time, there are high fiscal costs stemming from the 'construction of hydraulic infrastructure; from the institutional bureaucracy to support the design and execution of the projects and to set and collect water tariffs; and from the cost of operating and maintaining the system'.[10]

Too little emphasis has been placed on the planning and design of water delivery projects. A major reason for this is the perverse incentives resulting from political allocation. As Elinor Ostrom puts it, 'rent seeking and corruption' occur routinely in irrigation projects.[11,12] Indeed, irrigation projects, which are the largest water users in developing countries, have changed little since Helen Ingram found in 1973 that economic studies had been used to 'clothe politically desirable projects in the figleaf of economic respectability'.[13] In a similar vein, a comprehensive report for the World Bank in 1996 concludes that

> Many large multipurpose hydraulic projects (irrigation,
> hydropower, flood control, urban use, etc.) were undertaken on
> political rather than economic grounds. Costs tend to be high
> because of: inappropriate design, stemming in part from poor
> studies done prior to start-up; long gestation periods resulting

from funding shortfalls due to changing government priorities and poor capital programming and budgeting; few managerial incentives to control costs; and reported corruption that typically involves kickbacks from construction companies.[14]

An earlier World Bank report highlights some egregious examples of water mismanagement.[15] For instance, between 1974 and 1993 the Peruvian government invested $3.4 billion (in constant 1993 dollars) in nine coastal multipurpose projects. These projects achieved only 6.6% of the planned expansion in supply and none of the planned hydroelectric generation capacity. The primary justification for the projects was irrigation and, while the estimated cost per hectare ranged from $10,000 to $56,000, at completion irrigated land in the area sold for about $3,000 per hectare. Similar statistics can be found elsewhere. Sri Lanka invested 6% of its GDP in a single project, the Mahaweli Development Programme, which was vastly inefficient and led to severe social tensions.[16]

Economic inefficiency of administered allocation

The main reason for such waste is that water is often purposely sold at a very low price or no price at all. Authorities in many arid areas in both developing and developed countries ration water to urban, industrial enterprise while subsidising farmers to grow low-value, water-intensive crops. The effect of underpriced water is that farmers use inefficient irrigation technologies to produce uneconomic goods at the expense of lucrative alternative economic activities. The opportunity costs of this misallocation can be vast.[17] Furthermore, government control of water has often favoured the relatively wealthy and has not been effective in ensuring access to water for the poor.[18] The poor are often excluded from piped municipal water and must resort to expensive private water truckers to meet their daily consumption requirements. In its review of water vending, the World Bank showed that the unit cost of water supplied from water trucks to poor communities was between four and one hundred times greater than that of piped supplies.[19] In addition, the poor can rarely afford proper sewage arrangements. Government control has also often failed to address environmental issues,[20] for example, 10% of the Pakistani irrigation system faces chronic salinity problems.[21]

Historically, administrative approaches to water allocation have tended to favour large-scale investments over water conservation. There are few rewards for administrators who make painstaking improvements in water efficiencies via better pricing policies. In addition, the glamour of large projects and the attendant publicity and power they bring provide strong incentives to both administrators and the primary agricultural users.[22] Administrators are also often captured by interest groups.

Attempts to set prices that reflect the true cost of water provision are typically unpopular.[23] But the incentive to conserve water is weakened without such appropriate prices. A key feature of successful allocation mechanisms is the financial connection between suppliers and users of irrigation systems. Elinor Ostrom explains that allocation mechanisms that build in the eventual users' interests work well because the users naturally want to monitor resource use among themselves – at a very low cost to the system. When the users' interests are not satisfied, expensive auditing systems become necessary, but are rarely supplied.[24]

Discussing the failure of political allocation schemes in Africa, Robert Bates argues that 'inefficiencies persist *because* they are politically useful; economic inefficiencies afford governments means of retaining political power'.[25] Bates explains that when a government artificially lowers the price of water, supply from private sources is reduced, users demand more and the result is excess demand. One result of this process is that other agricultural inputs, particularly land, become more valuable, and the administratively created shortage in turn creates an economic premium for those who own such assets. As the market cannot match supply and demand without prices, the existing supply has to be rationed – usually by those who operate the political market. As Bates says, 'Public programmes which distribute farm credit, tractor-hire services, seeds and fertilizers and which bestow access to government-managed irrigation schemes and public land, thus become instruments of political organisation in the countryside of Africa.'[26]

Furthermore, central control of irrigation schemes gives local users no incentive to maintain the engineering facilities, which inevitably deteriorate. The resulting fall in reliability of the water supply stimulates greater government investment and central control, and farmers become even more reluctant to pay.[27]

Consultants, engineering firms and construction companies know this political process well and understand the mechanism whereby the allocation of funds is politically negotiated. Feasibility studies for new investments rarely warn that the construction of storage dams or the upgrading of canals may be financially unattractive.[28] When centralised administrative solutions fail – for example because supply augmentation is unsuccessful or simply leads to increased use – governments look for alternatives. The two most popular schemes are centrally administered quotas and prices.

Pricing
In principle, pricing enables public authorities to set user fees for water at levels that reflect the opportunity cost of provision, thereby inducing water conservation and making more water available for higher-value uses.[29] In practice, no central government has set water prices in this way and pricing is primarily used to recover costs of water delivery.[30,31] Nevertheless, where demand is sensitive to pricing it can have a considerable influence on the long-run quantity demanded.

Some countries with low water capacity per person have higher tariffs, such as Tunisia, but others, such as South Africa, do not. Countries with naturally high water levels have varied tariffs – in other words, scarcity of water is not a strong determinant of higher tariffs.[32] Farmers are the main users of water in semi-arid areas and oppose raising water prices because it increases their variable costs. Their assets also depreciate as higher water prices reduce the value of their land. Farmers' resistance to increased fees is therefore grounded in their incentives. If the fees charged for water on some projects were to be raised (and enforced) sufficiently to recover both the recurrent and capital costs, many farmers would be better off not irrigating. Robert Repetto found this to be the case for five of the six countries he analysed in Asia.[33] However, a common problem for pricing schemes is that increases in fees usually accrue to the central treasury and will only rarely be reinvested in better institutional facilities, unless bribes are paid. Farmers thus often have good reason to oppose price increases.

Occasionally, governments will allow local associations to keep water fees for reinvestment and farmer opposition to fees is diminished.[34] Robert Repetto found that in only one country out of six (the Philippines) did the fees collected cover the operating and maintenance costs of the systems (this was probably because in the Philippines revenues were hypothecated); in no country were the capital costs covered.[35] In several of the countries surveyed, the amount of bribes and fees paid to private tube-well operators demonstrated the farmers' willingness to pay far more than the subsidised price for reliably available water.

Ironically, it is poor farmers who suffer most from the underpricing of water. Low prices inflate demand, so authorities have to impose limits on water use. When this happens, the politically insignificant poor are excluded from receiving supply while better-off, politically relevant farmers obtain water at highly subsidised prices.[36]

Quotas

Quotas can constrain demand for water (if they are set lower than the quantity demanded).[37] Indeed, if demand is relatively unresponsive to changes in price (as is likely to be the case in places where water is extremely scarce),[38] quotas are more successful at constraining demand than water pricing.[39] This may be important if limiting water use to a specific maximum is vital to ensure sufficient water for ecosystems or subsistence users. Similarly, if demand for water increases due to economic development, quotas limit supply to a specific, ostensibly sustainable amount. Compared to water pricing, however, fixed, un-tradeable quotas provide less of an incentive to increase the efficiency of water usage.

Another important function of quotas is that they provide official recognition of access rights and can be given for free. In addition, if supply is increased through dam development and irrigation canals, farmers are more likely to avoid having to pay for developments from which they alone benefit under a quota scheme.[40] It is thus not surprising that of the two schemes, farmers in less developed countries seem to prefer water quotas over pricing regimes,[41] and quotas have been the favoured solution to restraining demand in the Least Developed Countries (LDCs).[42]

Overall, quota systems have proved insufficient to constrain demand. Often new quotas given to farmers (either incumbents or new arrivals) following supply augmentation eventually increase pressure on supply. Nevertheless, it is now the norm in LDCs to use quotas, coupled with low levels of pricing, to limit demand.[43]

Water markets

Quotas and prices, separately or in combination, have been criticised for not allowing sufficient flexibility in allocation.[44] Inflexible allocation usually leads to inequity and inefficiency, because as prices remain low, the value of quotas increases, with latent demand unfulfilled, which leads to economic stagnation, increased power to quota holders and even illegal exchanges of quotas. There are exceptions: where there is the administrative capability regularly to calculate shadow prices and change water usage, as is the case in countries such as France, pricing and quota strategies have been relatively flexible. But most developing countries do not have such administrative capacity. Scholars therefore suggest a third option, water markets, where quotas are legally traded among users.

Market allocation requires well-defined and freely exchangeable property rights. Unfortunately, transaction costs, which include the costs of creating, monitoring and enforcing such rights, are often large compared with the value of the water, making it difficult to establish market systems. Problems of externalities, inequity and devolution of power to local users also make markets politically unpopular.[45] Furthermore, water use is legally linked to land in most countries of the world, making the legal creation of tradeable rights to water technically complex. Meanwhile, at least one solution to this problem, tradeable quotas, tends to result in hostility.[46] Yet the flexibility and efficiency that come from the decentralised knowledge held in water markets has made them popular in many developing countries.

Tradeable water rights allow the price of water to reflect the value of its alternative uses, which creates incentives to put it to more productive uses. For example, if farmers were able to sell their water rights at freely negotiated prices, some might sell surplus water to a neighbouring farm where it has a higher value. Often, farmers can generate a surplus by using more efficient irrigation techniques or by switching to less water-intensive crops. In addition, buyers of water rights are likely to conserve water more efficiently.

Tradeable water rights can often shift water to higher value uses more cheaply and equitably than alternatives such as building hydraulic infrastructure, confiscating water from farmers, or raising water charges sufficiently to force farmers to conserve water. Although the conveyance infrastructure to transfer traded water must be built if it does not exist already, the cost of doing so may be less than that of generating new water rights.[47] Trading water rights is particularly beneficial for small farmers, who are often excluded from the political process and have therefore been most vulnerable to reductions in their water allocation over time, and have few other sources of collateral. Poor farmers are assured of sufficient water by their tradeable rights, which also help to reduce the abuses of administrative allocation. As rights are divisible, farmers can mortgage some part of their water rights for small loans, rather than their entire farm holdings.[48] Although the experience in some countries is that small farmers are generally bought out completely when they trade,[49] the more efficient ones that remain are able to expand by purchasing water use rights.[50]

Finally, when comparing the transactions costs of water markets with alternative allocation mechanisms, the 'hidden' transaction costs of the latter must also be taken into account. There are very high costs due to private rent-seeking by the managers of publicly administered irrigation systems. Allocation through markets in well-defined property rights in water will economise on rent-seeking costs.[51]

Case studies

So far the discussion has mostly focused on the problems of government control and the theoretical alternative of water markets. We now turn to a brief discussion of the practical implications of water trading, looking at various schemes that exist around the world, both formal and informal.

Informal markets

Failure of governments to allocate water to the satisfaction of users has led to informal, but often illegal, markets in water transfers in many countries of the world. In 1990, the Pakistan Water and Power Development Authority found active water trading on 70% of the water courses it studied.[52] Although trades were not officially sanctioned, it was found that where water had been traded agricultural incomes had increased by 40% due to greater control by farmers of their water supply.[53] Similarly in India, over half the area irrigated by tube-wells belonged to farmers who bought water.[54] The estimated gain from trading water in the whole of India was $1.38 billion per year. Yet the only policy statements and governmental actions on water markets in India have been to discourage them because they were illegally using electricity for pumping.[55]

Markets in India and Pakistan, and others like them, helped to resolve short-run water shortages. Scarcity drove the institutions to make the most efficient use of the available water,[56] but because informal water markets are not supported by existing laws, contracts are not enforceable. Agreements are only struck by users (usually farmers) who know and trust each other well. The lack of legal title also limits transactions to spot sales of water for brief periods of time, and never permanently, and so trades do not fully capture the benefits of an organised market in secure tradeable rights. Unfortunately, in many informal water markets (such as those in India and Pakistan) groundwater is depleted because of concerns that markets may be curtailed at any time. Nevertheless, informal markets can occasionally provide the benefits expected from legal markets, such as maintenance of canal delivery systems, because the canals transport purchased water.[57]

Chile

Chile has the most developed and one of the oldest regimes of water-use trading in the world.[58] All water rights were expropriated by the Chilean Government in 1966 and transferred to the state. But Chile's 1981 Water Code re-established tradeable water rights where existing water users (farms, industries, municipalities and power utilities) were granted rights to surface and groundwater.[59] New or unallocated water rights were auctioned. Except for a few restrictions, the allocated rights could be transferred or sold to anyone, for any purpose, at freely negotiated prices.

The agricultural sector in Chile accounts for 89% of the estimated 300,000 owners of water rights.[60] Administration is highly decentralised with the monitoring, distribution and enforcement of water rights carried out by water user associations at the local level – river basin, underground aquifer (for groundwater), primary canal and secondary or tertiary canal. Except for a few large dams and their associated main canals, all hydraulic infrastructure is owned and operated by water users themselves. Water users enjoy flexibility and control over water rights. In the arid areas north of Santiago there have been many mutually beneficial sales and leases of water, resulting in a voluntary transfer of water to more productive uses. By contrast, in the higher rainfall area south of Santiago, there have been few trades, since the transaction costs of registering the rights and conveying water are greater than the gains from transferring the water.[61]

Chile's transfer of water to more productive uses was carried out voluntarily and without having to increase water prices. In fact, water prices fell following the introduction of tradeable water rights. The decrease occurred because the Chilean government facilitated the transfer to user groups of the responsibility to carry out operations and maintenance activities and to set water tariffs. User groups were able to conduct these activities at a much lower cost than government. Despite the lower water prices, the opportunity to sell water reduces waste.[62]

Perhaps the greatest benefit of the trading approach has been that demands for environmentally destructive dam building have been abandoned. The city of La Serena in Chile is able to meet its rapidly growing demand for water by purchasing water rights from farmers at a lower cost, rather than contributing to the construction of a dam. Farmers receive an acceptable price for the water and are induced to use more efficient irrigation techniques.[63] Similarly, when Chile's main water company, Empresa Municipal de Obreros Sanitarios (EMOS), realised that it could no longer obtain free water rights, it invested in a programme to significantly reduce physical water losses.

Remarkably, Chile's sustained annual growth of 6% in agriculture during the 1980s was managed without public investments in new hydraulic infrastructure. While this was due in part to heavy investment in water infrastructure in previous decades, the tradeable water rights regime enabled new water uses, including the rapid expansion of fruit production.[64] Chile has also been successful in improving the access of the poor to potable water, as 99% of urban residents and 94% of rural residents are usually supplied for 24 hours a day. This contrasts sharply with comparable rates of coverage of 63% and 27% in Chile in 1970 and with developing countries elsewhere in the world.[65] While this is due to several factors, such as ensuring that regulated water tariffs reflected the true cost of water, allowing competition among water companies (Santiago alone has seven private companies) and subsidising water consumption for those with low incomes, the ability of water companies to buy water from farmers played a significant role.

Chile still has some problems with water use, particularly concerning quality. The obligations on holders of non-consumptive rights to release water for public consumption in times of shortage were not clearly defined, so dilution for effluent was occasionally low. This reduced water quality and led to conflict between the recently privatised hydropower companies and farmers. Some shortcomings in the law have also enabled one hydropower company to obtain huge blocks of non-consumptive rights without charge. Despite these problems, Chile has fewer conflicts and makes better use of its water than its neighbours.[66,67]

Mexico
In the past few years, the Mexican agricultural sector, and the economy as a whole, has become more market-oriented, and policymakers have increased security of water rights. According to the 1992 Water Law, and its 1994 regulations, users may convert their existing precarious water rights into more secure tradeable 'concessions' with a maturity of between 5 and 50 years (most are about 30 years), to ensure security of tenure.[68] However, the rights are not as secure as in

Chile. Under the Mexican Constitution, all water belongs to the nation, and the Water Law also mentions the possibility of forfeiture of water rights for the public interest if water is not being used efficiently, or if it has not been used for three years.

By 1995, 85% by volume of available water in Mexico had been allocated as water use rights and there was widespread leasing and selling of both surface and groundwater rights.[69] Water trades were common before 1994, but, as in India and Pakistan, these trades were limited, informal and illegal. Apparently, the authorities tolerated the trades but did nothing to monitor any externalities from them so, unfortunately, aquifers were drained. The new law recognised and encouraged trade (on either a permanent or temporary basis), which reduced total consumption and alleviated externalities (for example, slowing aquifer depletion).[70]

Most of the recent trades involve farmers selling to industries, water companies or more efficient farms, thereby encouraging investment in more productive activities. Water trading has also allowed unprofitable farmers to reduce their farming debts and to work as labourers on more efficient farms or to seek alternative employment. Although it may not be an ideal solution, having a tradeable asset in water rights gives an inefficient farmer some flexibility.

The western United States
Shortage of water in the western United States led to a system of property rights to water based on the 'prior appropriation doctrine';[71] whoever first diverted water and established beneficial use obtained primary rights. Successive claimants could only obtain rights that were contingent upon those with prior rights having received their allocations.

Although water rights regimes vary widely between states, their common characteristic is that water use cannot be changed without authorisation of state water authorities. Obtaining authorisation to change water use is often a lengthy and costly business, requiring consent from the relevant governing body after public hearings. Perhaps the most extreme example of restricting transfer between uses occurs in California. The agricultural sector makes up only 4% of GDP of the state, yet it receives about 44% of the water. Environmental use is allotted 44%, while urban and industrial users receive only 11%. Agricultural water rights vary widely, from cheap, inherited sources to highly subsidised ones. The anomalies that these restrictions cause are extreme; water is so cheap to some users (as low as $2.50 per acre-foot) that rice is cultivated in the desert, while some municipalities have built desalinisation plants to supplement their supplies of water at a cost of $2,000 per acre-foot.[72] Even worse are the perverse incentives to conserve water. Farmers are forced to operate under a 'use it or lose it' rule, while in towns, rationing during periods of drought is based on family use during periods of plentiful water, which encourages profligacy.

Reform is often discussed[73] but assigning to farmers the ability to simply sell their rights would give them millions of dollars in windfall gains on top of the large subsidies that they already receive – a politically unpopular result. On the other hand, farmers fear that their allocation will be reduced over time and with no compensation. Therefore, even in a country with well-developed institutions, there is poor administration of water allocation. The solutions used often defy logic and waste resources, and reform is slow.

A notable contrast to the various restricted water rights regimes which exist in the western United States is provided by the Big Thompson water trading scheme of 310,000 acre-feet of water in Colorado.[74] This scheme, which brings headwaters from the Colorado River through a tunnel in the Rocky Mountains to northeastern Colorado, was partially funded by subscribers in return for use rights. Soon after the scheme was fully operational it became apparent that water demand varied significantly between users and areas within the district. The Northern Colorado Water Conservancy therefore established a system that allowed permanent water rights trading. Trades had to demonstrate 'beneficial use' and no sales were allowed to areas outside the District. A central registry records ownership and transfers. The system has become so refined that a simple postcard is used to notify the Conservancy of a transfer.

An extremely sophisticated market has evolved for this water and many types of contracts are used, from straight transfers to the purchase and sale of options to water. Within the Conservancy District all of the complex infrastructure is in private hands. The Conservancy's role is to record transactions and to check that there is no cheating. The system appears to be operating efficiently within the water district, with supplies going to their highest valued use, although there is undoubtedly an opportunity cost to owners of water rights in not being able to sell their water outside the district.

Australia

Sturgess and Wright studied water transfers along the Murray-Darling River Basin, which stretches 2,530 km from the Snowy Mountains of eastern Australia to its mouth in South Australia.[75] In the worst drought years of 1987/8 there were 687 transfers, totalling 340 million cubic metres, with gains estimated at $17 million. In better years, a great deal of trading still took place but the total gains were lower: in 1988/9 the corresponding figures were 280 transfers, 85 million cubic metres and $5.6 million; in 1990/91 they were 435 transfers, 120 million cubic metres and $10 million. The researchers concluded that 'if benefits of this scale can be obtained by a system of water transfers circumscribed by regional barriers, the benefits that would flow from redefinition of water property rights to allow the free transfer of water between regions ... would be greater still'.[76]

Spain

Maass and Anderson examined the centuries-old water market of the farmers of Alicante in Spain.[77] The irregularity of water supply in the region led the Alicante farmers to build the Tibi Dam in the late sixteenth century, which became one of the most admired hydraulic works in Europe. Although this temporarily improved supply, it encouraged population growth and demand increased again. A flexible system of allocation subsequently developed to improve water use. Over the years, flexibility was achieved when the use of water was split from ownership of land and permanent and temporary transfers of water became legal. Although the water rights were based on allotted irrigation time from a canal, the rights were translated into volumetric units. By the 1970s the market was sophisticated enough to have temporary transfers, measured in minutes or fractions of minutes per day, up to entire seasons.

For the most part, water prices were freely negotiated and agreed at local taverns by the farmers themselves, although brokers did arrange some transactions. In spite of this very free system, concern was raised by officials and non-trading farmers that trades would lead to speculation and higher prices, and eventually would cause a reduction in farming. These opponents demanded a return to the time when water rights were legally tied to land sales, to ensure that water was always used on local farms. These demands were not acted upon. However, attempts to communalise private rights to water were enshrined in the 1985 Water Law, under which rights considered private in 1985 remain so until 2060, when the right will revert to the state, and no new rights will be allocated. Under the 1985 Law, water use will be maintained by the issuance of licenses, the right remaining with the State.[78]

Other examples
Water markets exist in other countries, including parts of North Africa,[79] South Africa[80] and Brazil.[81,82] These markets have similarities with the case studies discussed above and will not therefore be given detailed consideration here. Other markets also probably exist, but are yet to be documented, and many other countries are contemplating trading, for obvious reasons. In all the countries discussed in this chapter, allocative improvements have been made from trading and in some cases, such as Chile and India, significant economic gains have been made.

Summary and conclusions

Governments have sought to control water allocation in most countries of the world, often giving water to politically important users, such as farmers. The usual response to the inevitable, insatiable demand for free water has been construction of supply augmentation facilities, such as dams. As demand has continued to rise, governments have attempted to reduce water use by setting quotas and then imposing tariffs on the quotas.

For the most part, governments have resisted handing over allocative control to the market. Often political restrictions to trading have reduced the possibilities for better allocation. Many of these restrictions have emanated from concerns that overdepletion of water resources and environmental damage might occur. Concerns about concentration of power in the water market are also common but the literature is not clear on either point. Furthermore, much of the literature shows that existing allocation systems favour special interests, such as water bureaucracies. These interests differ from those that may dominate in a market, such as major farm estates or power companies. Water, like gas, electricity and telecommunications, is probably best allocated by private provision with government regulation.[83] This combination brings the flexibility and dispersed knowledge of the market, while leaving sufficient power in government hands to set maximum abstraction limits and control abuses of monopoly power.

Negative externalities (such as from pollution) have risen under certain trading conditions (usually informal markets), and fallen under others. Where formal markets have been permitted, overall environmental costs have been reduced, even where trading has reduced dilution for pollution.[84] On balance, water trading countries in arid areas have a better than average environmental performance.[85] There have been problems in Chile with concentration of power, but this was because of a mistake in allocating (non-consumptive) use rights to power companies. The companies (sometimes inadvertently) lowered the possibility of consumptive use trades by reducing flows in specific locations, although they never actually reduced net flow in the river taken as a whole. As the first to establish comprehensive modern water markets, Chile was bound to make mistakes, but now it and other countries have learnt their lessons and are resolving problems through regulation of non-consumptive use rights (ensuring that non-consumptive users return water to the same location from which they withdrew it, to ensure no 'dry' spots).

The theory and practice of water markets, as outlined in this chapter, provide a potential solution to inflexible allocations of water. As water scarcity increases around the globe, it is surely time to see more widespread use of such flexible solutions, not only because of their greater efficiency but also as a means of reducing conflict.

The Six Day War was fought partially over water. Israel refuses to leave the Golan Heights or West Bank in part because doing so would reduce the headwaters they control, putting thousands of Israelis at significant risk. Tensions are rising in Egypt over Ethiopian plans to expand water abstraction from the Blue Nile – Egypt draws over 85% of its fresh water from the Nile and any reduction in flow would harm its massive farming enterprises. Will it go to war over water, as Sadat suggested it might in 1979? Similar problems are occurring elsewhere in the world. In the past decade, armed conflicts have been fought over water in Bangladesh, Tajikistan, Malaysia, Yugoslavia, Angola, East Timor, Namibia, Botswana, Zambia, Ecuador and Peru.[86] Of course, water markets and good property rights systems would not by themselves resolve these tensions. But by improving efficiency of water use they would lower effective demand and hence the need to increase abstraction – the cause of the tension. Water markets in India and Pakistan stopped fighting among farmers and engendered cooperation. Markets replaced conflict.

Water markets will not settle historic border grievances such as that of the disputed territory of Kashmir, nor will they stop terrorism driven by religious fanaticism. But water markets can stop water wars. Just as Chile and Mexico have adopted markets to allocate water, so too can Israel and other parts of the world where tensions run high over dihydrogen monoxide.

Epilogue: What is sustainable development and how can we achieve it?

Julian Morris

The authors in this book have addressed a number of concerns that broadly relate to 'sustainable development'. In this epilogue I want briefly to draw together some of the themes that have emerged.

Two views of sustainable development

One popular interpretation of the term 'sustainable development' presumes that poverty, environmental degradation, disease and other problems afflicting the world are predominantly caused by, and therefore are the responsibility of, wealthy countries. According to this view – which is widely held by organisations claiming to represent the interests of the environment, consumers, the poor and the sick – people in the rich world consume too great a proportion of the world's resources and emit too great a proportion of the world's pollution; they exploit people in the poor world by paying too little for coffee and bananas and by making them pay too much for pharmaceuticals.

The solution typically offered by those who follow this interpretation of 'sustainable development' is to impose swingeing restrictions on the use of resources, wide-ranging interventions in the governance and behaviour of multinational companies and restrictions on international trade.

But an alternative view – and one that is more consonant with the thinking represented in this book – holds that the world is generally improving and that the rich world in particular has adopted, for the most part, institutions and policies that are sustainable. Broadly speaking, that means property rights, the rule of law, free markets, limited government and free speech.

According to this view, most of the problems of the poor world result not from the actions of those in the rich world but from the adoption of unsustainable policies by governments in the poor world. In particular, attempts to plan economies have proved disastrous in the Soviet Union and elsewhere.[1] Lack of adequately defined and readily enforceable property rights – often the result of well-meaning but utterly misguided government intervention – holds back economic development in many countries, while red tape stifles entrepreneurial activity and perpetuates poverty.[2]

The optimists' revenge

For millennia, pessimists have been telling us that everything is getting worse. As far back as the sixth century BC, Plato lamented the erosion of the soils of his native Attica, which were allegedly no longer farmed by 'true husbandmen'. In AD 200 Tertullian said:

> ... we men have actually become a burden to the earth, the fruits
> of nature hardly suffice to sustain us. There is a general pressure
> of scarcity giving rise to complaints, since the earth can no longer
> support us. Need we be astonished that plague and famine,
> warfare and earthquake come to be regarded as remedies, serving,
> as it were, to trim and prune the superfluity of population.[3]

In 1798, the Reverend Thomas Robert Malthus likewise averred that man's natural inclination to procreate, combined with the diminishing returns available from agricultural production, would lead to overpopulation and thus to war, pestilence and famine, unless kept in check by the social structures of Georgian England.

Our modern-day Tertullians are more numerous but no more numerically apt. As Mike Sierra, editor of the *Flummery Digest*, noted in April 1993:

> The *State of the World*, an annually updated book edited by
> Worldwatch Institute president Lester Brown, routinely predicts
> the imminent collapse of civilization through overpopulation,
> famine, resource depletion, and related environmental
> catastrophes. The 1993 edition proudly announced its tenth year
> of publication.[4]

The editorial continued:

Mr. Brown predicted imminent famine in 1967, 1974, 1984, and 1989. In 1984 he announced, 'If we go back to 1950 and look at the economic, agricultural, and social trends, we can see a clean breaking point somewhere around 1973.' In the late 1970s he also predicted that oil supplies would soon diminish sharply 'with production peaking around 1990.' And even 'more crucial than oil' is the world's topsoil, which Brown believes is being 'lost' to erosion to the tune of 415 million acres of cropland in America alone – half of its cultivated land.

Such apocalyptic predictions truly deserve the ironic derision afforded them by Sierra.[5] As Indur Goklany showed in chapter 2, on every indicator assessed – from the availability of food per capita to life expectancy and education – humanity as a whole is better off now than at any time since records began. Goklany argued, moreover, that we are in the midst of a virtuous cycle of progress 'composed of the mutually reinforcing, co-evolving forces of economic growth, technological change, and free trade'.[6] In other words, as long as we maintain the institutions that enable societies to become wealthier – and hence healthier – we will continue to see improvements in the human condition.

As Robert Bradley noted in chapter 10, the environment has also improved dramatically over the course of the past century in developed countries, with significant declines in air and water pollution.[7] The air in London is now cleaner than at any time since the sixteenth century! And even indoor air pollution – arguably among the biggest causes of early death among the world's poor – is improving, as people in poor countries switch from poorly flued wood and dung fires to using gas and electricity, or simply better, more efficient, stoves. But these changes are only possible with increases in income, which enable the purchase of superior technologies and encourage people to spend money on more efficient goods because their time is no longer efficiently spent gathering wood and dung for fuel.

Good business

But pessimists are reluctant to accept that the world is improving. They seem actually to prefer to think that the world is going to pot. To some extent it suits their world view, according to which all human activity should be treated with suspicion, especially when it involves profit, production, consumption, or anything else that might at a stretch be connected to business.

The ultimate villains of this piece are transnational companies (TNCs), who are presumed to be bad merely by virtue (vice?) of being big. Thus, the fact that many TNCs have incomes larger than the GDP of poor countries is given as justification for claiming that they have a responsibility to act more 'ethically' than other companies. Inasmuch as the provision of goods and services to people on a voluntary basis is a virtue rather than a vice, this argument seems upside down.

The possibility that TNCs might have become large primarily because they are good at providing people with what they want never seems to concern those who vilify them. Big is bad; small is beautiful; and, by this logic, nirvana is non-existent. Thus, the only truly 'ethical' company is one that makes no profits (because, as the inane slogan goes, 'people not profits'), produces enough of each good or service to satisfy everyone on the planet and charges nothing.

Such an 'ethical' company never has existed, never will exist, and probably is not desirable. The Soviets tried production without profit and it didn't work, as Charles Steele explained in chapter 6. Profits provide incentives to increase productive efficiency, reduce resource use and develop desirable new products. Destroy the profit motive and the incentives to discover what people want are destroyed, along with the incentive to produce better, more efficient things. The result would be a world full of Ladas: Lada cars, Lada houses, Lada computers. People don't like Ladas; they are small, smelly and inefficient. That's why Fiat stopped making them (or, rather, the 124 and 125, upon which all Ladas were based) in 1973.

In spite of their bad press, TNCs bring to poor countries muchneeded investment and relatively high-paying jobs. In many cases they also provide education and health care, not only to their workers but also to others in the communities in which they operate.[8] Even muchmaligned industries such as mining and forestry generally do far more good than harm.[9] However, in many poor countries these companies are discouraged from operating by government policies that limit their ability to repatriate profits, require them to partner with local companies, provide insufficient protection of their intellectual property, or require them to abide by all manner of absurd regulations.

The call for TNCs to comply with 'ethical investment' criteria, including compliance with global standards on environment and labour, is also cause for concern. While the ultimate objectives of such ethical investment are laudable – improving the environment and the conditions of employment for people in poor countries – it is questionable as to whether they are best achieved in this manner.

Labour standards would be difficult to enforce, as TNCs such as Levi's and Nike have already discovered: impoverished people clamour to work for foreign businesses and go to great lengths to get around rules. Such rules would also undermine the improvement of local standards, since TNCs and their contractors generally offer more favourable terms of employment than local companies. Given the alternatives that these people (especially women and young girls) face – prostitution, subsistence agriculture, begging – prohibitions on labour seem particularly worrisome. More generally, by raising the cost of doing business, the standards would discourage investment and thereby reduce the number of people who benefit, directly and indirectly, from the activities of TNCs. This will even feed through to the agricultural sector, as demand for food and other products will be lower than otherwise, reducing the value of the activities of peasant farmers and slowing down economic development.

Global environmental standards, meanwhile, would be equally counter-productive because they could not take into consideration the wide variety of circumstances that exist around the world. As Robert Bradley pointed out in chapter 10, if people in poor countries could rely on electricity for their energy needs, even the most polluting coal-fired power stations would cause far less harm than the poorly flued fires that cause human suffering and millions of premature deaths.

Moreover, as Pierre Desrochers showed in chapter 3, companies do not need government mandates to engage in activities that reduce consumption of resources and increase the efficiency of their operations. The market system itself provides huge incentives to engage in 'dematerialisation'.

TNCs have also been attacked for their failure to provide medicines to people in poor countries. Again, the criticisms are misdirected: Research shows that most medicines on the WHO's 'Essential Medicines' are not patented in most poor countries.[10] Even in India, which has over 20,000 pharmaceutical companies churning out generic copies of medicines (many of them on patent in other parts of the world, but not patentable in India), 60–70% of the population does not have access to medicines.[11] The access problem clearly has little to do with patents. Indeed, inasmuch as patents affect access it is to improve it – by giving research-based pharmaceutical companies an incentive to develop the drugs in the first place, in spite of huge costs. Rather, the access problem has many causes, including:

poverty, inadequate financing for pharmaceutical purchases, massively inadequate health care infrastructure (and infrastructure generally) and inadequacies in government controls on various health care activities, from the licensing of doctors to the regulation of pharmaceuticals.

Fortunately, some enlightened companies are stepping into the breach where corrupt and/or inefficient governments are failing. Coca-Cola has a programme for condom distribution in Southern Africa, which is aimed at reducing the region's growing HIV-transmission problem. Various mining companies have instituted comprehensive health care programmes, providing not only education and prophylactics but also treatment, even for people with AIDS, where medication can be relatively expensive. Many pharmaceutical companies have offered to supply their medicines at low or no cost to developing countries.

Companies are doing these things for a number of reasons. In part it is basic self-interest; ill workers are not productive. In part it is enlightened self-interest; improving the health of the poor makes for good PR. But for whatever reason they are doing it, they are doing it with little or no prodding from governments (indeed in many cases they are doing it in spite of all the restrictions imposed by governments), and they are doing it in places where governments are failing. Under such circumstances, it would be unwise to replace the ethical behaviour of TNCs with mandates that they behave in ways dictated by NGOs.

Promoting unsustainable development

While companies motivated by profits have undoubtedly improved our world, the same cannot be said for all the actions of the governments of rich countries. Colonialism, especially in Africa, directly harmed millions of people. It also caused enormous disruption to indigenous institutions, undermining what had in many cases been very effective political and economic systems.

Sadly, however, the guilt-inspired interventions by the rich world following the independence of the former colonies have hardly been a sparkling success. Fifty-five years of 'foreign aid' have probably done more harm than good. The billions of dollars taken from the middle class in rich countries and given to the elite in poor countries have propped up dictators, reinforced oppressive regimes and contributed to the starvation of millions.

In chapter 4, George Ayittey argued that most of Africa's problems stem from the inability of Africans to govern themselves appropriately, citing especially the failed experiments with socialism. However, he suggests that these problems have been compounded by foreign aid, which has in many cases supported corrupt governments and deterred reform. Zimbabwe is a case in point; the economy has halved in size over the past decade. In an attempt to cling to power in spite of the economic chaos, Robert Mugabe encouraged violent Zanu-PF supporters to occupy farms belonging to non-supporters. This only worsened the problems, destroying agricultural productivity and leading to famine. And now Mugabe is diverting food aid meant for famine victims to his Zanu-PF supporters.[12]

Latin America, meanwhile, has employed its own brand of unsustainable development, as Fabiano Pegurier and Gilberto Salgado showed in chapter 5. This really began in the 1950s, when many countries in the region adopted policies to promote 'import substitution industrialisation'. By restricting imports, and subsidising exports of industrial products, Latin America reduced its comparative advantage. Agricultural productivity collapsed, encouraging migration to shanty towns. In the name of industrialisation, the government caused social disruption and environmental chaos. But the industrialisation was short-lived. Governments propped up industries with subsidies, putting a strain on their finances. Looking for an easy way out, they inflated their currencies to reduce the external value of locally denominated debts, and forced banks to lend to them. The crunch came in the 1970s and 1980s, with stagflation and the debt crisis. Many countries are still reeling from the effects of these economically counterproductive policies.

Even as it preached reform during the late 1990s, Argentina's government increased spending but saw its revenue fall. To bridge the gap it compelled banks to loan it money and borrowed money from overseas organisations, including the IMF. But the burden of repayment was too great and in December 2001 it simultaneously defaulted on its loans and deflated the currency, thereby wiping out more than half the country's wealth in one fell swoop. The economy went from crisis to meltdown.

Bad as Africa and Latin America were – and for the most part continue to be – the prize for all-time star performance in the unsustainable development stakes must go to the Soviet Union, as Charles Steele showed in chapter 6. By removing the basic framework of the market economy and replacing it with a command system, the Soviets removed the very institutions that encourage efficiency and productivity. They solved the problem of 'market failure' by murder; replacing it with massive state failure. As with import substitution industrialisation, the Soviet system promoted industry by increasing throughputs, regardless of the consequences. While this increased output temporarily, the gains diminished rapidly and the damage to the environment and to people's lives grew. In their attempt to produce a socio-economic nirvana, the Soviet leaders instead merely caused misery.

The reason for the failure of central planning, as Martín Krause pointed out in chapter 7, is that central planners have no means of identifying what resources to use, when and where. Nor do they know what people want. As a result, they produce goods that nobody wants, inefficiently. Professor Krause argued that the same problems that affected the Soviet Union would also undermine any attempt to guide the world's economic activity by means of so-called 'green' accounting.

Unlike the kinds of indicators that Indur Goklany discussed, these alternative accounting systems aim to provide a detailed assessment of the sustainability of individual economies. Aside from the fact that green accounts are unable to take into consideration fundamental factors such as what resources will be important or useful in the future, there is the problem of discerning to what end the accounts will be used. Krause argued that the obvious purpose is to act as a guide to controlling economic activity in order to make it more 'sustainable'. Combining the impossibility of constructing a valid set of accounts with the inherent difficulties of attempting centrally to regulate economic activity is clearly a recipe for disaster.

Institutions for sustainable development

Krause also argued that if, instead of focusing on outcomes, policymakers were to focus on the institutional framework within which people act, it should be possible to design policies for sustainable development that would encourage individuals to make the best use of resources and to protect the environment, while at the same time improving both their lot and the lot of others. Such policies, he upheld, would focus on the key institutions of the free society: property rights, the rule of law, free markets and limited government. This idea is also discussed at some length in chapter 1.

Free trade and the risk of eco-protectionism

Statutory limitations on imports and exports have been common throughout history. Their purpose was typically some combination of revenue-raising for the state and preferential treatment for a favoured firm. They were often advocated as means of enhancing the wealth of a nation. These arguments were demolished by Adam Smith,[13] who showed that trade produces mutual gains, and David Ricardo,[14] who showed that this applies to trade between nations even when there is no absolute cost advantage.[15]

These insights still hold and have very clear implications for sustainable development. First, trade increases wealth, which, as Goklany noted in chapter 2, is broadly associated with improvements in human welfare. Second, trade increases the efficiency of resource use: in the absence of market distortions, production will occur in the most appropriate place, taking into consideration the cost of all factors. Third, trade can have direct environmental benefits. For example, trade in ivory increases the value of ivory to people living in poor parts of Africa, who then have stronger incentives to protect elephants and the habitat in which they live – if they have sufficiently strong rights to the wildlife. In sum, reducing trade barriers is essential for sustainable development.

In chapter 8, Alan Oxley argued that the agreement reached at Doha in November 2001 to launch a new round of trade liberalisation through the World Trade Organization (WTO) offers the opportunity of huge benefits to the people of the world. However, he cautions that these benefits will be reduced to the extent that trade sanctions are permitted on the basis of environmental concerns.

Whereas environmental protection may be used as a pretext for trade sanctions, Oxley warned that the EU might impose sanctions in order to protect its industries from lower-cost competition. For example, it might employ the 'precautionary principle' and invoke the Biosafety Protocol to justify restrictions on imports of agricultural goods from developing countries where biotechnology has been employed to improve yields. It might thereby more than wipe out the gains made possible by reduced tariffs on such products – harming poor countries in particular, which would be forced to choose between higher levels of exports to the EU or higher yields and crops better adapted to the climate of their countries. Either way, farmers in poor countries would lose and farmers in the EU get the protected markets they seek.

Are multilateral environmental agreements (MEAs) environmentally desirable?

Another possible use of trade sanctions for 'environmental' purposes would involve restrictions on imports from the US and other heavily industrialised countries that were not complying with the Kyoto Protocol on climate change. Oxley argued that if the EU implements Kyoto, the effect on its economies would be significant. In such circumstances, the pressure from European industry to impose tariffs on imported goods that are produced in energy-intensive ways would be huge. Such tariffs would, ironically, increase the costs of Kyoto.

Even under the most optimistic of scenarios, then, the costs of Kyoto would be large (a recent study suggested a 4 to 5% reduction in GDP in Germany and the UK by 2010) but the benefits would be negligible. In chapter 9, Robert Balling argued that our knowledge of the global climate remains sketchy; that most of the climate change that has been observed in the past century was not caused by man; and that in the future man's impact on the climate will be much smaller than the kinds of apocalyptic scenarios often bandied around. Under such circumstances, it seems to make little sense to impose swingeing restrictions on greenhouse gas emissions.

While others have noted scepticism regarding the utility of the Kyoto Protocol, many still conclude that 'no regrets' policies should be implemented. Often this is taken to include the promotion of 'alternative' energy. However, as Robert Bradley explained in chapter 10, hydrocarbon energy (coal, oil, gas) is becoming increasingly 'sustainable'. Indeed, it is far more sustainable than so-called 'renewable' alternatives (with the possible exception of some relatively isolated examples of hydroelectricity and wind power) and the drive towards these alternatives will cost human society by increasing the amount we pay for our energy – diverting resources into less efficient uses.

The aforementioned Biosafety Protocol is one of three multilateral environmental agreements (MEAs) which ostensibly address concerns about conserving endangered species, discussed by Jonathan Adler in chapter 11. Adler assessed the threat posed by species extinction and biodiversity loss and concluded that while man has definitely had an impact on the number and diversity of species, the likely extent of the problem is less and the consequences for humankind far less dramatic than some have claimed. Nevertheless, he concluded that there may be good reason to take measures to conserve biological diversity. However, Adler is sceptical that MEAs – and in particular the three MEAs that have so far been agreed – are of any help; indeed, they may be a hindrance:

- In places where property rights over wildlife are reasonably well defined and readily enforced (which is the case in much of Southern Africa), the restrictions on trade imposed under the Convention on International Trade in Endangered Species' (CITES) undermine the value of wildlife to people who must share their land with it, encouraging them to kill rather than conserve it.
- The Convention on Biological Diversity (CBD) does little to encourage practical *in situ* conservation. What it does accomplish is either ambiguous or harmful. The emphasis on the need to create official 'protected areas' is, as Adler pointed out, misguided. The experience globally with such protected areas has not been a happy one and they are especially problematic in countries with few financial resources available for conservation measures. Meanwhile, if governments nationalise physical and/or knowledge resources (a possible interpretation of Articles 15 and 16 of the CBD), they risk reducing the incentives for conservation by undermining the commercial incentives of locals.
- The Biosafety Protocol establishes measures that enable members to restrict trade in agricultural products on an arbitrary basis, enabling the EU and Japan to continue their protectionist policies without any justification as to their benefit to the environment or human health. Indeed, by discouraging the use of higher-yielding plant varieties, such measures would probably harm the environment because people in poor countries will increase their use of marginal land.

Property rights, intervention and conservation

One of the key themes of this book has been that, as a general rule, institutions that are compatible with human nature are more likely to result in appropriate levels of environmental protection and conservation of natural resources. One institution in particular – private property – has been shown to have such characteristics. When combined with the rule of law, which enables people to enforce and transfer what they own, private property encourages individuals to care for their possessions.

Where populations are scattered and the value of land is low, the costs of protecting habitat can be high relative to the benefits. In such circumstances, private property is still often superior to open access (or no property) and is almost always superior to state ownership (with all the perverse incentives of that system). However, under such circumstances it may not make sense for individuals to own plots of land, except for their dwellings. Rather, shared private property or 'common property' is often a superior solution, as Douglas Southgate argued in chapter 12.

Common property is almost ubiquitous in tropical forests. Where the local people have been left to their own devices, common property has in many places encouraged sustainable use of local resources. However, governments have often undermined the effectiveness of the traditional common property institutions. In some cases they have nationalised resources, or imposed regulations on their use – often with the best interests of everyone at heart. But good intentions are not enough to justify bad policies. In other cases, they have granted mining or logging licences to outside groups; these are rarely justified by anything other than the benefits, financial or political, which accrue to the government officials responsible for granting the licence.

While government intervention has been a significant factor promoting the conversion of forest to other uses, demand for agricultural land has played an even more important role. If land is more valuable for growing crops than for growing trees, people will tend to grow crops. Of course, not all such land conversion should be lamented; if growing populations in poor countries wish to use their land for agriculture and thereby improve their nutrition, what right does anyone else have to stop them?

In many places, however, land conversion is extremely inefficient because it is not converted permanently for sedentary agriculture. Rather, forest is slashed, burnt, used for a couple of years until the natural nutrients are depleted and then simply left. Where demand for land is low, such practices are not problematic, as the forest soon grows back. However, in areas where demand for land is high, the impact can be more severe. The solution in such cases is to encourage higher-yielding agriculture, which both better satisfies nutritional requirements and reduces pressure for land conversion. However, it also requires a shift from common to individual private property and for this to take place, people must be able to enforce their property rights.

In chapter 1, I noted that the inability to enforce property rights is probably the leading cause of poverty in the world. Now we see that the absence of property rights is also one of the leading causes of habitat destruction in the world. Changing that situation must therefore be the foremost priority of everyone who seeks to promote sustainable development.

Common property is also typical of coastal fisheries and has proved in many cases to be very successful, as Michael De Alessi showed in chapter 13. However, where the state has intervened, it has often destroyed these institutions, undermining incentives to conserve and creating conflict. Often that conflict is with industrial fishers, who have been favoured politically throughout the world. But, more recently, as industrial fishing has reached and exceeded the maximum sustainable yield of many fish stocks, the conflict is between different groups of fishers, each of which seeks to obtain as much of the remaining stock as possible. This is a classic open access problem, but the irony is that it has been caused by government. The solution, as De Alessi lucidly demonstrated, is to decentralise fisheries management; give the fishers a genuine stake in the fishery and they will have an incentive to conserve the stocks. New Zealand and Iceland have done this by creating individual transferable quotas (ITQs). These are a form of common property, similar to the kind of property one owns in a joint-stock company, and as such help fishers realise that what they do not consume today will be there for them tomorrow. This gives them an incentive to demand reductions in total allowable catch levels – quite the opposite of what happens in politicised management systems.

In addition, De Alessi showed that property rights in stands of water have encouraged the emergence of aquaculture – or fish farming – which is now responsible for a huge proportion of salmon and trout production and is likely in the future to be a significant source of cod production. By enabling high efficiency fish production, private property rights in water-based resources reduce the pressure on wild fish stocks, much as property rights in land encourage high-yield farming, which reduces the pressure on land-based species.

Even in extremely arid regions, private property and the rule of law are vastly superior to political management. Mary Tiffen and Michael Mortimore showed in chapter 14 that the conceptualisation of the desertification problem by the UNEP and other agencies has generally been inaccurate and has usually led to nothing but mischief. A more balanced assessment of the dynamics of the agronomy of dry regions indicates that people are highly adaptable and that changes in vegetative cover should not be interpreted always as a sign of permanent degradation. Like Douglas Southgate, Tiffen and Mortimore conclude that sedentary farming is the solution, as it leads to higher yields and lower levels of erosion. In order to achieve this, they argue, people in dry regions need: a stable currency; markets and ready access to them (on well-maintained roads, for example); advice about, and possibly government supervision of, animal health; and other services that people consider good value for money, such as education and health care (presumably this would be the case whether they are provided by government or not). And of course, in order for markets to exist, people need to own their own property and must be free to exchange it with others. Thus property rights and the rule of law become fundamental conditions for coping in arid environments, just as they are fundamental conditions for improving the lot of the common man – and the environment – across the world.

Property rights in water resources would help reduce the conflict that currently exists in so many parts of the world, as Roger Bate demonstrated in chapter 15. This concurs with what Hernando de Soto, the now-famous Peruvian economist and author of *The Mystery of Capital*, found when he studied the impact that poorly enforceable property rights and overbearing government regulations had on the people of his native country:

> The real remedy for violence and poverty is to recognise the property and labour of those whom formality today excludes, so that where there is rebellion there will be a sense of belonging and responsibility. When people develop a taste for independence and faith in their own efforts, they will be able to believe in themselves and in economic freedom.[16]

Or, as Stephan Schmidheiny, founder of the World Business Council for Sustainable Development, put it:

> ... efficient, transparent, reliable property rights are both an integral human right and a crucial tool in constructing this thing called sustainable development.[17]

So, to return to the theme begun in chapter 1, sustainable development is not about defining outcomes and putting in place grandiose schemes to achieve them. Humanity is too fallible, the world we inhabit too variable to accommodate such schemes. There may well be great changes afoot in the natural environment and man may even be responsible for some of them. But to suggest that we can control these changes is an arrogance that surpasses even the dreams of popes and princes. Humanity has adapted to the world in which it lives, carving out an ecological niche that is unique among species. But this adaptation did not stop ten thousand years ago when the first humans settled the plains of Mesopotamia. It has continued in the development of institutions – the norms, conventions, rules and laws that govern our behaviour. These institutions have enabled us to live with one another in intermittent peace and, in the past few centuries, have enabled a growing proportion of humanity to escape from the poverty in which their ancestors were mired. It would be a tragedy if, in the name of 'sustainable development', we were to allow ourselves to undermine these fine institutions and thereby propel ourselves back towards an age of darkness. Or, less extreme but still tragic, if we were to prevent ourselves from progressing.

It is our duty to ensure that the institutions we pass on to our children, and our children's children, enable them to progress just as we will progress. And we must strive to ensure that those institutions which enable progress are adopted widely, so that people alive today – wherever they are on this small blue-green globe – are able to improve their lot; to live rather than to subsist; to create rather than to copy; to be free rather than to be oppressed.

Notes

Chapter 1 – **Julian Morris**

1 WCED (1987), p. 43.
2 *See* p. 127.
3 http://www.un.org/esa/sustdev/index.html. Accessed 12 June 2002.
4 UN General Assembly resolution 55/2, para. 19, United Nations, New York.
5 The description is taken from Morris (1995).
6 Hancock (1989), pp. 192–3.
7 North and Thomas (1972).
8 de Soto (1989).
9 Portions of this section are taken from Morris (1995).
10 The meaning of 'private' property should be clarified: in the sense in which it is used here, private property means property for which an identifiable person or group of people is the principal 'residual claimant(s)', *see* Barzel (1989). Residual claimants have a right to any good produced by that property, and are liable for any externalities generated. Many fascinating alternative mechanisms for managing property, especially where individual rights are difficult to delineate, are discussed in Ostrom (1988, 1990) and Schlager and Ostrom (1992).
11 Alchian (1965), Demsetz (1967), Anderson and Hill (1975), Ault and Rutman (1979).
12 Brookfield and Padoch (1994).
13 Stahl (1993).
14 It is necessary only for the owner of B to show that this physical harm was most likely the result of the pollution emanating from A. However, it must be shown that the damage actually exists or is imminent; otherwise there is only the potentiality of an action, not an action as such: *Pemberton v Bright* [1960] 1 WLR 436.
15 *St Helen's Smelting Co v Tipping* (1865) 11 All ER 1483.

16 This section is taken from Morris *et al.* (2002).

17 'If later innovators cannot freely build on the work of others, or must pay to do so, they may be less likely to engage in inventive activity themselves' – Besen and Raskind (2001).

18 For example, the legal fees arising out of a battle between Kodak and Polaroid cost Kodak $100 million – Cole (2000).

19 It is important to distinguish here sound science from consensus science. Often interest groups on both sides of a particular argument will say that so many thousands of scientists have said x. While such statements probably persuade a certain section of the public, they rarely reflect the very real disputes that exist in the scientific literature. Ensuring that these disputes are taken into consideration is not an easy task – but forcing 'consensus' is no solution. In addition, any cost-benefit analysis must consider the opportunity costs of diverting resources towards one action rather than another. So, for example, if one believes that the global climate will warm by two degrees celsius by the year 2100 and that the cost of this will be 5% of total world output, then before taking action to prevent this harm one should calculate what the cost of taking action will be. If it turns out that no action can be taken that reduces world output by less than 5%, then it would be folly to take any action at all.

20 Of course, strict rules would be necessary to prevent abuse of power, such as a requirement that all tenders be clearly specified and bids be considered strictly on the basis of conformity with hurdle-type criteria and cost.

Chapter 2 – Indur Goklany

1 Barney (1980).

2 Simon (1995).

3 Simon (1995) p. 1.

4 Brown (1998) p. 4.

5 Maddison (1999).

6 UNDP (2000). The logarithm of per capita income is used to moderate the impact on the index from additional increases in income.

7 Ehrlich (1968), Paddock and Paddock (1967).

8 Mitchell and Ingco (1993), World Resources Institute (1998).

9 Goklany (1998).

10   FAO (1996a).

11   FAO (1996b), (1999).

12   World Resources Institute (1998).

13   This is the first of several curves plotting various indicators against GDP per capita (in 1995 US dollars at market exchange rates, MXR). To better illustrate the dependence of indicators at low- to mid-levels of economic development, the scales for this and similar figures are cut off at mid-levels of GDP per capita. Unless noted otherwise, the smoothed curves in all these figures were generated using log-linear relationships and the slopes, i.e. the coefficients of the log (GDP per capita) term, are significant (i.e. $p < 0.001$). In Figure 1, for 1961, the number of observations (N) was 92, and $R^2 = 0.61$. For 1994, $N = 150$ and $R^2 = 0.63$. Also, unless otherwise noted, the shifts in the indicator as we go from one year to the other, i.e. the y-intercepts, are also significant ($p < 0.001$). This shift informs us about the effect of technology over time in the level of the indicator. According to the regression analyses, if per capita income had been frozen at $300 (in 1995 US dollars, MXR), available food supplies would have increased from 2,004 calories per capita per day in 1961 to 2,148 calories per capita per day in 1994.

14   Goklany (1998).

15   Mitchell and Ingco (1993), World Resources Institute (1998).

16   Preston (1995).

17   UNDP (2000).

18   Floud and Harris (1997), p. 116.

19   Haines (1994).

20   N was 64 for 1970 and 51 for 1995. Because a number of countries were already at 100% in 1995, a Tobit model was used for truncation at that level. The untruncated log-linear regressions had R^2 of 0.35 and 0.55 for 1970 and 1995 respectively. The rise in the intercept was significant ($p < 0.001$), as were the slopes, i.e. coefficients for GDP per capita, for the individual years. *See also* note 13.

21   *See* Table 1 and Figure 1.

22   *See*, for example, Table 3.

23   World Bank (1999).

24   N and R^2 for 1962, 1980 and 1997 are 96 and 0.71, 121 and 0.71, and 148 and 0.65 respectively. If per capita income had been frozen at $300 (in 1995 US dollars), life expectancy would have increased from 44.7 years in 1962 to 55.0 in 1997. *See* note

13 above. Dollars for United States, China and India are all adjusted for purchasing power parity (Maddison 1995 and 1999).

25 Dollars for United States, China and India are all adjusted for purchasing power parity. Maddison (1995), (1999).

26 Bureau of the Census (1975).

27 World Bank (1999).

28 OECD (1998), Shalala (1998).

29 WHO (2000).

30 US Dept. of Health and Human Services (1997).

31 Figure 4 uses data from the World Resources Institute (1998) for 1950–55 and 1955–60 (plotted as 1952.5, and 1957.5, respectively). For Russia, it plotted the World Resources Institute data for 1960–65, 1965–70, 1970–75 as 1962, 1967 and 1972 data. The multiple years reflect five-year averages, using real or expected values. The rest of the data are from the World Bank (1999).

32 Becker and Bloom (1998).

33 Goklany (1998).

34 Becker and Bloom (1998).

35 UNDP (2000).

36 Hill (1995).

37 World Resources Institute (1998), UNDP (2000).

38 Bureau of the Census (1975) p. 60, (1999).

39 World Resources Institute (1998), UNDP (2000).

40 *See*, for example, Pritchett and Summers (1996), World Bank (1993).

41 World Bank (1999).

42 The curves in Figure 5 were fitted using a log-log relationship. N and R2 for each of the years 1962, 1980 and 1997 were 96 and 0.71, 123 and 0.74, and 147 and 0.79 respectively. The significant lowering of the curve over time is consistent with the creation and diffusion of new and existing-but-underused technologies. If GDP per capita had been frozen at $300 (in 1995 US dollars), the infant mortality rate would have declined from 147 per 1,000 live births in 1962 to 82 per 1,000 in 1997. *See also* note 13.

43 Bureau of the Census (1975) p. 57, (1999).

44 Maddison (1998), (1999).

45 International dollars are obtained using a special conversion factor, purchasing power parity, designed to reflect more accurately the purchasing powers of different currencies. Conversion is

based on the number of units of a country's currency required to buy the same amounts of goods and services in the domestic market as $1 would buy in the United States. In contrast, the market exchange rate (MXR) of a currency in US dollars (used elsewhere in this chapter) is the amount of the currency one can buy with one US dollar on the open currency market.

46 Goklany (1999c).

47 Ausubel and Grübler (1995).

48 World Bank (1999).

49 N and R2 for 1965, 1980 and 1996 were 82 and 0.54, 112 and 0.47 and 137 and 0.64 respectively. The increases in the intercepts, which are significant, are probably owing to increasing knowledge about the benefits of education and the willingness and ability of families and societies to incur the costs of longer periods of education. Globally, post-secondary enrolment increased from 6.8% in 1965 to 18.8% in 1996. *See also* note 13.

50 Maddison (1995), (1998).

51 World Bank (1999).

52 *Ibid.*

53 UNDP (2000).

54 Gwartney, Holcombe and Lawson (1998), Gwartney, Lawson and Samida (2000).

55 As noted previously, the index uses the logarithm of GDP per capita.

56 UNDP (2000).

57 *Daily Mail* and *Guardian* (1998), UNHCR (1998), (1999).

58 World Resources Institute (1998).

59 UNDP (2000).

60 CDC (1998), Martin *et al.* (1999) p. 28.

61 Costa and Steckel (1997), Maddison (1999).

62 UNDP (2000).

63 UNDP (1999) p. 11.

64 Maddison (1998), (1999).

65 UNDP (2000).

66 World Resources Institute (1998). The multiple years reflect five-year averages, using real or expected values.

67 FAO (1996b), (1999).

68 Easterlin (1996), Fogel (2000), Lerner and Anderson (1963).

69 Fogel (2000) p. 149.

70 UNDP (2000) p. 152.

71 Goklany (1998), (2000).

72 For 1961, there were 96 observations (N) and R2 was 0.34, for 1980, N=120 and R2 = 0.35 and for 1997, N=138 and R2 = 0.49. The slopes for each curve were significant (p < 0.001), as were the changes in the intercepts (for cereal yields) from 1961–80, and from 1980–97. *See also* note 13.

73 Goklany (1995), (1998).

74 *See*, for example, Figure 2.

75 Fogel (1995), (2000), WHO (1999).

76 Goklany (1999b), *see also*, Pritchett and Summers (1996), World Bank (1993).

77 Barro (1997), Bloom (1999), Fogel (1995), World Bank (1993), WHO (1999).

78 Fogel (1995) p. 65.

79 Easterlin (1996).

80 World Bank (1993), p. 18.

81 Malaria Foundation International (2000), *see also Guardian* (2000).

82 Easterlin (1996).

83 World Bank (1993) p. 19.

84 Watkins (1997).

85 Barro (1997), Goklany (1998).

86 Goklany (1995).

87 UNDP (1999).

88 Goklany (1995).

89 Barbour (1980), Seskin (1978).

90 UN (2000).

91 Goklany (1998).

92 Dollar and Kraay (2000), *see also* Frankel and Romer (1999).

93 Dollar and Kraay (2000).

94 Ravallion and Chen (1997).

95 Easterly and Rebelo (1993).

96 Dollar and Kraay (2000).

97 FAO (2000), McEvedy and Jones (1978) p. 342.

98 Bairoch (1982).

99 Bairoch (1982) defines manufacturing industry as industry in general except mining, construction, electricity, gas and water.

100 Smil (1994).

101 Maddison (1999).

102 This is calculated from GDPs provided by Maddison (1999) p. 40, for 1820 and 1995, and annual growth rates from 1700–1820 and 1978–95.

Chapter 3 – Pierre Desrochers

1 Simmonds, P.L. (1876) *Waste Products and Undeveloped Substances: A Synopsis of Progress Made in their Economic Utilisation During the Last Quarter of a Century at Home and Abroad*, Hardwicke and Bogue, London, pp. 11–12.
2 Worrell (2000), p. 1.
3 Nath *et al.* (2000), p. 1.
4 Hawken *et al.* (1999), p. 5.
5 *Ibid.*, pp. 8–9.
6 Florida and Davison (2001), p. 198.
7 *See*, for example, Resetar (1999) and the recent compilation of the *Harvard Business Review on Business and the Environment* (2000).
8 For a more detailed survey of the historical evidence, *see* Desrochers (2002).
9 Hertwich (1997).
10 Babbage (1835), p. 217.
11 The Bethnal Green Branch Museum was located in London's South Kensington and is now part of the Victoria and Albert Museum.
12 The Bethnal Green Branch of the South Kensington Museum (1875), p. 4.
13 Koller (1918 [1902]), p. vi.
14 Clemen (1927), p. vii.
15 *Ibid.*
16 *Ibid.*, p. vii.
17 *Ibid.*, p. 2.
18 Kershaw (1928), p. vii.
19 Carter (1939), p. 143.
20 Simmonds (1876) p. 5.
21 Quoted by Simmonds (1876), p. 1.
22 The Bethnal Green Branch of the South Kensington Museum (1875), p. 3.
23 *Ibid.*
24 Quoted by Rosenberg (1994), p. 104.
25 Hobson (1917), p. 75.
26 Marshall (1986 [1920]), p. 232.
27 Talbot (1920), pp. 13–14.
28 *See*, among others, The Bethnal Green Branch of the South Kensington Museum (1875), Kershaw (1928), Koller (1918), Simmonds (1862, 1876), Talbot (1920) and Desrochers (2002).

29 Talbot (1920), pp. 17–18.
30 e.g. Graedel and Allenby (1995).
31 e.g. Hawken *et al.* (1999).
32 Desrochers (2002).
33 Simmonds (1862), p. 2.
34 The Bethnal Green Branch of the South Kensington Museum (1875), p. 4.
35 Talbot (1920), p. 19.
36 Kershaw (1928), p. ix.
37 Cumbler (2000), p. 14.
38 *See* the authors selected by Neimark and Rhoades Mott (1999) in their documentary history of the environmental debate.
39 Riukulehto (1998), p. 51.
40 Chase (1926), Riukulehto (1998).
41 Spooner (1918), p. 198.
42 Thus Spooner (1918) spends less than 40 pages out of 300 on the topic of industrial by-product recovery in his *Wealth from Waste*. Chase (1926) devotes similarly limited space to the subject.
43 Chase (1926), p. 174.
44 *Ibid.*, p. 263.
45 Schwartz and Steininger (1997).
46 *Ibid.*
47 Talbot (1920), pp. 302–4.
48 Kneese and Bower (1979), OECD (1994).
49 Frosch (1997), p. 45.
50 Davies and Mazurek (1998), Environmental Law Institute (1998, 1999).

Chapter 4 – George B. N. Ayittey

  1 Africa has 40 per cent of the world's potential hydroelectric power supply, the bulk of the world's diamonds and chromium, 50 per cent of the world's gold, 90 per cent of its cobalt, 50 per cent of its phosphates, 40 per cent of its platinum, 7.5 per cent of its coal, 8 per cent of its known petroleum reserves, 12 per cent of its natural gas, 3 per cent of its iron ore, and millions upon millions of acres of untilled farmland (Lamb, 1983, p. 20). It also has 64 per cent of the world's manganese, 13 per cent of its copper, and vast bauxite, nickel and lead resources. It accounts for 70 per cent of cocoa, 60 per cent of coffee, 50 per cent of

palm oil, and 20 per cent of the total petroleum traded in the world market, excluding the United States and Russia.

2 *The African Observer*, 7–20 June 1999, p. 23.

3 The subsequent Asian economic crisis and collapse of Argentina will have affected these differentials but Africa itself has had major problems in the recent past (e.g. Zimbabwe's economic collapse and the decline in the value of the South African rand), which would also adversely affect its relative position. *See* World Bank (2001), p. 8.

4 Mazrui (1986).

5 *Ibid.*, p. 164.

6 This Mazrui ascribes to the 'shallowness of Western institutions', 'the lopsided nature of colonial acculturation' and 'the moral contradictions of Western political tutelage', *ibid.*, p. 202.

7 *Ibid.*, p. 199.

8 *Ibid.*, p. 164.

9 'The pervasive atmosphere in much of the land is one of rust and dust, stagnation and decay, especially within those institutions which were originally bequeathed by the West,' *ibid.*, p. 210.

10 *Ibid.*, p. 206.

11 *Ibid.*, p. 210.

12 *New African*, July 1988, p. 25.

13 *Zimbabwe Independent*, 27 April 1999, p. 25.

14 *The Independent*, 18 November 1999, p. 3.

15 *Panafrican News*, 8 September 2000.

16 Achebe (1985), p. 3.

17 *Ghana Drum* (1996).

18 *Free Press*, 29 March–11 April 1996, p. 2.

19 *Daily Graphic*, 12 July 2000, p. 5.

20 *The African-American Observer*, 25 April–1 May 2000, p. 10.

21 *The New York Times* (1996), p. 4.

22 *The Washington Times* (1995b), p. A18. Also see US Agency for International Development's website, http://www.usaid.gov/pubs/cp98/afr/countries/ke.htm, downloaded 5 June 2002.

23 *The Post Express*, 10 July 2000, p. 26.

24 *The New York Times* (2000).

25 *The Economist* (1990).

26 Eberstadt (2000).

27 Berkeley (1996).

28 *The Independent*, 16 November 1999, p. 1.

29 *The Washington Post* (1998).

30 Gourevitch (1998), p. 82.
31 *UN Recovery*, April 2000, p. 8.
32 *The Washington Times* (1996).
33 *The Washington Post* (1995).
34 *The Washington Post* (2000).
35 'Departing staff threaten Zimbabwe's health sector,' see http://www.suntimes.co.za/2000/12/17/politics/po104.htm, downloaded 5 June 2002. *Sunday Times*, Rosebank, South Africa, 17 December 2000.
36 *The Economist* (1997).
37 Eberstadt (2000).
38 Whitaker (1988), p. 68.
39 World Bank (1989), p. 1.
40 *The Washington Post* (1999).
41 Between 1980 and 1985, the United States alone gave Liberia's late President Samuel Doe more than $375 million in aid, most of which was squandered and looted, forcing Liberia to go into receivership on 2 May 1986.
42 Maren (1997) p. 11.
43 *The Washington Times* (1995a).
44 Maren (1997), p. 171.
45 UNCTAD (1998), p. xii.
46 World Bank (1993).
47 World Bank (1995).
48 *Financial Times* (1990).
49 Eberstadt (1988), p. 100.
50 *New African*, June 1992, p. 20.
51 *The New York Times* (1990).
52 World Bank (1990).
53 *The Economist* (1990a).
54 *The Economist* (1995).
55 *The Economist*, 9 October 1999, p. 52.

Chapter 5 – Fabiano Pegurier and Gilberto Salgado

 1 World Bank (2001), Thorp (1998). Precise estimates are difficult because of the chaotic economic situation in one of the region's largest countries, Argentina.
 2 In economic jargon, the income elasticity of such exports was believed to be less than unity.
 3 Haberler (1974), p. 152, for instance.

4 The first four countries listed were the ones that reached particularly high inflation rates in the 1950s and 1960s. Bolivia reached even higher rates in the 1950s, but it was going through a civil war.

5 Average tariffs and charges for semi-manufactured and durable consumer goods in 1957–9 are as follows: Brazil 143%, Argentina 139%, Chile 96%, Colombia 48%, Mexico 58%, Peru 25%. Moreover, negative interest rates were also used to reduce the cost of capital in the local market. In absolute values, these rates ranged from 21% in Brazil to 1.2% in Peru, following the above country sequence. Sheahan (1987), p. 87.

6 *Ibid.*, p. 90. The figures for the ratio of manufactured products to GDP are overestimated, especially in those countries where protection was greater and domestic prices were much higher than international prices. *Ibid.*, p. 86. What is clear is that industrial production was directed towards the domestic market. Since manufacturing did depend on protection, the growth in manufacturing had to rely on the level of domestic demand during a period in which international trade was booming.

7 *Ibid.*, pp. 95–6.

8 This fact is acknowledged on the historical background offered by the Internet site of the new version of Pacto Andino, Comunidad Andina (Andean Community).

9 Edwards (1997), p. 66.

10 *See* Bruton (1998) for a balanced, relevant discussion that considers South Korea's ISI efforts and relates the experiences of that country, after the mid-1960s, to that of Latin America. Our discussion is more straightforward, as is that of Edwards (1997), pp. 69–74 and 150–53.

11 Haberler (1974), p. 152.

12 But note that Mexico, Venezuela and Colombia were oil exporters, while Argentina, Chile and Peru were basically self-sufficient.

13 The average real interest cost of floating rate dollar debt rose from minus 8.7% in 1977–80 to nearly 16% in 1981–3. The fall in the prices of exports, in turn, had a serious impact even in a country such as Colombia, which did not otherwise have significant macroeconomic or current account imbalances. The same applied to countries that had engaged mainly in fixed interest rate contracts.

14 Net transfers to the region went from US $39.8 billion in 1979–81 to negative US $90.8 billion in 1983–5: that is,

transfers essentially became negative US$149 billion during the period between 1979 and 1985.

15 In South America, no country had a nominal devaluation of less than 200% in 1982–7. In Mexico, it was of 4,756%, and in the region as a whole 250,327%. Nevertheless, inflation was such that in some countries domestic currencies actually appreciated.

16 A study of seignorage revenue in the Bank of England Group estimates that the ratio of inflation tax to government revenue in 1979–93 was 43.7% in Argentina and 23.6% in Mexico – Fry *et al.* (1996), pp. 133ff.

17 IMF, *International Financial Statistics.*

18 Edwards (1997) ch. 3 discusses in detail the factors responsible for the emergence of interest in the market-oriented reforms of the late 1980s and the 1990s.

19 Fishlow and Cardoso (1992).

20 These policies were attempted with less emphasis also in Uruguay, where they had some measure of success, and in Argentina. Fiscal policies were lax, and hence inconsistent with the fixed exchange rate established by the plans, leading to overvaluation and loss of reserves. In Chile, a major inconsistency lay in fixing the nominal exchange rate while keeping wage indexation – inertia led to an appreciation of the peso.

21 *See* Edwards (1997), pp. 68–81 and Bruton (1998), pp. 626ff.

22 IDB (1998).

23 The 2001 rate is a projection from the IMF (2001).

24 In the televised words of the current President of the House of Representatives in Brazil, in response to recent measures by the US government to protect its steel industry from foreign competition.

25 For an analysis of the Peruvian case, *see* de Soto (1989). The issue is of literally tragic consequence, for these are poor countries that often are not so poor in resources. Entrepreneurship at all levels is the only activity that actually creates value. Entrepreneurship alone identifies hitherto overlooked, highly valued uses, for currently misemployed, undervalued resources.

26 ECLAC, projection made by mid-2001. Twelve out of seventeen of the largest economies of the region had current account deficits projected to be above 3.5% in 2001.

27 On the positive side it should be remembered that the 1980s were debt crisis years and that since 1994 the region has been affected by the Mexican, the Asian, and the Russian crises, which

in turn were followed by the slowdown in US and world economic activity. Therefore, with the smallest persistent improvement in external conditions, a better domestic environment should be able to deliver high growth rates over a depressed baseline.

28 Andersen (1999).

Chapter 6 – **Charles N. Steele**

1 Much of the information in the following presentation is based on the discussions in Boettke (1993), Gregory and Stuart (1997), Hewett (1988) and Kornai (1992).

2 The one-year plan was the actual set of operating instructions for the Soviet economy, and is described here. The more widely known five-year plans were largely indicative, and suggested goals which the one-year plans attempted to attain.

3 *See* Desrochers, this volume.

4 Goldman (1972b), Pryde (1991).

5 Kneen (2000).

6 In the Soviet experience, these constraints were exacerbated by the incentives for wasteful behaviour, previously mentioned. Additionally, official acceptance of the Marxist doctrine of the labour theory of value meant that raw resources had an implicit value of zero, in practice they were often treated this way, leading to additional wastefulness in harvesting of timber, extraction of oil, etc (Goldman, 1972a).

7 Aslund (2002), pp. 26, 36.

8 Romer (1991).

9 Estimates of the death toll range from 6 million to 14.5 million people, primarily Ukrainians – Conquest (1986), Werth pp. 159–68 in Courtois *et al.* (1999).

10 Easterly (1999).

11 It is not possible fully to document the effects of the system with a few statistics – for several reasons. First, statistical data for the Soviet Union (and the subsequent FSU countries) are notoriously inaccurate. The system encouraged false reporting at all levels, from the SOE (which misled planners as to capacity, inputs required, and output produced) through midstream planners (who reported successes, whether real or imagined, in order to avoid punishment) to the highest leaders (who trumpeted the supposed achievements of the economy to the citizenry and the world at

large, as part of their efforts to hold on to and increase power). Second, Soviet national accounts measured *gross material product*, rather than GNP or GDP, and thus are not directly comparable to national accounts of Western countries. Attempts by Western economists to estimate Soviet production were frustrated by the lack of data and the closed nature of the society, and the estimates are now believed to have been overly optimistic. Third, expressing Soviet production in monetary terms is extremely problematic. Soviet prices were set by the state, and did not reflect value or scarcity. Attempting to use world prices to value Soviet output fails to allow for quality problems, which are well known to have been chronic, yet nearly impossible to quantify, since data do not exist (the success indicator problem). And the partial dependence of the official economy on an unmeasured shadow economy makes official measures even less meaningful. These difficulties suggest that official economic data tend to overestimate economic activity.

12 Khanin and Selyunin (1987), cited in Boettke (1993), pp. 22–3, and Aslund (2002), p. 34.
13 EBRD (1999), p. 73.
14 Aslund (2002), p. 36.
15 OECD (2001), p. 10.
16 Aslund (2002), p. 38.
17 World Bank (1996), pp. 32–3, Hewett (1988), p. 85.
18 For one of the earliest claims to this effect, *see* Lange (1938).
19 Feshbach and Friendly (1992), pp. 113–14.
20 *Ibid.*, p. 201.
21 *Ibid.*, p. 189.
22 *Ibid.*, pp. 206–7.
23 *Ibid.*, p. 274.
24 Pryde (1991), pp. 22–3.
25 *Ibid.*, pp. 224–6, Micklin (1988).
26 Feshbach and Friendly (1992), pp. 76–82.
27 Pryde (1991), pp. 202–4.
28 *Ibid.*
29 *Ibid.*, p. 51.
30 Feshbach and Friendly (1992), pp. 175–8.
31 Courtois *et al.* (1999), p. 4.
32 Courtois *et al.* (1999), pp. 203–205.

Chapter 7 – **Martín Krause**

1 WCED (1987).
2 Kahn (1979), p. 53.
3 UNEP (1997).
4 Henderson (1991), p. 29.
5 *Ibid.*, p. 202.
6 *Ibid.*, p. 75.
7 OECD (1991).
8 Davis *et al.* (1997).
9 Hayek (1937, 1945).
10 UN (1994), p. 8.
11 Estimates vary from as few as 3 million to as many as 111 million species (*see* Adler, this volume).
12 UN (1994), ch. 5.
13 *Ibid.*, p. 18.
14 UNEP (1994).
15 There is in fact a huge literature on what is known as the 'contingent valuation method' (CVM). The interested reader is directed in particular to Kahnemann *et al.* (1986), Harrison (1992), Hanemann (1994) and Coursey (1998). This literature suggests that well-designed CVM studies provide a rank ordering of the public's willingness to pay for specific environmental or public goods but not much more.
16 Henderson (1991), p. 270.
17 Fundación Vida Silvestre (1993), p. 41.
18 Henderson (1991), p. 79.
19 UNEP (1994), p. 2.
20 Henderson (1991), p. 128.
21 Hardin (1968).
22 Quoted in Brailovsky and Foguelman (1991).
23 Bate (2001).
24 Anderson and Leal (1991), p. 139.
25 Foster and Hahn (1995).
26 *See* Steele (this volume).
27 Coase (1974).

Chapter 8 – **Alan Oxley**

1 The WTO dispute settlement body is the closest equivalent that the WTO has to a court system for settling disputes between members.

2 Griswold (2001).
3 Similar restrictions are permitted under the Sanitary and Phytosanitary Agreement, which covers trade in foodstuffs.
4 Technically speaking, restrictions could not be placed on 'non-product-related process and production methods (or PPMs)'.
5 WTO (1998), WTO (2001).
6 The Bush Administration does not follow the same environment policy objectives but it is bound to implement laws enacted by the US Congress, such as the unilateral trade sanctions against foreign exporters of shrimps who do not protect turtles according to US law. The recent ruling of the Appellate Body decreeing that those sanctions are legitimate under the WTO rules ironically creates fresh opportunities for the EU to pursue its preference for sanctions to secure compliance with its environmental standards in important new areas, such as climate change and against major trading partners such as the United States.
7 United Nations (1992).
8 *Ibid.*
9 For a technical description of CITES and its trade measures, *see* OECD (1999).
10 *See* Sugg and Kreuter (1994) for an analysis of the effect of an ivory trade ban on the protection of the African elephant.
11 't Sas-Rolfes (1995) shows that in the time since 1973 when a CITES ban was instituted, trade in rhino horn has not ceased nor has the decline in rhino numbers, except where those rhinos are well protected.
12 In its pursuit of donations from animal lovers, WWF has managed to convince people that buying ivory endangers elephants. Now a whole gaggle of more radical organisations, such as the Born Free Foundation and the Humane Society, continue that call in spite of strong evidence that such bans are often counterproductive – a fact that even WWF field officers now acknowledge.
13 Despite the concern that toxic waste from developed countries was being dumped illegally in developing countries, Montgomery (1995) argues that a careful assessment of the evidence compiled by Greenpeace indicates that there are only five recorded episodes of illegal export of hazardous waste from developed to developing countries, and four of these were cases of fraud.
14 Morris (2000).

15 For an insightful treatment of the shipbreaking issue, *see* Langewiesche (2000).

16 *See* Evans (1995).

17 *See* Raychaudhari *et al.* (2000).

18 *See* Jha and Hoffman (2000).

19 Morris (2000b).

20 Greenpeace, the EU and a small group of developing countries advised by Greenpeace and the Third World Network (an NGO lobby based in Malaysia with historic links to Public Citizen, Ralph Nader's US consumer lobby).

21 Wallach (1999).

22 Administration officials forecast privately that pressure from US green groups on the Executive Office would result in US officials being instructed to withdraw from negotiations as they drew to a close. The negotiations were completed in Montreal in February 2000.

23 Although it should be noted that after Doha Pascal Lamy wrote to Bob Zoellick stating that the EU did not intend to seek adoption of the Precautionary Principle within the WTO Agreement, it should also be noted he is Commissioner for Trade. The evidence suggests that environment officials in EU member states are unconcerned about legislating into the Biosafety Protocol provisions which create the right to block trade by invoking the Precautionary Principle and which undermine the provisions of the WTO.

24 The Directive has not yet been applied. National and possible subnational authorities in EU member states would be responsible for implementing the Directive. There is likely to be significant variation in the way it is applied by EU authorities in EU member states.

25 Yet, as Morris (1997) has pointed out, it is impossible to know whether such a label in fact reflects an objective assessment of the environmental impact of the product throughout its life cycle.

26 *See* Morris (2000a).

27 DRI/WEFA (2002).

28 WTO (1998), WTO (2001).

29 United Nations (1992).

30 *Ibid.*

31 *Ibid.*

Chapter 9 – **Robert C. Balling Jr**

1 For source of data, contact the author at robert.balling@asu.edu.
2 Jones (1994), pp. 1794–1802.
3 Balling *et al.* (1998), pp. 175–81.
4 Lean *et al.* (1995), pp. 3195–8.
5 Spencer and Christy (1990), pp. 1558–62.
6 Wallace *et al.* (2000).
7 Diaz *et al.* (1989), pp. 1195–1210.
8 IPCC (2001), p. 5.
9 Hansen *et al.*(1998), p. 12,753.
10 Wigley (1998), p. 2288.
11 Hansen *et al.* (2000), p. 9875.

Chapter 10 – **Robert L. Bradley Jr**

1 Simon (1996), p. 162.
2 *See*, for example, Linden (1997), p. 14, Amory Lovins (1975), p. 3.
3 WCED (1997), p. 168.
4 Ehrlich and Ehrlich (1974), p. 40.
5 Ehrlich *et al.* (1973), p. 279, Bradley (2000), pp. 21–2, 126–49.
6 In August 2000, consumers in Britain went so far as to abstain from buying petrol for several days in order to protest against high prices. Petrol prices in Britain are amongst the highest in the world – four times higher than in the United States – as a result of obscene taxes.
7 Even former US Vice President Al Gore, who warned against cheap energy in his book *Earth in the Balance*, complained about high petrol prices and vowed not to increase energy taxes during his campaign for the US presidency in 2000 – Seelye (2000), p. A2.
8 Holdren (2000), p. 21.
9 Ehrlich and Ehrlich (1996), p. 31.
10 Siteur (1996). Exceptions include Malaysia, which obtains only about 15% of its domestic energy from biomass, and Singapore.
11 Home stoves tend to be poorly flued, leading to horrific respiratory problems.
12 A great deal of time is spent gathering wood and creating dung pats that could otherwise be spent on more productive activities.
13 This is especially true of dung, which is often handled by young children and contains all manner of bacteria and other disease-causing agents.

14 Although some environmentalists claim that the depletion argument is no longer held, studies and books continue to argue the opposite, often in a sustainability context. *See* Campbell (1997), Deffeyes (2001) and McKenzie (1996).

15 These statistics come from Bradley (2000), pp. 28–31.

16 Orimulsion® is a registered trademark of Bitúmenes Orinoco, S.A (PDVSA-Bitor) and is licensed to Bitor America Corporation.

17 Herrick *et al.* (2002).

18 For a critical review that still finds Gold's hypothesis plausible, *see* Ehrlich (2001), ch. 7.

19 These statistics come from Bradley (2000), pp. 28–31.

20 *Ibid.*, pp. 47–53.

21 *See*, for example, Hayward and Jones (1999), Goklany (1999a), Lomborg (2001), pp. 163–77.

22 Lomborg (2001), p. 165, fig. 86.

23 Grossman and Krueger (1993), Shafik and Bandyopadhyay (1992).

24 As one might expect, this effect is more marked for urban air quality than aggregate emissions – reflecting the difference in impacts of emissions according to where they take place – Selden and Song (1994).

25 Goklany (1995).

26 Nathan (1996).

27 In many parts of the developing world, women are excluded from engaging in formal employment, so their time is undervalued. As a result, they are willing to spend more time than they might otherwise choose gathering fuel wood, which means that they are less concerned about the efficiency with which the wood burns – Nathan (1996).

28 Scarlett (1999).

29 Goklany (1999b).

30 FAO (1997, 1999).

31 In particular, restrictions on private ownership have undermined incentives to manage land sustainably – Morris (1995), Martin (2000).

32 Goklany (1998, 1999c).

33 Southgate (1998), Wilcove *et al.* (1998).

34 Goklany (1999b).

35 Goklany and Sprague (1992).

36 FAO (1997).

37 IIED (1996), Southgate (1998), Moore (2000).
38 Goklany (1995).
39 Perlack *et al.* (1992), Lorenz and Morris (1995).
40 Cook and Bayea (1997).
41 Bayea *et al.* (1992), Miles and Miles (1992), OTA (1995), Tolbert and Downing (1995), Tolbert and Schiller (1996).
42 Bradley (2000), pp. 91–5, 104–12.
43 IPCC (2001), pp. 5, 15–16, 33–4 and 104.
44 *Ibid.*, p. 7, Hansen (1998).
45 IPCC (2001), pp. 2, 4, 27, 30, 101, 104, 106, 108 and 129.
46 *Ibid.*, pp. 13, 67 and 116–17.
47 *Ibid.*, p. 16, IPCC (1996), p. 6.
48 IPCC (2001), p. 699.
49 Jenkins (2001).
50 Taylor and VanDoren (2002), p. 3. Shell has also tried to introduce social factors to supplement traditional profitability measures to better stack up against the 'super-majors' – Williams (2000).
51 *See*, for example, Romm and Curtis, (1996), pp. 57–74, Holdren (2002), pp. 65–6.
52 Bradley (1997), pp. 15–22, 26–36.
53 USEIA (1999), pp. 38–9, email communication from Patricia Smith, Energy Information Administration, March 2002.
54 Bradley and Fulmer (forthcoming).
55 Julian Morris, personal communication, 3 June 2002. *See also* 'Hither and Thither: Trends in Asian Power', *BusinessWorld* (Philippines), 6 August 1999.
56 Lieberman (2001).
57 WEC (2000), p. 5
58 UNDP, UNDESA, and WEC (2000), p. 15.
59 *See* de Soto (2000) and Yeatts (1997).
60 Lomborg (2001), pp. 305–24, 348–52. *See also* Goklany (2000), pp. 189–213.
61 Sarewitz and Pielke (2000), p. 63.
62 *See*, generally, Brack *et al.* (2000). On the clash between national sovereignty and the Kyoto Protocol, *see* Rabkin (1998), ch. 7. For the inherent problems of Kyoto's proposed international carbon trading scheme, *see* Victor (2001).
63 *See* Graham and Wiener (1995) and Hahn (1996).
64 International Energy Agency (2000), p. 21.
65 USEIA (2001), p. 176, Table A2.

66 WEC (2000), pp. 5, 66.
67 In 1976, Amory Lovins argued that government-engineered energy efficiency improvements could result in a 'modest, zero, or negative growth in our rate of energy use'. Lovins (1975), p. 83.

Chapter 11 – **Jonathan H. Adler**

1 In this chapter, the terms 'biological diversity' and 'biodiversity' are used interchangeably.
2 Edwards (1995), p. 213.
3 *World Resources 1996–7* (1996), p. 247.
4 Stork (1997), p. 65.
5 *Ibid.*, p. 44.
6 *World Resources* (1996), p. 247. There is even uncertainty about the actual number of species identified, and estimates range from 1.4 to 1.8 million. *See* Martin (1999), p. 207. Estimates vary because there is no single agreed-upon list of identified species, and many species may be known by more than one name.
7 *Ibid.*, p. 248, table 11.1.
8 Stork (1997), p. 41.
9 *Ibid.*, pp. 46–7.
10 *Ibid*, pp. 62–3, tables 5–6.
11 *See*, for example, Ryan (1992), p. 9.
12 Myers (1979), pp. 4–5.
13 Gibbs (2001), pp. 42–3.
14 Wilson (2000), p. 9.
15 *Global Biodiversity Outlook* (2001), p. 71.
16 Stork (1997), p. 45.
17 Quoted in Gibbs (2001), p. 43.
18 Edwards (1995), p. 218.
19 *Ibid.*, p. 219 fig. 7-2. *See also Global Biodiversity Outlook* (2001), p. 71.
20 *Ibid.*, p. 222.
21 Wilson (2000), p. 11.
22 Edwards (1995), p. 222.
23 Vitousek (1997), p. 494, Sala *et al.* (2000), p. 1771.
24 Goklany (1999a), p. 108, *see also* Sala *et al.* (2000), p. 1771.
25 Goklany (1999b), p. 164.
26 Martin (1999), p. 230.
27 *Ibid.*, p. 231.
28 *Global Biodiversity Outlook* (2001), p. 62.

29 Sedjo (1995), pp. 198–201.
30 FAO (1999), p. 1.
31 *Ibid.*
32 *Ibid. See also* Southgate's chapter in this volume.
33 Sedjo (1995), p. 188.
34 FAO (1999), p. 8.
35 Snape (1996), p. 85.
36 *World Resources 1998–9* (1998), p. 197.
37 *Ibid.*
38 Eberstadt (1999), pp. 64–5.
39 Georgia *et al.* (1999), pp. 242–3 (indicating that the 'medium projection' of the United Nations is for a global population just under 10 billion in 2050). It is worth noting, however, that some analysts expect population increases to slow more rapidly and top out at approximately 8 billion in 2040. *See also* Eberstadt (1999).
40 Paarlberg (2000), p. 21.
41 Mann (1999), p. 310.
42 *See* Georgia *et al.* (1999), pp. 256–7, 260–61 (indicating the continuous rise in per capita agricultural production and food production over the past four decades).
43 Mann (1999), p. 310. *See also* Conway (2000), p. 13.
44 Huxley (2000), p. 4
45 du Plessis (2000), p. 17.
46 'What is CITES?' available at <http://www.cites.org/eng/disc/what_is.shtml>.
47 Hutton and Dickson (2000a) p. xvi.
48 Edwards (1995), p. 246.
49 't Sas-Rolfes (2000), p. 72.
50 Jenkins (2000), p. 50.
51 Sugg and Kreuter (1994), p. 40.
52 Hutton and Dickson (2000b), p. xvi.
53 Webb (2000), p. 105.
54 *See* Morris (2000).
55 Brown and Leal (2000), p. 129.
56 McNeely and Scherr (2001), p. 10.
57 *See*, for example, James *et al.* (1999), p. 323, Inamadar *et al.* (1999), p. 1856.
58 Getz (1999), p. 1855.
59 *Ibid.*, Edwards (1995).
60 Blum (1993), p. 17.

61 *See* Revkin (2002).

62 The Rio Declaration provides that 'Where there are threats of serious or irreversible damage, lack of full scientific certainty shall not be used as a reason for postponing cost-effective measures to prevent environmental degradation' and that 'in order to protect the environment, the precautionary approach shall be widely applied by States according to their capabilities'. UN (1992).

63 AgBioWorld 'Scientists in Support of Agricultural Biotechnology' <http://www.agbioworld.org/petition.html>. The petition was opened for signatures on 18 January 2000 and released to the public at a press conference on 22 January.

64 *Ibid.* As of 3 March 2000, over 1,300 scientists had endorsed the petition. Signatories of the petition include Nobel Prize winners James Watson and Norman Borlaug, World Food Prize recipient Gurdev Khush and 1998 National Medal of Science recipient Bruce Ames. *See* 'Nobel Prize Winners Endorse Agricultural Biotechnology' <http://www.agbioworld.org/watson.html>.

65 Ye *et al.* (2000), p. 303.

66 Gugliotta (2000).

67 Miller and Conko (2000), p. 360.

68 *See* Adler (2000), pp. 202–04.

69 Goklany (1999a), p. 120.

70 *Ibid.*

71 *Ibid.*, p. 126.

72 Musters *et al.* (2000), p. 1760.

73 'Bioengineering of Crops Could Help Feed the World, Crop Increases of 10–25 Percent Possible', World Bank (9 October 1997) available at <http://www.worldbank.org/html/cgiar/press/biopress.html>.

74 Conway (2000), p. 14.

75 Moffat (1998), p. 2177.

76 *See* Goklany (1999a), p. 120.

77 Wambugu (1999), p. 15.

78 Paarlberg (2000), p. 22.

79 Barton (1996), pp. 95, 99.

80 NAS (1987), p. 11.

81 NBPBR (1992), p. 2.

82 Butler and Reichhardt (1999), pp. 651, 653.

83 Johnson (2000), p. 133.

84 *See* Paarlberg (2000), p. 20.

85 Cook (2000), p. 123.

86 Prakash (1999) (citing David Aaron of the US Commerce Department).
87 Miller (1999), p. 189.
88 Tangley (2000) quoting Calestous Juma, a Kenyan advisor to the Harvard University Center for International Development and former executive secretary of the CBD.
89 *See generally* Edwards (1995), Martin (1999).
90 Martin (1999), p. 231 and studies cited therein.
91 Sugg and Kreuter (1994), p. 52.
92 *Ibid.*
93 Kievit (2000), p. 93.
94 Norton (2002).
95 *Ibid.*
96 Norton (1998), p. 51.

Chapter 12 – Douglas Southgate

1 Wells and Brandon (1993).
2 Peters *et al.* (1989), pp. 655–6.
3 Peters (1990).
4 The site used in the Peruvian case study is located near a sizeable urban market for the *aguaje* (*Mauritia flexuosa*) fruit and other jungle products. In addition, it is in a floodplain where *aguaje* is unusually plentiful. Thus the case study does not offer a representative view of the current economics of harvesting non-timber products throughout the Amazon Basin. Furthermore, the price reductions that would be caused by a major expansion of this activity were not analysed. Analysis of the magnitude of these reductions would have to be undertaken before the adoption of a conservation strategy predicated on non-timber harvesting. These limitations are surveyed in Southgate (1998), pp. 45–9.
5 Peters *et al.* (1989), p. 656.
6 Browder (1992).
7 WCED (1987).
8 Wunder (2001).
9 Southgate *et al.* (1991).
10 Bohn and Deacon (2000).
11 Schneider (1995).
12 Of course, road construction may constitute intervention failure since government subsidies are being provided. Ironically enough, foreign governments, which profess concern about the

global environmental impacts of deforestation, have provided subsidies, in the form of aid, for the very infrastructure projects that facilitate land clearing.

13 Pearce (1996).

14 In the real world, of course, this second category of costs – relating to inter-agent negotiations within the ownership unit – never really reaches zero. Consider, for example, the negotiations that must occur within a firm holding private property that happens to employ two or more people.

15 North and Thomas (1973).

16 Anderson and Hill (1975).

17 Poteete and Ostrom (2002).

18 Goulding *et al.* (1996).

19 Southgate (1998), pp. 49–56.

20 Browder (1992).

21 Southgate (1998), pp. 59–82, Rice *et al.* (2001).

22 Southgate (1998), pp. 95–120.

23 Plotkin (1994).

24 Simpson *et al.* (1996).

25 Poteete and Ostrom (2002).

26 Bromley and Chapagain (1994).

27 Southgate *et al.* (2000).

28 Thiesenhusen (1995).

29 *Ibid.*

30 *Ibid.*

31 Shaw (1997).

32 Strasma (1989).

33 *Ibid.*

34 The disincentives for efficient management of community irrigation systems in northern Ecuador created by subsidisation of public systems are currently being investigated by Fabián Rodríguez, a doctoral candidate and advisee of mine at Ohio State University.

35 Gordon (1954).

36 Sader *et al.* (2000).

37 More information about the conservation initiative in northern Guatemala can be obtained from Georg (Jorge) Grunberg, an Austrian anthropologist and long-time Guatemalan resident. His email address is *grunberg@guate.net*

Chapter 13 – **Michael De Alessi**

1 FAO (2000).
2 *Ibid.*
3 Associated Press (1996).
4 Commercial extinction occurs when it is no longer economically viable to catch the remaining fish.
5 Myers *et al.* (1995).
6 *See*, for example, Brubaker (1999).
7 *See* Goklany (2000) and Goklany (this volume).
8 *See*, for example, Botkin (2001).
9 *See*, for example, Demsetz (1967), L. De Alessi (1980), Johannes (1981) and Ostrom (1990).
10 *See* Johannes (1981).
11 *See* Sugg and Kreuter (1994).
12 Hardin (1968) drew on the earlier work of economists such as Gordon (1954) and Scott (1955) and, unfortunately, did not initially recognise the exclusivity of some communal institutions, so his use of the word 'commons' has been the source of some confusion. Ostrom (1990), for example, documents numerous examples of successful common property management. The real problem seems to be not with commons *per se* but with resources that are not privately owned – that is *either* open access or controlled by the state.
13 Even under open access, harvests may be small either because costs of extraction are high (e.g. if the only technology available is sail boats and rod and line fishing tackle), or because demand for the resource is low.
14 Demsetz (1967), p. 348.
15 *See*, for example, Keen (1983), Scott (1988), Edwards (1994).
16 L. De Alessi (1980).
17 Libecap (1990).
18 Demsetz (1967).
19 Anderson and Hill (1975).
20 Ostrom (1990).
21 McKean and Ostrom (1995).
22 Unfortunately, anthropologists, economists and policymakers often promote either individual or group ownership at the expense of the other, even though the distinction is frequently muddled. Adding to the confusion are the varying definitions that different (and even often the same) schools of thought apply to terms like 'the commons', 'common property' and 'private prop-

erty'. For example, biologist Garret Hardin used the word 'commons' to mean open access, anthropologists often use it to mean a strictly monitored form of group ownership, and economists frequently dismiss the concept entirely under the assumption that only individual ownership institutions are private.

23 Acheson (1987).
24 Ostrom (1997).
25 Demsetz (1967).
26 Barber and Pratt (1997).
27 Johannes and Ripen (1996).
28 M. De Alessi (1997).
29 Johannes (1981).
30 *The Economist* (11 May 1996), p. 35.
31 Ruddle and Akimichi (1989).
32 Brooks (1996), p. 71.
33 Also known as 'freehold', this is the tenancy of *fee simple absolute in possession*.
34 M. De Alessi (1996).
35 *See* Iyambo (2000).
36 *See* McClurg (1997), Sharp (1997).
37 Quoted in *The Economist* (1994), p. 24, describing a 1993 decision by the hoki fleet not to fish an extra 50,000 tons of fish allocated to them by the government.
38 McClurg (1997).
39 Orange roughy has received a lot of attention in recent years due to new findings about their age and stock sizes, and the industry now fishes them much more conservatively.
40 Arbuckle (2000).
41 *Ibid.*
42 FAO (2000).
43 FAO (1993).
44 FAO (2000).
45 Bailey (1988).
46 Southgate (1992).
47 *Ibid.*
48 Weber (1996).
49 McKean and Ostrom (1995), p. 3.
50 Higgs (1982).
51 *Ibid.*, p. 59.
52 *See* M. De Alessi (1998) for a discussion of how advanced technologies may be used to enforce private rights to marine resources.

53 Cordell (1989), p. 1.

Chapter 14 – Mary Tiffen and Michael Mortimore

1 Mortimore (1998).
2 Dregne (1970).
3 UNEP (1977).
4 Mortimore (1998), p. 11.
5 Mainguet (1994).
6 UNEP (1990), Dregne *et al.* (1991).
7 *See* Warren and Agnew (1988), Thomas and Middleton (1994), Mortimore (1989, 1998), Morris (1995), and Swift (1996).
8 Stiles (1995).
9 The military language used in the CCD has been a feature of the discussion of anti-desertification efforts since at least the 1950s – Morris (1995).
10 UNEP (1997).
11 EC (1997).
12 It was included in a list of 34 treaties ratified without debate, which has since caused some controversy (*see* 'eco-logic on-line', at www.sovereignty.net/p/land/treaties.shtml).
13 The obsession with underfunding is not new: the main output of ICRISAT (the International Crops Research Institute for the Semi-Arid Tropics), which became the convening centre for the Desert Margins Initiative, 'an integrated national, regional and international research program ... to combat land degradation in sub-Saharan Africa' has been restricted by shortage of funds to a report on workshops in nine SSA countries, to review the state of current knowledge and to identify research priorities (Fletcher, 1996).
14 Warren and Khogali (1992).
15 Stiles (1995).
16 Tiffen (1998).
17 It would be desirable to be able to average data from several stations in a zone, since there can be considerable variations, due to local storms.
18 The slight recovery in the late 1970s was less marked in the two stations in the Diourbel, Senegal, for which we also collected data.
19 Tiffen and Mulele (1994).
20 Tiffen and Mulele (1994).

21 *See* Robert Balling's chapter.

22 Lambin *et al.* (2001).

23 It is also possible to exaggerate the extent of land-cover change, particularly at the boundaries. A well-known study shows how what were regarded as 'forest islands', supposed remnants of humid forest that would have previously extended further north into the savannah, were in fact a deliberate encouragement of trees around villages, and the myth of a past forest a generation back had been steadily reported since the 1890s, but disproved by aerial photo analysis and anthropological enquiries (Fairhead and Leach, 1996).

24 Voortman *et al.* (1999).

25 Faye *et al.* (2001).

26 Ariyo *et al.* (2001).

27 Tiffen and Mulele (1994).

28 In 1992 the former Machakos District was divided to form the present Machakos District and Makueni District, the latter named after its first official settlement.

29 Report by M.E.W. North, D.O. i/c Settlement areas, 4-5-1950, in Kenya National Archives.

30 Gichuki (2000a).

31 Meaning 'throwing upwards' – leading to the formation of a bench terrace.

32 Gichuki (2000b).

33 Gichuki (2000c).

34 Mbogoh (2000).

35 Nelson (2000).

36 Nzioka (2000).

37 Nelson (2000).

38 They suffer from the difficulty government officers have in getting out and about.

39 Mbogoh (2000).

40 Gichuki *et al.* (2000).

41 Mbuvi (2000).

42 Fall (2000).

43 Gichuki *et al.* (2000).

44 Issaka (2001).

45 Mortimore *et al.* (2001).

46 Diarra Doka (2001).

47 The masculine pronoun is appropriate. Women generally acquire land through their husband, who under some customs is

supposed to give them a portion of his land for their own use, not by inheritance from their father. In Niger and Nigeria they can, and sometimes do, buy land.

48 Okike *et al.* (2001).
49 Baba and Magaji (1998).
50 Mortimore and Adams (1998).
51 Mortimore and Adams (1999).
52 Ariyo *et al.* (2001).
53 Cline-Cole *et al.* (1990).
54 Dewees (1991), Patel *et al.* (1995).
55 Sadio *et al.* (2000).
56 Gaye (2000).
57 Gaye (2000), Badiane *et al.* (2000).
58 Coulon (1999), Wilson Fall (2000).
59 Snrech (1995).
60 Ariyo *et al.* (2001).
61 Lomborg (2001), p. 66.
62 Other recent case studies in dryland Africa reaching similar conclusions concern Burkina Faso (Mazzucato and Niemeijer, 2001), and Côte d'Ivoire (Dumont, 1998), while Reij *et al.* (1996) gives examples of good soil conservation from many countries.

Chapter 15 – Roger Bate

1 Quoted in Tadros (1996).
2 The Israel-Jordan peace treaty, signed on 26 October 1994, devoted much attention to water allocation decision-making.
3 Dinar and Xepapadeas (1998).
4 World Bank (2001).
5 Pearce (1992).
6 Becker (1995).
7 Ostrom (1990).
8 Shah (1991), Rosegrant and Gazmuri (1994), Anderson and Snyder (1997).
9 Holden and Thobani (1996), p. 3.
10 *Ibid.*
11 *Ostrom* (1992), p. 32.
12 Rent-seeking is essentially the legal manipulation of the political process by individuals or groups for personal/group gain.
13 Ingram (1973), p. 34.

14 Holden and Thobani (1996), pp. 3–4.
15 World Bank (1995a).
16 Frederiksen *et al.* (1993).
17 Holden and Thobani (1996).
18 Kemper (1997).
19 The median cost was 12-fold greater.
20 Kemper (1997).
21 Frederiksen *et al.* (1993).
22 Ostrom (1992), Kemper (1997).
23 Anderson and Snyder (1997), Holden and Thobani (1996).
24 Ostrom (1992).
25 Bates (1983) p. 128 (emphasis in original).
26 *Ibid.* (1983), p. 130.
27 Bates (1983).
28 Shanks (1981).
29 Thobani (1998).
30 Note that a policy of pricing water to cover the full cost of build-
     ing and managing the infrastructure (the long-run marginal cost)
     is not optimal if the infrastructure was ill conceived and built at
     high cost. If full-cost pricing could be enforced, most farmers,
     who typically account for the bulk of water use, would find irri-
     gation farming unprofitable (Thobani, 1998).
31 Water prices can also be used to reflect external costs, and this
     approach has been applied in some locations – *see* Howitt
     (1998).
32 Dinar and Subramanian (1997).
33 Repetto (1986).
34 *See* the case study on the Philippines National Irrigation Associ-
     ation by Bagadion (1988).
35 Repetto (1986).
36 Thobani (1998).
37 Quotas are quantitative limits on water use and can be based on
     time, volume, or can be use-specific (such as per crop).
38 Technically, the price elasticity of water demand is equal or close
     to zero.
39 Baumol and Oates (1988).
40 Bate *et al.* (1999).
41 Repetto (1986).
42 Easter *et al.* (1998).
43 Deacon (1997).
44 Anderson and Snyder (1997).

45 Strosser (1997).
46 Quotas may in fact change this legal linkage by exchanging a legal concept of 'reasonable use' of water with a stipulation of an exact amount of water. But this legal change is rarely obvious since water is still used on the same riparian land. However, trading in quotas gives a much stronger impression of alienation of water use from land. So, while establishing quotas is the key change to the legal status of the rights, hostility to quotas only occurs when they are exchanged.
47 Provision of conveyance infrastructure is almost certainly a job government will underwrite, if it does not fund it completely. Private finance is used in many schemes at the moment (IFC, 1998 – *Private Sector Bulletin*).
48 Holden and Thobani (1996).
49 Holtzhausen (1997).
50 Thobani (1998).
51 Rosegrant and Binswanger (1994).
52 Pakistan Water and Development Authority (1990).
53 Strosser (1997).
54 Shah (1991).
55 Saleth (1998).
56 Anderson (1994).
57 Easter *et al.* (1998).
58 Livingston (1995).
59 Anderson and Snyder (1997, p. 192) quote from the Chilean Constitution, which translated states that 'the rights to private individuals, or enterprises, over water, recognised or established by law, grant their holders the property over them'.
60 Ríos and Quiroz (1995).
61 Hearne and Easter (1997).
62 Rosegrant and Gazmuri (1994).
63 Hearne and Easter (1997).
64 *Ibid.* (1997).
65 Rosegrant and Gazmuri (1994).
66 Hearne and Easter (1997).
67 Bauer (1997) claims that some of the gains from markets have not been as substantial as originally claimed, and that external costs were not widely acknowledged in early studies. Nevertheless, these claims have been contested, particularly that external costs were relatively slight – Easter *et al.* (1998).
68 Hearne (1998).

69 Holden and Thobani (1996).

70 Hearne (1998).

71 Anderson and Snyder (1997).

72 Holden and Thobani (1996).

73 Anderson and Snyder (1997), Holden and Thobani (1996), Kemper (1997).

74 Kemper and Simpson (1995).

75 Sturgess and Wright (1993).

76 *Ibid.* (1993), pp. 23–4

77 Anderson and Snyder (1997).

78 *Ibid.*

79 Landry (1999).

80 Bate (2000).

81 Kemper (1997).

82 They are also allegedly forthcoming in Israel – Dinar and Subramanian (1997) and Peru – Easter *et al.* (1998).

83 Anderson and Snyder (1997).

84 Landry (1999).

85 Dinar and Subramanian (1997).

86 Gleick (1993).

Epilogue – **Julian Morris**

 1 *Supra* chapter 6.

 2 de Soto (2000).

 3 Quoted by Nisbet (1980), p. 52.

 4 http://www.oreilly.com/people/staff/sierra/flum/9304.htm#16. Accessed 10 June 2002.

 5 At least Malthus had the excuse that he was countering William Godwin's even more ridiculous idea that as man progressed he would soon live forever.

 6 *See* chapter 2, p. 38.

 7 *See also*, generally, Lomborg (2001).

 8 Hilton (2002).

 9 IIED (1997), MMSD (2002).

10 Attaran and Gillespie-White (2001); Dukes (1998).

11 Lanjouw (1998).

12 Lamont (2002).

13 Smith (1776).

14 Ricardo (1817).

15 That is to say, when the cost of producing all goods in country A

is greater than in B, there will still be trade if the *relative* cost of producing some goods is greater in B than in A. Thus, in Ricardo's famous example, although both wine and cloth may be more expensive to manufacture in Britain than in Portugal, the relative cost of producing wine compared to cloth is greater in Britain than in Portugal, so people in Britain will sell cloth to Portugal in exchange for wine.

16 de Soto (1989), p. 258.
17 Schmidheiny (1994).

Bibliography

Chapter 1 – **Julian Morris**

Alchian, A. (1965) 'Some Economics of Property Rights', *Il Politico* vol. 30, pp. 816–29, reprinted in Alchian, A. (1977) *Economic Forces at Work*, Liberty Press, Indianapolis.

Anderson, T. L. and Hill, P. J. (1975) 'The Evolution of Property Rights: A Study of the American West', *Journal of Law and Economics* vol. 18, pp. 163–75.

Ault, D. E. and Rutman, G. L. (1979) 'The Development of Individual Rights to Property in Tribal Africa', *Journal of Law and Economics* vol. 22, pp. 163–82.

Barzel, Y. (1989) *The Economic Analysis of Property Rights*, Cambridge University Press, Cambridge.

Besen, S. M. and Raskind, L. J. (1991) 'An Introduction to the Law and Economics of Intellectual Property', *Journal of Economic Perspectives* 3(1), Winter, pp. 3–27.

Brookfield, H. and Padoch, C. (1994) 'Appreciating Agro-diversity', *Environment* vol. 36, no. 5, June, pp. 6–11, 37–45.

Cole, Julio H. (2000) 'Patents and Copyrights: Do the Benefits Exceed the Costs?', paper presented at the Mont Pélerin Society, Santiago, Chile, 12–17 November.

de Soto, H. (1989) *The Other Path: The Invisible Revolution in the Third World*, Harper & Row, New York.

Demsetz, H. (1967) 'Toward a Theory of Property Rights', *American Economic Review* vol. 57, pp. 347–59.

Hardin, G. (1968) 'The Tragedy of the Commons', *Science* vol. 62, 13 December, pp. 1, 243–8.

Hancock, G. (1989) *The Lords of Poverty*, Macmillan, London and Atlantic Monthly Press, New York.

Morris, J. (1995) *The Political Economy of Land Degradation*, Institute of Economic Affairs, London.

Morris, J. Mowatt, R., Reekie, W. D. and Tren, R. (2002) *Ideal*

Matter: Globalisation and the Intellectual Property Debate,
Centre for the New Europe, Brussels.

North, D. and Thomas, R. P. (1972) *The Rise of the Western World*,
Cambridge University Press, Cambridge.

Ostrom, E. (1988) 'Institutional Arrangements and the Commons
Dilemma' in Ostrom, V., Feeny, D. and Picht, H. (eds.),
pp. 101–39.

Ostrom, E. (1990) *Managing the Commons*, Cambridge University
Press, Cambridge.

Ostrom, V., Feeny, D. and Picht, H. (eds.) (1988) *Rethinking
Institutional Analysis and Development*, ICS Press, San Francisco.

Schlager, E. and Ostrom, E. (1992) 'Property-Rights Régimes and
Natural Resources: A Conceptual Analysis', *Land Economics* vol.
68, pp. 249–62.

Stahl, M. (1993) 'Land Degradation in East Africa', *Ambio* vol. 22,
no. 8, December, pp. 505–8.

Wade, N. (1974) 'Sahelian Drought: No Victory for Western Aid',
Science vol. 185, 19 July, pp. 234–7.

WCED (1987) *World Commission on Environment and Development:
Our Common Future*, Oxford University Press, Oxford.

Chapter 2 – Indur Goklany

Ausubel, J. H. and Grübler, A. (1995) 'Working Less and Living
Longer', *Technological Forecasting and Social Change* 50, pp.
113–31.

Bairoch, P. (1982) 'International Industrialization Levels from 1750
to 1980', *Journal of European Economic History* 11, pp.
269–333.

Barbour, I. G. (1980) *Technology, Environment, and Human Values*,
Praeger, New York.

Barney, G. O. (ed.) (1980) *Global 2000 Report to the President*,
Pergamon Press, New York.

Barro, R. J. (1997) *The Determinants of Economic Growth: A
Cross-Country Empirical Study*, MIT Press, Cambridge, MA.

Becker, C. and Bloom, D. (1998) 'The Demographic Crisis in the
Former Soviet Union: Introduction', *World Development* 26, pp.
1913–19.

Bloom, B. R. (1999) 'The Future of Public Health', *Nature* 402
(supplement), pp. C63–4.

Brown, L. R. (1998) 'The Future of Growth' in Brown, Lester R.,

Flavin, C. and French, Hilary F. *The State of the World 1998*, W. W. Norton, New York, pp. 3–20.

Bureau of the Census (1975) *Historical Statistics of the United States, Colonial Times to 1970*, Government Printing Office, Washington DC.

Bureau of the Census (1997) *Statistical Abstract of the United States, 1997*, Government Printing Office, Washington DC.

Bureau of the Census (1999) *Statistical Abstract of the United States, 1999*, Government Printing Office, Washington DC.

Bureau of Economic Analysis (1998) 'GDP and Other Major NIPA Series, 1929–97' in *Survey of Current Business*, August, 147–66. Available at http://www.bea.doc.gov/bea/ARTICLES/NATIONAL/NIPA/1998/0898nip3.pdf

Burnette, J. and Mokyr, J. (1995) 'The Standard of Living through the Ages' in Simon, Julian L. (ed.) (1995), pp. 135–48.

CDC (1999) 'Summary of Notifiable Diseases, United States, 1998', *Morbidity and Mortality Weekly Report* 47(53), p. 84, Center for Disease Control and Prevention, Washington DC.

Costa, D. L. and Steckel, R. H. (1997) 'Long-Term Trends, Health, Welfare and Economic Growth in the United States' in Steckel, Richard H. and Floud, R. (eds.) (1997), *Health and Welfare during Industrialization*, University of Chicago Press, Chicago, pp. 47–89.

Daily Mail and *Guardian* (1998) 'Zim Commander "Not Killed in DRC"'. December 15.

Dollar, D. and Kraay, A. (2000) *Growth Is Good for the Poor*, Transition Newsletter, World Bank, Development Economics Research Group, Washington DC. Available at http://www.worldbank.org/research/growth/absdollakray.htm. Retrieved 3 September 2000.

Easterlin, R. A. (1996) *Growth Triumphant: The Twenty-First Century in Historical Perspective*, University of Michigan Press, Ann Arbor.

Easterly, W. and Rebelo, S. T. (1993) 'Fiscal Policy and Economic Growth: An Empirical Investigation', *Journal of Monetary Economics* 32(3), pp. 417–58.

Ehrlich, P. R. (1968) *The Population Bomb*, Ballantine Books, New York.

Floud, R. and Harris, B. (1997) 'Health, Height, and Welfare: Britain, 1700–1980' in Steckel, Richard H. and Floud, R. (eds.) *Health and Welfare during Industrialization*, University of Chicago Press, Chicago, pp. 91–126.

Fogel, R. W. (1995) 'The Contribution of Improved Nutrition to the Decline of Mortality Rates in Europe and America' in Simon, Julian L. (ed.) (1995), pp. 61–71.

Fogel, R. W. (2000) *The Fourth Great Awakening and the Future of Egalitarianism*, University of Chicago Press, Chicago.

FAO (1996a) *Assessment of Feasible Progress in Food Security*, Technical Background Documents 12–15, vol. 3, Food and Agricultural Organization, Rome, Italy.

FAO (1996b) *The State of Food and Agriculture*, Food and Agricultural Organization, Rome, Italy.

FAO (1999) *The State of Food Insecurity in the World* 1999, December, Food and Agricultural Organization, Rome, Italy. Available at http://www.fao.org/FOCUS/E/SOFI/home-e.htm. Retrieved 12 January 2000.

FAO (2000) *FAOStat* (FAO Statistical Databases). Available at http://apps.fao.org. Retrieved 31 October 2000.

Frankel, J. A. and Romer, D. (1999) 'Does Trade Cause Growth?' *American Economic Review* (June), pp. 379–99.

Goklany, I. M. (1995) 'Strategies to Enhance Adaptability: Technological Change, Sustainable Growth and Free Trade', *Climatic Change* 30, pp. 427–49.

Goklany, I. M. (1998) 'Saving Habitat and Conserving Bio-diversity on a Crowded Planet', *BioScience* 48, pp. 941–53.

Goklany, I. M. (1999a) *Clearing the Air: The Real Story of the War on Air Pollution*, Cato Institute, Washington DC.

Goklany, I. M. (1999b) 'The Future of Industrial Society', paper presented at the International Conference on Industrial Ecology and Sustainability, University of Technology of Troyes, Troyes, France, 22–25 September 1999. Available from author, Office of Policy Analysis, Dept. of the Interior, 1849 C St. NW, Washington DC 20240.

Goklany, I. M. (1999c) 'Meeting Global Food Needs: The Environmental Trade-Offs Between Increasing Land Conversion and Land Productivity', *Technology* 6, pp. 107–30.

Goklany, I. M. (2000) 'Potential Consequences of Increasing Atmospheric CO_2 Concentration Compared to Other Environmental Problems', *Technology* 7S, pp. 189–213.

Guardian (2000) 'Malaria Impedes Development in Africa', 12 May. Copy on file with the author.

Gwartney, J., Holcombe, R. and Lawson, R. (1998) 'The Scope of Government and the Wealth of Nations', *Cato Journal* 18, pp.

163–90.

Gwartney, J., Lawson, R. and Samida, D. (2000) *Economic Freedom of the World 2000*, Fraser Institute, Vancouver, BC.

Haines, M. R. (1994) *Estimated Life Tables for the United States, 1850–1900*, Historical Paper 59, National Bureau of Economic Research, Cambridge, MA.

Hill, K. (1995) 'The Decline in Childhood Mortality' in Simon, Julian L. (ed.) (1995), pp. 37–50.

Lee, J. and Feng, W. (1999) 'Malthusian Models and Chinese Realities: The Chinese Demographic System, 1700–2000', *Population and Development Review* 25, pp. 33–65.

Lerner, M. and Anderson, O. W. (1963) *Health Progress in the United States, 1900–1960*, University of Chicago Press, Chicago.

Maddison, A. (1995) *Monitoring the World Economy, 1820–1992*, Organization for Economic Co-operation and Development, Paris.

Maddison, A. (1998) 'Chinese Economic Performance in the Long Run', Organization for Economic Co-operation and Development, Paris.

Maddison, A. (1999) 'Poor Until 1820', *Wall Street Journal*, The Millennium, 11 January, R54.

Malaria Foundation International (2000) *Economic Analyses Indicate that the Burden of Malaria is Great*, executive summary for Harvard University Center for International Development and the London School of Hygiene and Tropical Medicine. Available at http://www.malaria.org/jdsachseconomic.html. Retrieved 2 October 2000.

Martin, J. A., Smith, B. L., Mathews, T. J. and Ventura, S. J. (1999) 'Births and Deaths: Preliminary data for 1998', *National Vital Statistics* 47(25).

McEvedy, C. and Jones, R (1978) *Atlas of World Population History*, Penguin, New York.

Mitchell, B. R. (1992) *International Historical Statistics: Europe, 1750–1988*, Stockton Press, New York.

Mitchell, D. O. and Ingco, M. D. (1993) 'The World Food Outlook', *Hunger Notes* 19 (Winter 1993–4), pp. 20–25.

OECD (1998) *Maintaining Prosperity in an Ageing Society*, Policy Brief 5–1998, Organization for Economic Co-operation and Development, Paris.

Paddock, W. and Paddock, P. (1967) *Famine 1975! America's Decision: Who Will Survive?*, Little, Brown, Boston, MA.

Preston, S. H. (1995) 'Human Mortality throughout History and

Prehistory' in Simon, Julian L. (ed.) (1995), pp. 30–36.

Pritchett, L. and Summers, L. H. (1996) 'Wealthier is Healthier', *Journal of Human Resources* 31, pp. 841–68.

Ravallion, M. and Chen, S. (1997) 'What Can New Survey Data Tell Us about Recent Changes in Distribution and Poverty?', *World Bank Economic Review* 11(2), pp. 357–82.

Seskin, E. P. (1978) 'Automobile Air Pollution Policy' in Portney, P. (ed.) *Current Issues in U.S. Environmental Policy*, Johns Hopkins University Press, Baltimore, MD.

Shalala, D. E. (1998) 'Eliminating Racial and Ethnic Health Disparities [sic]', speech delivered at the Patricia Harris Public Affairs Program, Howard University, 13 March. Available at http://www.hhs.gov/news/speeches/HOWARDPH.html. Retrieved 3 February 2001.

Simon, J. L. (ed.) (1995) *The State of Humanity*, Blackwell, Cambridge, MA.

Smil, V. (1994) *Energy in World History*, Westview Press, Boulder, CO.

UN (2000) 'Security Council Extends Iraq "Oil-for-Food" Program for Further 186 Days', press release SC/6872, 8 June. Available at http://www.un.org/News/Press/docs/2000/20000608.sc6872.doc.html. Retrieved 31 January 2001.

UNDP (1999) *Human Development Report 1999*, United Nations Development Program, Oxford University Press, New York.

UNDP (2000) *Human Development Report 2000*, United Nations Development Program, Oxford University Press, New York.

UNHCR (2000) *Appeals for Funds for Great Lakes Operations*, Press release, 2 March, United Nations High Commission on Refugees, Geneva, Switzerland.

——— (1999a) *1999 Global Appeal/Great Lakes*.

——— (1999b) *1999 Global Appeal/Southern Africa*.

US Department of Health and Human Services (1997) *Active Aging: A Shift in the Paradigm*, Office of Disability, Aging and Long Term Care, May. Available at http://aspe.hhs.gov/search/daltcp/Reports/ACTAGING.HTM. Retrieved 7 August 2000.

Watkins, Shirley R. (1997) 'Historical Perspective on the School Meals Programs: The Case for Strong Federal Programs', paper presented at Ceres Forum on School Meals Policy, Georgetown University Center for Food and Nutrition Policy, 24 November, Washington DC.

World Bank (1993) *World Development Report: Investing in Health*, Oxford University Press, New York.

World Bank (1999) *World Development Indicators*, CD-ROM, The
   World Bank, Washington DC.
WHO (1999) *The World Health Report 1999*, World Health
   Organization, Geneva.
WHO (2000) *The World Health Report 2000*, World Health
   Organization, Geneva. Available at http://www.who.int/
   aboutwho/en/promoting/nutrtion.htm. Retrieved January 5, 2000.
World Resources Institute (1998) *World Resources 1998–99
   Database*, Washington DC.
Wrigley, E. A. and Schofield, R. S. (1981) 'The Population History of
   England, 1541–1871: A Reconstruction', Harvard University
   Press, Cambridge, MA.

Chapter 3 – Pierre Desrochers

Babbage, C. (1835) [1832] *On the Economy of Machinery and
   Manufactures* (4th edition, enlarged), Charles Knight, London
   (reprinted 1986 by Augustus M. Kelley).
Bethnal Green Branch Museum (1875) *Descriptive Catalogue of the
   Collection Illustrating the Utilization of Waste Products*, George
   E. Eyre and William Spottiswoode for Her Majesty's Stationery
   Office, London.
Carter, H. D. (1939) *If You Want to Invent*, The Vanguard Press,
   New York.
Chase, S. (1926) *The Tragedy of Waste*, Macmillan, New York.
Clemen, R. A. (1927) *By-Products in the Packing Industry*,
   University of Chicago Press, Chicago.
Cumbler, J. T. (2000) 'Conflict, Accommodation, and Compromise:
   Connecticut's Attempt to Control Industrial Waste in the
   Progressive Era', *Environmental History* 5 (3).
Davies, J. C. and Mazurek, J. (1998) *Pollution Control in the United
   States. Evaluating the System*, Resources for the Future Press,
   Washington DC.
Desrochers, P. (2000) 'Market Processes and the Closing of
   "Industrial Loops": A Historical Reappraisal', *The Journal of
   Industrial Ecology* vol. 4, no.1 (Fall) pp. 29–43.
Desrochers, P. (2002) 'Industrial Ecology and the Rediscovery of
   Inter-Firm Recycling Linkages: Some Historical Perspective and
   Policy Implications', *Industrial and Corporate Change*, vol. 11,
   no. 5.
Environmental Law Institute (1998) *Barriers to Environmental*

Technology Innovation and Use, Environmental Law Institute, Washington DC.

Environmental Law Institute (1999) *Innovation, Cost and Environmental Regulation: Perspectives on Business, Policy and Legal Factors Affecting the Cost of Compliance*, Environmental Law Institute, Washington DC.

Florida, R. and Davison, D. (2001) 'Why do firms adopt advanced environmental practices (and do they make a difference)?' in Coglianese, C. and Nash, J. (eds.) *Regulating from the Inside: Can Environmental Management Systems Achieve Policy Goals?*, Resources for the Future, Washington DC, pp. 198–221.

Frosch, R. A. (1997) 'Closing the Loop on Waste Materials' in Richards, Deanna J. (ed.) *The Industrial Green Game: Implications for Environmental Design and Management*, National Academy of Engineering, Washington DC.

Graedel, T. E. and Allenby, B. R. (1995) *Industrial Ecology*, Prentice Hall, Englewood Cliffs, NJ.

Hawken, P., Lovins, A. and Lovins, L. Hunter (1999) *Natural Capitalism. Creating the Next Industrial Revolution*, Little, Brown and Company, Boston.

Hertwich, E. C. (1997) 'Eco-Efficiency and its Role in Industrial Transformation', Report to the International Dimensions of Global Change Workgroup.

Hobson, J. A. (1917) *The Evolution of Modern Capitalism. A Study of Machine Production*, Charles Scribner's Sons, New York.

Kershaw, J. B. C. (1928) *The Recovery and Use of Industrial and Other Waste*, Ernest Benn Limited, London.

Kneese, A. V. and Bower, B. T. (1979) *Environmental Quality and Residuals Management*, The Johns Hopkins University Press, Baltimore.

Koller, T. (1918 [1902]) *The Utilization of Waste Products: A Treatise on the Rational Utilization, Recovery, and Treatment of Waste Products of all Kinds* (3rd revised edition, translated from the 2nd revised German edition), D. Van Nostrand Company, New York.

Marshall, A. (1986 [1920/1890]) *Principles of Economics* (8th edition), Macmillan, London.

Nath, B., Hens, L. and Pimentel, D. (2000) 'Editorial', *Environment, Development and Sustainability* 1 (1).

Neimark, P. and Rhoades Mott, P. (1999) *The Environmental Debate. A Documentary History*, Greenwood Press, Westport, CT.

OECD (1994) *Managing the Environment: The Role of Economic Agents*, Organization for Economic Co-operation and Development, Paris.

Resetar, S. (1999) *Technology Forces at Work. Profiles of Environmental Research and Development at DuPont, Intel, Monsanto, and Xerox*, Rand Corporation, Santa Monica.

Riukulehto, S. (1998) *The Concepts of Luxury and Waste in American Radicalism, 1880–1929*, Finnish Academy of Science and Letters, Helsinki.

Rosenberg, N. (1994) *Exploring the Black Box. Technology, Economics, and History*, Cambridge University Press, Cambridge, UK.

Schwarz, E. J. and Steininger, Karl W. (1997) 'Implementing Nature's Lesson: The Industrial Recycling Network Enhancing Regional Development', *Journal of Cleaner Production* 5 (1/2), pp. 47–56.

Simmonds, P. L. (1862) *Waste Products and Undeveloped Substances; or, Hints for Enterprise in Neglected Fields*, Robert Hardwicke, London.

Simmonds, P. L. (1876) *Waste Products and Undeveloped Substances: A Synopsis of Progress Made in Their Economic Utilisation During the Last Quarter of a Century at Home and Abroad* (3rd edition), Hardwicke and Bogue, London.

Spooner, H. J. (1918) *Wealth from Waste. Elimination of Waste a World Problem*, G. Routledge, London, reprinted 1974 by Hive Publishing Company.

Talbot, F. A. (1920) *Millions from Waste*, J. B. Lippincott Company, Philadelphia.

Worrell, E. (2000) 'Editorial', *Resources, Conservation and Recycling* 28.

Chapter 4 – George B. N. Ayittey

Achebe, C. (1985) *The Trouble With Nigeria*, Fourth Dimension Publishing, Enugu, Nigeria.

Ayittey, G. B. N. (1982) *Africa Betrayed*, St Martin's Press, New York.

Ayittey, G. B. N. (1988) *Africa In Chaos*, St Martin's Press, New York.

Berkeley, B. (1996) 'An Encore for Chaos?' February, *Atlantic Monthly*, pp. 30–36.

Eberstadt, N. (2000) 'Pursuit of south of the Sahara', *Washington*

Times, 27 August, p. B4.

The Economist (1990a) 'Tanzania; A teacher retires', 2 June, p. 48.

The Economist (1990b) 'Africa's French-franc zone; time to devalue', 21 July, p. 82.

The Economist (1995) 'Aid for Kenya. Stop, go', 19 August, p. 37.

The Economist (1997) 'Nigeria. Privatisation? Forget it', 25 January, p. 41.

The Economist (1999) 'Who's fooling whom?, 9 October, p. 52.

The Financial Times (1990) 'Western aid for Africa seen as a failure', 7 June, p. 7.

Gourevitch, P. (1998) *Stories From Rwanda*, Farrar, Strauss and Giroux, New York.

Lamb, D. (1983) *The Africans*, Random House, New York.

Maren, M. (1997) *The Road to Hell: The Ravaging Effects of Foreign Aid and International Charity*, The Free Press, New York.

Mazrui, A. (1986) *The Africans*, BBC Publications, London.

Nafziger, E. Wayne (1993) *The Debt Crisis In Africa*, Johns Hopkins University Press, Baltimore.

The New York Times (1990) 'Nyerere and Tanzania: no regrets at socialism', 24 October, p. A8.

The New York Times (1996) 'Not quite democracy, Africans look east for new model', 4 February, p. 4

The New York Times (2000) 'Against tough odds, Nigeria bets on reform', 20 August, p. 1.

UNCTAD (1998) *Trade and Development Report, 1998: Financial Instability and Growth In Africa*, United Nations Commission on Trade and Development, New York.

The Washington Post (1995) 'Disaffected in Zambia; citizens caught by economic ills, power struggle', 12 September, p. A12.

The Washington Post (1998) 'Corruption Flourished in Abacha's regime; leader linked to broad plunder', 9 June, p. A01.

The Washington Post (1999) 'Generosity shrinks in an age of prosperity', 25 November, p. A01.

The Washington Post (2000) 'Besieged Mugabe turns from reconciliation to rage', 5 May, p. A01.

The Washington Times (1995a) 'Has Mobutu Sese Seko really converted to democracy?', 6 July, p. A18.

The Washington Times (1995b) 'Sanctions' record mixed for Kenyans; rights abuses still occur despite legal opposition', 3 August, p. A18.

The Washington Times (1996) 'Guinea moves boldly to boost

development; prime minister plucked from Ivory Coast',
17 October, p. A19.

Whitaker, Jennifer (1988) *How Can Africa Survive?* Harper & Row,
New York.

World Bank (1989) *Sub-Saharan Africa: From Crisis to Self-
Sustainable Growth*, World Bank, Washington DC.

World Bank (1990) *World Development Report*, World Bank,
Washington DC.

World Bank (1993) *Adjustment in Sub-Saharan Africa*, October,
World Bank Operations Evaluation Department, Washington DC.

World Bank (1995) 'Ghana: is Growth Sustainable', Precis No. 99,
Operations Evaluation Department of World Bank, 1 December
1995. Available at http://wbln0018.worldbank.org/oed/oeddoclib.
nsf/d6e15766d406a12d85256808006a000c/
7a2194020508073a852567f5005d8a39?OpenDocument,
downloaded 5 June 2002.

World Bank (2001) *Can Africa Claim The 21st Century?*, World
Bank, Washington DC.

Chapter 5 – **Fabiano Pegurier and Gilberto Salgado**

Arthur Andersen (1999) 'Pesquisa sobre tributação', mimeo.

Bruton, H. (1998) 'A Reconsideration of import substitution', in
Journal of Economic Literature vol. XXXVI, June, pp. 903–36.

de Soto, H. (1989) *The Other Path – The Invisible Revolution in the
Third World*, Harper & Row, New York.

Edwards, S. (1997) *Crisis y Reforma en América Latina: del
Desconsuelo a la Esperanza*, Emecé Editores, Buenos Aires,
Argentina.

Fishlow, A. and Cardoso, E. (1992) 'Desarrollo económico en
América Latina: 1950–1980' in Barbosa, Fernando H. *et al. De la
Estabilizacion al Crescimiento en Latin America*, CINDE and
FGV, San Francisco, CA and Rio de Janeiro, Brazil.

Fry, M., Goodhart, C. and Almeida, A. (1996) *Central Banking in
Developing Countries, Objectives, Activities and Independence*,
Routledge, London.

Haberler, G. (1974) *Economic Growth and Stability: An Analysis of
Economic Change and Policies*, Nash Publishing, Los Angeles, CA.

IDB (1998) *Annual Report*, Inter-American Development Bank,
Washington DC.

IMF (2001) *World Economic Outlook, December 2001*,

International Monetary Fund, Washington DC.

IMF, *International Financial Statistics*.

Sheahan, J. (1987) *Patterns of Development in Latin America*, Princeton University Press, Princeton, NJ, p. 87.

Thorpe, R. (1998) *Progress, Poverty and Exclusion: An Economic History of Latin America*, Inter-American Development Bank, Washington DC.

World Bank (1990) *World Development Report*, World Bank, Washington DC.

World Bank (2001) *World Development Report*, World Bank, Washington DC.

Chapter 6 – Charles N. Steele

Aslund, A. (2002) *Building Capitalism: The Transformation of the Former Soviet Bloc*, Cambridge University Press, Cambridge, UK.

Boettke, P. (1993) *Why Perestroika Failed: The Politics and Economics of Socialist Transformation*, Routledge, London.

Conquest, R. (1986) *The Harvest of Sorrow: Soviet Collectivization and the Terror-Famine*, Oxford University Press, New York.

Courtois, S., Werth, N., Panné, J.-L., Paczkowski, A., Bartosek, K., Margolin, J.-L. (1999) *The Black Book of Communism: Crimes, Terror, Repression*, Harvard University Press, Cambridge, MA.

Easterly, W. (1999) 'The Ghost of Financing Gap: Testing the Growth Model of the International Financial Institutions', *Journal of Development Economics* 60(2), pp. 423–38.

EBRD (1999) *Transition Report 1999: Ten Years of Transition*, European Bank for Reconstruction and Development, London.

Feshbach, M. and Friendly, A. Jr (1992) *Ecocide in the USSR: Health and Nature Under Siege*, BasicBooks, New York.

Goldman, M. I. (1972a) 'Externalities and the Race for Economic Growth in the USSR: Will the Environment Ever Win?' *Journal of Political Economy* 80(2), March–April, pp. 314–27.

Goldman, M. I. (1972b) *The Spoils of Progress: Environmental Pollution in the Soviet Union*, MIT Press, Cambridge, MA.

Gregory, P. and Stuart, R. (1997) *Comparative Economic Systems*, Houghton-Mifflin, Boston.

Hewett, E. A. (1988) *Reforming the Soviet Economy: Equality versus Efficiency*, Brookings Institution Press, Washington DC.

Kneen, P. (2000) 'Political Corruption in Russia and the Soviet Legacy', *Crime, Law and Social Change* 34, pp. 349–67.

Kornai, J. (1992) *The Socialist System: The Political Economy of Communism*, Princeton University Press, Princeton, NJ.

Lange, O. (1938) 'On the Economic Theory of Socialism' in Lippincott, B. (ed.) (1938 – reprinted 1964) *On the Economic Theory of Socialism*, McGraw-Hill, New York.

Mickin, P. P. (1988) 'Desiccation of the Aral Sea: A water management disaster in the Soviet Union', *Science* 241, pp. 1170–6.

Murdock, D. (2002) 'Russians Do Taxes Right', *National Review Online*, 1 March 2002. Available at: http://www.nationalreview.com/murdock/murdockprint030102.html

OECD (2001) *Transition at a Glance: 2001 Edition*, Organization for Economic Co-operation and Development, Paris.

Pryde, P. R. (1991) *Environmental Management in the Soviet Union*, Cambridge University Press, Cambridge, UK.

Romer, P. (1991) 'Increasing Returns and New Developments in the Theory of Growth' in Barnett, W. *et al.* (eds.) *Equilibrium Theory and Applications: Proceedings of the 6th International Symposium in Economic Theory and Econometrics*, Cambridge University Press, Cambridge, MA.

Svejnar, J. (2002) 'Transition Economies: Performance and Challenges', *Journal of Economic Perspectives* 16(1), pp. 3–28.

Tullock, G., Seldon, A. and Brady, G. (2000) *Government: Whose Obedient Servant?*, Institute of Economic Affairs, London.

World Bank (2002) *Transition, the First Ten Years: Lessons for Eastern Europe and the Former Soviet Union*, World Bank, Washington DC.

World Bank (1996) *World Development Report 1996: From Plan to Market*, Oxford University Press, Oxford.

Chapter 7 – Martín Krause

Anderson, T. and Leal, D. R. (1991) *Free Market Environmentalism*, Pacific Research Institute for Public Policy, San Francisco.

Bate, R. (2001) *Saving Our Streams*, Institute of Economic Affairs, London.

Coase, R. H. (1974) 'The Lighthouse in Economics', *Journal of Law and Economics* 17, pp. 357–76.

Brailovsky, A. E. and Foguelman, D. (1991) *Memoria Verde: Historia Ecológica de la Argentina*, Ed. Sudamericana, Buenos Aires.

Coursey, D. (1998) 'The revealed demand for a public good: evidence from endangered and threatened species', Symposium on Endangered Species Act, *New York University Environmental Law Journal* 6, pp. 411–49.

Davis, Lance E., Gallman, Robert E. and Gleiter, K. (1997) *In Pursuit of Leviathan: Technology, Institutions, Productivity and Profits in American Whaling, 1816–1906*, University of Chicago Press, Chicago.

Foster, V. and Hahn, R. W. (1995) 'Designing More Efficient Markets: Lessons from Los Angeles Smog Control', *Journal of Law and Economics* 38(1), pp. 19–48.

Fundación Vida Silvestre (1993) 'Situación Ambiental de la Argentina: Recomendaciones y prioridades de acción', Boletín Técnico no. 14.

Hanemann, M. (1994) 'Valuing the Environment Through Contingent Valuation', *Journal of Economic Perspectives*, vol. 8, no. 4, pp. 19–43.

Hardin, G. (1968) 'The Tragedy of the Commons', *Science* 162, pp. 1243–8.

Harrison, G. W. (1992) 'Valuing Public Goods with the Contingent Valuation Method: A Critique', *Journal of Environmental Economics and Management* 23:3, pp. 248–57.

Hayek, F. A. von (1937) 'Economics and Knowledge', *Economica* 4, pp. 33–54.

Hayek, F. A. von (1945) 'The Use of Knowledge in Society', *American Economic Review* 35(4), pp. 519–30.

Henderson, H. (1991) *Paradigms in Progress: Life beyond Economics*, Adamantine Press Limited, London.

Kahn, H. (1979) *World Economic Development: 1979 and Beyond*, Croom Helm, London.

Kahneman, D., Knetsch, J. L. and Thaler, R. H. (1986) 'Fairness as a constraint on profit seeking: Entitlements in the market', American Economic Review 76(4), pp. 728–41.

OECD (1991) 'Environmental Indicators: a Preliminary Set', Organization for Economic Co-operation and Development, Paris.

UN (1994) *Contabilidad ambiental y económica integrada*, United Nations, New York.

UNEP (1994) 'Workshop on Environmental and Natural Resource Accounting with Particular Reference to Countries in Transition to Market Economies', United Nations Environment Programme

(UNEP), *Environmental Economics Series Paper N° 9*. Session 2. Web version: http://www.unep.org/unep/products/eeu/ecoserie/ ecos9/eco93.htm

UNEP (1997) Global Environmental Outlook-1, United Nations Environment Programme, Global State of the Environment Report. Web version: http://www.grida.no/geo1/index.htm, chap. 3, Box 3.16.

WCED (1987) *World Commission on Environment and Development: Our Common Future*, Oxford University Press, Oxford.

Chapter 8 – Alan Oxley

DRI/WEFA Inc. (2002) 'Kyoto Protocol and Beyond: The High Cost to the United Kingdom', study prepared for American Council for Capital Formation's Center for Policy Research, Washington DC. Available at http://www.scientific-alliance.com/dri4.doc. Retrieved 10 June 2002.

Evans, R. (1995) 'The Basel Convention: Internationalism's Greatest Folly', Competitive Enterprise Institute, Washington, DC.

Griswold, D. (2001) 'Seven Moral Arguments for Free Trade', *Cato Policy Report* vol. XXIII, no.4, pp. 1, 12–14. Available at http://www.cato.org/pubs/policy_report/v23n4/freetrade.pdf. Accessed 10 June 2002.

Jha, V. and Hoffman, U. (2000) *Achieving Objectives of Multilateral Environmental Agreements: a package of trade measures and positive measures. Elucidated by Results of Developing Country Case Studies*, United Nations Conference on Trade and Development, Geneva.

Langeweische, W. (2000) 'The Shipbreakers', *The Atlantic Monthly*, August, pp. 31–49. Available at http://www.theatlantic.com/issues/2000/08/langewiesche.htm. Accessed 10 June 2002.

Montgomery, M. (1995) 'Reassessing the Waste Trade Crisis: What Do We Really Know?', *Journal of Environment and Development* 4 (1), pp.1–28.

Morris, J. (1997) *Green Goods? Consumers, Product Labels and the Environment*, Institute of Economic Affairs, London.

Morris, J. (2000a) 'From Seattle's Front Lines: Environmentalists, Organized Labor Attempt to Capture WTO Agenda', *Organization Trends*, January, Capital Research Center,

Washington DC. Available at http://www.capitalresearch.org/
publications/organizational_trends/2000/0001.htm. Accessed 10
June 2002.

Morris, J. (2000b) *Rethinking Risk and the Precautionary Principle*,
Butterworth-Heinemann, Oxford.

OECD (1999) 'Experience with the Use of Trade Measures in the
Convention on International Trade in Endangered Species of Wild
Fauna and Flora (CITES)' in *Trade Measures in Multilateral
Environmental Agreements*, Organization for Economic Co-
operation and Development, Paris, pp. 11–62.

Raychaudhari, A. and Hoffman, U. (2000) 'The Effectiveness of the
Provisions on Transfer of Technology to Developing Countries in
the Basel Convention: The Case of Used Lead-Acid Batteries in
India' in Jha, V. and Hoffman, U. (2000).

't Sas-Rolfes, M. (1995) *Rhinos: Conservation, Economics and
Trade-Offs*, Institute of Economic Affairs, London.

Sugg, I. and Krueter, U. (1994) *Elephants and Ivory: Lessons from
the Trade Ban*, Institute of Economic Affairs, London.

UN (1992) 'Rio Declaration on Environment and Development',
A/CONF.151/26 (vol. I), 12 August, United Nations Conference
on Environment and Development, New York.

Wallach, L. (1999) *Whose Trade Organization?*, Public Citizen,
Washington DC.

WTO (1998) *United States – Import Prohibition of Certain Shrimp
and Shrimp Products*, Report of the Appellate Body,
WT/DS58/AB/RW, 12 October, World Trade Organization,
Geneva.

WTO (2001) *United States – Import Prohibition of Certain Shrimp
and Shrimp Products: Recourse to Article 21.5 of the DSU by
Malaysia*, Report of the Appellate Body, WT/DS58/22, 22
October, World Trade Organization, Geneva.

Chapter 9 – **Robert C. Balling Jr**

Balling, R. C. Jr, Michaels, P. J. and Knappenberger, P. C. (1998)
'Analysis of winter and summer warming rates in gridded
temperature time series', *Climate Research* 9.

Diaz, H. F., Bradley, R. S. and Eischeid, J. K. (1989) 'Precipitation
fluctuations over global land areas since the late 1800s', *Journal
of Geophysical Research* 94.

Hansen, J. E., Sato, M., Lacis, A., Ruedy, R., Tegen, I. and

Matthews, E. (1998) 'Climate forcings in the Industrial era', *Proceedings of the National Academy of Sciences* 95, pp. 12, 753–8.

Hansen, J. E., Sato, M., Ruedy, R., Lacis, A. and Oinas, V. (2000) 'Global warming in the twenty-first century: An alternative scenario', *Proceedings of the National Academy of Sciences* 97, pp. 9875–80.

IPCC (2001) *Climate Change 2001: The Scientific Basis*, Cambridge University Press, Cambridge, UK.

Jones, P. D. (1994) 'Hemispheric surface air temperature variations: A reanalysis and an update to 1993', *Journal of Climate* 7.

Lean, J., Beer, J. and Bradley, R. (1995) 'Reconstruction of solar irradiance since 1610: Implications for climate change', *Geophysical Research Letters* 22.

Spencer, R. W. and Christy, J. R. (1990) 'Precise monitoring of global temperature trends from satellites', *Science* 247.

Wallace, J. M., Christy, J. R., Gaffen, D. J., Grody, N. C., Hansen, J. E., Parker, D. E., Peterson, T. C., Santer, B. D., Spencer, R. W., Trenberth, K. E. and Wentz, F. J. (2000) *Reconciling Observations of Global Temperature Change*, National Academy Press, Washington DC.

Wigley, T. M. L. (1998) 'The Kyoto Protocol: CO_2, CH_4 and climate implications', *Geophysical Research Letters* 25, pp. 2285–8.

Chapter 10 – **Robert L. Bradley Jr**

Anderson, T. (1983) *Water Crisis – Ending the Policy Drought*, Cato Institute, Washington DC.

Avery, D. (1999) 'The Fallacy of the Organic Utopia' in Morris and Bate (1999), pp. 3–18.

Bailey, R. (ed.) (1995) *The True State of the Planet*, Free Press, New York.

Bayea, J., Cook, J., Hall, D., Socolow, R. and Williams, R. (1992) *Toward Ecological Guidelines for Large-Scale Biomass Energy Development: Report of a Workshop for Engineers, Ecologists and Policy Makers*, National Audubon Society, New York.

Brack, D., Grubb, M. and Windram, C. (2000) *International Trade and Climate Change Policies*, The Royal Institute of International Affairs, London.

Bradley, R. (1997) 'Renewable Energy: Not Cheap, Not "Green"', *Cato Policy Analysis* No. 280, 27 August.

Bradley, R. (2000) *Julian Simon and the Triumph of Energy Sustainability*, American Legislative Exchange Council, Washington DC.

Bradley, R. and Fulmer, R. (forthcoming) *Energy: The Master Resource*, Institute for Energy Research, Houston.

Campbell, C. (1997) *The Coming Oil Crisis*, Multi-Science Publishing Company, Essex.

CEI (1996) Comments on Proposed Reform to the EPA National Ambient Air Quality Standards For Particulate Matter, Docket no. A-95-54, 61 Fed. Reg. 65,637, 13 December.

Cook, J. H. and Bayea, J. (1997) 'An Analysis of the Environmental Impacts of Energy Crops in the USA: Methodologies, Conclusions and Recommendations', presented at the European conference 'Environmental Impact of Biomass for Energy', held 4–5 November 1996 in Noordwijkerhout, The Netherlands. Available at http://www.panix.com/~jimcook/data/ec-workshop.html. Retrieved 3 March 2000.

Deffeyes, K. (2001) *Hubbert's Peak*, Princeton University Press, Princeton, NJ.

de Soto, H. (2000) *The Mystery of Capital*, BasicBooks, New York.

Ehrlich, P. and Ehrlich, A. (1974) *The End of Affluence*, Rivercity Press, Rivercity, MA.

Ehrlich, P. and Ehrlich, A. (1996) *Betrayal of Science and Reason*, Island Press, Washington DC.

Ehrlich, P., Ehrlich, A. and Holdren, J. P. (1973) *Human Ecology: Problems and Solutions*, W. H. Freeman & Company, San Francisco.

Ehrlich, R. (2001) *Nine Crazy Ideas in Science*, Princeton University Press, Princeton, NJ.

FAO (1997) 'State of the World's Forests, 1997', Food and Agricultural Organization, Rome, Italy.

FAO (1999) 'The State of Food Insecurity in the World, 1999' (December). Food and Agricultural Organization, Rome, Italy. Available at http://www.fao.org/FOCUS/E/SOFI/home-e.htm.

Gaston, K. J. (2000) 'Global patterns in biodiversity,' *Nature* 405, pp. 220–7.

Goklany, I. M. (2000) 'Potential Consequences of Increasing Atmospheric CO_2 Concentration Compared to Other Environmental Problems', *Technology* vol. 75, pp. 189–213.

Goklany, I. M. (1993) *Key Issues Related to Sustainable Development, Issue: Reconciling Human Demands on Land and*

Other Natural Resources with Those of Nature, background paper, Office of Policy Analysis, US Department of the Interior, Washington DC, October.

Goklany, I. M. (1995) 'Richer is Cleaner: Long-Term Trends in Global Air Quality' in Bailey (1995), pp. 339–77.

Goklany, I. M. (1998) 'Saving Habitat and Conserving Biodiversity on a Crowded Planet', *BioScience* 48, pp. 941–53.

Goklany, I. M. (1999a) *Clearing the Air: The True Story of the War on Air Pollution*, Cato Institute, Washington DC.

Goklany, I. M. (1999b) 'The Future of Industrial Society', paper presented at the International Conference on Industrial Ecology and Sustainability, University of Technology of Troyes, France, 22–25 September.

Goklany, I. M. (1999c) 'Meeting Global Food Needs: The Environmental Trade-offs Between Increasing Land Conversion and Land Productivity', *Technology* 6, pp. 107–30.

Goklany, I. M. and Sprague, M. W. (1992) *An Alternative Approach to Sustainable Development: Conserving Forests, Habitat and Biological Diversity by Increasing Efficiency and Productivity of Land Utilization*, Office of Program Analysis, US Department of the Interior, Washington DC.

Graham, J. and Wiener, J. (eds.) (1995) *Risk versus Risk: Tradeoffs in Protecting Health and the Environment*, Harvard University Press, Cambridge, MA.

Grossman, G. M. and Krueger, A. B. (1993) 'Environmental Impacts of the North American Free Trade Agreement' in Garber, P. (ed.) *The US–Mexico Free Trade Agreement*, MIT Press, Cambridge, MA.

Hahn, R. (ed.) (1996) *Risk, Costs, and Lives Saved*, Oxford University Press, New York.

Hansen, J. (1998) 'Climate Forcings in the Industrial Era', *Proceedings of the National Academy of Sciences*, October, p. 12753.

Hayward, S. and Jones, L. (1999) *Environmental Indicators for North America and the UK*, Institute of Economic Affairs, London. Available at http://oldfraser.lexi.net/publications/critical issues/1999/env indic/

Herrick, T., Lifsher, M. and Whalen, J. (2002) 'As Oil Supplies Grow, US Is Less Reliant on the Middle East', *Wall Street Journal*, 15 March, p. A1.

Holdren, J. (2000) 'Memorandum to the President: The Energy-

Climate Challenge' in Kennedy, D. and Riggs, J. (eds.) *U.S. Policy and the Global Environment: Memos to the President*, The Aspen Institute, Washington DC.

Holdren, J. (2002) 'Energy: Asking the Wrong Question', *Scientific American*, January, pp. 65–6.

International Energy Agency (2000) *World Energy Outlook*, OECD/IEA, Paris.

IIED (1996) *Forest Resources and Forestry Practices of Selected World Regions*, International Institute for Environment and Development, London.

IPCC (1996) *Climate Change 1995 – The Science of Climate Change*, Cambridge University Press, Cambridge, UK.

IPCC (2001) *Climate Change 2001: The Scientific Basis*, Cambridge University Press, Cambridge, UK.

Jenkins, H. (2001) 'How to be Agreeable About Global Warming', *Wall Street Journal*, 25 July, p. A17.

Leach, M. and Mearns, R. (eds.) (1996) *The Lie of the Land: Challenging Received Wisdom on the African Environment*, International African Insitute/James Currey, London.

Lieberman, B. (2001) 'Another Gas Spike: The Energy Crisis, Take Two', National Review Online, 21 September. Available at http://www.cei.org/gencon/019,02168.cfm. Accessed 10 June 2002.

Linden, H. (1997) 'Operational, Technological and Economic Drivers for Convergence of the Electric Power and Gas Industries', *The Electricity Journal*, May, p. 14.

Lomborg, B. (2001) *The Skeptical Environmentalist*, Cambridge University Press, Cambridge, UK.

Lorenz, D. and Morris, D. (1995) *How Much Energy Does it Take to Make a Gallon of Ethanol?*, MS Institute for Local Self-Reliance, Minneapolis.

Lovins, A. (1975) *World Energy Strategies: Facts, Issues, and Options*, Friends of the Earth International, New York.

Lovins, A. (1976) 'Energy Strategy: The Road Not Taken?', *Foreign Affairs*, October, pp. 76–7, 83.

Martin, R. B. (2000) 'Biological Diversity: Divergent Views on Its Status and Diverging Approaches to Its Conservation' in Bailey, R. (ed.) *Earth Report 2000*, McGraw-Hill, New York.

McKenzie, J. (1996) 'Oil as A Finite Resource: When is Global Production Likely to Peak?', World Resources Institute, Washington DC.

Miles, T. R. Sr and Miles, T. R. Jr (1992) *Environmental*

Implications of Increased Biomass Energy Use, National Renewable Energy Laboratory, Golden, CO.

Moore, P. (2000) *Greenspirit: Trees are the Answer*, Hushion House, Toronto.

Morris, J. (1995) *The Political Economy of Land Degradation*, Institute of Economic Affairs, London.

Morris, J. and Bate, R. (eds.) (1999) *Fearing Food: Risk, Health and Environment*, Butterworth-Heinemann, Oxford.

Mortimore, M. (1990) *Adapting to Drought: Farmers, Famines and Desertification in West Africa*, Cambridge University Press, Cambridge, UK.

Myers, N., Mittermeier, R. A., Mittermeier, C. G., Da Fonseca, G. A. B. and Kent, J. (2000) 'Biodiversity Hotspots for Conservation Priorities', *Nature* 403, pp, 853–8.

Nathan, D. (1996) 'Economic Factors in the Adoption of Improved Stoves', *Wood Energy News* vol. 12, no. 1.

OTA (1995) *Renewing Our Energy Future*, US Office of Technology Assessment, Washington DC.

Perlack, R. D., Ranney, J. W. and Wright, L. L. (1992) *Environmental Emissions and Socioeconomic Considerations in the Production, Storage, and Transportation of Biomass Energy Feedstocks*, Oak Ridge National Laboratory, Oak Ridge, TN.

Pomerance, R. (1999) *Coral Bleaching, Coral Mortality, and Global Climate Change*, Report to the US Coral Reef Task Force, Bureau of Oceans and International Environmental and Scientific Affairs, US Department of State, 5 March 1999.

Rabkin, J. (1998) *Why Sovereignty Matters*, American Enterprise Institute, Washington DC.

Romm, J. and Curtis, C. (1996) 'Mideast Oil Forever?', *Atlantic Monthly*, April, pp. 57–74.

Sarewitz, D. and Pielke, R. (2000) 'Breaking the Global-Warming Gridlock', *Atlantic Monthly*, July, pp. 55–64.

Scarlett, L. (1999) 'Doing More with Less: Dematerialization – Unsung Environmental Triumph?', in *Earth Report 2000*, ed. Ronald Bailey, McGraw-Hill, New York

Seelye, K. (2000) 'Bush Says Gore Has Oil on His Own Shoes', *New York Times*, 29 June, p. A2.

Selden, T. M. and Song, D. (1994) 'Environmental Quality and Development: Is there a Kuznets Curve for Air Pollution Emissions?', *Journal of Environmental Economics and Management* 27, pp. 147–62.

Shafik, N. and Bandyopadhyay, S. (1992) 'Economic Growth and Environmental Quality: Time-Series and Cross-Section Evidence', Policy Research Working Paper no. 904, The World Bank, Washington DC.

Simon, J. (1996) *The Ultimate Resource 2*, Princeton University Press, Princeton, NJ.

Siteur, J. (1996) 'Energy Balances in RWEDP Member Countries', *Wood Energy News*, vol. 11 (2), p. 4.

Southgate, D. (1998) *Tropical Forest Conservation in Latin America*, Oxford University Press, New York.

Stott, P. (1999) *Tropical Rain Forest: A Political Ecology of Hegemonic Mythmaking*, Institute of Economic Affairs, London.

Taylor, J. and VanDoren, P. (2002) 'Evaluating the Case for Renewable Energy: Is Government Support Warranted?', *Cato Policy Analysis* no. 422, 10 January.

Thomas, D. S. G. and Middleton, N. J. (1994) *Desertification – Exploding the Myth*, John Wiley, Chichester.

Tolbert, V. R. and Downing, M. (1995) 'Environmental Effects of Planting Biomass Crops at Larger Scales on Agricultural Lands' in *Proceedings of the Second Biomass Conference of the Americas: Energy, Environment, Agriculture and Industry*, National Renewable Energy Laboratory, Golden, CO, pp. 1628–35.

Tolbert, V. R. and Schiller, A. (1996) 'Environmental Enhancement Using Short-Rotation Woody Crops and Perennial Grasses as Alternatives to Traditional Agricultural Crops' in *Proceedings of the Conference, Environmental Enhancement Through Agriculture*, Tufts University, Medford, MA.

UNDP, UNDESA and WEC (2000) *World Energy Assessment: Energy and the Challenge of Energy Sustainability*, United Nations Publications, New York.

USEIA (2001) 'Many European countries witnessed growing consumer anger over high motor fuel prices in the third quarter of 2000', *International Energy Outlook 2001*, US Energy Information Administration, Government Printing Office, Washington DC.

Victor, D. (2001) *The Collapse of the Kyoto Protocol and the Struggle to Slow Global Warming*, Princeton University Press, Princeton, NJ.

Warren, A. and Khogali, M. (1992) Assessment of Desertification and Drought in the Sudano-Sahelian Region, 1985–91, United Nations Sudano-Sahelian Office (UNSO), New York.

Wilcove, D. S., Rothstein, D., Dubow, J., Philips, A. and Losos, E. (1998) *Bioscience* 48, pp. 607–15.

Williams, B. (2000) 'Comment: Is Shell Report 2000's Sustainable Development Focus an Anomaly or Sign of the Future?', *Oil & Gas Journal*, 13 November, pp. 74–7.

WCED (1997) *Our Common Future*, Oxford University Press, Oxford.

WEC (2000) *Energy for Tomorrow's World—Acting Now!*, World Energy Council, London.

Yeatts, G. (1997) *Subsoil Wealth: The Struggle for Privatization in Argentina*, Foundation for Economic Education, Irvington-on-Hudson, New York.

Chapter 11 – **Jonathan H. Adler**

Adler J. (2000) 'More Sorry than Safe: Assessing the Precautionary Principle and the Proposed International Biosafety Protocol', *Texas International Law Journal* vol. 35, no. 2.

Barton, J. H. (1996) 'Biotechnology, the Environment, and International Agricultural Trade', *Georgetown International Environmental Law Review* vol. 9.

Blum, E. (1993) 'Making Biodiversity Conservation Profitable', *Environment* vol. 35, p. 17.

Brown, M. and Leal, D. R. (2000) '… Or should Private Enterprise Take Over', *Nature* vol. 403, p. 129.

Butler, D. and Reichhardt, T. (1999) 'Long-term Effect of GM Crops Serves Up Food for Thought', *Nature* vol. 398, p. 651.

Conway, G. (2000) 'Food for All in the 21st Century', *Environment* Jan/Feb, p. 11.

Cook, R. J. (2000) 'Science-Based Risk Assessment for the Approval and Use of Plants in Agricultural and Other Environments', in *Agricultural Biotechnology and the Poor*, Consultative Group on International Agricultural Research, Washington DC, p. 133.

du Plessis, M. A. (2000) 'CITES and the Causes of Extinction' in Hutton and Dickson (2000a).

Eberstadt, N. (1999) 'World Population Prospects for the Twenty-First Century: The Specter of "Depopulation"?' in Bailey, R. (ed.) *Earth Report 2000*, McGraw-Hill, New York.

Edwards, S. R. (1995) 'Conserving Biodiversity: Resources for Our Future' in Bailey (ed.) *The True State of the Planet*, The Free Press, New York.

FAO (1999) *State of the World's Forests 1999*, United Nations Food and Agriculture Organization, Rome.

Georgia, P. *et al.* (1999) 'Benchmarks: The Global Trends that Are Shaping Our World' in Bailey, R. (ed.) *Earth Report 2000*, McGraw-Hill, New York.

Getz, W. M. (1999) 'Sustaining Natural and Human Capital: Villagers and Scientists', *Science* vol. 283, p. 1855.

Gibbs, W. W. (2001) 'On the Termination of Species', *Scientific American*, November.

Global Biodiversity Outlook (2001) Secretariat of the Convention on Biological Diversity, Montreal, Quebec.

Goklany, I. M. (1999a) 'Meeting Global Food Needs: The Environmental Trade-Offs Between Increasing Land Conversion and Land Productivity', *Technology* vol. 6.

Goklany, I. M. (1999b) 'Richer Is More Resilient: Dealing with Climate Changes and More Urgent Environmental Problems' in Bailey, R. (ed.) *Earth Report 2000*, McGraw-Hill, New York.

Gugliotta, G. (2000) 'New Vitamin A-Rich Rice Strain Termed Nutrition Breakthrough', *Washington Post*, 14 January, p. A6.

Hutton, J. and Dickson, B. (2000a) *Endangered Species, Threatened Convention: The Past, Present and Future of CITES*, Earthscan, London.

Hutton, J. and Dickson, B. (2000b) 'Introduction' in Hutton and Dickson (2000a).

Huxley, C. (2000) 'CITES: The Vision' in Hutton and Dickson (2000a).

Inamadar, A. *et al.* (1999) 'Capitalizing on Nature: Protected Area Management', *Science* vol. 283, p. 1856.

James, A. N. *et al.* (1999) 'Balancing the Earth's Accounts', *Nature* vol. 401, p. 323.

Jenkins, R. W. G. (2000) 'The Significant Trade Process: Making Appendix II Work' in Hutton and Dickson (2000a).

Johnson, B. (2000) 'Genetically Modified Crops and Other Organisms: Implications for Agricultural Sustainability and Biodiversity' in Persley, G. J. and Lantin, M. M. (eds.) *Agricultural Biotechnology and the Poor*, Consultative Group on International Agricultural Research, Washington DC.

Kievit, H. (2000) 'Conservation of the Nile Crocodile: Has CITES Helped or Hindered?' in Hutton and Dickson (2000a).

Mann, C. C. (1999) 'Crop Scientists Seek a New Revolution', *Science* vol. 283, p. 310.

Martin, R. B. (1999) 'Biological Diversity' in Bailey, R. (ed.) *Earth Report 2000*, McGraw-Hill, New York.

McNeely, J. A. and Scherr, S. J. (2001) *Common Ground, Common Future: How Ecoagriculture Can Help Feed the World and Save Biodiversity*, IUCN, Gland, Switzerland.

Miller, H. I. and Conko, G. (2000) 'The Protocol's Illusionary Principle', *Nature Biotechnology* vol. 18, p. 360.

Miller, H. I. (1999) 'UN-based Biotechnology Regulation: Scientific and Economic Havoc for the 21st Century', *Trends in Biotechnology* May 1999.

Moffat, A. S. (1998) 'Toting Up the Early Harvest of Transgenic Plants', *Science* vol. 282, p. 2177.

Morris, J. (2000) 'Defining the Precautionary Principle' in Morris, J. (ed.) *Rethinking Risk and the Precautionary Principle*, Butterworth-Heinemann, Oxford.

Musters, C. J. M. et al. (2000) 'Can Protected Areas Be Expanded in Africa?' *Science* vol. 287, p. 1760.

Myers, N. (1979) *The Sinking Ark: A New Look at the Problem of Disappearing Species*, Pergamon Press, Oxford.

NAS (1987) *Introduction of Recombinant DNA Organisms into the Environment: Key Issues*, National Academy Press, Washington DC.

NBPBR (1992) *1992 National Biotechnology Policy Board Report*, National Institutes of Health, Washington DC.

Norton, S. W. (1998) 'Property Rights, the Environment and Economic Well-Being' in Hill, P. J. and Meiners, R. E. (eds.) *Who Owns the Environment?* Rowman & Littlefield, Lanham, MD.

Norton, S. W. (2002) *Population Growth, Economic Freedom, and the Rule of Law*, PERC Policy Series no. 24, Bozeman, MT.

Paarlberg, R. (2000) 'Promise or Peril? Genetically Modified Crops in Developing Countries', *Environment*, Jan/Feb, p. 21.

Prakash, C. S. (1999) 'Feeding a World of Six Billion', *AgBioForum* Summer/Fall.

Revkin, A. C. (2002) 'Biologists Sought a Treaty; Now They Fault It', *New York Times*, 7 May.

Ryan, J. C. (1992) 'Conserving Biological Diversity' in Brown, L. (ed.) *State of the World 1992*, W.W. Norton, New York.

Sala, O. E. *et al.* (2000) 'Global Biodiversity Scenarios for the Year 2100', *Science* vol. 287, p. 1771.

Sedjo, R. A. (1995) 'Forests: Conflicting Signals,' in Bailey, R. (ed.) *The True State of the Planet*, The Free Press, New York.

Snape, W. J. III (1996) 'International Protection: Beyond Human Boundaries' in Snape, W. (ed.) *Biodiversity and the Law*, Island Press, Washington DC.

Stork, N. E. (1997) 'Measuring Global Biodiversity and Its Decline' in Reaka-Kudla *et al.* (eds.) *Biodiversity II: Understanding and Protecting Our Biological Resources*, Joseph Henry Press, Washington DC.

Sugg, I and Kreuter, U. (1994) *Elephants and Ivory: Lessons from the Trade Ban*, Institute of Economic Affairs, London.

Tangley, L. (2000) 'Engineering the Harvest', *U.S. News & World Report*, 13 March, p. 46.

't Sas-Rolfes, M. (2000) 'Assessing CITES: Four Case Studies' in Hutton and Dickson (2000a).

UN (1992) *Rio Declaration on Environment and Development*, A/CONF.151/5/Rev.1, 12 August, United Nations Conference on Environment and Development, New York.

Vitousek, P. M. *et al.* (1997) 'Human Domination of Earth's Ecosystems', *Science* vol. 277, p. 494.

Wambugu, F. (1999) 'Why Africa Needs Agricultural Biotech', *Nature* vol. 400, p. 15.

Webb, G. J. W. (2000) 'Are All Species Equal? A Comparative Assessment' in Hutton and Dickson (2000a).

Wilson, E. O. (2000) 'Biodiversity: Wildlife in Trouble' in Novacek, M. (ed.) *The Biodiversity Crisis*, New Press, New York.

World Resources 1996–97 (1996) World Resources Institute, Washington DC.

World Resources 1998–99 (1998) World Resources Institute, Washington DC.

Ye, X. *et al.* (2000) 'Engineering the Provitamin A (B-Carotene) Biosynthetic Pathway into (Cartenoid-Free) Rice Endosperm', *Science* vol. 287, p. 303.

Chapter 12 – Douglas Southgate

Anderson, T. and Hill, P. (1975) 'The evolution of property rights', *Journal of Law and Economics* 18, pp. 163–79.

Bohn, H. and Deacon, R. (2000) 'Ownership risk, investment, and the use of natural resources', *American Economic Review* 90, pp. 526–49.

Bromley, D. and Chapagain, D. (1994) 'The village against the center', *American Journal of Agricultural Economics* 66, pp. 868–73.

Browder, J. (1992) 'The limits of extractivism', *Bioscience* 42, pp. 174–181; Southgate (supra note 5), pp. 56–7.

Gordon, H. Scott (1954) 'The economic theory of a common property resource', *Journal of Political Economy* 62, pp. 124–42.

Goulding, M., Smith, N. and Mahar, D. (1996) *Floods of fortune*, Columbia University Press, New York.

North, D. and Thomas, R. (1973) *The rise of the western world*, Cambridge University Press, Cambridge, UK.

Pearce, D. (1996) 'Global environmental value and tropical forests' in Adamowicz, W., Boxall, P., Luckert, M., Phillips, W. and White, W. (eds.) *Forestry, economics, and the environment*, CAB International, Wallingford.

Peters, C. (1990) 'Population ecology and management of forest fruit trees in Peruvian Amazonia' in Anderson, A. (ed.) *Alternatives to deforestation*, Columbus University Press, New York.

Peters, C., Gentry, A. and Mendelsohn, R. (1989) 'Valuation of an Amazon rainforest', *Nature* 339.

Plotkin, M. (1994) *Tales of a shaman's apprentice*, Penguin Viking, New York.

Poteete, A. and Ostrom, E. (2002) 'An institutional approach to the study of forest resources' in Poulson, J. (ed.) *Human impacts on tropical forest biodiversity and genetic resources*, CAB International, Wallingford.

Rice, R., Sugal, C., Ratay, S. and Fonseca, G. (2001) 'Sustainable forest management', *Advances in Applied Biodiversity Science* 3, pp. 1–29.

Sader, S., Sozd, C. and Schwartz, N. (2000) 'Time-Series Forest Change, Land Cover/Land Use Conversion, and Socio-Economic Driving Forces in the Petén District, Guatemala' (Progress Report), NASA-ESE-LCLUC Science Program.

Schneider, R. (1995) *Government and the economy on the Amazon frontier* (environment paper 11), World Bank, Washington DC.

Shaw, C. (1997) 'Rural land markets' (report 16253-ES), World Bank, Washington DC.

Simpson, D., Sedjo, R. and Reid, J. (1996) 'Valuing biodiversity' *Journal of Political Economy* 104, pp. 163–85.

Southgate, D., Sierra, R. and Brown, L. (1991) 'A statistical analysis of the causes of deforestation in eastern Ecuador', *World Development* 19, pp. 1145–51.

Southgate, D. (1998) *Tropical forest conservation*, Oxford University Press, New York.

Southgate, D., Salazar-Canelos, P., Camacho-Saa, C. and Stewart, R. (2000) 'Markets, institutions, and forestry', *World Development* 28, pp. 2005–12.

Strasma, J. (1989) 'Unfinished business – consolidating land reform in El Salvador' in Thiesenhusen, W. (1995) *Broken promises*, Westview Press, Boulder, pp. 139–58.

Thiesenhusen, W. (1995) (ed.) *Searching for agrarian reform in Latin America*, Unwin Hyman, Boston.

Wells, M. and Brandon, K. (1993) *People and Parks*, World Bank, Washington DC.

WCED (1987) *World Commission on Environment and Development: Our common future*, Oxford University Press, New York.

Wunder, S. (2001) 'Poverty alleviation and tropical forests', *World Development* 29, pp. 1817–33.

Chapter 13 – Michael De Alessi

Acheson, J. M. (1987) 'The Lobster Fiefs Revisited' in McCay and Acheson (eds.) *The Question of the Commons*, University of Arizona Press, Tucson, pp. 37–65.

Anderson, T. and Hill, P. J. (1975) 'The Evolution of Property Rights: A Study of the American West', *Journal of Law and Economics* 12, pp. 163–79.

Arbuckle, M. (2000) 'Fisheries Management under ITQs: Innovations in New Zealand's Southern Scallop Fishery', Oregon State: IIFET proceedings. Available at http://www.orst.edu/Dept/IIFET/2000/papers/arbuckle.pdf. Accessed 10 June 2002.

Associated Press (1996) press release 7 June.

Bailey, C. (1988) 'The Social Consequences of Tropical Shrimp Mariculture Development', *Ocean and Shoreline Management*, pp. 31–4.

Barber, C. V. and Pratt, V. (1997) *Sullied Seas: Strategies for Combating Cyanide Fishing in Southeast Asia and Beyond*, World Resources Institute/International Marinelife Alliance, Washington DC.

Botkin, D. (2001) *No Man's Garden: Thoreau and a New Visitor for Civilization and Nature*, Island Press, Washington DC.

Brooks, W. K. (1996) [1891] *The Oyster*, Johns Hopkins University Press, Baltimore.

Brubaker, E. (1999) 'Cod Don't Vote', *The Next City*, January.

Chase, A. (1987) *Playing God in Yellowstone: the Destruction of*

America's First National Park, Harvest Books, San Diego.

Cordell, J. (1989) *A Sea of Small Boats*, Cultural Survival, Inc., Cambridge, MA.

De Alessi, L. (1980) 'The Economics of Property Rights: A Review of the Evidence', *Research in Law and Economics* vol. 2, pp. 1–47.

De Alessi, M. (1996) 'Oysters and Willapa Bay', Private Conservation Case Study, Center for Private Conservation, Washington DC.

De Alessi, M. (1997) 'Holding out for some local heroes', *New Scientist*, 8 March, p. 46.

De Alessi, M. (1998) *Fishing for Solutions*, Institute of Economic Affairs, London.

Demsetz, H. (1967) 'Toward a Theory of Property Rights', *American Economic Review* vol. 57, pp. 347–59.

Economist, The (1996) 'Cyanide Sauce', 11 May, p. 35.

Edwards, S. (1994) 'Ownership of Renewable Ocean Resources' *Marine Resource Economics* 9, pp. 253–73.

FAO (1993) *Aquaculture Production 1985–1991*, Food and Agriculture Organization of the United Nations, Rome.

FAO (2000) *The State of World Fisheries and Aquaculture: 2000*, Food and Agriculture Organization of the United Nations, Rome.

Goklany, I. (2000) 'Richer is More Resilient: Dealing with Climate Change and More Urgent Environmental Problems' in Bailey, R. (ed.) *Earth Report 2000*, McGraw-Hill, New York, pp. 155–88.

Gordon, H. S. (1954) 'The Economic Theory of a Common-Property Resource: The Fishery', *Journal of Political Economy* vol. 62, pp. 124–42.

Hardin, G. (1968) 'The Tragedy of the Commons', *Science* vol. 162, pp. 1243–8.

Higgs, R. (1982) 'Legally Induced Technical Regress in the Washington State Salmon Fishery', *Research in Economic History* 7, pp. 55–86.

Iyambo, A. (2000) 'Managing Fisheries with Rights in Namibia: A Minister's Perspective' in Shotten, R. (ed.) *Use of property rights in fisheries management*, FAO Fisheries Technical Paper 404/1, Rome.

Johannes, R. (1981) *Words of the Lagoon*, University of California Press, Berkeley.

Johannes, R. and Ripen, M. (1996) 'Environmental, economic and social implications of the fishery for live coral reef food fish in Asia and the Western Pacific', *SPC Live Reef Fish Information Bulletin*, March.

Keen, E. (1983) 'Common Property in Fisheries: Is Sole Ownership an Option?' *Marine Policy* 7, pp. 197–211.

Libecap (1990) *Contracting for Property Rights*, Cambridge University Press, Cambridge, UK.

McClurg, T. (1997) 'Bureaucratic Management versus Private Property: ITQs in New Zealand after Ten Years' in Jones, L. and Walker, M. (eds.) *Fish or Cut Bait!* The Fraser Institute, Vancouver, pp. 91–105.

McKean, M. and Ostrom, E. (1995) 'Common Property Regimes in the Forest: Just a Relic from the Past?', *Unasylva* vol. 46, no. 180, pp. 3–15.

Myers, R. A., Barrowman, N. J, Hutchings, J. A. and Rosenberg, A. A. (1995) 'Population Dynamics of Exploited Fish Stocks at Low Population Levels', *Science* 269, pp. 1106–08.

Ostrom, E. (1990) *Governing the Commons: The Evolution of Institutions for Collective Action*, Cambridge University Press, Cambridge, UK.

Ostrom, E. (1997) 'Private and Common Property Rights', in Bouckaert, B. and De Geest, G. (eds.) *Encyclopedia of Law and Economics*. Edward Elgar, London and University of Ghent, Ghent, Belgium. Available at http://allserv.rug.ac.be/~gdegeest/generali.htm.

Ruddle, R. and Akimichi, T. (1989) 'Sea Tenure in Japan and the Southwestern Ryukus' in Cordell, J. (ed.) (1989), p. 364.

Scott, A. (1988) 'Development of Property in the Fishery', *Marine Resource Economics* 5, pp. 289–311.

Scott, A. (1955) 'The Fishery: The Objectives of Sole Ownership', *Journal of Political Economy* 63, pp. 63–124.

Sharp, B. (1997) 'From Regulated Access to Transferable Harvesting Rights: Policy Insights from New Zealand', *Marine Policy* 21(6), pp. 501–17.

Southgate, D. (1992) 'Shrimp Mariculture Development in Ecuador: Some Resource Policy Issues', Working Paper #5 of the Environment and Natural Resources Policy and Training Project, University of Wisconsin.

Sugg, I. and Kreuter, U. (1994) *Elephants and Ivory: Lessons from the Trade Ban*, Institute of Economic Affairs, London.

Weber, M. (1996) 'The Fish Harvesters: Farm Raising Salmon and Shrimp Makes Millionaires, and also Creates Dead Seas', E Magazine, Nov/Dec.

Chapter 14 – Mary Tiffen and Michael Mortimore

Ariyo, J. A., Voh, J. P. and Ahmed, B. (2001) 'Long-term change in food provisioning and marketing in the Kano Region', *Drylands Research Working Paper* 34, Drylands Research, Crewkerne, UK.

Baba, K. M. and Magaji, M. D. (1998) 'Fadama crop residue production and utilisation in north-western Nigeria' in Hoffmann, I. (ed.) *Prospects of pastoralism in West Africa*, Tropeninstitut, Giessen, pp. 247–62.

Badiane, A. N., Khouma, M. and Sène, M. (2000) 'Région de Diourbel: Gestion des sols', *Drylands Research Working Paper* 15, Drylands Research, Crewkerne, UK.

Barry, A., Ndiaye, S., Ndiaye, F. and Tiffen, M. (2000) 'Région de Diourbel: Les aspects démographiques', *Drylands Research Working Paper* 13, Drylands Research, Crewkerne, UK.

CCD Secretariat (2001) 'Down to Earth: The newsletter of the convention to combat desertification', Convention to Combat Desertification Secretariat, Bonn.

Cline-Cole, R. A., Main, H. A. C., Mortimore, M., Nichol, J. E. and O'Reilly, F. D. (1990) *Wood fuel in Kano*. United Nations University Press, Tokyo.

Coulon, C. (1999) 'The Grande Magal in Touba: a religious festival of the Mouride Brotherhood of Senegal', *African Affairs*, 98/391, pp. 195–210.

Dewees, P. A. (1991) 'The woodfuel crisis reconsidered: observations on the dynamics of abundance and scarcity', *World Development* 17, pp. 1159–72.

Diarra Doka, M. (2001) 'Évolutions à long terme de l'organisation sociale et économique dans la région de Maradi', *Drylands Research Working Paper* 26, Drylands Research, Crewkerne, UK.

Dregne, H. E. (1970) 'Arid lands in transition', *Publication* 90, American Association for the Advancement of Science, Washington DC.

Dregne, H. E., Kassas, M. and Rosanov, B. (1991) 'A new assessment of the world status of desertification', *Desertification Control Bulletin* 20, pp. 6–18.

Dumont, M. (1998) *Trajectoire d'evolution des systèmes de production senoufo – Le cas de Dikodougou, Nord Côte d'Ivoire*, Institut de Savanes, Bouake, Côte d'Ivoire; Centre National d'Etudes Agronomiques des Régions Chaudes, Montpellier, France.

EC (1997) *Addressing diversification – A review of EC policies*, *programmes, financial instruments and projects*, European Commission, Luxembourg.

Fairhead, J. and Leach, M. (1996) *Misreading the African landscape: society and ecology in a forest-savanna mosaic*, Cambridge University Press, Cambridge, UK.

Fall, A. (2000) 'Makueni District profile: Livestock management, 1990–1998', *Drylands Research Working Paper* 8, Drylands Research, Crewkerne, UK.

Faye, A., Fall, A., Mortimore, M., Tiffen, M. and Nelson, J. (2001) 'Région de Diourbel: Synthesis', *Drylands Research Working Paper* 23e, Drylands Research, Crewkerne, UK.

Fletcher, A. (1996) *Desert Margins Initiative. Consolidated report on national workshops*, International Crops Research Institute for Semi-Arid Tropics, Sahelian Center, Niamey, Niger.

Gaye, M. (2000) 'Région de Diourbel: Politiques nationales affectant l'investissement chez les petits exploitants', *Drylands Research Working Paper* 12, Drylands Research, Crewkerne, UK.

Gichuki, F. N. (2000a) 'Makueni District profile: Farm development, 1946–1999', *Drylands Research Working Paper* 1, Drylands Research, Crewkerne, UK.

Gichuki, F. N. (2000b) 'Makueni District profile: Soil management and conservation, 1989–1998', *Drylands Research Working Paper* 4, Drylands Research, Crewkerne, UK.

Gichuki, F. N. (2000c) 'Makueni District profile: Tree management, 1989–1998', *Drylands Research Working Paper* 5, Drylands Research, Crewkerne, UK.

Gichuki, F. N., Mbogoh, S. G., Tiffen, M. and Mortimore, M. (2000) 'Makueni District profile: Synthesis', *Drylands Research Working Paper* 11, Drylands Research, Crewkerne, UK.

Hamadou, S. (2000) 'Politiques nationals et investissement dans les petites exploitations à Maradi', Drylands Working Paper 33, Drylands Research, Crewkerne, UK.

Issaka, M. (2001) 'Évolution à long terme de la fertilité de la sol dans la région de Maradi', *Drylands Research Working Paper* 30, Drylands Research, Crewkerne, UK.

Kelly, V. (1997) 'Are structural adjustment programs and sustainable soil fertility management incompatible? Evidence from the Senegalese Peanut Basin' in Renard, G. *et al.* (eds.) *Soil Fertility Management in West African Land Use Systems*, International Crops Research Institute for Semi-Arid Tropics, Niger.

Lambin, E. F., Turner B. L. II, Geist, H. J. *et al.* (2001) 'The causes of land-use and land-cover change: moving beyond the myths', *Global Environmental Change* 11, pp. 261–9.

Lomborg, B. (2001) *The skeptical environmentalist: Measuring the real state of the world*, Cambridge University Press, Cambridge, UK.

Mainguet, M. (1994) *Desertification. Natural background and human mismanagement*, 2nd Edition, Springer-Verlag, Berlin.

Mazzucato, V. and Niemeijer, D. (2001) 'Overestimating land degradation, underestimating farmers in the Sahel', *Issues Paper 101*, International Institute for Environment and Development, Drylands Programme, London.

Mbogoh, S. G. (2000) 'Makueni District profile: Crop production and marketing, 1988–1999', *Drylands Research Working Paper 7*, Drylands Research, Crewkerne, UK.

Mbuvi, J. P. (2000) 'Makueni District profile: Soil fertility management', *Drylands Research Working Paper 6*, Drylands Research, Crewkerne, UK.

Morris, J. (1995) *The political economy of land degradation: Pressure groups, foreign aid and the myth of man-made deserts*, Institute of Economic Affairs, London.

Mortimore, M. (1989) *Adapting to drought: farmers, famines and desertification in West Africa*, Cambridge University Press, Cambridge, UK.

Mortimore, M. (1998) *Roots in the African dust: Sustaining the Sub-Saharan drylands*, Cambridge University Press, Cambridge, UK.

Mortimore, M. and Adams, W. M. (1998) 'Farming intensification and its implications for pastoralism in northern Nigeria' in Hoffmann, I., von C. Schäfer, M.; Steinbach, J.; Willeke-Wetstein, C. (eds.) Prospects for Pastoralism in West Africa, Giessener Beiräge zur Entwicklungsforschung, Tropeninstitut Giessen, pp. 262–73.

Mortimore, M. and Adams, W. (1999) *Working the Sahel: Environment and society in Northern Nigeria*, Routledge, London.

Mortimore, M., Tiffen, M., Boubacar, Y. and Nelson, J. (2001) 'Department of Maradi: Synthesis', *Drylands Research Working Paper 39e*, Drylands Research, Crewkerne, UK.

Nelson, J. (2000) 'Makueni District profile: Income diversification and farm investment, 1989–1999', *Drylands Research Working Paper 10*, Drylands Research, Crewkerne, UK.

Nzioka, C. (2000) 'Makueni District profile: Human resource

management, 1989–1998', *Drylands Research Working Paper* 9, Drylands Research, Crewkerne, UK.

Okike, I., Jabbar, M. A., Manyong, V., Smith, J. W., Alinwumi, J. A. and Ehui, S. K. (2001) 'Agricultural intensification and efficiency in the West African savannahs: Evidence from northern Nigeria', *Socio Economics and Policy Research Working Paper* 33, International Livestock Research Institute, Nairobi, Kenya.

Patel, S. H., Pinckney, T. C. and Jaeger, W. K. (1995) 'Smallholder wood production and population pressure in east Africa: Evidence of an environmental Kuznets curve?', *Land Economics*, 71/44, pp. 516–30.

Reij, C., Scoones, I. and Toulmin, C. (1996) *Sustaining the soil, indigenous soil and water conservation in Africa*, Earthscan, London.

Sadio, S., Dione, M. and Ngom, S. (2000) 'Région de Diourbel: Gestion des ressources forestières et de l'arbre', *Drylands Research Working Paper* 17, Drylands Research, Crewkerne, UK.

Snrech, S. (1995) *Preparing for the future: A vision of West Africa in the year 2020: Summary Report of the West Africa Long Term Perspective Study*, Club du Sahel/OCDE/Organisation for Economic Cooperation and Development, Paris.

Stiles, D. (1995) 'An overview of desertification as dryland degradation' in Stiles, D. (ed.) *Social aspects of sustainable dryland management*, John Wiley, Chichester, pp. 3–20.

Swift, J. (1996) 'Desertification: narratives, winners and losers', in Leach, M. and Mearns, R. (eds.) *The lie of the land. Challenging received wisdom in African environmental change and policy*, James Currey, Oxford, pp. 73–90.

Thomas, D. S. G. and Middleton, N. (1994) *Desertification: Exploding the myth*, John Wiley, Chichester.

Tiffen, M. (1998) 'Demographic growth and sustainable land use' in Blume, H.-P. *et al.* (eds.) *Towards sustainable land use: Furthering co-operation between people and institutions* 2, Catena, Reiskirchen, Germany, pp. 1333–47.

Tiffen, M. (2001) 'Profile of demographic change in the Kano-Maradi Region, 1960–2000', *Drylands Research Working Paper* 24, Drylands Research, Crewkerne, UK.

Tiffen, M., Mortimore, M. and Gichuki F. (1994) *More people less erosion: environmental recovery in Kenya*, John Wiley, Chichester.

Tiffen, M. and Mulele, M. R. (1994) *The environmental impact of the 1991–2 drought on Zambia*, International Union for the

Conservation of Nature, Gland, Switzerland and Lusaka, Zambia.

UNEP (1977) *Report of the United Nations Conference on Desertification, 29 August–9 September 1977*, United Nations Environment Programme, Nairobi.

UNEP (1990) *World map of the status of human-induced soil degradation*, United Nations Environment Programme, Nairobi.

Voortman, R. L., Sonneveld, B. G. J. S., Langveld, J. W. A., Fischer, G. and van Velthuizen, H. T. (1999) *Climate change and global agricultural potential: A case study of Nigeria. 99–06. Staff Working Paper*, Stichting Onderzoek Wereldvoedselvoorziening van de Vrije Universiteit, Amsterdam.

Warren, A. and Agnew, C. (1988) *An assessment of desertification and land degradation in arid and semi-arid areas*, International Institute for Environment and Development, London.

Warren, A. and Khogali, M. (1992) *Assessment of desertification and drought in the Sudano-Sahelian region*, United Nations Sudano-Sahelian Office, New York.

Wilson Fall, W. (2000) 'Région de Diourbel: The family, local institutions and education', *Drylands Research Working Paper 20*, Drylands Research, Crewkerne, UK.

Chapter 15 – **Roger Bate**

Anderson, T. L. (ed.) (1983) *Water Rights: Scarce Resource Allocation, Bureaucracy and the Environment*, Pacific Institute for Public Policy Research, San Francisco.

Anderson, T. L. (ed.) (1994) *Continental Water Marketing*, Political Economy Research Center, Montana.

Anderson, T. L. and Snyder, P. (1997) *Water Markets*, Cato Institute, Washington DC.

Backeberg, G. R. (1997), 'Water institutions, markets and decentralized resource management', *Agrekon* 36 (4), pp. 350–84.

Backeberg, G. R. (1995) 'Towards a Market in Water Rights: A pragmatic institutional Economic Approach', Discussion paper, University of Pretoria.

Bagadion, B. U. (1988) 'The evolution of the policy context: An historical overview' in Korten, F. F. and Siy Jr, R. Y. (eds.) *Transforming a Bureaucracy: the Experience of the Philippine National Irrigation Administration*, Kumarian Press, West Hartford, CT.

Bate, R., Tren, R. and Mooney, L. (1999) 'An econometric and institutional economic analysis of water use in the Crocodile River catchment, Mpumalanga Province, South Africa', Water Research Commission Project K5/855, Pretoria.

Bates, R. H. (1983) *Essays on the Political Economy of Rural Africa*, Cambridge University Press, Cambridge, UK.

Bauer, C. J. (1997) 'Bringing water markets down to earth: The political economy of water rights in Chile, 1976–95', *World Development* 25 (5), pp. 639–56.

Baumol, W. J. and Oates, W. E. (1988) *The Theory of Environmental Policy*, Cambridge University Press, Cambridge, UK.

Becker, N. (1995) 'Value of moving from central planning to a market system: lessons from the Israeli Water system', *Agricultural Economics* 12, pp. 11–21.

Deacon, E. (1997) Compiled Papers, unpublished.

Dinar, A. and Subramanian, A. (eds.) (1997) 'Water Pricing Experiences: An international perspective', World Bank Technical Paper no. 386, Washington DC.

Dinar, A. and Xepapadeas, A. (1998) 'Regulating water quantity and quality in irrigation', *Journal of Environmental Management* 54, pp. 273–89.

Easter, K. W., Rosegrant, M. W. and Dinar, A. (eds.) (1998) *Markets for Water: Potential and performance*, Kluwer Academic Publishers, MA.

Frederiksen, H., Berkoff, J. and Barber, W. (1993) 'Water resources management in Asia', World Bank Technical Paper 212, Asia Technical Department, Washington DC.

Gleick, P. H. (1993) *Water in Crisis*, Oxford University Press, New York and Oxford.

Hearne, R. R. (1998) 'Institutional and organisational arrangements for water markets in Chile' in Easter, K. W. *et al.* (1998).

Hearne, R. R. and Easter, K. W. (1997) 'The economic and financial gains from water markets in Chile', *Agricultural Economics* 15, pp. 187–99.

Holden, P. and Thobani, M. (1996) 'Tradable Water Rights: a property rights approach to resolving water shortages and promoting investment', World Bank Policy Research Working Paper 1627, Washington DC.

Holtzhausen, K. (1997) Archive of Papers, unpublished.

Howitt, R. E. (1998) 'Spot prices, options prices and water markets:

an analysis of emerging markets in California' in Easter, K. W., Rosegrant, M. W. and Dinar, A. (eds.) *Markets for Water: Potential and performance*, Kluwer Academic Publishers, MA.

Ingram, H. M. (1973) 'The political economy of regional water institutions', *American Journal of Agricultural Economics* vol. 55, no. 1, pp. 10–18.

Kemper, K. E. (1996) *The Cost of Free Water: Water resources allocation and use in the Curu Valley, Ceará, Northeast Brazil*, Linköping Studies in Arts and Science 137, Linköping University, Sweden.

Kemper, K. E. and Simpson, L. D. (1995) *A Water Market in Practice: The Northern Colorado Water Conservancy District*, Linköping: Department of Water and Environmental Studies (mimeo), Linköping University, Sweden.

Landry, C (1999) 'Market transfers of water for environmental protection in the western United States', *Water Policy* vol. 1, no. 5, pp. 457–69.

Livingstone, M. L. (1995) 'Designing Water Institutions: Market Failures and Institutional Response', *Water Resources Management* 9, pp. 203–20.

Maas, A. and Anderson. R. (1978) *And the deserts shall rejoice: Conflict, growth and justice in arid environments*, MIT Press, Cambridge, MA.

Ostrom, E. (1990) *Governing the Commons*, Cambridge University Press, Cambridge, UK.

Pearce, F. (1992) *The Dammed: Rivers, Dams, and the Coming World Water Crisis*, The Bodley Head, London.

Pakistan Water and Power Development Authority (1990) 'Trading of canal and tubewell water for irrigation purposes', Planning and Investigation Directorate Publications 358 (December), Lahore, Pakistan.

Repetto, R. (1986) *Skimming the Water: Rent-seeking and the performance of public irrigation systems*, Research Report no. 4, World Resources Institute, Washington DC.

Ríos, M. and Quiroz, J. (1995) 'The market for water rights in Chile: Major issues', *Cuadernos de Economica* 97, pp. 291–315.

Rosegrant, M. W. and Binswanger, H. P. (1994) 'Markets in tradable water rights: Potential for efficiency gains in developing country water resource allocation', *World Development* 22 (11), pp. 1613–25.

Rosegrant, M. W. and Gazmuri-Schleyer, R. (1994) 'Reforming

Water Allocation Policy Through Markets in Tradable Water Rights: Lessons from Chile, Mexico, and California', International Food and Production Technology Division, EPTD Discussion Paper no. 6, Washington DC.

Saleth, R. M. (1998) 'Water markets in India: Economic and Institutional Aspects' in Easter, K. W., Rosegrant, M. W. and Dinar, A. (eds.) *Markets for Water: Potential and performance*, Kluwer Academic Publishers, MA.

Shah, T. (1991) 'Managing Conjunctive Water Use in Canal Commands: Analysis for Mahi Right Bank Canal, Gujarat' in Meinzen-Dick, R. and Svendsen, M. (eds.) *Future Directions for Indian Irrigation*, International Food Policy Research Institution, Washington DC.

Shanks, B. (1981) 'Dams and Disasters: the social cost of water development policies' in Baden, J. and Stroup, R. (eds.) *Bureaucracy v. Environment: The environmental costs of bureaucratic governance*, The University of Michigan Press, Ann Arbor.

Strosser, P. (1997) *Analyzing alternative policy instruments for the irrigation sector*, Wageningen Agricultural University, The Netherlands.

Sturgess, G. L. and Wright, M. (1993) *Water Rights In Rural New South Wales: The Evolution of a Property Rights System*, The Centre For Independent Studies, St Leonards, Australia.

Tadros, N. (1996) 'Shrinking Water Resources: The National Security Issue of This Century', *NorthWest Journal of International Law and Business* 17, pp. 1091–1131.

Thobani, M. (1998) 'Meeting water needs in developing countries: Resolving issues in establishing tradable water rights' in: Easter, K. W. *et al.* (1998).

UNCED (1992) *Agenda 21: Chapter 18*, United Nations Conference on Environment and Development, United Nations, New York.

World Bank (1995a) 'Water Policy and Water Markets', Selected Papers and Proceedings for the World Bank's Ninth Annual Irrigation and Drainage Seminar, Annapolis, MD, December 8–10, 1992.

Epilogue – Julian Morris

Attaran, A. and Gillespie-White, L. (2001) 'Do Patents for Antiretroviral Drugs Constrain Access to AIDS Treatment in

Africa?', *Journal of the American Medical Association*, vol. 286, pp. 1886–1892.

de Soto, H. (1989) *The Other Path*, Harper and Row, New York.

de Soto, H. (2000) *The Mystery of Capital*, BasicBooks, New York.

Dukes, G. (1998) 'Change and Growth in Generic Markets in Developed and Developing Countries', in Felix Lobo and German Velasquez (eds.) *Medicines and the new economic environment*, World Health Organization and University Carlos III, Madrid.

Hilton, S. and Gibbons, G. (2002) *Good Business: Your World Needs You*, Texere, London.

IIED (1996) *Towards a Sustainable Paper Cycle*, International Institute for Environment and Development, London.

Lamont, J. (2002) 'Rights group fears Harare manipulating food relief', *Financial Times*, June, p. 10.

Lanjouw, J. O. (1998) *The Introduction of Pharmaceutical Product Patents in India: 'Heartless Exploitation of the Poor and Suffering'*? NBER Working Paper no. w6366, National Bureau of Economic Research, Cambridge, MA.

Lomborg, B. (2001) *The Skeptical Environmentalist*, Cambridge University Press, Cambridge.

MMSD (2002) *Breaking New Ground: Mining, Minerals and Sustainable Development*, International Institute for Environment and Development, London.

Nisbet, R. (1980) *History of the Idea of Progress*, BasicBooks, New York.

Ricardo, D. (1817) *On the Principles of Political Economy and Taxation*.

Schmidheiny, S. (1994) 'Property Rights and Sustainable Development' in *Property for the Poor: The Path to Development*, proceedings of a conference organised by the Institute for Liberty and Democracy, 12 April, Washington DC.

Smith, A. (1776) *An Inquiry Into the Nature and Causes of the Wealth of Nations*.

Acknowledgements

I would like to thank everyone who has helped and encouraged me to produce this book. Special thanks to the authors, who produced brilliant material at very short notice; to Kendra Okonski, who read the entire manuscript and provided many helpful comments, clarifications and changes; to Paul Forty at Profile, who made the book possible and chivvied me along; and to Fiona Screen, whose commitment to copy-editing went beyond the call of duty. Thanks also to all those in the Sustainable Development Network, who have provided support and shown commitment to the cause of real sustainable development.

Julian Morris
London
June 2002

The Sustainable Development Network

The Sustainable Development Network comprises individuals and groups around the world who are concerned about the way that sustainable development is currently conceptualised and who seek to promote an alternative vision underpinned by the institutions of the free society. To find out more about the network, please visit its website, www.sdnetwork.net.

Index

Page numbers in *italics* refer to Figures and Tables.